Culture
and Society in
Venice
1470–1790

STUDIES IN CULTURAL HISTORY
SERIES EDITOR:
Professor J. R. Hale

Culture
and Society in
Venice

1470-1790
The Renaissance and its Heritage

OLIVER LOGAN

Lecturer in History, School of European Studies,
University of East Anglia

B. T. Batsford Ltd *London*

for
Mary

First published 1972
© Oliver Logan 1972

Made and printed in Great Britain by
C. Tinling & Co. Ltd, London and Prescot
for the publishers B. T. Batsford Ltd,
4 Fitzhardinge Street, London W.1

ISBN O 7134 1524 X

Contents

List of Illustrations vi

Acknowledgments vii

Map of sixteenth-century Venetian Republic viii

one The Mythology of Venice 1

two Venetian Society 20

three The Venetian Dominions and their Cultural Setting 38

four The Active and the Contemplative Life 49

five Intellectual Life 68

six Literature 93

seven Artistic Theory and Propaganda for the Artist 129

eight Patronage and Collecting of Art 148

nine The Visual Arts 220

ten Music and Music Patronage 256

eleven Continuity and Change in Venetian Tradition 269

Appendix 295

Bibliography 322

Index 333

List of Illustrations

facing page

1 Giorgione, *The Three Philosophers* — 24

2 Detail from Fig. 1 — 24

3 Daniele Barbaro by Titian — 25

4 Cardinal Pietro Bembo by Titian — 56

5 Andrea Odoni by Lorenzo Lotto — 57

6 Titian, *Vendramin Altarpiece* (detail) — 88

7 Portrait of Alvise Corner attributed to Tintoretto — 89

8 G. M. Falconetto, the Loggia Cornaro, Padua — 120

9 Palladio, Villa Barbaro, Maser — 121

10 J. Sansovino, the Public Library, Venice — 121

11 Titian, *Cain and Abel*

12 Titian, *Diana and Callisto* — *between pages 136 & 137*

13 Titian, *Diana and Actaeon*

14 Paolo Veronese, *The Triumph of Mordecai*

15 Paolo Veronese, *Feast in the House of Levi* — 152

16 Jacopo Tintoretto, *Miracle of the Slave* (detail) — 153

17 Jacopo Tintoretto, *Presentation of the Virgin* — 184

18 Jacopo Tintoretto, *Transportation of the Body of St Mark* — 185

19 Illustration from *Hypnerotomachia Polifili*

20 Palazzo Vendramin-Calergi, Venice — *between pages 200 & 201*

21 J. Sansovino, Palazzo Corner di S. Maurizio, Venice

22 M. Sanmicheli, *Palazzo Bevilacqua*, Verona

23 Palladio, church of the Redentore, Venice — 216

24 A. Vittoria, bust of Doge Nicolò da Ponte — 217

25 G. B. Tiepolo, *Allegory of Marriage* — 248

26 Ca Rezzonico, Venice — 249

Acknowledgments

I wish to express my deep gratitude to Professor Gaetano Cozzi who first initiated me into the study of Venetian history and to Dr Richard Cocke, Mr Anthony Gable, Professor J. R. Hale and Dr B. S. Pullan who examined the draft of this book and made many helpful suggestions.

O.L.

The Author and Publisher would like to thank the following for permission to reproduce photographs: Terisio Pignatti, *Giorgione* (Phaidon, 1971) and the Kunsthistorisches Museum, Vienna (Figs 1 and 2); Museo del Prado (Fig. 3); Galleria Nazionale di Capodimonte, Naples (Fig. 4); Fig. 5 by gracious permission of Her Majesty the Queen; Fig. 6 is reproduced by courtesy of the Trustees, The National Gallery, London; Hans Tietze, *Tintoretto: the paintings and drawings*, Phaidon, 1948 (Figs 7 and 17); J. S. Ackerman and the Fogg Art Museum, Harvard University, Mass., U.S.A. (Fig. 8); Countess Luling Buschetti (Fig. 9); Salute, Venice (Fig. 11); Duke of Sutherland Collection, on loan to the National Gallery of Scotland (Figs. 12 and 13); Juergen Schulz, *Venetian Painted Ceilings of the Renaissance*, University of California Press, 1968 (Fig. 14); Galleria dell' Accademia, Venice (Figs 15, 16 and 18); Mrs Dearborn Massar (Fig. 23); Seminario, Venice (Fig. 24); the Director, Ca Rezzonico, Venice (Figs. 25 and 26). The jacket illustration is derived from Veronese's *The Family of Darius before Alexander* and is reproduced by courtesy of the Trustees, The National Gallery, London,

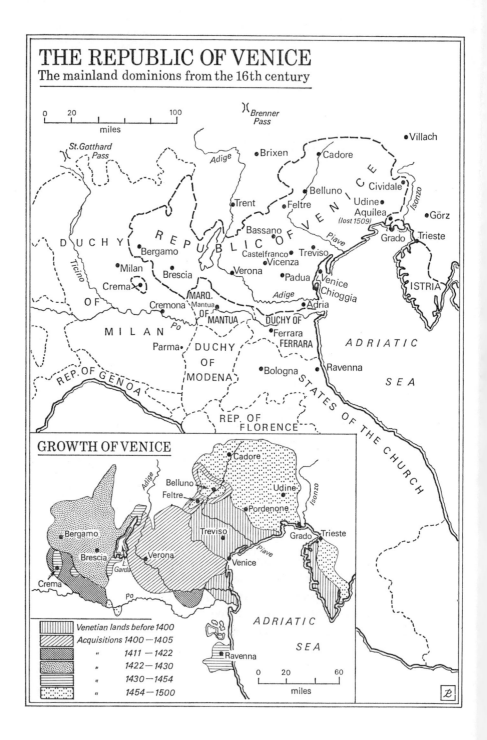

THE REPUBLIC OF VENICE
The mainland dominions from the 16th century

0 20 100
miles

Brenner Pass

St. Gotthard Pass

● Villach

Adige

● Brixen

● Cadore

V E N I C E

● Belluno

● Cividale

● Udine
Aquilea
(lost 1509)

● Görz

● Trent

● Feltre

Isonzo

Trieste

D U C H Y

R E P U B L I C

Bassano ●

O F

Piave

● Grado

● Bergamo

Castelfranco ●

● Treviso

Vicenza ●

● Milan

● Brescia

● Verona

Ticino

Crema ✕

MARQ.

● Padua

Venice
Chioggia

ISTRIA

O F

Cremona ●

Mantua
OF
MANTUA

Adige

Adria ●

Po

DUCHY OF

A D R I A T I C

M I L A N

Parma ●

DUCHY
OF
MODENA

● Ferrara
FERRARA

● Bologna

Ravenna ●

S E A

REP. OF GENOA

S T A T E S   O F   T H E   C H U R C H

REP. OF
FLORENCE

GROWTH OF VENICE

Adige

● Cadore

Belluno ●

● Udine

Feltre ●

● Pordenone

Isonzo

● Bergamo

Treviso ●

● Grado

Trieste

Brescia ●

Verona ●

Piave

Garda

Venice

Crema ●

Po

A D R I A T I C

S E A

● Ravenna

	Venetian lands before 1400
	Acquisitions 1400 – 1405
"	1411 – 1422
"	1422 – 1430
"	1430 – 1454
"	1454 – 1500

0 20 60
miles

£

one

The Mythology of Venice

Puis ils sont vivans a la loi d'Epicure
Faisant yeulx, nez et oreilles jouyr
De ce qu'on peut veouyr, sentir et ouyr,
Au gré des sens, et traictans ce corps commes
Si là gisoit le dernier bien de l'homme.
D'or et d'azure, de marbres blancs et noirs
Sont enrichiz leurs temples et manoirs
D'art de paincture et medailles dorées
Sont a grand cout leurs manoirs decorées,
Mais a leurs pieds (hélas) sont gémissans
Les povres, nuds, pasles et languissans . . .[*][1]

So wrote the French Protestant poet Clément Marot to Calvin's patroness Renée Duchess of Ferrara in 1536. Marot's Venice, like the Venice of Montaigne, with its richly caparisoned *filles de joie*,[2] is very different from that one which recent studies of religious life and sentiment have made known to us, the city of Gerolamo Miani, the noble protector of orphans, or of the tortured, severe Gasparo Contarini, scholar, statesman and religious reformer; the work of these two men was reaching its climax at the time Marot wrote. The significance of his *Epître*, however, lies not in what it tells us about Venice but in what it implied for Europe's vision of the City of the Lagoons. The great myth of *Venezia città galante*, which Marot helped to create and which was fostered by other foreign descriptions of the city in the sixteenth and early seventeenth centuries such as that of Thomas Coryat,[3]

[*] 'They live by the law of Epicurus. They give eyes, nostrils and ears all that can be seen, smelt and heard with sensual pleasure and they treat the body as if the final good of man lay therein. Their Churches and villas are enriched with gold and silver, with black and white marbles, their houses are decorated with paintings and gilded medallions at great cost. But at their feet, the naked, pale poor languish groaning.'

has continued to exercise its fascination up to the present day.

Yet in the European consciousness of the sixteenth and seventeenth centuries, the myth of *Venezia città galante* if anything took second place to the myth of 'Venice state of liberty' and the allied vision of Venice as the supreme exemplar of the 'mixed constitution'. In an age in which many republican and princely governments had foundered in Italy, Venice appeared as a model of stability and as the most powerful surviving exponent of free political institutions. Like the myth of ancient Rome, the myths of *Venezia stato di libertà* and *Venezia stato misto* provided a framework within which thinkers both in Italy and beyond the Alps could work out their ideas of the best practicable form of state. The material for these myths was provided both by the constitutional system of Venice and by her apparently miraculous survival of the upheavals of the Italian wars, more particularly the disaster which had nearly overwhelmed her in 1509.

Sovereignty over the aggregation of north Italian, Dalmatian and eastern Mediterranean territories that formed the Venetian Republic resided in the patrician government of the *città dominante* of Venice itself. This government was the fruit of the process whereby, over the centuries, the Rialtine aristocracy had curbed the power of the Doge and eliminated the ancient popular assembly (*concio*) of the Commune. From the mid-twelfth century we find a council of 'sages' (*sapientes*) placed alongside the Doge as a brake on his power. From this body of sages had developed two organs, the small Consiglio proper and the Maggior Consiglio or Great Council. The Maggior Consiglio, which was evidently dominated from its inception by the Rialtine aristocracy, expanded to become the assembly of the entire Venetian nobility and replaced the *concio* as the supreme forum. By the two 'closures' (*serrate*) of the Maggior Consiglio of 1297 and 1307–16, the membership of this council was confined to certain families; a new block of families was given entry in 1381, but from then until the mid-seventeenth century it was essentially a closed body. All male members of the designated families (barring illegitimacy and legal degradation) had right of entry and were defined as noble; nobility and right of entry into the Great Council were synonymous. In the early sixteenth century there were some 2,500 male nobles. The Consiglio proper, or Minor Consiglio retained the character of an inner core, being composed of the Doge and his councillors; when it sat with the *Capi di Quarantia*, the chief judicial magistrates of the city, it was known as the Signoria and when the Signoria sat with the administrative magistrates known as the *Savii*, it became the Collegio. The Senate or Pregadi can be basically regarded as a further expansion of the Collegio: to be precise it took its origins from a new body of councillors set up to advise the Doge, probably in the early thirteenth century in the first instance, and to this body had been subsequently added members of various magistracies emanating from the Maggior Consiglio; as an end product, the Senate was composed of the members of the Collegio together with various other administrative and judicial magistrates, either senators in ordinary or other magistrates holding seats *ex officio*. By the sixteenth century it had, together with its appendage the *Zonta*, a membership of between 200 and 300.

Theoretically the Maggior Consiglio was the supreme forum. In point of fact, its legislative powers had limited practical exercise in our period and its main function was the election of office-holders. Theoretically again, the highest, although not exactly the supreme, organs of government were the Signory and the Collegio. Their active importance, however, derived principally from the primacy enjoyed by their members in the other main administrative organs and although the Collegio had a number of specified duties—including receipt of ambassadors and tutelage over Church–State relations—it had few deliberative powers. Effective legislative power belonged mainly to the Senate, and this was the chief cog that set the various administrative departments and magistracies in motion. It was composed of men who had at least reached the middling rungs of the *cursus honorum*, through either proven administrative ability, political pull or the wealth needed to support office. The precise spheres of competence of the various councils and supreme politico-administrative organs were never very clearly defined and within this ill-defined framework, increasing power was passing in the early years of the sixteenth century into the hands of the Council of Ten and its Zonta—a body in fact of forty men—which had evolved from the early fourteenth century as the organ designed to expedite urgent or secret matters involving state security; this was the bastion of the small group of families of established wealth and political power.

The inevitable tensions within the Venetian nobility were to become more evident as the sixteenth century progressed. From the 1580s, the party of the Giovani, which basically represented the political 'outsiders' among the patriciate, or those who had only recently acquired high office, was to attack the exorbitant powers of the Council of Ten and wage a vendetta against the *case vecchie*, the families of established political eminence. An attack on the *case vecchie* was again to be led in the 1620s by the 'demagogue' Renier Zeno, supported by the rabble of poorer nobles. Among the population of Venice as a whole, however, murmurs of dissension were surprisingly absent, not least among the so-called 'citizens'. These formed the privileged class of legally-defined membership of which shared trading rights with the nobles; in the sixteenth century they were some 2,000–2,500 in number. Within this group, there was the inner élite of the *cittadini originarii* from whom the incumbents of the main government secretarial and chancery posts were drawn. The citizens had access to certain honours, but no political powers. Their apparent contentment was an object of admiration to many contemporary observers who regarded it as marvellous evidence of the sagacity of the Venetian system. In the Terraferma, Venice's possessions on the Italian mainland, the picture was rather less idyllic. There had been sinister movements among the provincial nobilities in 1509, but in the end Venice had been saved, apparently, by the loyalty of her subject populations.

In 1509, following the defeat of Agnadello, the Terraferma was over-run by French and Imperial armies. As a result of her incursions into Papal and Habsburg territory, Venice had been faced at the beginning of the year by the League of Cambrai, a grand coalition of the Papacy, France and the Holy Roman Emperor, these being subsequently joined by Aragon. The ensuing military disaster meant that Venice had to cede her recent conquests together with the parts of Lombardy she had seized when she joined with France in the dismemberment of the Milanese state in 1499, but after 1517 she basically retained her pre-1499 boundaries. Her survival was due partly to a shift in diplomatic align-ments but also in some measure to the loyalty of a significant portion of the peoples of the Terraferma; the aristocratic groups in Vicenza, Padua and Treviso who had sought to make common cause with the invaders had been countered by risings of the urban populace while the peasantry had rallied against the ravaging armies even where they had initially shown signs of rebellion against their old masters. Not a few contemporary observers sought the explanation of the apparent miracle of Venice's survival in the hope of finding lessons for their own troubled times.

Venice, often regarded in the fifteenth century as aspiring to the dominance of Italy and an active aggressor in the first decade of the six-teenth century, was now seen almost as a victim in a period when French and Habsburg power threatened the independence of the Italian states. As the Habsburg grip tightened on the peninsula after 1525

Venice was left as perhaps the most powerful of the independent Italian states and appeared as the bastion of liberty. While generations of her historians sought to present Venice as the heroic victim rather than the foolhardy aggressor in the War of the League of Cambrai, outside observers, first Italians and later foreigners, sought the causes of her stability. Apparently immutable through the centuries, she had stood firm among the turmoils of the Italian wars and the upheavals which these had provoked inside other Italian states. Observers sought the causes in the structure of her governmental system and in the fibre of her governing class and here they stressed the elements both of strength and of freedom.

Outside admiration of Venice's constitution and the myth of the 'state of liberty' can certainly be traced back before the crisis of 1509. The origins of the myth can perhaps be seen in the first half of the fifteenth century when Florentines had intermittently looked to Venice as a bastion of republican freedom against the encroaching despotism of Visconti Milan. Again, after the expulsion of the Medici from Florence in 1494, those who attempted to frame a new republican constitution had a close eye on the Venetian system, the Savonarolian 'popular' constitution being partly based on it. Yet if Venice had been regarded as an exemplar before 1509, it was perhaps more than anything her survival of the War of the League of Cambrai that helped to bring the Venetian myth to fruition and give it a place in the consciousness of sixteenth-century Europe, while the splendours of the myth were undoubtedly highlighted against the sombre background provided by the failures of the two Florentine Republics and the Medici restorations of 1512 and 1530. Thus in the second decade of the century, those Florentines, most notably the members of the Rucellai circle, who devoted themselves to the comparative study of political institutions in the hope of finding a framework of government for their own unhappy city, saw Venice as providing the outstanding example of a modern constitution to be placed alongside the ancient constitutions of Athens, Sparta and Rome. The third decade of the century saw the two classic studies of Venetian institutions, the Venetian Gasparo Contarini's *De magistratus venetorum* (1524) and the Florentine Tommaso Gianotti's *Dialogi della Repubblica Veneziana* (1526). With Contarini came the perfection of the myth; Venice was the ideal state of justice, superior even to ancient Athens and Rome.

The myth of the Venetian state was all the more potent for the very uncertainty as to how its constitution actually worked. To modern eyes it offers a supreme example of aristocratic dominance. To the men of the sixteenth century, however, who understood a popular government as one in which constitutional rights belonged to a restricted élite of 'citizens', Venice might appear to have an element of popular government in the shape of the fairly extensive Great Council. Thus some observers saw Venice as a true aristocracy, others as having a 'mixed' form of government, a democratic element being provided by the Great Council, an element of government by the few in the Senate and a monarchical element with the Doge; in this way Venice had admirers among all shades of anti-Medici opinion, both among the aristocratic party and among those who called for a constitution giving substantial power to a citizen body.

For Gianotti, the exiled Savonarolian, Venice was a testimony to the success of democratic institutions. For Contarini it was the supreme example of the 'mixed state', but he no longer saw the democratic element as lying in the Great Council. Rather he added a new dimension to the concept of the mixed state by maintaining that the element of popular participation extended outside the limits of the aristocratic caste. While the Great Council and the state magistracies were a noble preserve, there were honorific posts to which the citizens were admitted and they played a dignified role in the great charitable confraternities of the city. Contarini was obviously thinking here in the first place of the offices of Grand Chancellor and the Secretaryships of the Great Council and Senate and in the second place of the Scuole Grandi. In the confraternities, Contarini said, 'they imitate the nobility, for the heads of these societies do in a manner imitate the Procurators among the people'.[4]

The polarity of visions of the Venetian constitution which we have already encountered among the early sixteenth-century Florentines is again illustrated by two Italian writers of the early seventeenth century, Traiano Boccalini and Giovanni Botero. For Boccalini, Venice's preservation of her freedom was due to the cohesion and indeed the closed character of her ruling class.[5] Botero, on the other hand, saw the constitution as a 'mixed polity' and followed Contarini in attempting to prove its open character by examining the compensations open to non-nobles.[6]

Fascination with the Venetian constitution was not a purely Italian affair. In France, not long after Agnadello, the tones of strident jingoism which had lashed Venice as the enemy par excellence were modified in certain quarters by tones of profound respect. French ambassadors there gave glowing accounts of both her culture and her political institutions. Admiration for the latter came to be particularly marked among defenders of constitutional monarchy as against royal absolutism in the first half of the century, notably Claude de Seyssel[7] and Étienne la Boetie. For la Boetie, the tyrant-hater, the Venetians were the supreme example of a people attached to liberty.[8] It was Jean Bodin, however, who did most to add new dimensions to the vision of Venice in his *Methodus ad facilem historiarum cognitionem* (1566); here his researches were conducted with a view to formulating a concept of sovereignty, which he subsequently defined in his *Six livres de la République* (1576). For Bodin, the Venetians, who were not particularly distinguished for their military prowess or religious zeal and inferior to the Spaniards in trade and in their administration, excelled by their laws and 'counsels of sagacity'. He stressed the freedom under which Venice's inhabitants lived, but, although he referred to the openings given to plebeians, he had no truck with ideas of 'government by the many'. For him, as for Boccalini later, the strength of Venice lay in the coherence and indeed exclusiveness of her aristocratic caste and it was Bodin who delivered the most erudite attack on the myth of the 'mixed state'; he showed how Venice had evolved from a popular state into an aristocracy to the point where the control of the Great Council was very limited and real power belonged to an inner core of magistrates.[9, 10]

Bodin had perceived, what scarcely any writer had stated before him, that not only was the government nominally in the hands of some two thousand men or fewer but also that within this caste the reins of power belonged to an inner oligarchy. Modern historians would tend to see in this a reflection of social and economic distinctions within the aristocracy itself; control belonged, for much of the sixteenth century, to a group of families of established political prestige and the wealth needed to support it. Their power lay not so much in the main decision-making organs but in the bodies that could influence or check them: not so much in the Senate, as Bodin believed, but rather in the Collegio as the inner nucleus of the Senate and, above all, in the Council of Ten; the latter, seen as an instrument of terror by contemporary foreign observers, was more a relatively benign instrument of oligarchical control. How far the more generally aristocratic structure of the Venetian state was modified by the opportunities open to citizens is subject to doubt. The chief Chancery and secretarial posts and the leading offices of the scuole which were substantially confined to them were certainly highly prestigious, but the former, at least, were substantially the preserve of a small élite within the class of the *cittadini originarii*.

Admiration for Venice was shared in the sixteenth century by men of varying political orientations, with different views of the nature of the Venetian state-system and laying individual stresses on what its prime merits were, whether freedom, justice, symmetry of parts or simple pragmatic effectiveness. The myths of 'Venice state of liberty', 'Venice the mixed state' possessed their potency, exercised their creative function as myth not only because of what Venice was but also because the very uncertainty as to her nature enabled men to see in her the concrete confirmation of their own different ideals.

For rather different reasons, Italian liberals of the post-Risorgimento generation again saw the confirmation of their ideals in the Venice of the sixteenth and early seventeenth centuries, but this time not so much in the structure of the Venetian state as in Venice's politico-religious history. The leaders who had made the Risorgimento and brought about the unification of Italy had come into conflict with the Church over the abolition of ecclesiastical privileges and the temporal power of the Papacy. To liberals of the post-Risorgimento generation the history of Venice's relations with the Church in the sixteenth and early seventeenth century perhaps seemed to offer testimony that opposition to the Church's temporal pretensions, anti-clericalism even, were good old Italian traditions. Venice's policy appeared to be one of religious tolerance and defence of the integrity of secular power.[11]

Religious tolerance had appeared as one aspect of the famed 'liberty of Venice' to not a few Italian Protestants of the sixteenth century. Magnificent hopes were reposed in her. She was called upon to embrace the Reformation; to Bernardino Ochino, Venice would be the 'gateway' through which it would spread into Italy and even Luther had been optimistic.[12] Such expectations probably took their roots as much in the hospitality which Venice offered to the Florentine exiles as in her very limited religious tolerance; significantly many of the Protestants active in Venetian territory were Tuscans. The myth of 'Venice state of liberty' may have coloured beliefs in her openness to new ideas, especially for those imbued with a Savonarolian vision of a combined renewal of religion and politics bringing a resurgence of civic freedom and a purification of the Church. As a result, too much significance may have been attached to the haphazardness with which, at certain times, religious heterodoxy was prosecuted in Venice. It is advisable to speak of haphazardness of prosecution rather than a consistent policy of tolerance as such. In comparison with that of many other Italian states, Venetian government policy regarding censorship and the Inquisition was relatively liberal; in marginal cases, persons accused of heresy obtained an exceptionally fair deal. Much depended, however, upon the composition at any given time of the body of lay magistrates attached to the ecclesiastical tribunals and upon the opportunities for pulling strings on behalf of accused persons. While at some periods the ecclesiastical authorities accused the government of being remiss in its measures against heresy, at other times such measures were undertaken with considerable energy. Thus, while the hopes of some Protestants may have been raised in the 1530s, a series of heresy-trials in the early 1540s lead to widespread disillusion. Nevertheless, prophesies of extraordinary optimism on the part of individual Italian Protestants continued to be made throughout the sixteenth century and Venice's relative religious tolerance was again stressed by certain liberal historians of the late nineteenth century and continues to be so by many present day ones.

Venice was placed under interdict by Julius II in 1509 and by Paul V in 1606: administration of the sacraments under normal circumstances was prohibited and members of the government were excommunicated. Although the occasion of the first interdict was Venice's refusal to hand back her conquests in the Papal States, the relations between the civil power and the Church within the Venetian dominions was also an issue in both cases. It would be dangerous, however, to regard the Republic's dispute with Paul V as necessarily forming part of a general movement stretching back to the struggle with Julius. While there were many serious disputes in the intervening period, it is not easy to see a clear pattern in Veneto–Papal relations, although many historians have been prepared to see a fairly consistent and quintessentially 'Venetian' policy on the part of the Signory of resistance to the political ambitions of the Papacy and refusal to allow the exercise of civil power to be limited by the Church's claims to privileged and independent status. If Venice's individual disputes with the Papacy in the latter half of the sixteenth century are taken in isolation and ranged in chronological order, a certain progression in the direction of worsening relations might seem to present itself; here the emergence of militant counter-reformatory Papacy in the 1560s and that of a more politically ambitious Papacy from the mid-1580s might be seen as turning points. If, however, the documentation of these disputes is studied simply as part of the vast and jumbled mass of diplomatic correspondence between

Venice and Rome in the period, major policy disputes, petty squabbles, effusions of amity and benevolence are seen to succeed one another, often interspersed by extensive periods in which nothing much happened, and it is difficult to form a coherent picture. It would be hard to deny, however, that increased potentialities for tension came from the 1580s with the rise to prominence of the anti-clerical party of the Giovani and in the first decade of the seventeenth century unsettled disputes had accumulated to an alarming degree.

Although the consistency of Venetian policy regarding the Church may be doubted, it cannot be denied that the Signory repeatedly insisted on exercising extensive powers where public order, the distribution of property and the material well-being or lives and liberties of Venetian subjects were concerned. Thus it kept almost exclusive control over hospitals and other philanthropic institutions and over lay charitable confraternities. It was made clear that the *de facto* control of the ecclesiastical authorities over censorship was ultimately exercised under the aegis of the state; lay representatives of the secular power exercised surveillance over the Inquisition to ensure that proper rules of evidence were followed. Greeks and foreign Protestants in Venetian territory were protected from molestation on the part of the ecclesiastical authorities. At various stages laws were enacted curtailing the ability of ecclesiastical bodies to acquire real property or embark on building programmes. Furthermore, the desire to prevent covert pressures by any pro-ecclesiastical parties is evident in laws preventing close relatives of churchmen from holding certain offices or sitting in the Senate or Consiglio when matters concerning the Church or relations with the Papacy were under discussion. Doubtless the Papacy found the Venetian Signory considerably less docile than, say, the Dukes of Savoy. On the other hand, its intransigence in maintaining its powers *vis-à-vis* the Church was probably less than that of the crowns of France and Spain. To the liberal mentality of the late nineteenth century, however, Venetian policy seemed to provide a model of discriminating insistence on the integrity of secular power. Stress was laid above all on the events surrounding the interdict of 1606 and here the hero was Fra Paolo Sarpi.

The ostensible pretext for the imposition of the interdict was provided by recent mortmain laws and by the government's insistence on submitting two clergy of the Terraferma accused of nefarious crimes to the justice of the secular tribunals instead of handing them over to the spiritual arm; the mortmain laws of 1605 had extended to the Venetian dominions as a whole the restrictions on the power of ecclesiastical bodies to acquire real property which had hitherto only applied to Venice and the immediately adjoining region of the Dogado; in the case of the criminous clerks the Signory was attempting to extend to the Terraferma a privilege which it already enjoyed by papal concession for the city of Venice. It was mainly on these two issues that the papal ultimatum was based. In point of fact, Paul v was probably attempting to cut the gordian knot of a complex entanglement of disputes that had arisen in recent years involving, among other things, state appointments to the Patriarchate of Venice, the temporal jurisdiction of certain bishops and, perhaps the most important of all, Adriatic navigation. The interdict was imposed from April 1606 to May 1607 and it was raised without concessions of substance being made on the part of the Serenissima. Meanwhile a pamphlet war had broken out, sustained on the papal side mainly by certain Jesuits and on the Venetian side by a group of secular clerics and members of religious orders. The dispute and the polemic to which it gave rise were avidly watched all over Europe, not least in Protestant countries; even the Wisest Fool in Christendom felt impelled to unburden the royal mind in a pamphlet. For historians in England and France throughout the seventeenth century the Interdict dispute remained one of the wonders of the age and not a few modern historians have seen Venice's resistance as dealing the death-blow to papal pretensions to dominion over secular states.

Above all, it was the writings of Fra Paolo Sarpi that seized the attention of Europe at the time. His works were extensively printed and translated in England, France and the Netherlands in the course of the seventeenth century and no other Venetian writer in either the sixteenth or the seventeenth century can have enjoyed a European reputation of similar dimensions. To many late nineteenth-century historians he appeared as the animating soul of Venice's resistance to the Papacy and here, indeed, almost as the incarnation of a long-standing Venetian tradition. There is little evidence for such a contention, however, and his role appears to have been a relatively modest one. Although he had links with various high-ranking members of the government, he wrote essentially as a servant of the Signory—as its Consultant in Theology to be precise—and here he was held under a tight discipline which curtailed the expression of his own very radical views.

Nevertheless, those pamphlets in which Sarpi defended Venice's orthodoxy, asserted the supremacy of the secular power and rebutted contentions that the ecclesiastical estate was exempt from its control, surpassed in sheer bulk those of any other pro-Venetian pamphleteer and were unique in departing from the limited repertoire of arguments which the others repeated one after another; with him alone were the individual arguments related to a comprehensive and fully articulated theory of Church–State relations, although the full scope of his theory was only revealed in writings that were not published at the time. It was, however, to his *History of the Council of Trent*, written *c.* 1612–15 and first published in England in 1619, that Sarpi's European reputation was primarily due. Here he developed the thesis that the Council had brought the degradation of the Church to completion by finally subjecting her to papal absolutism; behind this thesis lay the vision of a decline from a primitive Church of apostolic simplicity and republican in structure to one corrupted by worldly possessions, tarnished by the proliferation of novel doctrines and in slavery to the papal will.

The very fact that Sarpi had the greatest European reputation of any Venetian writer has for centuries coloured the vision of the society to which he belonged. Indeed, a very one-sided picture of Venice's culture would result from a study purely of those of her writers on religion and politics who enjoyed a European fame, for in many cases they appealed to Protestant prejudices or to the preoccupations of those 'Gallican' Catholics who asserted the substantial independence of national churches *vis-à-vis* the Papacy. With regard to Sarpi, quite apart from the fact that his views were too radical for the government to allow their full expression in print, it is open to question how far he was representative of any Venetian tradition. His most obvious affinities were perhaps with certain Italian Protestants of the mid-sixteenth century and with those Italian bishops who, at the Council of Trent, asserted episcopal independence of the Papacy, and here it is Tuscans rather than Venetians that come to mind; the Venetian dominions, while subject to extensive Protestant propaganda and infiltration had produced few prominent Protestant thinkers and while there was doubtless a widespread tacit assumption there of the individual bishop's rights of initiative, there is little evidence of the strident episcopalism that had distinguished certain Tuscan bishops at Trent.

It is by no means obvious that any consistent principles had animated the Serenissima's policy regarding Church and Papacy in the century or so before the Interdict. Much obviously depended upon the composition of the government at any one time. It is possible that for much of the period the Serenissima's position was less that of a militant defender of the integrity of secular power than that of a courted damsel intent on securing every advantage from a favoured position. To many six-teenth-century popes, Venice must have appeared as a most desirable ally, a strong Italian power, less overweening than Spain, more reliable than a France undermined by the forces of Protestantism; under the circumstances it was perhaps only natural that the Serene Republic should assert a position of independence. Alleged points of principle could be put forward as bargaining counters by both sides and on many occasions they perhaps raised their demands beyond what they really hoped to attain; the rounds of diplomatic haggling between Venice and the Papacy often suggest the trading tactics of the oriental bazaar. Frequently enough compromise agreements were reached which only saved the formal structure of what had hitherto appeared as rigid posi-tions of principles. What emerged in the history of Veneto–Papal relations was not a precise delimitation of the spheres of Church and State but rather a very complex system in which Signory and Papacy both shared extensive control over almost all aspects of Church life.

Veneto–Papal relations were conditioned by the presence of both papalists and anti-papalists within the government and the place which étatiste anti-clericals held in Venetian society and culture should not be over-estimated. A line of prominent statesmen imbued with mistrust of ecclesiastical pretensions can be traced from the time of the War of the League of Cambrai, but it would be dangerous to look for the pre-sence of a coherent anti-clerical party before the 1580s. From this time, however, the party of the Giovani began to crystallise and gain in prominence and it secured a temporary triumph in the years 1605–6. Its leading members, as most notably with Nicolò da Ponte, Leonardo Donà and Nicolò Contarini, were often animated in their mistrust of the Papacy by a vision of the dignity of state power, zeal for political reform and even a severe personal piety. At the turn of the seventeenth century, many such men played a leading role in Venetian and Paduan intellectual milieus. Alongside the anti-clerical idealists, how-ever, must be set the members of the powerful and affluent dynasties which, doubtless by means of some entente with the Roman court, revelled in the lush pastures of the ecclesiastical beneficiary system; undoubtedly their hold over this system was severely weakened from the 1530s and their entrenched positions of political power seriously challenged from the 1580s, but their privileged position in Church and state was never completely destroyed. Such families did much to set the tones of lavishness and urbane refinement in Venetian society.

Again we must not forget that those austere ecclesiastics who, with predominantly religious preoccupations, were unyielding in their devotion to the Papacy, were not necessarily obscurantists inhabiting a closed world of the Church but were in certain cases men of wide culture and among the most respected intellects of their day.

We have seen that the myth of *Venezia città galante* was balanced by myths imbued with a more serious and indeed practical ethos, those of *Venezia città di libertà* and *Venezia stato misto* and the myth, if so it can be called, of 'Venice the lay state'. It is the first and the last that are, to some extent, still with us. Enthralment by them may lead us to forget that Venetian society and culture were profoundly influenced by the severe ethos of the Catholic reform movement. It is worth remembering that, in the city which immediately struck the eye by its opulence and extravagance, there lived and worked a body of men of severe personal piety, in certain cases profoundly preoccupied with the poverty and misery around them, some of whom were to play a leading role in the purification of the Catholic Church. Furthermore, concentration on the more exuberant and lavish aspects of Venetian culture would give a very one-sided picture of that culture as a whole.

Venice gave much to the Catholic reform movement and was in turn profoundly influenced by it. In the years 1510–11, two high-ranking nobles, Tomaso (Fra Paolo) Giustiniani and Vincenzo (Fra Pietro) Querini had left their city and families to join the hermit order of Camaldoli; subsequently they became the leaders of a movement for a strict eremetical observance within the order and their famous reform programme, the *Libellus ad Leonem X* presented to the Lateran Council in 1513, showed an acute awareness of the challenges faced by the Church in the sixteenth century. Giustiniani can be seen as an important link between fifteenth-century movements for monastic revival, so strong in the Venetian dominions, and the group of Catholic reformers of the Reformation period. The late 1520s and early 1530s saw the emergence in Venice of a number of important religious confraternities and looser reform-minded groups. These centred in the main upon the fiery, and later highly intolerant Neopolitan bishop Gianpietro Caraffa, General of the Theatine order and subsequently Pope Paul IV, and upon the cultivated reforming abbot of S. Giorgio Maggiore, the Modenese Gregorio Cortese. Caraffa's links were more particularly with zealant movements within the religious orders and with persons engaged in work for mendicants, syphilitics, prostitutes and orphans; of the several nobles engaged in charitable work, Gerolamo Miani, later the founder of a chain of orphanages extending over northern Italy, was perhaps the most distinguished. Around Cortese at S. Giorgio there gathered a group of churchmen and scholars, including Caraffa, Gasparo Contarini and Reginald Pole, apparently devoted in the main to discussions of a learned nature. Members of this circle and their correspondents outside Venice substantially formed the nucleus of the reforming group brought into positions of power in Rome in the mid-1530s.

With little doubt, the outstanding figure in the Venetian religious revival of the first half of the sixteenth century was Gasparo Contarini, a member both of the Giustiniani circle and of the S. Giorgio group. After a lifetime spent as a layman in the service of the Venetian state, mainly engaged in diplomacy, he was made a cardinal in 1534 and became perhaps the most powerful member of the reforming group at the papal court. On the basis of private studies while still a layman, he became one of the outstanding exponents in Italy of a theology based primarily on the Bible and the early Church Fathers. This, and a spiritual crisis in 1511, not dissimilar to that of Luther, particularly qualified him for his role as one of Europe's leading Catholic eirenicists; he sought conciliation with the German Protestants through a rigorous examination of theological points in a spirit of mutual charity and as Papal Legate at Ratisbon in 1541 he presided over one of the last and most heroic attempts to heal the religious schism. Contarini was also the author of the *Office of the Bishop*, one of the most noteworthy pieces of Italian reforming literature of the period. Contarini's ideal of a learned and dignified pastor, following a life of ordered routine, taking his occasional leisure in dignified pastimes and the converse of learned men, exercising his solicitude both for the succour of the poor and for the promotion of learning, was perhaps quintessentially the vision of a scholar-aristocrat and it had its limitations; he delineated the pastoral office in predominantly organisational terms. But it was precisely here, in the detailed points Contarini raised, that he appears as the prophet of later episcopal reform programmes, both in the legislation of the Council of Trent and in the work of individual bishops. Contarini, by his *De magistratibus venetorum* was one of the chief propagators of the myth of 'Venice state of liberty'. There is danger of erecting another myth on the basis of Contarini's own life, but the harmony between religious and civic zeal which it shows does perhaps exemplify one facet of the Venetian aristocratic ethos.

In the period after the Council of Trent, the Venetian dominions were well-placed to receive the new reforming wind blowing from Milan; St Charles Borromeo's activities here were to provide the model for much of post-Tridentine pastoral reform both in Italy and in Europe as a whole. Borromeo stood for a strong organisational reform, puritanical in a way and often somewhat bureaucratic in character, designed to transform the rabble of lower clergy into a presentable priestly caste and to curb popular licence among the laity. Borromeo and the austere, rigorous Pope Pius v made a strong impression on certain members of the Venetian aristocracy. It was to Borromeo that a phalanx of bishops drawn from Venetian nobility were looking in the 1570s and 80s and the fact that most of these were former government servants probably reinforced their tendency towards organisational rigorism. Outstanding among Borromeo's followers was Agostino Valier, Bishop of Verona. A public lecturer in philosophy for some years and recognised as one of the outstanding intellects in the Venice of his day, Valier combined moral and spiritual rigour with the outlook of the scholar. His affirmation of the primacy of the spiritual over the secular, of the other-worldly over the things of this life, his rejection of the earlier humanist vision of a harmony between antique culture and Christianity, may have been the marks of a rigid man, but they were not those of a man with narrow intellectual horizons. Perhaps, with his profound erudition, he had a clearer vision than many of his predecessors of the true nature of antique civilisation, and where he rejected so much of what are vulgarly called 'Renaissance values', he put forward vital and stimulating insights of his own; against classical poetry, he set the poetry of the Old Testament, against the cult of Petrarch, the Christian vision of Dante.

It has often been implied that Venice 'kept the Counter-Reformation at bay'. If the Counter-Reformation is understood as an aggressive quasi-political movement, vowed to the extirpation of heresy by persecution and military force and tending towards the creation of a papal autocracy within the Church, then this statement does contain a certain element of truth. But the Counter-Reformation, inasfar as it was a rigorist and even puritanical reform-movement, profoundly affected Venetian society. To disregard its influence while laying heavy stress on the tradition of *étatiste* anti-clericalism would give a highly distorted picture. At the same time, it would be misleading to suggest that the Catholic reform movement and the ideals of the Giovani were necessarily antithetical. Gasparo Contarini, although a staunch defender of papal supremacy within the Church, evidently held a most unfavourable view of the Roman court of his time, and this not least because of his reforming conscience, while the leading anti-papalist Leonardo Donà was an admirer of Borromeo and was himself highly regarded by Valier. Anti-clericalism and religious zeal were not necessarily opposed to one another; indeed they could be intimately connected. It has even been suggested that Giovani like Leonardo Donà and Nicolò Contarini, with their austere, moralistic vision, were the spiritual heirs of Gasparo Contarini.

A comprehension of the impact of the Catholic reform movement must also modify our picture of *Venezia città galante*. It influenced culture not in the direction of the baroque exuberance which has sometimes been regarded as the hall-mark of so-called 'counter-reformatory art' but which was in fact patronised by the more indulgent churchmen of the early seventeenth century; rather the ethos was one of austerity and mistrust of extravagance and, where artistic commissions were involved, the preoccupations were often distressingly utilitarian. This is not to say that the art of the great Venetian colourists was uninfluenced by new currents of popular piety but that it had little connection with the true leaders of Venetian Catholic reform.

The world of Titian was far removed from that in which many of the leaders of Venetian society moved. In any case, the art of the great colourists reveals only one facet of Venetian art as a whole. If, in painting, the dominant strain was one of colour, sensuousness and measured exuberance, marked by a generally free attitude towards classical norms, the tendency in sculpture was towards a severe, often austere, neoclassicism. This strain received considerable impetus from a weighty antiquarian scholarship and it is perhaps here that the most obvious links can be seen between art and the intellectual interests of the Venetian aristocracy. It would be dangerous to assume a parallel between this neo-classicist tradition and the ethos of the Counter-Reformation, but there may have been an indirect link inasfar as the ponderous antiquarian scholarship, of which archaeological study was one form, was probably a type of secular erudition that the counter-reformatory ethos regarded as safe and indeed dignified.

Monumental erudition, the patient accumulation of facts, whether concerning the arts, the humanities or the natural sciences, was something on which Venetians of scholarly inclination prided themselves and in which they excelled. As the sixteenth century progressed, it increasingly replaced a merely elegant classical culture as the intellectual passion of the Venetian ruling class. It had great potentialities in what it implied for archaeological, historical and scientific studies, but it was hardly glamorous.

But then, few Venetian nobles would have liked to think that they inhabited a *città galante*, although they might pretend that they did so for the benefit of distinguished visitors like Henry III of France, a featherbrained northerner who would be impressed by show. Their extravagance, as foreign observers admitted, was lavished on their palaces rather than on the adornment of their persons.[13] *Gravità* was seen as the distinguishing characteristic of Venetian nobles. They did not, so Agostino Valier asserted, approve of ornate speeches; brevity was what they relished. Venetian thought, indeed, has little of the elegance that we associate with the Tuscans and the style in which it was expressed carries with it the ponderous, almost lumbering cadences of the Venetian dialect. The thought of the great Venetian historians, political theorists and art-critics has, for all its originality, an element of the prosaic, but this very prosaic quality can come to be respected and, in the end, loved.

Notes

[1] *Epistre envoyée de Venise à Mme la Duchesse de Ferrare par C. Marot*. Variant D. In C. Marot, *Les Epîtres. Edition critique* ed. C. A. Mayer (London 1958)

[2] *Voyage en Italie* in Montaigne, *Oeuvres complètes* (ed. Pleiade, 1962), pp. 83–4

[3] T. Coryat, *Coryat's Crudities*, I (Glasgow 1905), pp. 302, 599, 401–5, 427

[4] G. Contarini, *De magistratus venetorum*, 1st ed. Venice 1524, 2nd ed. Paris 1540, English trans. by Lewes Lewkenor, London 1598

[5] Traiano Boccalini, *Ragguagli di Parnasso*, 1st ed., see critical edition ed. G. Rua, 3 vols (Bari 1934–48), I, pp. 30–31, 78–81

[6] G. Botero, *Relatione della republica veneziana* (Venice 1605)

[7] Claude de Seyssel, *La monarchie de France*, 1st ed. Paris 1515, see critical edition ed. J. Poujol (Paris 1961) pp. 107–10

[8] Etienne La Boetie, *De la servitude volontaire*, 1st ed. 1587, see Paris 1963 ed. p. 65. (According to Montaigne it was written in 1548)

[9] J. Bodin, *Method for the Easy Comprehension of History*, trans. B. Reynolds (New York 1966) pp. 165, 185–98, 273–8, cf. *Six Books of the Commonwealth*, trans. M. J. Tooley (Oxford 1955) pp. 193–5, 209

[10] On the subject of the myths of the Venetian state generally, see: F. Gaeta, 'Alcune considerazioni sul mito di Venezia', *Bibliothèque d'Humanisme et de Renaissance*, XXIII, (1961), pp. 58–75; R. Pecchioli, 'Il "mito" di Venezia e la crisi fiorentina intorno al 1500', *Studi Storici*, III, (1962) pp. 451–92; B. S. Pullan, 'Service to the Venetian State. Aspects of Myth and Reality in the Early Seventeenth Century', *Studi Secenteschi*, V,

(1964), pp. 95–147; F. Simone, 'I contributi della cultura veneta allo sviluppo del Rinascimento francese', in *Rinascimento europeo e Rinascimento veneziano*, ed. V. Branca (Florence 1967), pp. 153–7; F. Gilbert, 'The Venetian Constitution in Florentine Political Thought' in *Florentine Studies* ed. N. Rubinstein (London 1968), pp. 463–500

[11] As examples of such liberal historiography I am thinking especially of B. Cecchetti, *La repubblica di Venezia e la Corte di Roma nei rapporti della religione*, 2 vols., (Venice 1874); A. Battistella 'La politica ecclesiastica della Repubblica di Venezia', *Archivio Veneto*, XVI (1896), pp. 386–420

[12] E. Pommier, 'La société vénitienne et la Réforme Protestante', *Boll. Ist. Stor. & Stat. Ven.* I (1959), pp. 4–5 and seq.

[13] Note *Coryat's Crudities*, I, pp. 397–8, 415

two

Venetian Society

The Venetian dominions in the sixteenth century included a large area of the north Italian plain, the Dalmatian littoral and a number of eastern Mediterranean islands. A small mainland area immediately adjoining the Lagoon was known as the Dogado, but the remainder of the north Italian territories went under the collective name of the Terraferma. Between the seaboard and the river Mincio, lay the lowland region now known as *Venezia Eugeniana*, its principal towns being Padua, Vicenza and Verona, and further west still, bordering on the confines of the Milanese state, a section of Lombardy including Bergamo, Brescia and Crema. This general lowland region was a rich agricultural one supporting a wide range of semi-rural industries and including a number of flourishing cities. To the northeast of Venice, between the seaboard and the Giulian Alps, lay Friuli, a wild, lethargic, feudalised area, alternating between rich plainland and unproductive hill country. A wedge of Habsburg territory separated Friuli from Istria, Venice's Italian territory on the eastern shore of the Adriatic. From here, Venetian dominion was prolonged into the Slav lands by a narrow strip of the Dalmatian littoral. Here the towns were mainly Italian colonies in a Slav countryside. The most important Italian colony, and Venice's great commercial rival, Ragusa lay outside Venetian territory and in the course of the sixteenth century Venice's Dalmatian possessions were subject to Turkish encroachments. Of the eastern Mediterranean islands, the most important were Crete and Cyprus, rich corn, wine and sugar producers. Cyprus, however, was lost to the Turks in 1570, certain other islands having been lost to them in 1540.

The eastern Mediterranean sections of the empire were ruled basically as colonial territories by a small body of Venetian administrators who did not always desist from the cruder forms of exploitation and who did not have to consult local representative organs. The *Città dominante*'s relations with the Terraferma and the Dalmatian territories were more complex, however. Here the ancient communes had accepted Venetian dominion, mostly around the turn of the fifteenth century, by very precise treaties of submission; thereby they retained their customary legal systems and their communal assemblies. The purview of the latter had, however, been rapidly reduced to the more petty details of local government and real power had passed into the hands of Venetian *rettori* who controlled not only military administration, but also civil administration. This process was combined in the Terraferma, although not apparently in Dalmatia, with a government policy favouring the dominance in city councils of the privileged groups of nobles and 'citizens'. The aristocracies of the Terraferma were of considerable significance and we shall speak more of them in due course.

The Economy

The strength of the Venetian economy was based not only upon a European and Mediterranean trade-network but also upon the considerable resources of the Terraferma as well as Venice's own industries. In the eastern Mediterranean, Venice enjoyed a powerful trading position in Constantinople, Syria and Egypt and one that was, up to the 1570s, little challenged by the merchants of other Christian powers, with the exception of Genoa, whose position in the Levant had in any case been seriously weakened in the late fifteenth century. Constantinople was the entrepôt for a wide range of products, including wood, corn and sugar, from the Black Sea area. Aleppo, Damascus, Alexandria and Cairo were the major points of debouchement for the trans-Arabia spice trade and the lesser luxury trades, such as that in silk, which it carried with it. Venetian trade with northern Europe, so important in the fifteenth century, continued to be significant up to the 1570s and Venice continued into the early seventeenth century to provide the main link between southern Germany and the Mediterranean, although the trade from the Venetian dominions into Germany was substantially in the hands of German merchants of whom there was a large community in the city. In the course of the sixteenth century, the agriculture and industries of the Terraferma came to play an increasingly important role in the Venetian economy and by the mid-seventeenth century they were its main support.

The sixteenth century had seen serious threats to Venice's mercantile position. There had been a temporary depression in ship-building at the end of the fifteenth century. The effects of the development after 1494 of the Cape route which enabled the Portuguese to tap the spice trade at its source and, for a very brief period, to block the entry of spices into Arabia and the Red Sea, was registered with surprising rapidity by a dearth of spices at the Levantine ports in the years 1500-1. The gravity of the threat posed by the Cape route was increased by the fact that groups of bankers from Genoa, Florence and central Germany moved to Lisbon and managed to participate with their capital and their ships in eastern voyages. The moving of the Portuguese spice-staple to Antwerp in 1507 exposed Venice to the danger of completely losing her German clientèle. The Portuguese were unable, in the long run, to maintain their hold in the Persian Gulf, but obstacles to the recovery of the Mediterranean spice trade were imposed by the Turkish wars of conquest in Syria and Egypt between 1516 and 1523 and for some years the new Turkish rulers, by a rapacious policy of levying imposts, showed themselves less sensitive to the needs of trade than their Mameluke predecessors. The Levant trade continued, however, and while Venetian construction of the small, fast galleys diminished, there was increased employment of the large round ships, more suited to bulky cargoes. Around the middle of the century came a general efflorescence of Mediterranean trade in which Venice shared and it is probable that between about 1550 and 1570 her spice trade rose to a level never hitherto reached. Throughout the century her cloth-manufacture, which had rapidly expanded up to the 1560s, continued to flourish and to provide an important article of exchange for the merchandise of the East.

From about 1570, however, Venice's Levant trade was increasingly damaged by competition on the part of merchants from England, the United Provinces and France; moreover, she ceased to be the main carrier of silks and spices to these countries, although she continued into the first decade of the seventeenth century to be the main purveyor of these products to the German lands. By the 1590s her ship-building industry was declining. In the first decade of the seventeenth century she was further hit by a decline of the Levantine spice market caused by a renewed exploitation of the Cape route, this time by the English and Dutch, and with the turn of the century the gradual beginnings of the long decline in her cloth industry can be detected. Around the 1620s Venetian trade and the Venetian cloth industry succumbed to a crisis, one which was, however, evidently common to much of Europe.

Economic life and especially industry were probably disrupted by the serious fall in population caused by the plague of 1630–1: decimation of the labour force evidently pushed up wages and hence the price of manufactured articles to an uncompetitive level. Venetian cloth, which, for reasons of the materials available and of craft traditions, had always tended to be of high quality but expensive, was in an especially weak position in a period when manufacturers of such cloths all over Europe were succumbing to the competition of manufacturers of cheap, coarse cloths such as the English and Dutch. Luxury industries and agriculture were to form the main basis of the Venetian economy.

While empire waned and commerce declined, the increasingly landward orientations of Venetian interests continued to develop. There had been extensive purchases of lands in the Padovano in the fifteenth century, following the Serenissima's acquisition of the region in 1405. Reliable statistics of Venetian landholding are not available before the early seventeenth century, but the evidence available suggests a steady increase in acquisitions from the late fifteenth century. The diarist Gerolamo Priuli, in the second decade of the sixteenth century, wrote in terms suggestive of a fairly recent scramble for land. This may have been accentuated by the trade contraction after 1500. It is probable that the main period of land reclamation was between about 1540 and 1580. The crucial period of change to landed activities in general, however, may have been in the period c. 1570–1630, while the increase in Venetian landholding continued steadily throughout the seventeenth century. Not only nobles, but virtually all Venetians with funds to dispose of had joined in the land scramble. Lands were extensively purchased and developed all over the fertile area to the east of the Mincio, but predominantly in the arc of territory stretching from the southern end of Venice's Adriatic seaboard, through the Padovano towards the Trevigiano to the north. The Venetians were active not only in land drainage but also in land-improvements generally, they introduced new crops, notably maize, which was to save the Veneto from famine in the seventeenth century, and they are to be regarded as being among the pioneers of the minor agrarian revolution that affected various countries of western Europe in the course of that century. The great spokesman of the movement for the exploitation of the mainland was Alvise Corner who had himself restored his ruined patrimony by means of his activities on his estates in the Padovano. Corner, in a memorandum to the Signory of 1556, noted that the population had increased and was putting heavy pressure on food supplies, while existing arable land was being progressively exhausted; he claimed that it was necessary for the Venetian state to increase grain-production in order to reduce imports which were responsible for loss of specie, and he put forward an ambitious programme of land-drainage. Agrarian autarchy was by no means achieved in the Venetian dominions, but it is probable that increased acquisition and exploitation of lands in the Terraferma helped to counter-balance the decline in trade.

Among recent historians there has been a strong reaction against the picture of a general Venetian decline in the sixteenth century and this was not the picture seen by contemporaries. A political decadence is now minimised and a serious economic decline placed only in the second quarter of the seventeenth century. This was a period in which many other European countries were experiencing economic stagnation, but Venice showed no particular signs of recovering from it. It would be safest, however, when speaking of the 'decline' of the Venetian economy to regard this as meaning in the long run that the latter failed to keep pace with expansion elsewhere in Europe, more particularly the north, rather than as implying an overall fall in prosperity.

Whatever the troubles of the Venetian economy, Venice in the sixteenth and early seventeenth centuries managed to support heavy expenditure on buildings, works of art and general ostentation. It is probable that a major increase in such expenditure took place around the middle years of the sixteenth century. It seems reasonable to connect it, in the first instance, with the boom in Mediterranean trade in the years 1550–70. The wave of massive expenditure continued, however, long after the trade boom had weakened. It is possible that decreased opportunities for secure investment in trade may have lead men to put their money into buildings and objets d'art instead of trade. Carleton, the English Ambassador, writing in the 1620s thought that the passion for luxury increased as trade declined. Heavy artistic expenditure is a sign of recent wealth, but not necessarily of expanding or stable wealth.[1]

Venetian Society

We have already seen that political power lay in the hands of the corpus of nobles, that is of persons entitled to sit in the Maggior Consiglio; there were some 2,500 of them at the beginning of the sixteenth

1 Giorgione, *The Three Philosophers* (see pp. 79–81, 227–9)

2 Detail from Fig. 1

3 Daniele Barbaro (1513–70), scholar and patron, by Titian (see pp. 59–61, 173)

century and some 1,600 by 1630. Their number was substantially confined to the descendants of those included in the Maggior Consiglio at the time of the great 'closure' of 1296–7 or those brought in by the block of ennoblements of 1381; after this, apart from members of foreign ruling houses and the families of a few persons who had distinguished themselves in the Italian wars of the fifteenth and early sixteenth centuries, scarcely any families were added to the nobility until the period 1646–69 when, under pressure of the Cretan war, a number were admitted in return for a payment of 100,000 ducats each. The genealogies of the nobility were guarded by the Magistracy of the *Avogadori di Commun* and no one who was not inscribed in their 'Golden Book' might sit in the Maggior Consiglio. Only nobles possessed voting rights in the executive committees and councils of state such as the small Consiglio proper, the Collegio, the Senate and the Council of Ten. To the nobles were effectively confined the so-called *magistrati* or what we may call, for lack of a better name, the 'responsible' governmental posts, including provincial governorships and also official ambassadorships.

As we have seen, membership of the various councils of State signified a certain *de facto* hierarchy among the nobility. The 'senatorial nobility' comprised a stratum of moderate elevation, while an inner core of families of established political pre-eminence exercised their power through the Collegio and, above all, the Council of Ten. Gradations within the nobility were also reflected in tenure of the *magistrati*. Of the 'responsible' offices of state, the least distinguished were the castellanships and the governorships of minor towns; these posts were attractive enough to small nobles, however, since they gave opportunities for perquisites. Of middling importance were the majority of judicial and financial magistracies; again of only middling importance were the governorships of Verona, Vicenza, Bergamo and Treviso; officials at this level were often members of the Senate. At the summit of the *cursus honorum* were the civil and military governorships of Padua and Brescia, the Lieutenancy of Friuli, and full ambassadorships: the key post that formed the habitual opening to the highest offices was that of *Savio di Terraferma*. The supreme honorific positions in the state, apart from the Dogado, were the *Cavaleriato* and the Procuracy (i.e. wardenship) of the basilica of St Marks. The highest offices demanded the maintenance of a more than dignified 'state' and involved their holders in considerable expense. They therefore necessitated extraordinary wealth as well as considerable talent.

B

Nobility was a purely legal status. Many nobles were, in fact, paupers. It has been suggested that the nobility was in decline in the first half of the seventeenth century. Certainly governing circles were beginning to regard pauperism as a danger by the early years of the century. Already many nobles of the better sort were experiencing difficulty in maintaining their position in an age of extravagance and ostentation, in supporting the costs of high government offices that fell upon the holder, and in marrying off their daughters. Yet it would be dangerous to posit an overall decline of the nobility and we do not possess a sufficiently general picture of the Venetian economy to argue it from any decline in Venice's total wealth. Moreover, a decline in numbers of the nobility might have meant increased *per capita* wealth.[2]

Below the nobles came the citizens, who fell into several classes: the *cittadini originarii* proper, the allied group capable of entering the corps of scribes and notaries and 'citizens by grace'. *Cittadini originarii* had to be legitimate descendants of two generations of Venetian citizens and must possess 'honourable status', that is neither they nor their father might have exercised a 'mechanical' occupation. Apart from the requirements of citizen forbears, essentially the same qualifications were required for admission to the body of public notaries and to that of the accountants and holders of lesser secretarial posts in the bureaucracy. Citizenship 'by grace', either *de intus*, bestowing rights to trade inside Venice or *de extra* giving rights to trade outside, needed certain qualifications of residence or marriage. These trading rights, of course, belonged automatically to the upper two ranks of citizens, as well as to nobles.

Citizens had no voting rights in the committees and councils of state, yet they could play an important role in the 'non-responsible' permanent bureaucratic posts or *ministeri*. Given the rapid circulation of nobles from one government office to another, citizens of the two upper ranks would have provided the bureaucracy with its backbone of personnel with specialised experience and their official subordination to noble 'magistrates' must often have been no more meaningful than the subordination in the modern British army of regimental sergeant-majors and quartermasters to commissioned subalterns. Indeed in the 1620s complaints were being raised against the enormous power of the secretaries of the Council of Ten and the Senate. The 'ministerial' posts of the Ducal chancery were confined to *cittadini originarii* by a law of 1478, nobles being thereby excluded (a ruling that was slightly altered by laws of 1486 and 1559 allowing a newly elected Doge to make appointments notwithstanding this law). This meant that the secretaries of the Senate and the Council of Ten and also the Cancelliere Inferiore who supervised the city's notaries, were normally *cittadini originarii*. Only a *cittadino originario* might obtain the extremely honourable post of the Cancelliere Grande who headed the Chancery. The latter had charge of all government documents including treaties; his office gave him entry into all Councils of State and one of the chief positions of honour there, although not a deliberative voice; he had a place in all public functions and his funeral was equal to that of a doge.[3] Citizens, drawn from the ranks of the secretaries, were sometimes employed in the fully 'responsible' post of resident or agent in a foreign country, who performed many of the functions of an ambassador without enjoying the honours normally due to one. Residencies might be used for diplomacy with subject states, like Milan or Naples, or with Protestant states; in the case of the latter, the despatch of a full ambassador would have caused embarrassments with the Papacy and the despatch of an unobtrusive citizen was advisable; for certain missions in oriental countries it was not always possible to find nobles with the necessary linguistic knowledge. Citizens frequently held high positions in the armed forces, such as that of *Amiraglio dell'Armar*, a post that was, however, officially subordinate to the noble post of *Capitaneo General del Mar*.

The official posts of the great lay religious confraternities, the Scuole Grandi, were confined to citizens. The officers of the Scuole supervised the disbursement of large sums for charitable purposes and performed impressive ceremonial functions.[4]

Within the body of the *cittadini originarii* it is possible to detect a species of administrative caste. Between the mid-fifteenth and the mid-seventeenth centuries, the Grand Chancellorship and leading secretarial posts were held with particular frequency by members of the Padavin, Franceschi, Antelmi and Ottobon families; the latter two were ennobled in 1646. The Ottobon family was the most distinguished of all; it was to produce a Pope, Alexander VII (1689–91); it was intermarried with several noble families and connected by marriage with high-ranking government servants from other citizen families.[5]

Marriage both between nobles and women of citizen class and between citizens and noble women were, in fact, quite common, although the former were, it might be assumed, more attractive since nobility could only be transmitted through the male line. The dowry of a citizen's daughter would have been a worth-while prize for not a few nobles.

Citizens may often have been among the wealthier members of Venetian society. The 100,000 ducats paid by citizens for admission to the nobility was no paltry sum even in 1650. We know that Gianfranco Labia, one of those elevated around this time, was very rich (in addition to being connected to several noble houses through marriage).[6] The family background of Bertoldo and Paolo Vidman, two citizens who were ennobled in 1646 and whose brother Christoforo was a cardinal, is particularly noteworthy; their father Giovanni, a Carinthian merchant with a generation of Venetian residence behind him, revealed himself in his testament of 1630 as a man of stupendous wealth.[7] Unfortunately no study has been made of citizens' wealth from tax-rolls and indications of wealth are difficult to draw from testaments —testators were too reticent about their total possessions—but the most lavish pious bequests often came from citizens.[8] When nobility was sold to 80 families in the years 1646–69, it was, moreover, hardly a question of letting in a horde of parvenus. Some were parvenus certainly, but in the enrolment lists, alongside the names of provincial noble families, the eye is continually struck by the names of citizen families which had been prominent for over a century, sometimes from the fifteenth century; some families had found themselves narrowly excluded from the nobility at the time of the great 'closure' of 1297.[9] The *cittadinanza* was not a rigid caste like the nobility—it was easy enough to enter—but it possessed an inner élite core of relative stability and the importance of its members must not be forgotten.

Even in a city remarkable for a large, erudite and educated aristocratic milieu, many of the more lettered members of society were citizens. It is significant that the school of S. Marco, the Venetian humanist academy par excellence, had been founded around 1450 for the education of members of the Ducal Chancery. While the Venetian Cancelliere Grande never exercised any scholarly role comparable to that of the Florentine Cancelliere, the government secretariate included a number of distinguished scholars, including Gian Battista Ramusio, a fine linguist and famous geographer, Celio Magno, a poet learned in ancient and modern languages, and Antonio Milledonnis, one of the first historians of the Council of Trent.

Having examined the Venetian caste-system, it is now desirable to say something about Venetian family structure. It is necessary to be clear, however, as to what we mean by 'family'. The Venetian aristocracy was composed in the sixteenth century of some seventy *case*. Thus the *serrata* of 1296 had granted entry into the Maggior Consiglio to entire *case* and henceforth any Contarini, Loredan or Corner, say, who was of legitimate descent and whose escutcheon was not blemished by some 'infamy' was a noble. The *case* had various branches or *rami* which often took their name from a particular palazzo or the parish in which it was situated. The group which actually inhabited a particular palazzo would often be very much smaller, however.

By our period, many members of individual *case* had ceased to be 'relatives' in any meaningful sense of the term—the Contarini house, for instance, comprised some two hundred male nobles—and it is open to doubt whether any substantial clan-organisation or 'clan-spirit' existed. Sometimes an entire *casa* exercised the right of presentation to an abbacy. A testator might occasionally make a bequest for the education of the sons of his *casa* or sometimes he would provide that its eldest member should be his executor in the case of death or default of other executors. In general, however, testaments do not suggest any strength of 'clan-spirit'. Members of the individual *ramo* might only be related in the twelfth degree of kinship and there is little to suggest that it had a particularly tight structure.

Families proper, within the first and second degrees of kinship were often closely knit, however. The family partnership or *fraterna* was the predominant form of business organisation. Furthermore, a group of brothers, together with their families and un-married sisters, would often share the same palazzo and manage the family affairs in common, or so many a paterfamilias hoped; rather pathetic entreaties for such family unity often occur in testaments. The bulk of the ancestral wealth would often be vested in a 'family trust' for the benefit of all the male heirs. Entail by primogeniture seems to have been fairly rare in Venice at this time; by the adapted form of *fidecommesso*, or family trust, commonly found there, the bulk of the family wealth, funds as well as immoveables, was bequeathed to all of a testator's sons equally to be passed on to their descendants, those without male issue leaving their portions to the lines that continued. The practicability of this system substantially depended upon the fact that many Venetian nobles apparently never married.

Partly as a result of this system, Venice did not have a 'problem of younger sons'. Furthermore it was often younger sons who married and the eldest ones not infrequently remained celibate. The classic picture of a flock of noble cadets entering the Church does not apply in

Venice; often it was the eldest sons, who had perhaps received the best
education, who became prelates. Besides, government office provided
sons of the Venetian patriciate with openings for employment that
few other European nobilities possessed.

Possession of an empire provided the upper strata of Venetian
society with certain financial opportunities. For the nobles there were a
large number of civil and military governorships and castellanships.
These were not necessarily particularly profitable, however. Tenure
of the more important governorships could involve heavy personal
expenditure, while the official revenues of the minor ones were very
small indeed. Furthermore, many posts were subject to a period of
contumacia during which a recently retired official was temporarily
ineligible for further office. It is impossible to estimate what Venetian
officials drew from perquisites and the fruits of corruption.

Another way in which the Venetian nobility exploited the resources
of the Republic's dominions was through tenure of ecclesiastical office.
Quite apart from abbacies and canonries, many of which were held by
Venetian nobles, there were 44 bishoprics in the Venetian dominions.
Disregarding the two poor bishoprics of Caorle and Chioggia, the 16
sees of the north-Italian plain and Friuli were attractive enough to pro-
spective incumbents, all having revenues of over 2,000 ducats in the
first half of the seventeenth century; the richest were apparently Padua,
Aquilea, Verona, Vicenza, Bergamo, Brescia and Adria most of which
had revenues of between 5–10,000 ducats around this time; Padua had
revenues of 15,000 ducats in 1494 and was obviously one of the richest
bishoprics in Italy and while figures are lacking for Aquilea, the great
see of Friuli, it was clearly again one of the most affluent. The bishoprics
of Istria, Dalmatia and the eastern Mediterranean were less attractive
on account of both distance and small revenues; only about nine of
them had revenues of over 2,000 ducats in the early seventeenth
century. The sees in these regions were often held by natives or by
southern Italians. The more affluent bishoprics, most notably those of
the Italian mainland, were substantially a preserve of the Venetian
nobility, however. In the first half of the sixteenth century only some
17 non-Venetians, mostly papal favourites, held any of the 16 major
bishoprics in the Terraferma, while in the latter half of the century,
only about seven did so. A number of Venetian *cittadini* held bishoprics,
but these were minor ones. It is not altogether clear how the hold of
Venetian nobles over the better ecclesiastical preferments was obtained.
The Signory only possessed rights of presentation to the sees of Venice

and Candia, but the Papacy certainly paid close attention to the recommendations which the Serenissima from time to time put forward and it doubtless realised that it was necessary to promote Venetian patricians to the more important sees if it wished to remain on good terms with the Republic. The near monopoly by Venetian patricians, which was consolidated around the middle years of the sixteenth century, was not disturbed by subsequent tensions between Venice and the Papacy.

Certain patrician families enjoyed a particularly privileged position in the ecclesiastical beneficiary system and established a firm hold over certain bishoprics and benefices. In the early part of the sixteenth century, a small group of families had acquired vast accumulations of these. From about the mid-1530s, partly it would seem as a result of pressure from the Venetian government and partly, doubtless, on account of the reforming preoccupations of the Papacy, these systems of pluralities began to break down, but certain ecclesiastical preferments virtually remained family heirlooms until well into the seventeenth century. The frequency with which relatives succeeded one another in bishoprics did not decrease vastly during the period of reform in the middle and latter years of the sixteenth century, indeed highly conscientious bishops were quite prepared to resign sees to their nephews. It should be said that the hold which certain families acquired over bishoprics was based not on any juridical rights but on judicious manipulation of the system of resignation.

Two groups of families enjoyed an especially large share of ecclesiastical preferments in the sixteenth century: the Grimani-Barbaro consortium and the Corner-Pisani consortium. The Corner di ca Grande of S. Maurizio and S. Polo and the Pisani di S. Maria Zobenigo (later di S. Stefano) were linked by marriage. The Grimani of S. Maria Formosa and the Barbaro of S. Maria Mater Domini also appear to have had familial links. The Grimani were ultimately linked to the Pisani by intermarriage with the Querini and Giustiniani who shared in the patronage system of the two groups and with the Priuli who accumulated a large number of church preferments on their own account. The branches of the Grimani, Corner and Pisani concerned were families of high political distinction, greatly enriched by trade and, in the case of the Pisani, banking. All three families achieved their position with regard to the Church by similar methods; Domenico Grimani in 1493, Francesco Pisani in 1518 and Francesco Corner in 1527 used their family wealth and probably a certain amount of political intrigue to gain the cardinalate; once they had achieved this eminence they were able to make their vast accumulations of ecclesiastical preferments. Domenico Grimani and his nephews Marco, Marino and Giovanni kept the sees of Aquilea, Ceneda and Concordia, together with a number of lesser preferments in their hands by a complex system of nominal resignations to one another. The heyday of Grimani accumulations was over by 1546, but they continued to hold Aquilea for another eighty years while intermittently sharing it with the Barbaro; probably their tenure of it was favoured by the Venetian government which feared that it might fall into the hands of a Habsburg subject. Bishoprics were held by members of the Corner family on no less than 18 occassions between 1527 and 1626. Between 1524 and 1630, the see of Padua was almost continuously in their hands or in those of their Pisani relatives to whom it was intermittently resigned, while the Pisani shared with them their own control over the see of Treviso. While the power of individual prelates to accumulate bishoprics was curbed from the 1530s, the Corner family's share of Venetian bishoprics and other ecclesiastical preferments did not notably diminish until after the 1630s and it continued to be prominent in the Church up to the eighteenth century. With the early seventeenth century, a new dynasty of ecclesiastical potentates emerged in the shape of the Delfin who, after holding a number of bishoprics, most notably Vicenza, in the first half of the century, acquired a near monopoly over Aquilea from 1659 until the fall of the Republic.

The Venetian government often envisaged grants of ecclesiastical preferments as a means of aiding noble houses. It was probably not pauperised ones exactly that it had in mind—bishoprics of any importance usually went to families at the level of senatorial nobility—but rather relatively distinguished ones whose fortunes were not in as healthy a state as they might have been; in particular ecclesiastical office was envisaged as a way of compensating families whose members had diminished their fortunes in government service. Yet if the distribution of ecclesiastical preferments represented in a small measure an attempt to provide outdoor relief for families of ailing though not exactly extenuated fortunes, more generally, and especially where the most important preferments were involved, it only mirrored the dominance of certain families within Venetian society. The Grimani, Pisani and Corner were among its leaders on account both of wealth and of political prestige. The Corner above all, perhaps, represented the inner core of *case vecchie* who made their weight felt through the Council of Ten, and when the reformist anti-clerical party of the

Giovani in the latter decades of the sixteenth century simultaneously attacked the dominance of the Council of Ten and sought to counter the influence of the Roman court and its paladins among the Venetian nobility, it was families like the Corner that they were ultimately opposing. The Barbaro, although very wealthy, belonged less obviously to the monied interest and had none of the shadiness of the Corner; rather they were a family distinguished by loyal service to the Venetian state at high levels and represented a remarkable union of administrative competence with intellectual distinction. The Delfin were quite probably trying to repair the family fortunes by tenure of ecclesiastical office; Giovanni Delfin, who became bishop of Vicenza in 1603 after a long political career and had been for some time suspected of angling for ecclesiastical dignities, was in financial difficulties, but he had been one of the leading figures in Venetian politics; the Delfin, again, were among the leaders of Venetian society. In due course we shall be examining the artistic patronage of the Grimani, Barbaro and Corner; the role of the Delfin in this respect belongs primarily to the eighteenth century.[10]

The Terraferma also possessed its élites in the old feudal territorial nobilities and in the urban aristocracies and citizenries which had emerged since the fourteenth century. From this time, a distinction between *popolani* and *cittadini* had become increasingly common. The marks of the *cittadino* were generally recognised as being his family's residence in a city and its abstention from 'mechanical trades' for a fairly extensive period. By the sixteenth century, the terms *cittadino* and *nobile* were becoming substantially synonymous in several major cities, notably Padua, Vicenza, Verona and Brescia. The emergence of these aristocracies was in large measure connected with the process whereby membership of the city councils had become increasingly hereditary, while artisan representation was progressively reduced. Throughout the fifteenth century, the Venetian government had abetted this process and continued to do so after the War of the League of Cambrai, despite the fact that groups of the urban nobility and citizenry, most notably in Verona, Vicenza, Padua and Treviso, had sided with the Imperialist invaders, while it was more the *popolani* who had shown themselves loyal to Venice. While it was basically in the fifteenth century that closed castes had asserted their hegemony in the towns and cities and acquired *de facto* the majority of seats on city councils and a monopoly of administrative posts, it was in the sixteenth century that this situation was given legislative form. The aristocratisation of the city councils continued up to the eighteenth century.

The effective powers of these councils were, on the other hand, being progressively whittled away as the reins passed into the hands of the *podestà* and *capitanei*, the civil and military governors sent from Venice. Not only the governorships of the main towns and cities, but also the important military governorships in the countryside passed into the hands of Venetians, although a few of the lesser ones, together with various communal offices, were left for provincial nobles and citizens. These did not enjoy opportunities for service in the administration of the Serenissima properly speaking. At the same time, few of them were employed in Venice's army; her numerous mercenaries tended to come from her Balkan possessions or from outside her dominions altogether. Furthermore, as far as ecclesiastical office in the Venetian dominions went, they were virtually confined to abbacies and canonries. Those numerous provincial nobles who followed a career of arms usually did so in the armies of other European powers, particularly the Imperial ones, and provincial aristocracies often looked sympathetically towards the Habsburgs, in whose adjacent dominions nobles were, they believed, better treated. In general, provincial nobilities and citizenries had reason for resentment against Venice. Provincial proprietors were increasingly giving way to Venetians in the economic dominance of the Terraferma, although more particularly in the Polesine, Padovano and Trevigiano. Around the turn of the sixteenth century, many provincial proprietors had been induced to alienate their lands in return for what had appeared at the time to be generous cash payments and in the ensuing decades had consumed their liquid capital, while Venetian landlords, often with the aid of land-improvements, had drawn extensive profits from agriculture in a period of rising food prices; moreover, a certain proportion of the land acquired by Venetians had, in fact, been confiscated from provincial nobles guilty of treasonable activities.

As has been seen, there were in the Terraferma two main strata of aristocracy, the old territorial nobility of fief-holders and castellans and the 'civic aristocracies', of which the most notable were those of Padua, Vicenza, Verona and Brescia. Friuli was the region par excellence of the feudal baronage, here an unruly caste, for the most part hostile to Venice at the beginning of the sixteenth century. The faction-struggles which had long divided the region broke out into conflagration after Venice's defeat in 1509, when the pro-Venetian Savorgnan had attempted to settle accounts with their adversaries, profiting from a wave of popular violence. Venice had suppressed the open faction-war, but throughout the sixteenth century was unable to eliminate the chronic conditions of vendetta and brigandage. In Brescia, civic and feudal aristocracies lived side by side, not without tension. Here again, the *mores* of the feudal caste made for disorder, although the Brescian nobility was noted for its relative loyalty to Venice. Notoriously the most haughty of the Venetian Terraferma, the Brescian civic aristocracy had assumed the character of a closed caste earlier than others. The nobilities and citizenries of Verona, Vicenza, Padua and Treviso, if less patient of Venetian rule, were evidently more civilised. The aristocracy of Vicenza, a civic nobility with extensive landed interests was apparently the most numerous, the most prosperous and the most cultivated of the Terraferma. It had, however, few outlets for its energies and considerable talents. A large number of Vicentine nobles served as *condottieri*, generally in the pay of other Italian and European powers. Some attached themselves to courts both inside and outside Italy and, while opportunities for bishoprics in the Venetian dominions were lacking, several achieved prominence in the Papal Curia. Little is known, as yet, of Vicenza's idiosyncratic culture and society, but it was obviously the most brilliant of all the capitals of the Veneto. The peculiarly aristocratic character of this culture was a symptom of the change which had taken place in the societies of the Terraferma as a whole. Not only had the civic aristocracies asserted their hegemony in the towns, but furthermore they were acquiring in the sixteenth century all the characteristics of a caste ethos. Thus involvement in trade and industry appears to have been regarded with disfavour in the latter part of the sixteenth century. It could raise difficulties regarding entry into the citizen body. It certainly did not automatically disqualify a person, but it did raise doubts as to whether he had disqualified himself by physically soiling his hands with merchandise. A business-man was a person who might have these skeletons in his cupboard; a noble, it was often indicated, lived off rents and dues.[11] We should not overstress here the contrast with the Venetian nobility in a period of massive transfer from mercantile to landed interests. It would, however, be a century or more before Venetian nobles came in any substantial way to share the haughty attitudes already revealed by provincial nobilities in the late sixteenth century. Furthermore, the retreat from sea to land involved for Venetians an active participation in the management and improvement of properties which many provincial nobles disdained.

Venice was not only a great commercial emporium but also a capital
with a large and prosperous hinterland, her nobility not merely a
mercantile patriciate but increasingly a landed aristocracy as well.
Venetian nobles were, as landlords, coming into increasingly closer
contact with the Terraferma. For all this, there was, apparently, surprisingly little contact with the aristocracies of the Terraferma. Venetian administrators obviously took pains to be on good terms with
them; the elaborate mutual courtesies between the *Rettori* of Vicenza
and the city's nobility are well-documented and the former participated
extensively in the city's social life. A large number of provincial
nobles, perhaps more particularly from Friuli were prepared to pay for
entry into the Venetian nobility in the middle years of the seventeenth
century; the haughty isolationism of the provincial nobilities evident at
the end of the eighteenth century had certainly not been reached. On
the other hand, there is little evidence of social contact between Venetian and provincial nobilities in general, with the notable exception
of the intellectual circles of Padua, and certainly intermarriage was
rare.

For all this, Venice's cultural debt to the Terraferma was considerable
and she tended to drain it of its talent, although the degree to which she
did this should not be overestimated. The weakened provincial aristocracies were not in a good position to compete with Venetian nobles as
patrons. Of the great provincial centres, Vicenza was peculiar in her
ability to retain her more talented artists. At the beginning of the sixteenth century, Venice housed a somewhat idiosyncratic and isolated
culture, but as the century progressed it showed the fruits of an increased intimacy between the *città dominante* and the mainland. At the
same time, testimony of Venetian penetration into the Terraferma was
provided by a new art-form: the country villa.

Notes

[1] For sources on Venetian economic history see Bibliography section 2(d)

[2] For sources on the nobility see Bibliography section 2(e); note also M. Ferro,
Dizionario del diritto commune et veneto VIII (Venice 1780) pp. 67–81 under *Maggior
Consiglio* and pp. 85–102 under *magistrato*

[3] Ferro, *Dizionario* III, pp. 189–93 under *cittadinanza*, pp. 70–76 under *cariche* pp. 5–11
under *Cancelleria*

[4] B. S. Pullan, *Rich and Poor in Renaissance Venice, the Social Institutions of a Catholic
State to 1620* (Oxford 1971), esp. pp. 99–111

5 A. S. Ven., M. Todarini, *Cittadinanza veneta* XI, f. 1598 and *ivi*. G. Tassini, *Cittadinanza veneta* XI, f. 1564; cf. *ibid.* 1 f. 104, IX, ff. 918–20

6 Nationalbibliothek Vienna, Fondo Foscarini Cod. III, n. 6144, *Breve historia* etc. under 1646

7 A. S. Ven. *Notarile. Testamenti.* B 1181, f. 207v. Tassini, *Cittadinanza* XII

8 cf. U. Tucci, 'The psychology of the Venetian merchant in the sixteenth century' in *Venetian Studies* ed. J. R. Hale (London 1972)

9 *Fondo Foscarini* Cod. III, n. 6144 cit.

10 The role of the nobility in the church is discussed in detail in my thesis *Studies in the Religious Life of Venice in the Sixteenth and Early Seventeenth Centuries: the Venetian Clergy and Religious Orders 1520–1630* (Cambridge, Ph. D. 1964)

11 For Terraferma society, see especially A. Ventura, *Nobiltà e popolo veneto del '400 e '500* (Bari 1964)

three

The Venetian Dominions
and their Cultural Setting

Between the fifteenth and the seventeenth centuries, Venice developed from being a Mediterranean power into a north Italian one, from an international emporium into the nucleus of a province. In the sixteenth century, she had her feet firmly planted on the mainland and her preoccupations with it increased. At the same time, not only her trading interests but also the need to defend her landward possessions through diplomacy gave her European preoccupations. Ultimately her history can only be comprehended fully against a European background as well as a purely Italian one.

Her culture, so strikingly individual and, at the turn of the sixteenth century, even at first sight rather isolated, derived part of its character from general European and Mediterranean influences and from the tensions that her international position imposed. Likewise, although physically removed from the routes by which marauding armies and foreign potentates normally passed through Italy, she was able in the long run to make her cultural influence felt in Europe as a whole, often in unobtrusive and roundabout ways, partly by means of the network of her cultural-cum-diplomatic relations. At the same time, we must not forget the constant cultural interchange between Venice and the Veneto, which did not in fact mean that the capital completely drained local centres of their intellectual and artistic talent.

Across the southern frontiers of the Veneto lay Mantua and Ferrara. Between the mid-fifteenth and the mid-sixteenth centuries they were the sites of two of the most cultivated Italian courts. In the mid-fifteenth century they had seen the educational experiments of Vittorino da Feltre and Guarino Veronese, who had both aspired to combine training in letters with the development of personal character, and the University of Ferrara, which had grown out of Guarino's school, was the only Italian university primarily devoted to the study of Latin letters. In the ages of Isabella d'Este (Duchess Consort and subsequently Dowager 1490–1530) and Federico II Gonzaga (Duke 1519–40) the Mantuan court provided extensive employment for Venetian artists and under Federico Mantua became a point of diffusion for central Italian influences. Here the crucial figure was Giulio Romano, Raphael's artistic chief pupil, who worked in Mantua in the years 1524–46, building the Palazzo del Tè and executing there and in the main Ducal Palace ambitious mural cycles which were soon to be emulated in Venice.

Further south, Venice's natural links were with the eastern side of Italy. Her primary Italian trading connections were with such ports as Rimini and Ancona and in the fifteenth century strong links had existed with courtly Urbino and the Marches. At that time, a number of Venetian painters, notably Carlo Crivelli, had worked in the Marches and the painters of that region had exercised perhaps the dominant influence on those of the Venetian school. The influence of the more westward regions of central Italy often tended to pass through the Veneto before it reached Venice, Padua having been perhaps the main intermediary of Tuscan artistic and scholarly currents in the fifteenth century. This is not to say, however, that there were not strong links between Venice and Florence at the level of the aristocratic humanist élite around the turn of the sixteenth century.

Venice's trading position in Constantinople, Syria and Egypt has already been examined. The main importance of the Levant for Venetian culture had lain more in the thirteenth and fourteenth centuries. Venetian builders and masons had then learnt much from the Byzantine art of Constantinople and possibly from the Islamic art of Syria as well. In the sixteenth century, the artistic influence of the Levant can be clearly seen only in minor arts such as book-binding. With regard to Greek scholarship, Venice evidently drew her resources less from Constantinople than from her own possession of Crete.

Crete, after the fall of Constantinople in 1453, had become the main centre of Greek cultural life. In the early sixteenth century, a number of exiles from its fractious and overcrowded scholarly community moved to Venice where they played a major role in the development of Hellenistic studies, not least in Aldus' editorial enterprises. By this time a flourishing Greek community was developing in Venice, enjoying its own Church under the fiction that it was a Catholic 'Uniate' one, and among the artists and craftsmen who formed a significant section of this community were to be found the typographers who provided the skilled manpower for Europe's first fully effective Greek presses and the group of Cretan miniaturists and icon painters, one of whom, Dome-nico Theotocopoulos, later to be known as El Greco, passed for a brief period through Titian's studio.

Of the other foreign groups in Venice, it was probably the Germans and Flemings who ranked next in importance as far as regards the history of Venetian culture. The location of the main trade-routes from Germany into Italy, that from Augsburg through the Brenner and the Adige valley to Verona and that passing from Carinthia, via Villach, into Carniola and Friuli, made Venice a natural entrepôt for German trade, especially in view of the high consumption of spices in Germany. The German merchant community in Venice was highly organised, possessing the imposing 'factory' of the Fondaco dei Tedeschi and enjoying a tacit religious toleration. The significant German presence in the city would appear to account in part for the extensive emigration to Venice in the decade 1470–80 of German printers who were sub-stantially responsible for the foundation there of what later became one of her most important skilled industries. Furthermore, certain German and Flemish merchants, including the Fugger, were patrons of the arts in Venice and played a significant role in the transmission of Venetian paintings and musical scores to their native lands.

The forays of Venetian merchants and indeed of Italian merchants in general into Germany would appear to have been relatively few. On the other hand, Venice had extensive trading interests in the Low Countries in the fifteenth and early sixteenth centuries, in contrast to the Florentines who were obliged to restrict their commercial commit-ments in this region around the turn of the sixteenth century. The pre-sence of a large number of Flemish paintings in Venetian collections in the early sixteenth century was doubtless in part the fruit of well-developed commercial and diplomatic relations with the Low Coun-tries and these may have helped to foster the taste in Venice for the Flemish musical tradition. The first three *Maestri di Capella* of St Marks, Petrus de Fossis (1491–1537), Adriaan Willaert (1527–63) and Ciprian Rore (1563–4) were Netherlanders, although it should be said that none of them were appointed as the result of searches in the Low Countries. It is unclear how far Venetian painters of Giovanni Bellini's generation were directly influenced by the great fifteenth-century Flemish masters, with whom they had so much in common, but it is probable that access to Flemish works did at least help to mould the taste of Venetian patrons.

The temporary contraction of Venice's Mediterranean trade in the early decades of the sixteenth century and the long-term decline of both her Mediterranean and her northern-European trades after about 1570 did not mean that she became less aware of the outside world. With difficulties in trade, the interests of her patriciate turned increasingly landwards. The attempt to increase her mainland possessions in the first decade of the sixteenth century did, indeed, lead to disaster and only from the latter years of the sixteenth century were there again consistent demands from a section of the patriciate for a more active Italian and European policy; for much of the sixteenth century, the dominant section of the patriciate thought primarily in terms of a policy of conservation, the question being made all the more critical as Habsburg power tightened on the peninsula. In the long run, however, preoccupations with the mainland, whether linked to an active or to an essentially passive foreign policy, meant that Venice had to take account of other European powers and of the balance of power in Europe. The passionate interest in the internal condition of other European states, which produced the masterly analyses found in certain *comptes rendus* of ambassadors and in many works of Venetian historians, certainly drew some of its impetus from anxiety about Venice's security and her place in Europe. Sections of the patriciate might find themselves sympathetically disposed towards the institutions and cultures of states from which they hoped Venice might receive support. In the latter years of the sixteenth century, while the members of the party of the Vecchi, who were mostly drawn from the families of long-established political power and who tended to come from the older generation, thought in terms of a policy of conservation and were disposed to be conciliatory towards Spain, their opponents of the Giovani, the party of 'outsiders', who were for the most part of the younger generation, called for an active Italian and European policy and looked with favour on the powers hostile to Spain, principally France, but also England and the United Provinces of the Netherlands. Among the leaders of the Giovani, certain of whom moved in the academic circles in which politics and history were a major topic of discussion, there was considerable enthusiasm for French institutions and traditions; this extended both to the Gallican Church's position of independence *vis-à-vis* the Papacy and to the views of the *Politique* school. With Fra Paolo Sarpi, not a patrician but a man closely linked to the leading Giovani, sympathies of a political nature for France, England and the United Provinces helped to cement the links with a wide circle of correspondents among the intelligentsia of these countries, with whom he exchanged views on political, religious, historical and scientific topics.

Venice's increasingly landward preoccupations had involved concern, both political and economic, with her possessions of the Terraferma themselves, on which her administrative grip had in any case been tightening throughout the fifteenth century. As we have seen, Venetians were extensively acquiring and exploiting lands there. It is uncertain when it first became common for Venetians to have residences on their country estates, but the habit was probably fairly common by the late fifteenth century. Even without Venice's increasing involvement with the Terraferma, the cultural interchanges between capital and provinces would doubtless have been considerable, but inevitably it made them all the more numerous. Furthermore, the penetration of Venetian proprietors into the lands of the Terraferma had evidently increased the economic weight of the Venetian patriciate as against the provincial noble and citizen classes, who had lost out to Venetians in the land-scramble and in the agrarian boom. It is probable that the Venetian nobility, enriched by the profits of agriculture and by the trade-boom of the 1550s and 1560s disposed of means of patronage which the bulk of the provincial nobilities did not possess and it was only natural that the *Città dominante* should become a magnet for aspiring artists and craftsmen from the Terraferma.

Venice's most obvious rival as a centre of attraction was Mantua which, unlike her, possessed a court. Andrea Mantegna, who was born on the borders between Paduan and Vicentine territory and who had studied and commenced his career in Padua, had in fact permanently settled in Mantua in 1459, on the invitation of Ludovico Gonzaga. In the sixteenth century, however, while Venetian artists received commissions from the Mantuan court, none of any note settled in the city; even G. M. Falconetto, the Veneto artist who perhaps worked there the most extensively, did not remain for long. Mantua did not perhaps offer outstanding opportunities for permanent employment: Isabella d'Este was too intent on obtaining works from as many distinguished artists as possible to provide it and Federico II was doubtless too well-satisfied with the style of Giulio Romano and his followers to choose court-painters from the Venetian dominions. Ultimately, Mantua and the great cities of the Veneto could hardly compete as centres of attraction with a city of between 115,000 and 170,000 souls and with some 120 churches. Already in the first half of the sixteenth century there was an appreciable body of private art collectors in

Venice and between the 1550s and the end of the century there were dazzling opportunities for employment on the decorative schemes in public buildings. Furthermore, Venice in the sixteenth century offered outstanding facilities for training under great masters of the art of painting. It was perhaps Giovanni Bellini, himself a Venetian citizen, who first made Venice a natural centre for aspiring artists. Cima da Conegliano, Giorgione da Castelfranco, Tiziano Vercellio da Cadore and the Bergamese Jacopo Palma, Lorenzo Lotto and Andrea Previtale all may have studied under him. With Giorgione and Titian, a great tradition was firmly established. This is not to say that there were not still recognisable Terraferma schools of painting in the sixteenth century, most notably the Brescian school (Vincenzo Foppa, Gerolamo Savoldo, il Moretto and the Rossi) and a Veronese school (Anselmo Canera, Bernardo India, Battista Zelotti, Battista del Moro, Paolo Farinati, Cristoforo Sorte, Benedetto Caliari and ultimately Paolo Caliari, 'il Veronese', et al.).

For painters from the north of Venice and from Friuli, the city of the Lagoon was the natural centre. Padua and Treviso were too close to be able to compete. Friuli, however, was a region that nursed a traditional resentment against the *Città dominate*. It is perhaps significant that the two most distinguished Friulian artists of the first half of the sixteenth century, Giovan Antonio Regillo da Pordenone and Giovanni Ricamatori da Udine moved out of the Veneto in the first instance. Pordenone subsequently re-settled in his native town, being perhaps the outstanding example of a Veneto artist with an Italian reputation who firmly based himself in the provinces. Giovanni da Udine, when he accepted Venetian patronage after 1539, worked in Friuli. The Trevigiano, from which Cima and Giorgione came, was, on the other hand, regarded as being remarkably patient of Venetian rule. Titian, who was born on the borders of the Empire, came of a family with a tradition of loyalty to the Serenissima and for him the only road to the great cities lay down the Piave Valley towards Treviso; from there it was but a step to Venice. Artists from the regions of Vicenza and Verona, with their proud local traditions, were not perhaps so likely to feel the pull of the *Città dominante*. The Brescians were noted for their loyalty to Venice, perhaps reinforced by their opportunities for observing life in the Milanese state. Milan certainly does not seem to have held much attraction for Brescian artists, but they evidently tended to stay in their native city or, as in the case of Savoldo, to move out of the Venetian dominions altogether. By contrast, Bergamese painters seem to have looked naturally to Venice: Palma Vecchio settled there permanently, Previtale studied there and then returned to his native town, while Lotto, born in Venice of Bergamese parents, seems to have had dual allegiances. Venice's reliance upon Bergamese masons may have been significant here: the example of the master-builders Mauro Coducci and Bartolomeo Bon, who had moved to Venice, may have encouraged their compatriots with painterly skills to follow the same road to fortune.

The mid sixteenth-century group of artists from the Veronese and the Vicentino were mainly active in the provinces, Paolo Caliari being a notable exception. Verona evidently provided opportunities for training of a sort: most of its artists seem to have undergone at least part of their apprenticeship there. Chances of employment there certainly existed, but not, it would seem, brilliant ones: Veronese nobles did not play a notable role as patrons of the arts and the amount of church building there in the sixteenth century was limited. Vicenza can hardly be said to have possessed a painterly school of its own in the sixteenth century—its two most notable resident painters Giovan Battista Maganza and the Lombard Antonio Fasolo were pupils of Titian and Veronese respectively—but the Vicentine nobility were active patrons of the arts. It was, however, not so much the attraction of the great urban centres but the spread of the country villa that kept Veronese and Vicentine artists in the provinces. Fasolo and the Veronese group, with their skill in fresco and their lightness of style were admirably equipped to decorate the elegant new villas. Fasolo, G. B. Maganza and his son Alessandro seem to have been definitely based on Vicenza. The Veronese painter Battista Zelotti, on the other hand, worked fairly generally in the Vicentino, Padovano and Trevigiano. The Da Ponte of Bassano, who remained strongly attached to their home town, did not of course belong to the group of frescoists. Technically they were residents of Vicentine territory, but Bassano is not much further removed from Venice than from Vicenza, and they had fairly strong links with the capital, while working extensively in Vicenza and in the Terraferma generally.

The Veronese and Vicentine painters of the sixteenth century were the practitioners of a fresco tradition that Venice did not really possess. Furthermore, Verona was important as a gate of entry for central Italian artistic influences coming through Mantua, and from Verona they naturally passed to Vicenza. It was in Verona and Vicenza that the impact of Giulio Romano's style was most marked.

While Venice had a number of outstanding native painters (including the Bellini, Vittore Carpaccio, Vincenzo Catena, Sebastiano del Piombo, the Robusti—Tintoretto—and Palma Giovane), she produced few architects and sculptors of note before Baldassare Longhena. Of the main sculptors and master-builders working there in the last three decades of the fifteenth century and the first two decades of the sixteenth, only Giorgio Spavento comes to mind; for the most part, they came from beyond the Mincio, from Bergamo or from Milanese territory.[1] The sculptural school that developed in Venice from the 1530s was essentially founded by artists with central Italian training, notably the Florentine Jacopo Sansovino and the Ligurian Danese Cattaneo, and those who carried on the tradition were not in the main Venetians: the Aspetti were Paduans and Alessandro Vittoria a Trentino. In the latter half of the sixteenth century there were, in fact, extremely active master-builders of Venetian origin in Antonio Ponte, Giovan Antonio Rusconi and Simon Sorella, but these tended to be more concerned with the execution of building projects than with designs. Vicenza, on the other hand, produced in the middle years of the sixteenth century a remarkable school of architects and master-builders. Palladio may in fact have been Paduan, but much of his working life was spent in Vicenza and there were a number of minor masters there whose work is very difficult to distinguish from his, while the most distinguished exponent of the Mannerist tradition in the Veneto, Vincenzo Scamozzi, was a Vicentine. The mid sixteenth-century architectural revolution in the Veneto was only to a limited degree a Venetian affair. Jacopo Sansovino, the architect of the Serenissima, was undoubtedly a crucial figure, but the buildings of the Veronese painter and architect Giovan Maria Falconetto in Padua, those of Palladio in Vicenza and, perhaps to a lesser degree, those of Michele Sanmicheli in Verona, were of cardinal importance.

Of all the cities of the Veneto, the *Città dominante* apart, Vicenza and Padua were obviously the most important for its cultural life. As we have seen, the Vicentine patriciate was probably the most important noble class of any of the subject cities from the point of view of numbers, wealth and cultivation, but its members could often only find an outlet for their energies outside the dominions of the Serene Republic. The frustration of this highly talented and energetic caste doubtless explains in part that sentimental bias towards the Holy Roman Empire which could reveal itself in literary form in a vague pro-Imperial idealism and in more disturbing concrete forms, as when a section of the nobility rallied to Maximilian's standards in 1509.

It was here perhaps, rather than in Venice, that the traditions of courtly cultivation found in nearby Mantua found the most ready acceptance. Modern scholarship has found difficulty in penetrating beyond the outward manifestations of a cultural life which veered between exuberant public display and a highly academic and scholarly literary tradition. The difficulty is experienced not least with the highly formalised literary productions of Count Giangiorgio Trissino, undoubtedly the city's most distinguished humanist and writer in the first half of the sixteenth century, and with the records of the great Olympian Academy in the latter half of the century; here reports of lectures on classical, philosophical and scientific topics, of lavish dramatic performances of tragedies and pastorals, of the building of Palladio's magnificent theatre, are interspersed with notices of requests by members for at least the occasional tournament. Trissino's *Italia liberata dai Goti*, which sought to apply the form of the Homeric-Virgilian epic to a history of Christian-Imperial valour, did perhaps unite some of the disparate strands of this extraordinary cultural tradition in which a highly formalised classicism mingled with hankerings after chivalric display and an ideology of Messianic imperialism. The erudite tradition of Vicenza must certainly have contributed powerfully towards the development of Trissino's great protégé, Andrea Palladio, through whom the Vicentine cultural milieu made its greatest contribution to the culture of the Veneto and that of Europe as a whole.

If Vicenza was a great provincial centre with an independent and indeed rather idiosyncratic culture of its own, Padua was more firmly linked to the *Città dominante* some fifteen miles away. This is not to say that the city itself did not have a distinctive cultural life which reacted on that of the capital in the long run. In the fifteenth century it was more open to artistic influences from other regions of Italy. In the sixteenth century it had, in the playwright Beolco Ruzzante, a spokesman for a provincial sentiment that was positively anti-Venetian in tone. The University of Padua, however, was essentially the university of Venice, being the only one in the Venetian dominions after 1405, when the Signory had ordered the closures of the *studia* of Vicenza and Treviso. Long renowned for juridical and Aristotelian studies, the University had been the scene of the first extensive development of humanist studies in the Veneto in the early years of the fifteenth century and, by the turn of the seventeenth century, it had become Europe's leading centre for medical and scientific studies. Attendance at other universities was forbidden to Venetian subjects, and although many of them were in fact seeking higher education elsewhere in the latter years of the sixteenth century, the University was increasingly attracting students from all over Europe, becoming in fact an international, rather than a specifically Venetian centre of learning. It was not only the University that forged links between the Venetian and Paduan intelligentsia. In the sixteenth and early seventeenth centuries, scholars and writers from both cities met together in a number of learned circles in Padua.

It was not only the living but also the dead culture of the Veneto that was of value to Venice. Few regions north of Rome can have been as rich in antique remains, even if few of these were of notable artistic value. Brescia possessed a temple, Verona a theatre and an arena. Although Aquilea was known at the time to have been an important area of settlements in late antiquity, it is doubtful whether the rich archaeological remains of the site (lost to the Imperialists in 1509) had been notably exploited in the Renaissance period, but those of Adria (Rovigo) certainly were and a fair amount of material appears to have been gathered in Este and also in the region of the Lagoon, where the island of Torcello is still covered with late antique fragments. Furthermore, contacts with the Levant facilitated the importation of antiques, both statuary and small-scale pieces. For a variety of reasons, therefore, the Veneto, and especially Padua, had become by the mid-fifteenth century the main centre of the Italian trade in antique objects. The stimulus of archaeological resources to antiquarian and epigraphical studies in Venice is obvious. The degree of direct stimulus offered to artists is less certain, but Palladio obviously profited from what archaeological research had to teach, if only with regard to ground-plans and building techniques. Furthermore, the fashion for antiquarian studies among the Venetian intelligentsia would appear, as we shall see in due course, to have encouraged the development of the Venetian art-collection.

In the middle ages, Venice's commercial relations had exposed her to the influence of Byzantine and Islamic art, in the sixteenth century they exposed her to the artistic and musical traditions of northern Europe, in particular to the lavish and colourful culture of the Netherlands. Her links with the Greek-speaking areas, combined with the scholarly traditions of Padua and the facilities offered by her printing-presses, enabled her to become, in the early sixteenth century, the main European centre of Hellenistic studies and for the printing of classical texts.

Her special position also favoured the development of antiquarian studies. Venice was one of the most cosmopolitan cities of Europe. It would be dangerous to suggest, however, that her culture was an outstandingly cosmopolitan one. The presence within Venetian palaces of paintings by Van Eyck, Memlinc and Raphael, Cretan icons, antique sculptures from Rome and the eastern Mediterranean, carpets and brocades from the Levant, testified however to the wide-ranging tastes of collectors. The potential lessons were not apparently lost on Venetian artists. Members of the Venetian ruling class were aware of the need for observing the outside world. Such an awareness had been required of Italian statesmen in general with the wars at the turn of the sixteenth century which had turned Italy into an international cockpit, but in the middle and latter years of the century it was perhaps above all Venetians who showed it. Its fruits can be seen in the work of the Venetian historical school.

Note

[1] Mauro Coducci and Bartolomeo Bon were Bergamese. Andrea Briosco (Riccio) and Antonio Abbondi (lo Scarpagnino) were Milanese. Giovanni Buora was from Lugano, Antonio and Paolo Bregno from Como. The family of Pietro Solaro (Lombardo) was from Carona in Lombardy and he settled in Padua before coming to Venice, his sons Tullio and Antonio can be regarded as of Veneto-Paduan origin. Antonio Rizzo was evidently Veronese

four

The Active and the Contemplative Life

Debate on the relative values of the *vita contemplativa*, the life of religious and scholarly contemplation in retirement, and the *vita activa*, the life of service to the community and the pursuit of honour, was a recurrent literary topic in the Renaissance. Within its framework it was asked how far the pursuit of intellectual excellence was totally identified with the *vita contemplativa* and involved detachment from worldly concerns. It would be dangerous to regard the debate as a contraposition of supposed 'this worldly' values of the Renaissance to equally problematical 'other worldly' values of the Middle Ages. It took its inspiration as much as anything from debates in antiquity and, perhaps especially, from the dual facets of Cicero's literary personality. The ideal of a life of scholarly meditation aloof from the world was doubtless more particularly marked with the fourteenth-century humanism of Petrarch, the late Salutati and Vergerio. Professor Baron has suggested that this outlook received a major challenge with the rise in the early fifteenth century of Florentine 'civic humanism', represented most notably by the Chancellor Leonardo Bruni; this asserted the superiority of the *vita activa* over 'selfish' withdrawal into scholarship, put forward the ideal of the citizen who, in addition to his studies, consummated his *humanitas* by service to the community in public office, and posited an intimate connection between a flourishing political life in a state and cultural excellence.[1] The great debate was never firmly decided one way or the other, however, and it is wrong to regard the ideal of the *vita contemplativa* as one that became progressively more *démodé* as time went on. In Venice, the debate became particularly poignant in the sixteenth century and it was then perhaps that the most explicit doubts were raised as to the dignity of the active life. It is tempting to see Venice as the true depository of the ideals of civic humanism in that period. Undoubtedly many of her leading intellectuals achieved a remarkable union of service to the community with intellectual pursuits and even, in some cases, a genuine life of contemplation. It was, indeed, one factor that gave Venetian civilisation its distinctive character. This union, however, was not without tensions and certain of Venice's leading intellectuals, coming precisely from the ruling caste, chose to opt out of the *vita activa*; some were devotees of letters, others imbued with the ascetic outlook of the Catholic Reform movement.

Although the division of time between scholarship and affairs could be a painful issue, it is doubtful whether anxieties about the harmony between the *vita activa* and the *vita contemplativa* as ways of life in themselves ever seriously perturbed the minds of the great triad of late fifteenth century Venetian humanism, Gerolamo Donà, Bernardo Bembo and Ermolao Barbaro. All three combined devotion to humane letters with an active life of service to the state in *magistrati* and ambassadorial posts; above all Ermolao Barbaro (1455–93), who here continued a tradition established by his grandfather Francesco, a distinguished humanist, politician and military man. Having lectured on Aristotle at Padua in the years 1474–9, Ermolao became a senator in 1483. In the following year he was teaching the Greek poets at Padua and lecturing on Aristotle at his own house in Venice. In the years 1485–91 he held a variety of major diplomatic posts and in the latter year, while he was Orator in Rome, the Pope made him Patriarch of Aquilea, to the anger of the Signory which did not wish its ambassadors to accept such offices. Exiled in disgrace in Rome, he there completed his great work of the textual correction of Pliny before his premature death in 1493. Barbaro did more than anyone of his age, with the exception of Politian, to put the techniques of a scientific textual criticism at the service of encyclopaedic knowledge. The other facet of his achievement was represented by the *De officio legati*, written in the years 1490–1, the first realistic literary description of the duties of an ambassador. Realistic but not cynical. The man who described the duties of the ambassador as being 'to do, say, advise and think whatever may best serve the preservation and aggrandisement of his own state' was not a different person from the one who wrote:

> *Musa malos odit, Musae improbitate fugantur,*
> *Musas et vitium non capit una domus*[2]

'The Muses hate the wicked, they shun dishonesty; the Muses and vice cannot live together.'

The ambassador must not stoop to any demeaning action such as be-having like a spy in fulfilling his crucial task of gathering information; he must incarnate the dignity of the state he represents.[3] The lustre which Barbaro himself brought to his diplomatic functions was doubt-less increased by his almost mythical reputation among the European scholarly community. It is hardly surprising, however, that with his many active engagements, his massive programme for purification and elucidation of the Aristotelian texts was little more than begun by the time of his death at the age of 38.[4] His friend Gerolamo Donà, who devoted his spare moments to the search for a truly antique philo-sophy based on a harmony between Plato and Aristotle, had been conscious of the difficulties of dividing time between the service of culture and that of the state: 'public and private affairs constrain me so', he wrote to Politian, 'that our studies are less studies than thefts from our time'.[5]

Bernardo Bembo fulfilled an exceptionally heavy round of state duties by any standard and, although a noted figure in erudite circles, was primarily a diplomatist rather than a scholar. He, however, saw culture as a means to a political end. He regarded his Latin orations not so much as literary exercises, but as examples of eloquence designed to persuade in the public arena; rhetorical pursuits of this kind, he be-lieved, could be combined with philosophy and science.[6]

He was sadly disappointed in his son Pietro, whose intensive devo-tion to letters was diverting him from the duties of a patrician. Pietro's successive failures in elections to state office suggest that his father's misgivings may have been generally shared. To make matters worse, he had not followed his early promise as a philologist, but had become a poet, a poet of love at that. By the time he was 36, in 1506, it was clear that he must either fulfil his duties as a patrician or seek advance-ment elsewhere and he broke with family and friends to go to Urbino. It was the courts, those of princely Urbino and the Rome of Leo x, that were to provide the fitting milieu for Bembo's considerable talents. When he returned to the Venetian dominions in 1525, having failed to obtain the longed-for cardinalate, it was to retirement at his Paduan villa where he celebrated the joys of a life spent *procul negotiis* in cultivating the Muses and gathering strawberries. His nomination as Public Historiographer in 1530, represented, perhaps, the offer of an olive branch by the Venetian government, but the fact remains that the most distinguished Venetian man of letters of the first half of the six-teenth century, while not exactly ostracised, was unable to find his true niche in the milieu of the governing class and was felt to have evaded its responsibilities by an exclusive concentration on cultural pursuits.[7]

Gasparo Contarini, the propagator of the 'Venetian myth', a myth himself for later generations, seemed exemplary in his combination of the lives of religion, scholarship and service to the state, but this harmony was probably not achieved without an element of personal crisis. Certain of his most intimate links were with persons who denied its possibility, notably Tomaso Giustiniani and Vincenzo Querini, the two prophets of the Catholic Reform movement. Originally among the leaders of the Venetian intelligentsia, they had eschewed the study of profane letters to devote themselves exclusively to sacred duties and had buried themselves in the Hermitage of Camaldoli. Their departures in the years 1510–11 had caused consternation among their friends and relatives and was perhaps regarded as something of a betrayal of their city at a time when Venice lay under papal interdict. Giustiniani had tried to recruit Contarini and others of his circle to the hermit life as the only sure way to salvation, pointing to the vanity of earthly pursuits. For Contarini, Giustiniani's letters provoked a crisis in the spring of 1512. This crisis in its most obvious aspects concerned the role of human endeavour in the process of justification before God, but it also perhaps involved the status of the active life in the world.[8] It was this life, however, that Contarini decided, in all humility, to follow.

It was the life of a celibate statesman aristocrat who devoted his leisure to scholarship and religious meditation. Having taken a private vow of chastity around 1512, he held a variety of major ambassadorships between 1520 and 1534; he was among the most distinguished diplomatists of his age. He shared, nevertheless, something of Giustiniani's outlook. His wide-ranging intellectual formation had originally centred mainly upon Aristotelian philosophy, but in 1511 he had decided on the primacy of sacred sciences and, although he never repudiated his debt to scholastic theology and philosophy, it was towards the Bible and the early Church Fathers that he moved. The fruits of his theological studies were revealed in his courteous polemic against Luther, while his continuing philosophical interests were utilised in his equally courteous confutation of Pomponazzi's denial of the natural immortality of the soul. The dual orientations of Contarini's life are perhaps most clearly illustrated, however, by his two books, the *Office of the Bishop* and the *Magistracies of Venice*. The delineation of the servant of God and the paen to Venice as the embodiment of civil justice were essentially complimentary. Contarini's moralistic attitude towards statesmanship, as well as the primarily philosophical nature of his more secular intellectual interests, did perhaps partly account, however, for the limitations of the latter treatise. The detailed sections hardly went further than accounts of constitutional procedures, while the remarks on the general nature of the constitution did little more than attempt to align it with abstract philosophical categories derived from Aristotle. It was the work of a moralist versed in Aristotle rather than of a man fascinated by the tug of political forces.[9]

Governments had traditionally shown a disposition to employ outstanding practitioners of humane letters in two main fields, secretarial work and diplomacy, doubtless as supposed masters of elegant and urbane expression. In Venice, in point of fact, the secretarial functions were exercised by citizens, not nobles. Those serving in the Ducal Chancery and secretariat were given a grounding in humane letters at the school of St Mark. In practice, however, the Venetian government, in contrast, say, to the Popes Leo x and Clement vii, showed relatively little preoccupation with fostering an exquisite latinity in its secretariate and probably felt little need for it, except when it came to the formal addresses of ambassadors presenting their credentials and delivering messages of congratulations or condolence. Significantly, those members of the government secretariate who distinguished themselves intellectually did so in the main outside the field of classical scholarship. At the same time, it is doubtful how far classical cultivation was really of utility to Venetian statesmen of the sixteenth century and certainly the government had little use for a creature of the study like Pietro Bembo. The business of composing Latin addresses could be left to the secretariate, although it probably helped to have the state represented by a scholar of international repute like Ermolao Barbaro and, in the case of Bernardo Bembo, common intellectual interests helped to cement an intimate personal relationship with Lorenzo the Magnificent from which the Signory could hope to draw profit.

The statesmen-scholars we have examined so far were in fact primarily distinguished in diplomacy and undoubtedly they were excellent classical scholars. It needs to be said, however, that, with all these men, literary interests were substantially subsumed by philosophical ones, and with Gasparo Contarini these clearly predominated. Indeed, it would seem that, very broadly speaking, the main intellectual formative influences on the Venetian patriciate in the first half of the sixteenth century were exercised not so much by the literary-humanist school of St Mark—although this was by no means a predominantly plebeian educational centre—as by the philosophical and legal faculties at Padua and by the highly aristocratic philosophy school of the Rialto in Venice.

It is doubtful whether the strong philosophical interests of Venetian patricians could ever be integrated with service to the state, although there appears to have been a curious connection between political stance and approaches towards Aristotelian studies: the leading anti-clericals Sebastiano Foscarini and Nicolò da Ponte sought to disengage the original thought of the Stagirite from the accumulation of mediaeval interpretations, while by contrast Gasparo Contarini and Agostino Valier, who were among the most outstanding exponents of a Thomist Aristotelianism that sought to resolve apparent conflicts between Aristotle and Christian dogma, were the leading proponents of an intimate collaboration between church and state. However great the hiatus might appear between philosophical studies and service to the state, it is significant that the chief philosophy chair at the Rialto school was held continuously by patricians from 1455. Between 1505 and 1550, with Sebastiano Foscarini, it was occupied by a patrician who was not only recognised as one of the best-informed Aristotelian scholars of his day but was also a powerful figure on the political scene. His teaching of logic, natural philosophy, mathematics and theology was, however, interrupted on various occasions when he was called to fulfil high government office and his most obvious successor, Nicolò da Ponte, the subsequent patriarch of the Giovani party and a future Doge, who had acted as his locum in the years 1521–3 in fact confined himself to the career of statesmanship.[10]

The great figures of Venetian politics and culture of the mid-sixteenth century meet in Paolo Paruta's *Della perfezione della vita politica* ('The perfection of political life') published in 1579, the finest literary contribution to be made by a Venetian to the debate on the active and contemplative lives. Here the debate in the first instance is not exactly on the respective claims of scholarship and affairs, but rather on those of political life and religious-cum-philosophical meditation. In the course of the discussion, however, religion, philosophy and meditation are shown as distinct and separate elements. The initial discussion ultimately branches out into ones on the value of material goods, on the nature of virtue and on the best form of state. Paruta's book purports to describe a series of conversations taking place at Trent in 1563 in the shadow of the Church Council. The leading roles are taken by a number of prelates from the Venetian dominions and a group of Venetian diplomats returning from Germany. Here Paruta uses figures drawn from real life. The most insistent protagonist of the position that the highest form of life is that of action directed towards the well-being of the many—political life in short—is one Michele Surian, who in real life was a highly distinguished statesman. The most rigid defense of the ultimate primacy of contemplation is put forward by three bishops, the Friulian Michele della Torre, bishop of Ceneda, and the Venetians Giovanni Grimani Patriarch of Aquilea and Filippo Mocenigo, archbishop of Cyprus. Della Torre had fulfilled a long career as a diplomat in the papal service. Grimani was a gentleman of leisure, scion of an immensely wealthy family; it is perhaps worth mentioning that his own version of the contemplative life had involved the amassing of a vast collection of antiques in his Venetian palace, far from the cares of his diocese which, for rather complex technical reasons, he only visited after some forty years as Patriarch. Mocenigo was a philosopher of some repute. These prelates appear to substantially identify the life of philosophical speculation with that of religious meditation. For them, political life binds man's spirit to the ground and it is, indeed, tinged with corruption. Where the discussion branches out into one on the value of earthly goods, it is Surian, supported by the great Nicolò da Ponte, who maintains that they are a necessary adornment to virtue, while Grimani attacks this position asserting that virtue requires no adornment by things mortal and fading.

In view of what is known about Paruta's personages in real life, it is unlikely that it is exactly 'secular' and 'spiritual' values that are being counterposed. For contemporary Venetians, della Torre and Grimani would have been prime examples of prelates who meddled in the secular sphere. Both had incurred the mistrust of the Serenissima by their obstinate defence of certain rights of temporal jurisdiction annexed to their particular bishoprics. It is probably not without deliberation that Paruta sets della Torre, who had been a trusted instrument of papal politics, against Surian who, in real life, had attacked the Papacy's abuse of its authority in its interventions on the international scene. It is possible that Paruta really means to suggest that those who, having made a sharp distinction between 'spiritual' and 'secular', assert the absolute supremacy of the former, are in fact liable to confound the two in a very dangerous fashion. Furthermore, there is no particular reason for thinking that either of the three prelates, least of all Grimani, were particularly authentic representatives of the ascetic spirituality of the Catholic reform movement, and they were probably not regarded by Paruta as such. If any of the speakers stood for it in real life it was probably Agostino Valier, who in fact adopts a moderate position in the debate. In Paruta's book, della Torre, who prefers 'the quiet of Ceneda' and 'pleasurable retirement' to the travails of diplomatic service and the uncertainties of political life is perhaps above all the symbol of a world-weary cynicism leading to abandonment of responsibilities; perhaps Grimani would also have been regarded as a symbol of irresponsibility by his contemporaries. The ideal of aloof detachment put forward by the three prelates is not, indeed, truly religious in spirit.

The more authentic representative of the religious spirit in the debate is Daniele Barbaro. A notable scholar, the real-life Barbaro, after a short but distinguished career in government service had become coadjutor to Grimani and Patriarch Elect of Aquilea. While adopting a less intransigent stance in the debate, Barbaro is, in the last analysis, on the side of Surian. He asserts the dignity of civil life and the value of patriotism, but it is also Barbaro who posits an essential harmony between philosophy and the promotion of public well-being. Regarding the dignity of the contemplative life, Barbaro refuses to accept the unity of religion and philosophical speculation which the other three prelates had assumed; God is approached through the virtuous life, not through the feeble resources of the human intellect. Here his discourse, redolent of the language of the Psalms, takes on tones of ecstatic rapture. Paruta appears to be counterposing the concrete, fervent piety of Barbaro to the cerebral rigorism of the other three prelates. It is significant that Barbaro takes an intermediate position between Surian and Grimani on the worth of material goods, treating these as instruments of the virtues and firmly rejecting Grimani's studious contempt of them. In reality, Grimani and his coadjutor were both munificent artistic patrons, but it is to the pious Barbaro that Paruta entrusts the defence of material possessions and magnificence properly used. The last word lies with Matteo Dandolo, perhaps the most distinguished Venetian statesman of his day. Appealing to the authority of the late Cardinal Gasparo Contarini, he points to the ideal of a state devoted to justice and peace; above all its security and dignity lie in the promotion of true religion to whose service material splendour may also be devoted.[11]

What was Paruta's own position? Speaking with his own voice at the beginning of Book II, he says that true philosophy consists in teaching virtuous civil life. At the time of writing the *Della Perfezione*,

4   Cardinal Pietro Bembo (1489–1547), man of letters and patron, by Titian
    (see pp. 95–102, 156)

5　Andrea Odoni, collector, by Lorenzo Lotto (see pp. 315–16)

he presumably inclined towards the position of Surian and Barbaro. The *Della Perfezione* only marked a stage in his development, however. In the *Soliloquio*, written shortly before his death in 1598, he retracted the ideals of his youth; he had loved profane culture, he had sought riches and honour, but now he knew that worldly things were but vanity.[12] If he had ever accepted the ideals of Michele Surian, he now rejected them, but not perhaps exactly for those of Della Torre, Grimani and Mocenigo.

It should be noted that the debate in the *Della Perfezione* about the active and contemplative lives does not preoccupy itself with the status of cultural pursuits in general, but quite specifically with that of philosophy, understood in the broadest sense. Whatever Paruta's real views may have been, he is obviously anxious to question any straight-forward dichotomy between politics and philosophy. The question at issue is whether philosophy is purely speculative, directed towards the contemplation of some quasi-celestial truth, or whether it can have a practical end. Involved in this question is that of the relationship of philosophy to religious life: is it akin to contemplation of the divine? In denying this, Daniele Barbaro fragments the vision of the *vita contemplativa* which had animated, say, Petrarch and Salutati in their later phases and certain of Gasparo Contarini's friends, notably Reginald Pole. The religious outlook Barbaro expresses is, of course, nothing if not conventional and if there is any originality at all in this part of his discourse it lies in the insertion of this position into the framework of a debate on the *vitae activa et contemplativa*. Barbaro's contention that philosophy relates to the promotion of public well-being can perhaps best be understood against the background of Venetian interest in Aristotle's *Politics* and may be regarded as an indirect testimony to the way in which Venetians had helped to broaden the vision of antique philosophy. Surian, Barbaro and the three prelates who espouse 'pure contemplation' all represented outlooks to be found among the Venetian patriciate; it would be futile to search for any 'quintessentially Venetian' ethos in the mouths of any of the speakers. What is of considerable interest, however, is the way in which Paruta appears to align certain cultural attitudes, more specifically regarding historical writing, with attitudes towards the *vitae activa et contemplativa*, or at least with certain ways of life, those of the statesman, the scholar and the ecclesiastic.

For Barbaro, history offers material for acquiring prudence in civil affairs, such as the experience of any individual lifetime could not pro-

C

vide. Grimani agrees with him, but specifies that historians should not
be content with simple narration, but should insert frequent didactic
passages. He is not impressed by the recent example of narrative history
provided by Guicciardini; he prefers to look to the ancients. Surian, on
the other hand, is opposed to mingling narrative with philosophical
precepts and regards the ancient writers who indulged in this as
'political philosophers' rather than historians; it is the task of the
historian 'simply to narrate human affairs as they took place'. Barbaro
agrees only up to a point; insertions, which can help to tie a narrative
together, should be made for the comparison of cases as well as to
explain causes; his models are Thucydides and Guicciardini. Grimani,
with his predominantly didactic considerations, in fact echoes the
demands that many fifteenth-century humanists had made of historical
writing. It was an outlook that had been substantially jettisoned by
those sixteenth-century historians, like Guicciardini, who sought above
all to understand the situation in which Italy found herself. Barbaro's
vision of history as a storehouse of examples also attaches him in a certain measure to a somewhat antiquated humanist tradition, but,
through his mouth, Paruta shows a consciousness of the preoccupation
with causality which Guicciardini had helped to stimulate. Surian was
perhaps speaking for the kind of unpretentious annal writing that had
been produced by Marino Sanudo between the 1490s and the 1530s. His
views are suggestive of hostility towards the historiography with strong
moralistic-cum-patriotic preoccupations that had asserted itself in
Venice in the middle years of the sixteenth century but which in some
measure marked a return to fifteenth-century Italian humanist tradition. In the event a severely factual historiography shorn of moralising
general reflections and of grandiose literary trappings was to assert itself
strongly in Venice in the decades following the publication of the *Della
Perfezione*. It would be too much to suggest that Paruta deliberately
intended to delineate differences between old and new traditions of
historiography, but he probably did mean to indicate that statesmen
and men of the study might write history in very different ways. The
ideal of a didactic history, treating the past as a storehouse of examples,
was perhaps par excellence that of humanist scholars, while a starkly
factual historiography with a strong focus on causality was, in Venice,
more particularly the work of statesmen anxious about the Republic's
position in Europe; the substantial identity of the real-life Surian's
political stance with that of the Giovani party is perhaps of significance
here. In due course we shall see a certain contrast between the historio-

graphical outlook of men with strong religious and ethical preoccupations like Barbaro and Valier with that of men like Paruta, Morosini
and Nicolò Contarini whose concerns were primarily political.

Paruta's book is also of interest in what it implies of the author's
vision of certain prominent Venetians of the period, most notably
Daniele Barbaro. None of the figures represented in the book, perhaps
no Venetian in the 1550s and 1560s, more effectively represented the
combination of scholarship, politics and religion than did Daniele
Barbaro (1513–70). To English historians he is the author of the famous
Relazione on the affairs of England of 1550, the first really comprehensive account of English life and customs by an Italian, which is recognised as one of the *chefs d'oeuvre* of Venetian diplomatic reporting. To
art historians he is known as the editor of the classic sixteenth-century
edition of Vitruvius and as the patron of Palladio. In fact his intellectual
interests were extremely wide. Up to the 1540s he moved primarily in
the Paduan intellectual milieu, devoting himself to philosophy, mathematics, science and *belles lettres*, but more particularly to Aristotelian
studies. He published a number of treatises in this field and was also
responsible for the publication of certain Aristotelian works by his
great-uncle Ermolao. He probably shared the latter's botanical interests
for he was entrusted by the Senate with the foundation of the Botanical
Garden at Padua, in fact the first in the world. With the late 1540s and
the 1550s Daniele's spheres of interests and experiences widened. Up to
the early 1540s, he had devoted himself to study and only fulfilled the
indispensable duties of a patrician, but by 1548 he was Venetian
ambassador in England. It was at the time of his embassy, which he held
until 1550, that he appears to have developed historical and theological
interests, while he had probably commenced his translation of Vitruvius
shortly before his appointment. The *Relazione* on English affairs, that is
the general report which he submitted to the Great Council on his
return, reveals many of the qualities of a historian. It is a sober and
apparently unpretentious work which eschews the petty detail and
court gossip that fill so many Venetian *relazioni*. It does not attempt, as
so many do, to assess the balance of power at court and the international
orientations of the government on the basis of imprecise information.
Rather, it seeks to present the more permanent features of the English
governmental, parliamentary and legal system in the simplest terms.
Barbaro was obviously interested in governmental forms as such—he
evidently wished to compare the English parliamentary system with
that of the Venetian Great Council—and here perhaps he was bringing

to bear on a concrete situation, theoretical preoccupations derived in the first instance from a study of Aristotle's politics. It was perhaps the *Relazione* which secured a government commission to write a history of Venice in 1552. The appointment did not have a happy outcome, however. The Council of Ten was dissatisfied with the portions he produced, perhaps on account of its polemical tone: it was imbued with a spiritualistic vision of the Church, of which he presented Venice as the paladin against the secularist tendencies of the Roman court.

In any case, his energies were now substantially preoccupied with theological studies and with art. In 1550 he had been made coadjutor Patriarch of Aquilea and by 1563 he had definitely been consecrated as priest and bishop. There is no evidence that he actually exercised government in his diocese, but it is not unlikely that Grimani, the titular Patriarch, impeded him from doing so. He did, however, make a number of notable interventions at the Council of Trent, where he distinguished himself for his opposition to an indiscriminate ecclesiastical censorship. He had probably been promoted to the see of Aquilea in the first instance primarily on account of his relationship with Grimani and as a man the Serenissima could trust. It would be an exaggeration to describe him as one of the leading religious lights of his day, but he was obviously a man of religious sensibility and he devoted himself to religious scholarship. He had commenced writing theological treatises during the English mission in order to protect himself, according to his own account, from infection of his beliefs while resident in a heretical country. As bishop, he had allegedly abandoned Aristotelian studies for theological ones. He translated works of the Greek Church Fathers into Latin, but he was better known for his translations of the Psalms. In fact, however, his range extended to the publication of the Vitruvian *Ten Books of Architecture* with commentaries in 1565 and a treatise on perspective, utilising the discoveries of Dürer, in 1569. The commentaries on Vitruvius, which far outweigh the original text, were written very much from the viewpoint of an Aristotelian and Platonist scholar, dealing extensively with abstract philosophical topics such as the relationship of the arts and sciences to truth and the role of the intellect in artistic creation. He was also anxious, however, to elucidate Vitruvius's verbal descriptions of antique architectural forms and building practice by presenting the fruits of recent archaeological research and observation to the public; here it was substantially upon Palladio that he relied. Barbaro obviously had strong artistic interests. The Villa Maser which Palladio built for him and his brother Marcantonio, richly adorned by Veronese and Vittoria, is the most splendid of all Venetian Renaissance villas. Yet in his testament Daniele asked to be buried not in the family chapel at S. Francesco della Vigna, which he had had decorated by Battista Franco, but in a wooden coffin in the churchyard, robed as Patriarch with mitre ring and cross; for a Venetian noble, churchyard-burial was a relatively serious sign of self-abnegation.[13] It is tempting to regard the fictional Barbaro presented by Paruta as the defender of 'Renaissance values' against the ethos of the Counter-Reformation. Yet just as the fictional Barbaro was also the spokesman of a mystical religion of the heart, the real-life Barbaro, the translator of the Psalms, had not a little in common with the great exponent of the post-Tridentine reform movement in the Venetian dominions, Agostino Valier.

After the deaths of Sebastiano Foscarini and Daniele Barbaro, Agostino Valier (1531–1606) was probably the most authoritative, although not necessarily the most brilliant member of the Venetian intelligentsia. In youth, he had undergone the traditional apprenticeship for high government office by entering the Collegio as *Savio ai Ordini*, but does not appear to have proceeded further in his political career. In 1558, he was made public lector in philosophy at the Rialto School; he was a leading exponent of a Thomist Aristotelianism. In 1562 he went to Rome with his uncle Cardinal Bernardo Navagero and moved in the erudite circles patronised by the youthful Carlo Borromeo. He succeeded his uncle as Bishop of Verona in 1565 and subsequently revealed himself as an enthusiastic exponent of the Borromean reform current. As a teacher at Rialto and more generally, he appears to have exercised a formative influence on many patricians.[14]

Valier appears in Paruta's *Della perfezione della vita politica* but does not intervene strongly in the debate on the active and the contemplative lives. In fact, however, the position put forward by della Torre, Grimani and Mocenigo represented in crude and exaggerated form the position to which the real-life Valier subscribed; Paruta probably found it more convenient to put assertions of the primacy of contemplation in the mouths of certain notoriously troublesome prelates than in that of the revered bishop of Verona. Such an assertion, albeit in moderate and subtle form, is to be found in Valier's 'Memorial to Luigi Contarini on the studies befitting a Venetian Senator' written in 1574 (although not in fact published until 1803).[15] Valier's disciple Luigi (Alvise) Contarini was returning from the governorship of Verona and had expressed the intention not to seek honours in Venice. Valier praised this resolution. Worldly honour was a vanity. Contarini should not seek office, but, at the same time, he should not avoid it, for Venetian patricians were under an obligation to serve their city to which they owed a debt of patriotism. Even without holding office, a Venetian noble could find true honour by exercising his voting rights in the Maggior Consiglio. Those who did not attend it and banished themselves from the company of their fellows deserved no praise. Valier's ideal was fulfilled by the great patrician humanist Trifon Gabriel, who lived a quiet life in the midst of his fellows, like Socrates among the Athenians, setting an example to Venetian youth of detachment from worldly things. Valier praised Contarini's intention to devote himself to study, 'a noble exercise truly befitting a gentleman', which held the passions in check, moderated the senses, promoted detachment from the world and taught prudence. Regarding subjects for study, philosophy took precedence over literary studies and the ultimate priority must be accorded to sacred science. Valier's scheme of intellectual priorities will be examined further in due course. Here attention will be confined to the manner in which it mirrored his attitude towards the active and contemplative lives. 'Since you are not of such an age as to have to praise any prince on his death and you do not intend to be *Avogadore di Commun* (one of the chief judicial officers) and you avoid honours,' Valier remarks, 'it is not necessary for you to study the precepts of rhetoric.' In the long run, however, Valier obviously does not believe that oratorical skills learnt from the classics are of much utility to a Venetian statesman. He would seem to have set a lesser value on literary classicism that on historical study. Here his stress was particularly upon ecclesiastical history and the history of Venice. He developed his views on historiography in another epistle to Contarini, entitled 'Advice on writing the history of Venice in the present times'.[16] With regard to historical writing, it would seem that Valier's very considerable patriotic preoccupations both provided motivation and imposed certain limitations of vision. He evidently regarded it as having a utilitarian purpose. Xenophon he praised for having written 'things useful to the citizen', Sallust, for whom he had the greatest admiration, for 'political prudence' (*prudentia civile*). Valier's evident rejection of the primarily literary preoccupations which had characterised so many humanist historians, and his own strong preoccupations with issues of factual description and analysis may perhaps be seen partly within this context. It is not altogether clear, however, what he meant exactly by 'political prudence' and his historical thought was heavily marked by patriotic and moralistic preoccupations rather than by pragmatic ones. In his own draft of a Venetian history, his interest was shown not so much in politics in itself but as an instrument for the realisation of a state's moral and religious ideals.[17] It was perhaps to be expected of a man who considered that the debt of patriotism might impose active duties but who at the same time regarded the actual political game and political appetites as somewhat unworthy.

Yet from the time of the War of the League of Cambrai, Venetian historians had shown a passionate interest in politics, not so much in order to draw lessons from the study of the past as in order to understand the world in which Venice found herself. Perhaps at no time was the passion for such an understanding so strong as at the turn of the seventeenth century. In the early sixteenth century, Agnadello had opened Venetians' eyes to sinister realities which they had sought to comprehend. Yet, almost as if they were still in a state of shock, their capacities for dispassionate analysis were limited. Historians sought to apportion the blame for their own misfortunes and those of Italy; they tried to make apologies for Venice; they consoled themselves and counted their mercies in contemplation of the grandeurs of their own political institutions. They probably realised that there was little that Venice could do to influence the European scene, although this did not prevent some writers like Sanudo from trying to understand it. By the end of the century, however, the analytical powers of Venetian historians had reached a new maturity at a time when a general European conflagration seemed increasingly imminent and when Venetian statesmen were again calling for the Serene Republic to assume an active role in the international field. Paolo Paruta and Andrea Morosini writing at the very end of the sixteenth century were cautious men whose detailed analysis pointed in the direction of a policy of neutrality, but with Nicolò Contarini, a prominent member of the Giovani party, writing in the 1620s, the search for comprehension of the international scene was bound to enthusiasm for an activist policy: with Contarini, more than any of his predecessors, historical writing was shorn of didactic and apologetic considerations and became a politician's tool.[18]

With the turn of the seventeenth century, we again find Venetian statesmen immersed in the intellectual milieu of their time, but the interests were no longer primarily in antique literature and philosophy. Some, indeed, buried themselves in antiquarian studies, but it is probable that these rather tended to be political conservatives drawn from ancient and affluent families. Those associated with the Giovani party, the young activists, often political 'outsiders' who were breaking into the bastions of power, tended to move in circles, most notably those of Andrea Morosini and Nicolò Contarini, where scientific and historical studies, together with political observation, were probably the main topic of discussion. Morosini himself was in fact one of the more conservative members of the Giovani party and devoted to the memory of Gasparo Contarini. Religious conservatives were certainly to be found in his circle, but so also were dangerous characters like Giordano Bruno, Sarpi and Micanzi. It is doubtful whether the young political militants imbibed any genuine religious heterodoxy in these circles, but it is not unlikely that their intolerance of ecclesiastical pretensions was nourished there, as well as in the intellectual milieu of Padua where Cesare Cremonino, commonly regarded as being more an Aristotelian than a Christian and a cantankerous anti-clerical, was very much the grand old man. Often they would have mingled with the adepts of a ponderous and undigested historical antiquarianism, but it was a milieu in which a factual historiography counted rather than an elegant, literary, didactic one.[19]

It would be as misleading to regard the leaders of the Giovani as subscribing to a crude and uncompromising ideal of the superiority of the active life as it would be to regard their anti-clericalism as implying any indifference to religious values. It would be too much to say that they made intellectual enquiry the servant of public utility but they obviously aspired towards a harmony of the two and ultimately it was in the political arena that they expanded their main energies. Nicolò Contarini obviously came to feel that his duties as a patrician imposed limits on the range of his intellectual activities. As a young man in 1576, he had published the *De perfectione rerum*, a work of natural philosophy examining the divine action in the Universe. The opening sections breathe the conviction that philosophy is a preparation for the active life; Contarini obviously declines to see a tension between them, but, he says, it is clear that philosophical knowledge 'is highly defective when it does not have as its illustrious aim the profit of the state and human affairs and endeavour'. Contarini's position was not dissimilar to that of Daniele Barbaro in Paruta's *Della perfezione*—the affinities are with Barbaro perhaps more than with Surian—and like Barbaro he firmly separated contemplation of the divine from philosophical speculation, pointing towards a mystical spirituality as the essence of religion. For Contarini, man fulfilled himself in prayer and action.[20] Yet the *De perfectione rerum* was, in its main lines, a work of neo-scholastic philosophy and it was probably on this account that Contarini had become rather ashamed of the treatise by 1609. He had now, he said, been attracted by 'higher and more useful endeavours' (*altioribus et utilioribus studiis*) and by these he doubtless meant political labours and historical studies.[21]

The significance of the debate over the active and contemplative lives in the Renaissance lay less in the ways in which it was decided than in the fact that it existed at all; a tension between them was obviously felt to be potentially, at least, a real one. Thus it was not for nothing that Paruta used the form of the symposium-debate in the *Della perfezione della vita politica*, for it is unlikely that he approached the question with a rigid *a priori* conviction; his eventual stance, as manifested in the *Soliloquio*, particularly suggests that he felt drawn in different directions. So did many other Venetian scholars and statesmen.

The question of the division of time and effort was probably connected in some measure, in practice, with the issue of celibacy. Ermolao Barbaro had been convinced of an incompatibility between marriage and the life of scholarship. It was probably not so much that he feared a nagging wife and noisy children. Rather marriage and procreation necessitated the regulation of complex personal and economic relationships between offspring and with other members of the family, who probably held the family estate in common—*in fraterna*—and might inhabit the same palazzo; here, as many testaments suggest, there could be considerable tension. The Venetian system of the *fraterna* probably made for considerable strains in family life, but, on the other hand, it might enable a celibate, who left the heavier responsibilities of domestic and business management to his brothers, to devote untrammelled energies to politics and scholarship. As has been noted, perhaps the larger proportion of Venetian nobles never married and the aristocratic celibate, like Ermolao Barbaro, Gasparo Contarini and Daniele Barbaro, was quite a common figure among the Venetian intelligentsia. It is perhaps of relevance here to note the strong philosophical-cum-theological interests of a number of Venetian patricians. Celibate statesmen knew that a bishopric might await them at the end of their political careers and, although such studies were probably of relatively small help in actually obtaining one, they would provide a fitting adornment for episcopal office.

It was not without reason that many humanists had been conscious of a tension between study and political action. The demands of public office incumbent on patricians evidently left little enough time for the painstaking researches of developed humanist philology. It was, perhaps, precisely because advanced classical study in Venice was in large measure an aristocratic affair that its achievements there were fragmentary, even though certain particular topics were examined in considerable depth. On the other hand, while classical scholarship may have been regarded as a qualification of some value for the diplomat at the end of the fifteenth century, this was probably ceasing to be the case as the sixteenth century progressed. What remains remarkable, and ultimately puzzling, is the devotion to philosophy of so many Venetian statesmen. It cannot be said, however, that the combination of traditional philosophy with the study of politics as an intellectual exercise was, in general, particularly fruitful; with Aristotelian spectacles it was difficult to see politics as a network of tensions or in any more than static terms. So long as the intellectual interests of the Venetian aristocracy lay primarily in classical scholarship and antique or scholastic philosophy, political life and the life of the study must essentially exist in separate compartments and make conflicting demands upon a patrician's time and energies. It was, perhaps, historical studies directed towards the understanding of the contemporary world that offered the most fruitful possibilities for a harmony of the two ways of life.

Notes

[1] H. Baron, *The Crisis of the Early Italian Renaissance. Civic Humanism and Republican Liberty in the Age of Classicism and Tyranny* (revised ed. Princeton 1966)

[2] Carme IX in Hermolaus Barbarus, *Epistolae, orationes et Carmina*, ed. V. Branca (Florence 1943)

[3] Reproduced in V. E. Grabar (or Hrabar), *De legatis et legationibus tractatus varii* (Dorpat 1905), pp. 65–70

[4] See especially A. Ferriguto, *Almorò Barbaro, l'alta cultura del settentrione d'Italia nel '400* etc. (Venice, 1922)

[5] *Ibid.*, p. 70; on Donà see V. Branca, 'Late quattrocento Venetian humanism' in *Venetian Studies*, ed. J. R. Hale (London 1972)

[6] *Dizionario biografico degli Italiani* (Rome 1960–)

[7] See especially C. Dionisotti, introduction to P. Bembo, *Prose della volgar lingua* (Turin 1960)

[8] This interpretation has been put forward in F. Gilbert, 'Religion and Politics in the Thought of Gasparo Contarini' in *Action and Conviction in Early Modern Europe*, ed. T. K. Rabb and J. E. Seigel (Princeton 1969). For Contarini's crisis see H. Jedin, 'Ein Turmerlebnis des Jungen Contarini', *Historisches Jahrbuch*, 70 (1951), pp. 115–30;

'Contarini und Camaldoli', *Archivio Italiano per la Storia della Pietà*, II (Rome 1959), pp. 51–118

[9] The standard life of Contarini is F. Dittrich, *Gasparo Contarini (1483–1542)* (Braunsburg 1885)

[10] B. Nardi, 'La Scuola di Rialto e l'Umanesimo veneziano', in *Umanesimo europeo e Umanesimo veneziano*, ed. V. Branca (Florence 1963), pp. 93–139, esp. 116–20 and 130

[11] P. Paruta, *Opere politiche*, ed. C. Monzani (Florence 1852), I. For an interpretation of the work and biographical details of the personages portrayed see G. Cozzi, 'La Società veneziana del Rinascimento in un'opera di Paolo Paruta: Della perfettione della vita politica' in *Atti della Deputazione di Storia Patria per le Venezie* (1961)

[12] Paruta, *Opere politiche*, II

[13] For Barbaro see especially: P. Laven, *Daniele Barbaro Patriarch Elect of Aquilea, with special Reference to his Circle of Scholars and to his Literary Achievement*, Ph.D. Thesis 1957, Modern History, University of London (copy in Senate House Library, London); P. Paschini, 'Daniele Barbaro letterato e prelato veneziano nel Cinquecento', *R.S.C.I.*, XVI(1962), pp. 73–106; id., 'Gli scritti religiosi di Daniele Barbaro', *R.S.C.I.*, V (1961), pp. 340–9; R. Wittkower, *Architectural Principles in the Age of Humanism* (London 1952), pp. 59–61; G. Cozzi, 'Cultura politica e religione nella "pubblica storiografia" veneziana del '500', *Boll. Ist. Stor. Soc. & Stat. Ven.*, V (1963), pp. 23–4. The *Relazione d'Inghilterra* is in E. A. Alberì, *Relazioni degli ambasciatori veneti*, Ser. I, Vol. 2 (Florence 1840)

[14] Cozzi, 'La Società veneziana' etc., pp. 32–4; id., 'Cultura politica e religione' etc., pp. 30–41; A. M. Querini and G. Gradenigo, *Tiara et purpura veneta ab anno 1379 ad annum 1759* (Brescia 1761), pp. 235–41

[15] A. Valier, *Memoriale . . . a Luigi Contarini Cavaliere sopra gli studi ad un senatore veneziano convenienti*, ed. G. Morelli (Venice 1803)

[16] A. Valier, *Ricordi per scriver le historie della Republica di Venetia di questi tempi a M. Alvigi Contarini Cavalier* in *Anecdota Veneta*, ed. G. B. M. Contarini, II (Venice 1757), p. 173 and sqq.

[17] Cozzi, 'Cultura politica e religione' etc. pp. 37–41

[18] See Cozzi, 'Cultura politica e religione' etc. *passim*

[19] See below

[20] A. Tenenti, 'Il *De perfectione rerum* di Nicolò Contarini', *Boll. Ist. Soc. & Stat. Ven.*, I(1959), pp. 155–68

[21] G. Cozzi, *Il Doge Nicolò Contarini. Ricerche sul patriziato veneziano agli inizi del seicento* (Florence 1959), p. 56

five

Intellectual Life

At the beginning of the sixteenth century, Venice was the great European centre for hellenistic studies and for the editing and printing of classical texts in general. In the Venetian dominions a particularly remarkable synthesis was achieved between traditional philosophical disciplines and 'humanist studies', which will here be treated basically as the cultivation of classical letters; it was in Venice and Padua that some of the most distinguished contributions of Renaissance Aristotelianism were made around the turn of the sixteenth century. As the century progressed, classical studies were subsumed into an omnivorous antiquarianism that embraced archaeology and historical studies. Often it was combined with the accumulation of scientific data. The accumulation of data in both the scientific and historical fields often seems to have been animated by a passion for information for information's sake, compilatory rather than critical in its manifestations, but it probably helped to provide a basis for certain highly creative work in these areas. The institutional and mechanical aids to these various intellectual achievements were provided by the schools of St Mark and Rialto, the University of Padua, numerous academies and learned societies and the printing-press.

In order to understand the institutional forms of the Venetian academic system, and ultimately in order to comprehend the nature of Venice's intellectual achievements, it is necessary to say something of the conceptual division of academic disciplines in Renaissance Italy. A common distinction was made between *humanistae* and *philosophi*. In sixteenth-century parlance, the *humanistae* were scholars of 'humane letters' or the 'liberal arts', which were recognised as comprising grammar, rhetoric, poetry, moral philosophy and history.[1] For practical purposes, we can regard them as being scholars of antique literature and language in the first instance. If they were teachers, they might exercise their profession in humanities schools outside the university framework, or they might hold university chairs of grammar, rhetoric or moral philosophy. 'Moral philosophy', as a recognised academic discipline, was discursive rather than systematic in form, closely allied to the study of rhetoric and tending, initially at least, to be based on Plato rather than Aristotle. It was distinguished from logic, metaphysics (the study of 'being') and 'natural philosophy' (basically natural science, but having close affinities with metaphysics). These, as traditional university disciplines, originally introduced into Italy from Northern Europe around the turn of the fourteenth century, were primarily based on Aristotle and his commentators. The theoretical distinction between 'humane letters' and 'philosophy' became increasingly less clear-cut in practice. From the early fifteenth century, Italians had been applying the techniques and outlook of humanist classical scholarship to the study of Aristotle. These endeavours reached their high-water mark in Venice and Padua at the turn of the sixteenth century. In the Venetian educational system, however, there was a fairly clear division between 'humane letters' and philosophy *in viam Aristotelis*.

Although there were numerous private schools in Venice, at which grammar and rhetoric were taught, often by scholars of considerable distinction, the main teaching institutions were the two public schools, the philosophy school of Rialto, which was in action by 1408, and the humanities school of St Mark, founded in 1450. While the orientations of the Rialto School were primarily towards logic, metaphysics, natural philosophy and science, with a strong Aristotelian bent, those of the rival academy of St Mark were towards classical letters and moral philosophy, with an inclination towards Platonism. Its list of distinguished teachers in the latter half of the fifteenth century included Filelfo, George of Trebizond, Giorgio Merula and Giorgio Valla. It had originally been founded for the education of the young men of the Ducal Chancery, but it also took many nobles and ordinary citizens. It would appear, however, to have been more the Rialto School that was the main nursery of the aristocracy's intellectual élite.[2]

In the middle years of the fifteenth century, it had seemed that the Rialto School might develop into a university, but here the aspirations of its professor, Paolo della Pergola, had been curbed by the Council of Ten. The latter had evidently wished to preserve Padua's monopolistic position as *studium generale* of the Venetian dominions. Many Venetian patricians attended this great international university, although the lack of comprehensive matriculation rolls makes an estimate of their numbers impossible; it seems clear that many nobles attended without actually taking degrees. It often tends to be forgotten that the early developments of Venetian humanism, around the beginning of the fifteenth century, had primarily occurred in Padua and, in the early sixteenth century, Venetian classical scholars were still drawing profit from teachers there. It was, however, primarily for legal studies, philosophy, more particularly of an Aristotelian bias, and natural science that Padua was chiefly famous.

The Aristotelian tradition had always been strong at Padua, but from the late fifteenth century it showed novel orientations when research came to be based on the Greek text, or at least recent Latin translations of it, rather than on mediaeval Latin translations from Arabic ones. At this time, the great debate in Paduan philosophical circles concerned interpretations of Aristotle's doctrine of the soul, the Averroists, who maintained the soul's essential autonomy of the body, battling with the Alexandrists, who maintained its essential unity with all other human functions. The former ascribed to Aristotle the doctrine of a collective 'world soul', which alone was immortal, the latter, while asserting the individuality of the soul, claimed that any concept of its natural immortality was alien to Aristotle's thought. With the early sixteenth century, the Alexandrists substantially asserted their dominance in Padua, thus marking a victory for antique over Arab and mediaeval commentaries of the Stagyrite. Here a major blow was struck by the publication in 1516 of the *De immortalitate animae* by Pietro Pomponazzi who had held a chair of philosophy at Padua in the years 1495–1509. The debate on the soul had been substantially conducted within the framework of scholastic concepts and preoccupations, although Nicoletto Vernia, the great master of late fifteenth century Paduan Aristotelianism, more a precursor of Pomponazzi than a strict Averroist, and Pomponazzi himself probably utilised in some measure the deeper knowledge of Aristotle brought about by humanist research. It was, however, Leonico Tomeo (professor from 1497 to 1531) who, of the Paduans, revealed the greatest debt to the humanists. One gift of humanism was a broader vision of the encyclopaedic scope of the Aristotelian corpus and while Paduan Aristotelianism remained, throughout the sixteenth century, strongly preoccupied with problems of metaphysics and, in particular, the nature of the soul, it did branch out in new directions. Thus Tomeo turned towards natural science, while Sperone Speroni (1500–88) studied Aristotle's rhetoric and claimed to have applied its principles in his own literary compositions.

The anatomists Santorio, Acquapendente and Vesalius and the young Galileo were only the most brilliant of a phalanx of scientists working at

Padua in the late sixteenth and early seventeenth centuries. While it is difficult to evaluate the mass of work done there in this period on mechanics, optics and the circulation of the blood, it is generally considered that the discoveries of Galileo and Harvey (himself an alumnus of Padua) were considerably indebted to the accumulated labours of observation and ratiocination undertaken by Paduan professors.

An important place in the intellectual life of Venice was held by the large number of *cenacoli* or groups of scholars and men of letters. Some of these had statutes and styled themselves academies. Information of their activities, especially in the first half of the sixteenth century, tends to be fragmentary, however. The Accademia Filosofica founded by Ermolao Barbaro in 1484 had evidently been devoted primarily to Latin studies. We know little of the circle of Tomaso Giustiniani in the first decade of the sixteenth century and that of Abbot Cortese in the late 1520s apart from details of their membership; this comprised scholars of the classics and philosophy with strong religious preoccupations and interests in Biblical scholarship. We are well informed, however, concerning the Neacademia founded by the great publisher Aldus Manutius around 1501, obviously the most distinguished of Venetian academies in the first half of the sixteenth century. Closely integrated with Aldus's editorial enterprises, it was primarily devoted to the promotion of Hellenistic studies. Its members included such outstanding classical scholars as Erasmus, Bembo, Egnazio and Musurus; modern annalistic historiography was also represented by Marcantonio Sabellico and Marin Sanudo and cosmography by Giovan Battista Ramusio, the Secretary of the Senate. Towards the middle of the century, groups gathered round two other distinguished printers occupied in the publication of grammars and modern and antique literature, Paolo Manuzio, Aldus's son, and Gabriele Giolito of Ferrara.

It would appear that, in the first half of the sixteenth century, the main orientation of academies and the more informal learned groups was towards the study of antique literature and philosophy. In the latter half of the century, however, they became encyclopaedic in their interests, a prominent place being assigned to historical and antiquarian studies and natural science. The most ambitious project was that of the Accademia Veneziana or Accademia della Fama founded in 1557, with heavy financial support from his own resources, by the patrician Federigo Badoer. Its members included the poet Bernardo Tasso, Francesco Patrizi the Paduan mathematician and natural philosopher, Francesco Sansovino, son of the architect, a jurist, antiquarian and compiler of guide-books, and Giuseppe Zarlino, the musical theorist and *Maestro di Capella* at St Mark's, as well as a number of nobles. Lectures were held at the Academy daily, allegedly on *every* subject. The supplications of the Academy to the Signory contained grandiose phraseology about the utility of learning to the state and a concrete example of this was, in fact, provided by the Consiglio Politico, a section of the Academy designed to help the education of Venetian statesmen by the collection of foreign intelligence. A project was also set on foot for the compilation and editing of Venetian laws. This was part of a wider scheme for publications under the auspices of the Academy which possessed its own printing-press, donated by Paolo Manuzio. Of the 300 volumes projected, about a third were scientific, 66 being classical treatises and 23 Arabic, mediaeval and modern works; here can be seen the reflection of the curious literary-humanistic science, focusing on the study of ancient texts, which had been a tradition in Venice from the time of Ermolao Barbaro. A number of works of jurisprudence with new commentaries were also proposed. In fact only 22 books were printed, for the Academy was closed on government orders in 1561, following Badoer's bankruptcy. Although its achievements were limited, its history provides an interesting testimony of the range of interests of the Venetian intellectual milieu. An attempt was made to revive it with the foundation of the second Accademia Veneziana in 1593. The membership of the latter included the two Tintorettos and the sculptor Alessandro Vittoria. Especially important groups of a less formal nature were those of Domenico Venier and Paolo Paruta and that of Andrea Morosini, to which we have already referred. Interests in science, history and politics appear to have been particularly strong among the members of the latter who allegedly included Sarpi, Micanzi, Galileo, and several prominent members of the Giovani party, including Nicolò Contarini and Leonardo Donà. The Venier circle seems to have been more a literary and poetical one. The Paruta and Morosini circles would appear to have been fairly strongly aristocratic in character, but this was not so evidently the case with the Accademia della Fama, the second Accademia Veneziana and the Venier circle; the latter two in particular contained a substantial number of non-Venetians.[3]

A word must be said about the academies and *cenacoli* of Padua and Vicenza. The intellectual life of Venice was closely linked to those of Padua and while the connections of the Vicentine Accademia Olympica with Venice were limited, it was of great significance for the culture of the Veneto as a whole. In Padua, the Accademia degli Infiammati was founded in 1540 by Daniele Barbaro, Leone Orsini, later bishop of Fréjus and probably also the Paduan philosopher and man of letters Sperone Speroni, who certainly became the leading figure of the Academy in due course. It provided a meeting ground between professors of the University and members of the Venetian aristocratic intelligentsia. It is not clear whether it was closed in 1545 or 1550 or even later.[4] In the final years of the century, the house of Giovan Vincenzo Pinelli in Padua provided a meeting ground for men of letters, antiquarians and scientists, including Speroni, Galileo and Micanzi, Pinelli's own interests being primarily antiquarian. Although aspersions were cast on the religious orthodoxy of certain of the circle's members, Pinelli had strong personal links with the Jesuits and leading thinkers of the Counter Reformation, including Agostino Valier, Bellarmine and Baronius.[5]

The Accademia Olympica was founded in 1555 by a group of Vicentine nobles and scholars. Regular lectures were given on such subjects as philosophy, mathematics, cosmography, anatomy and aesthetics. For the purposes of study, a collection was made of casts of antique and modern sculptures and of modern works of art, together with mathematical and cosmographical instruments and maps. The academy had its own orchestra and a succession of magnificent theatrical performances was put on; masques, pastorals, classical tragedies in translation or the new classicising drama of Trissino. In the early years, Palladio, himself a founder-member of the academy, designed the scenery and temporary theatres and it was he who designed the famous Teatro Olympico, upon which work was begun in 1580. The major performances were attended by foreign ambassadors and by nobles from all over the Veneto. The academy was entrusted with the conduct of certain major civic solemnities, such as receptions of royalty and foreign statesmen or the solemn leave-takings of Venetian governors.[6]

One of the great resources available to Venetian scholars lay in the city's libraries. In 1468, Cardinal Bessarion had bequeathed to the Serenissima his great collection of Greek codices, perhaps the finest ever to be formed in the Renaissance period, which became the basis of the Marciana Library. This public collection was enriched by the bequests of the Cardinals Domenico and Marino Grimani. We possess only fragmentary information about private libraries in the first half of the sixteenth century, but, from the 1560s, guide books drew attention to them as being among the city's great treasures and listed the chief bibliomanes. It would seem that the treasured core of the collections was formed by manuscripts, which might often include chronicles of Venetian history, as well as classical works. The passion for collecting antiques, coins and mathematical and cosmographical instruments cannot be seen in isolation from this bibliomania and certain of the chief collectors of antiquities and works of art possessed major libraries, notably the Grimani cardinals, Daniele Barbaro and Giacomo Contarini, whom we shall examine in another chapter.

It was probably in part the manuscript resources of Venetian libraries as well as the textual skills of Venetian and Paduan scholars that attracted so many printers to Venice. An enlightened government policy with regard to the printing trade and access to supplies of good quality paper from the Riviera di Salò on Lake Garda were further factors. In the early sixteenth century, the Venetian printing industry was the most important in Europe. The first enterprises using moveable type, conducted by John of Speyer and the Frenchman Nicholas Jenson around the 1460s[7] had been followed in the 1470s by a substantial immigration of German printers and by the 1490s, with further immigration by Italians and foreigners, there were about 150 presses in Venice (as against 60 in Milan, 42 in Bologna, 37 in Rome and 22 in Florence). Most of the main typographers appear to have come from outside Venice. Although printing with moveable type came to Venice relatively early, in few of the late fifteenth-century innovations was it original, but each expansion of the art of printing in Italy reached its highest development there; in particular, the Greek press achieved its greatest initial expansion in the city. Immigrants were probably encouraged by the state's willingness to grant monopolies for technical innovations, although they were loosely applied, and it was in Venice that the first known system of copyright developed. The first example of copyright was one granted to Sabellico for his history in 1486 and the first legislation dates from 1517. With regard to censorship, however, the relative liberalism of the Venetian government should not be overestimated. Control over publication became tighter after 1562 and with the institution of the papal Clementine Index in 1596, which the Venetian government accepted after some misgivings, censorship became quite oppressive, its target being supposed licentiousness as well as suspected religious heterodoxy.

By the 1490s, not only had Venetian printers attained the highest typographical standards but they were also prepared to take the greatest pains to obtain the best readings of texts and to employ the best scholars for editorial work. For Greek works, a distinguished body of emigré Cretan scholars was available for consultation. If Venice stole the lead on Florence as the main centre of humanistic textual work in these years, it was in some measure due to her residue of publishing skills. Here the most distinguished contribution was obviously that of Aldus Manutius. It is significant that when Aldus settled in Venice, some time in the early 1490s, probably attracted in part by the presence of Bessarion's library, his background was not that of a printer but of a scholar, having studied Latin in Rome and Greek at the great Ferrarese humanities school and acted as tutor to the della Mirandola family at Carpi. His contribution was based on harnessing sober scholarship with outstanding typographical skills. He had grasped the need for accurate texts in a readable, aesthetically pleasing and easily manageable format. In the field of typography, he revolutionised both Greek and Roman founts; here founts modelled on cursive handwriting made for extreme legibility in combination with small format and his 'Bembo' type remains with us to this day; for Greek founts he utilised the skills of Cretan calligraphers and workmen. In editorial work, he made use of the distinguished scholars of his academy, which we have already examined. His aim in the publication of classical works was to make the best texts available rather than to provide the reader with a wealth of philologial erudition; he renounced attempts to amend readings, but a certain editorial scholarship did lie in the very selection of sources for the bare, unglossed texts which he presented to the public. Up to 1500, he was mainly occupied with Greek texts and ones which catered for the interests of philosophers and students of medicine rather than literary humanists. This is not to say that he had not published certain works of Greek poets and prose-writers, but these must be primarily seen within the context of his publications of lexicons and grammars, as serving an ancillary function in providing linguistic knowledge. From 1500, however, the publications of his house became predominantly literary in character and mirrored the general range of interests of the Italian humanist tradition, both Greek, Latin and vernacular: works of Dante, Petrarch, and Pietro Bembo appeared alongside those of the ancient poets, historians, tragedians, comedists and moralists.

Aldus's dazzling reputation must not lead us to forget the other highly distinguished publishers working in Venice, notably the Cretan Zacharia Calergi, who commenced printing in Greek shortly after Aldus, Aldus's own son Paolo, like him a distinguished scholar at the centre of the intellectual life of his day, Gabriele Giolito of Ferrara and the Giunta family. In the long run, moreover, classical texts and erudite works in general only formed a fraction of the output of Venice's presses. From all over Italy, volumes of poetry, plays, *romanze* and works of popular piety were sent to be printed there; in particular, Florentine *volgare* writers, who did not have a particularly flourishing or cost-effective press close at hand, often turned to Venetian publishers; there was even a fairly extensive clandestine production of religious works for consumption by Protestant publics abroad, the Venetian book-trade in general having an appreciable German market. With the latter half of the sixteenth century, however, Venice's printing industry began to encounter serious difficulties. Ecclesiastical censorship was one factor. The Tridentine Index of 1564 evidently damaged both home and foreign markets and Paolo Paruta's prophesies of the disastrous effects of the Clementine Index of 1596 appear to have been fulfilled. Typographers began to leave Venice in large numbers within a few months of its publication and the number of presses fell from 125 to 40. Ecclesiastical censorship was probably not the only factor, however. The crisis of the book trade in the 1590s was probably connected in some measure with the general economic crisis in this decade, caused by high grain-prices, famine and plague. Moreover, Paruta alleged that the trade was being damaged by a severe decline in typographical quality and standards of accuracy; these factors were again mentioned in a government decree of 1603. In the seventeenth century, the book-trade was still an important item in the commerce of the Republic, but she had lost her European leadership in this field, having succumbed, in particular, to competition from the Low Countries. It was a symbol: Venice was a distinguished member of the European intellectual community, but no longer among its leaders.[8]

★   ★   ★

The importance of *cenacoli* in Venetian intellectual life has already been noted. Here Aldus Manutius and Andrea Morosini stand out particularly as men who helped to bring the outstanding minds of their generations together. Gasparo Contarini is also significant as the link between the humanist and reforming groups which met under the aegis of Tomaso Giustiniani and Abbot Cortese. The network of relationships between scholars and thinkers cannot be studied here in detail, but an examination of certain of its aspects, with particular regard to a number of family trees of the Venetian intelligentsia, will help to elucidate developments in Venetian scholarship and letters and also features of artistic patronage in Venice, which will be examined more fully in a later chapter.[9]

Several important lines of descent radiate from the late fifteenth century group of Ermolao Barbaro, Bernardo Bembo and Gerolamo Donà, all of whom were friends. It may be noted that Ermolao was himself the grandson and nephew of distinguished humanists, Francesco and Ermolao Barbaro the Elder, respectively. The younger Ermolao began his humanist education under his uncle, who was bishop of Verona and it is significant that the latter, like his nephew later, had entered the vexed contemporary debate on the relationship between letters and philosophy. As we shall see in a future chapter, certain of Giorgione's patrons had links with Bembo and Donà. Bernardo Bembo was the possessor of an important library, a patron of men of letters and a Platonist scholar of some repute. Pietro Bembo, the Ciceronian scholar, poet and systematiser of the *volgare*, and also an important art collector, was his son. It was doubtless from his father that Pietro first absorbed his enthusiasm for Petrarch. Bernardo who was, after Ermolao Barbaro, perhaps the most cosmopolitan Venetian scholar of his time, probably introduced his son into the cultured circles of Ferrara and Rome which he frequented in the course of his diplomatic activity. It is also worth noting Bernardo's circulation in the Florentine intellectual milieu and his close links with the Medici family, which had been forged while he was ambassador in Florence, and which may have ultimately aided Pietro's promotion as secretary to Leo X. In his own day, Pietro was the Venetian *letterato* with the most extensive knowledge of cultural centres elsewhere in Italy and was perhaps, intellectually, the most Tuscanised. Daniele Barbaro, the Aristotelian scholar, editor of Vitruvius and patron of Palladio was the great-nephew of Ermolao the Younger, certain of whose works he edited. His foundation of the Paduan botanical garden catered for interests which Ermolao had originally helped to stimulate. Although Ermolao died twenty years before Daniele's birth, the two men were alike in their combination of heavy philosophical erudition with artistic sensitivity. Evidently the links between the Barbaro and Bembo families were maintained, for Daniele corresponded with Pietro Bembo, who had been a friend of the great Ermolao in his youth.

The Barbaro of S. Maria Mater Domini and the Grimani of S. Maria Formosa were evidently related in some way,[10] and this probably aided Daniele's appointment as Patriarch of Aquilea Elect and coadjutor to

Giovanni Grimani. We have already seen how Cardinal Domenico Grimani had acquired a vast accumulation of ecclesiastical preferments which he subsequently passed on to his nephews Marino, Marco and Giovanni. Domenico was described by Erasmus as the most learned prelate of the Roman court and he possessed an important library and an outstanding collection of antiques and modern works of art. His nephews were not outstandingly distinguished intellectually, but the Cardinal Marino again built up a major library and both he and Giovanni Grimani had remarkable antique collections. If the Bembo had strong Florentine and Medici links, the Grimani, in the first half of the sixteenth century were partly Roman-based, and, in the case of the Cardinal Domenico at least, this helps to account for their antiquarian interests. Little is known of Giovanni Grimani's relations with Daniele Barbaro, but they were both munificent artistic patrons, with somewhat classicising tendencies and to some extent employed the same artists. The intellectual traditions of the Barbaro family were in some measure continued by Daniele's nephews Francesco and Ermolao, who followed Grimani as Patriarchs of Aquilea.

Most of the numerous Contarinis who distinguished the Venetian intellectual scene were in no way closely related. Alvise (Luigi) Contarini, the historian and disciple of Agostino Valier was, however, the nephew of the great Cardinal Gasparo. He was the editor of his works, and although still a layman at the time of his own early death, was imbued with the same religious and reforming ideals. Valier's relations with him are significant, for the bishop of Verona, although possibly of a more rigid outlook, was in many respects the true heir to Gasparo Contarini's mantle as a scholar and divine, as the spokesman of a severe moral ethic and exponent of a moralistic vision of the state and as a writer on episcopal reform. There are other indications of close links between the Contarini and Valier families, although there is no evidence that they were related by marriage.

The pattern of personal and family relationships between many of Venice's great thinkers and *cognoscenti* is hardly surprising. Repeatedly we find that such men, more particularly in the late fifteenth century and the first half of the sixteenth century, came from the high strata of the nobility, not so much the senatorial nobility in general but its inner élite from which members of the *Collegio* and incumbents of ambassadorships and major governorships tended to be drawn, an élite of men well-known to one another and probably, within certain limits, an endogamous caste. Association of particular families with the Church, and the frequent intermarriage of these, probably also provided certain linkages and traditions. Here the particularly close relationship between nephew and celibate uncle, which the peculiar structure of the Venetian family system promoted, was probably of significance. Bishops, even the most conscientious ones, were inclined to see nephews as heirs to their office and often acted as their mentors; with regard to the figures we have examined, the relationship between the two Ermolao Barbaros and that between Agostino Valier and his scholarly uncle the Cardinal Bernardo Navagero are cases in point. Furthermore, the duties of high-ranking patricians, whether laymen or ecclesiastics, often led them out-side the Venetian dominions and to young nobles who accompanied them this opened up possibilities for a wider intellectual apprenticeship than they could have undergone in Venice; they might, like Pietro Bembo, accompany their fathers on diplomatic missions, or, like, Agostino Valier, visit Rome with prelate-uncles. Ultimately, however, the manner in which a family like the Barbaro repeatedly gave forth distinguished scholars cannot be explained in purely objective terms. The most obvious tradition of the Barbaro of S. Maria Mater Domini was one of service to the state rather than of scholarship, yet it was this branch of the Barbaro that stood out more than any other Venetian family for its intellectual distinction, while Ermolao the Younger and Daniele are perhaps the great heroes of our story; both came the nearest of any Venetians to being *uomini universali* of truly creative capacity.

★　　★　　★

Giorgione's painting in the Vienna Kunthistorisches Museum, known as the 'Three Philosophers', and already known as such in 1525, may well contain a poetic vision of the new humanist philosophy and naturalistic enthusiasms represented, par excellence, by Ermolao Barbaro. Its subject matter is, however, an enigma. It seems to fall within the genre of representations of the 'three ages of man', showing a bearded elder, a man in his prime and a youth. Behind them is a verdant landscape, detailed by the rays of a low sun just outside the picture. To the left of the picture is a curious mass of earth and rock, the entrance to a cave perhaps, across which leaves are blowing, coming from the landscape behind. The old man, on the extreme right, is dressed in what could be taken for monastic garb, only the draperies are saffron and the hood a rich maroon colour. He holds a sheet covered with astrological figures and stares before him with a severe and some-

what irascible expression. The middle-aged man, in the centre, is
dressed in oriental costume. His face is curiously expressionless, tinged
perhaps with a certain resigned sadness, and his half-closed eyes are cast
somewhat downwards, apparently in the direction of the sheet of
figures in the hands of the old man, towards whom he seems to incline.
The youth, seated on the left, is clothed in white draperies, which could
be classical dress or equally an ecclesiastical alb, and a green cloak is
thrown over them. He holds a set-square and dividers. The other two
figures have their backs towards the landscape, the youth's body is
partly directed towards it; his serene, concentrated gaze is directed, not
perhaps exactly towards the landscape, but towards the very edge of
the rock-face across which the leaves are blowing.

Various conflicting interpretations of this picture have been put forward. Perhaps the most interesting are those of Bruno Nardi and
Arnaldo Ferriguto. Nardi suggests that the figures represented are
mathematicians and astronomers. He is disposed to identify the old man
with Ptolemy and the oriental with one of a number of Arab astronomers or mathematicians. For the youth he suggests a recent Paduan
astronomer or mathematician and inclines towards an identification
with Copernicus, who studied at Padua in the years 1501–5; Nardi
considers that there are marked similarities with a known portrait of
the latter.[11] It is, however, upon Ferriguto's interpretation that we
especially wish to concentrate.

He suggests that the theme of the three ages of man, itself probably
inspired by a passage in Aristotle's *Rhetoric*, is used to depict the philosophical tendencies of three successive generations at Venice and Padua,
in a period of rapid change in philosophical milieux between about
1475 and 1525. Bearing in mind the prominence of Aristotelianism in
Venetian and Paduan philosophical thought, he suggests that the three
men are Aristotelians. The severe, bearded elder is the representative of
a theologising scholastic Aristotelianism which, in its primary preoccupations with logic and metaphysics, has substantially reduced the
thought of the Stagyrite to the realm of the abstract. The oriental is the
representative of an 'arabist' scholasticism, based on Averroes, which
has a similarly limited vision. The Averroists had for long been
attacked by the ecclesiastical authorities, but by the turn of the sixteenth
century, however, there was a certain *rapprochement* between them and
guardians of religious orthodoxy, in the face of the 'Alexandrists' who
denied any natural immortality to the soul. In Professor Ferriguto's
view, the alliance was also against the new humanist philosophy. Hence,

Ferriguto suggests, the oriental's almost deferential inclination towards the hooded elder. He is a dignified yet tragic figure, hesitating, Ferriguto believes, between the old man and the youth. The latter is the incarnation of the new humanism. While the other two men have their backs turned to the world of nature, this elegant Grecian figure serenely regards it. He is the symbol of an Aristotelianism which has rediscovered the true thought of Greek antiquity and a philosophy orientated towards the natural world, of an outlook represented, above all, by Ermolao Barbaro.[12] The face of the youth could indeed be an idealised version of the delicate yet faintly porcine features of Ermolao as we know them from more or less contemporary portrayals and the green mantle could be a reference to the ecclesiastical status of the young Patriarch of Aquilea; green, in ecclesiastical symbolism, is not only the colour of hope but is, above all, the episcopal colour. Further suggestions could be added to Ferriguto's. The rock-face could be the entrance to a cave and the picture might represent a modified version of Plato's parable of the cave. The old man, representing scholastic philosophy, may be regarding the shadows of the outer world cast upon the cave wall, while the Arab regards only the mathematised representations of the universe; the humanist philosopher's vision is not bound to the cave and, if not actually directed towards the full contemplation of the world of nature, is moving towards it and can at least perceive the fragments of it that are wafted in.

All this is pure hypothesis. We shall never know whether the picture was really intended to represent the new encyclopaedic Aristotelianism and natural science of Ermolao Barbaro, the resurrected philosophy of ancient Greece, turning away from an obscure and arid world of stone and shadows towards the light and the world of nature. In the eyes of learned contemporaries, however, the symbolism would certainly have appeared appropriate to Ermolao Barbaro and his intimate circle.

This may come as a surprise to those accustomed to regard a reaction against Aristotle as integral to the humanist movement. Admittedly, certain adepts of humane letters, whose preoccupations were primarily literary, might make slighting reference to Aristotle. Those, however, who endeavoured to combine systematic philosophy with humanistic textual science normally had a profound respect for the thought of the Stagyrite. Needless to say, unlike the schoolmen of the mediaeval universities, they sought to recover this thought from the Greek text and to disengage it from the accumulation of mediaeval and Arab commentaries, at the same time setting it within the general context of antique thought. From these endeavours a broader vision of Aristotle emerged. If, in the later Middle Ages, almost the whole of the surviving Aristotelian corpus had been fairly generally known in western Europe and the Stagyrite had been regarded as 'the master of those who know', he had been treated more particularly as the master of metaphysicians and logicians. Now more extensive attention was given to his science, ethics, politics, economics and poetics: he was seen more fully as an encyclopaedic philosopher.

In Italy, it was above all the Venetians who distinguished themselves in recovering the Greek Aristotle and broadening the vision of him. They were able to do this, in part, because their outlook was fertilised by wide knowledge of other areas of antique thought. Thus Platonist studies helped to direct attention towards Aristotle's politics, ethics and poetics. The discovery of antique commentators cast new light on his thought. An encyclopaedic Aristotelianism within the context of a broad philosophical and literary culture was rather more the attainment of Venetian aristocrat-humanists than of Paduan professors of philosophy. Although certain of these did much to deepen knowledge of the Greek Aristotle, showing an awareness of humanist discoveries, such men tended to be rather narrow Aristotelian specialists. On the other hand, Venetian 'Aristotelianism' at its best, with Ermolao Barbaro, Gerolamo Donà and Bernardo Bembo, opened up new vistas because it was not exclusively based on Aristotle. Thus while Peripatetic science, in the hands of exclusivist Aristotelians, only lead to sterility, with certain Venetians, notably Ermolao Barbaro, it only formed part of a broader enquiry into the natural world which, in the case of the latter involved active observation. At the same time, a wide literary and philological culture made possible a deeper understanding of the precise meaning of the Aristotelian texts.

The strain of Renaissance culture, sometimes referred to as *cultura filosofica*, which sought to apply the textual techniques developed by humanist scholars to the elucidation of the actual content of antique thought, more particularly ancient philosophy, reached its high-water mark in Italy with the Florentine Angelo Poliziano and with Ermolao Barbaro. These two men were regarded by Erasmus as the two greatest Italian philologists in the final decades of the fifteenth century. With regard to the application of philological science to the study of philosophy, indeed, Politian seems to have been substantially Barbaro's disciple and it was the latter who also formed the chief middle link between the *cultura filosofica* of Florence and that of Budé and Ramus in

France. He was a man of encyclopaedic interests, a practicing botanist and one of the most renowned scientists of his day, sensitive to all forms of poetry, whether antique or the most advanced modern Italian genres and probably an appreciator of the art of Carpaccio and Gentile Bellini. His major importance was not only as a practitioner of *cultura filosofica* but also as one of the main initiators of interest in science and natural history in the Veneto. It has been said that Barbaro was a *letterato* rather than a philosopher. This was so inasfar as his aim was to elucidate texts rather than to expound any particular philosophical system as such. As an Aristotelian scholar, his main contribution was twofold; to have sought to determine Aristotle's meaning in terms of the vocabulary available to him and to have directed attention to the need for examining the Aristotelian corpus as a whole and not merely the portions commonly taught in university faculties; it was his constantly reiterated ambition to give public readings of, and ultimately to translate *all* the works of the Stagyrite. He repeatedly urged the necessity of sound linguistic knowledge for an understanding of Aristotle and pointed to the dangers of relying upon Arab and Mediaeval commentators. His most ambitious work was, in fact, the 'Emendations of Pliny' (*Castigationes Pliniae*, 1492) in which he corrected some 6,000 passages of the *Natural History*. Here grammar and a profound knowledge of Greek and Latin etymology were used to elucidate passages which were hitherto obscure or to emend ones which copying errors had rendered meaningless. Furthermore, Barbaro evidently realized that first-hand knowledge of natural history was needed to elucidate Pliny's scientific vocabulary and, where necessary, he was prepared to 'castigate' Pliny's own errors. In this way, Barbaro combined his textual skills with his own active scientific interests and in doing so he contributed towards the creation of an international scientific vocabulary. Barbaro was convinced of an essential unity between the pursuits of philosophy, natural science and literary studies. Mastery of 'the word' was indispensable to the comprehension of the ancient philosophers and to the presentation of philosophical propositions. Behind this conviction lay an understanding of words, not as mere labels arbitrarily invented for the sake of human convenience, but as complex manifestations of the wealth of human experience. Not only did he assert that a man ignorant of Greek had no right to call himself an Aristotelian, but he also attacked those who tried to separate philosophy from *eloquentia*. By the latter he evidently meant not merely literary elegance but proper use of language in the widest sense. The separation, he believed, had damaged the substance of philosophy as well as its form. 'Whatever of life's span God pleases to give me,' he wrote to Gerolamo Donà, 'I will dedicate to this sole end; inasfar as in me lies to restore the harmony between natural philosophy and humane letters.' (*Ut naturalis plulosophia cum studiis humanitatis in gratiam redeat.*)[13] Premature death, however, cut short his endeavour.[14]

As an exponent of *cultura filosofica*, Barbaro found distinguished disciples in France, but no true successor in Venice. Gerolamo Donà, who shared his aspirations in some measure, was too immersed in affairs of state. At one time, it seemed that Pietro Bembo might inherit Barbaro's mantle, but, to the disappointment of contemporaries, he turned from scientific classical philology to the pursuit of literary elegance. Aldus declined to patronise advanced textual criticism and confined himself to the humbler task of finding the best source for the naked, unglossed text. The fragments of Barbaro's heritage can be seen everywhere: in a more totalistic vision of Aristotle, in a respect for the Greek text and for classical commentators, in the enthusiasm for Pliny, in the development of botanical studies and in a curious literary-humanistic science which relied on the appreciation of classical texts while trying, in certain cases, to align them with modern discoveries. This latter tradition was nourished by Aldus's publications and found exponents in the Bembo circle and the Accademia della Fama: it can be seen even with the early Pietro Bembo in his study of Mount Etna.[15] In the long run it probably fostered scientific enquiry if only by bringing to light discrepancies between antique authorities. The combination of science, philosophy and classical culture was pursued by many patrician scholars, but it is probably fair to say that none of them made textual and linguistic science the servant of other branches of learning in quite the same way as Ermolao Barbaro had done. Venetian classical scholarship, in the main, pursued humbler aims.

From the mid-fifteenth century to the late sixteenth century, Venetian students of classical antiquity produced a mass of sober textual and philological scholarship. As yet, it is difficult to evaluate it or to assess very clearly how it developed man's vision of antiquity. What can be said, however, is that, if fifteenth-century Florence had been the main centre for the gathering of rare classical manuscripts, Venice, at the turn of the sixteenth century, had become the main centre for the editing of texts and for philological work designed to elucidate them: the provision of commentaries, studies of orthography and the technicalities of metre and prosody, the compilation of grammars and lexicons. The impulse which all this gave to studies of vernacular usage will be examined in another chapter.

Questionings as to the relationship between the pursuit of classical culture and the life of the citizen, the statesman and the Christian cannot have left the minds of Venetians untouched. Fifteenth-century apologists for 'humane letters' had given clear guidance on the issue. Fluency of tongue and pen based on the study of the ancients, they asserted, was invaluable to the statesman. But was the language of Cicero, serviceable enough perhaps in late fifteenth century Italy, in the golden days of the concert of Peninsular powers, the language to be used with the ravening wolves beyond the Alps? Vergerio and Piccolomini had asserted, among others, that the study of the ancient historians would provide guidance for the conduct of politics. But did Livy really offer any lessons for an Italy at the mercy of foreign invaders? A long line of writers from Petrarch and Salutati to the early Erasmus had stressed the utility to the Christian of the moral precepts to be found in the writings of the ancients and had professed to see a profound harmony between the ethics of Cicero and Seneca and those of St Paul. It is doubtful, however, whether Venetians of the mid-sixteenth century would have taken for granted a harmony between antique pagan ethics and those of Christianity. For one thing, they probably had a stronger historical sense, a clearer perception of the context of antique thought. For another, the Counter-Reformatory ethos was too mistrustful of human capacity, too preoccupied with the role of divine Grace and too conscious of the heritage of the Christian people of God to accept such a harmony without severe qualifications.

With Agostino Valier, the rejection, on religious grounds, of classical cultivation as the mark par excellence of the scholar was particularly explicit and, at the same time, unusually sophisticated. He was obviously well-enough versed in antique literature and he believed that much was to be gained from it, but considered that the study of the Bible and Christian writers must ultimately take precedence. Thus far, he shared some of the deepest convictions of the Christian humanists of Erasmus's generation. Furthermore, however, he showed an explicit consciousness of a difference, not only between Christian religion and pagan ethics, but also between a Christian morality and a pagan one. Epictetus and Seneca, though putting forward excellent precepts on contempt for the world, were blind in their failure to perceive human weakness, but the Stoics were truly enemies of human nature in regarding *misericordia*, the capacity for being affected by others' misfortunes, as a disease. Valier

was anxious to assert the moral inferiority of the ancient Greek and
Roman heroes and sages to the Old Testament heroes and the Christian
saints. Furthermore, he implied the superiority of a Christian culture to
a pagan one precisely as a culture. He would not have accepted Erasmus's contention that the pagan moralists inculcated the precepts of an
almost Christian virtue with literary powers that Christian writers did
not possess. It was not, perhaps, an unreflecting oratorical device but,
rather, the indication of an unusual if restricted sensitivity when Valier
counterposed the Psalms of David to antique classical poetry and claimed
for the former a superiority in 'the delineation of the most profound
sentiments, with fine comparisons and fitting metaphors'. Where the
Christian humanists of Erasmus's generation had discovered the grandeurs of the early Church Fathers, Valier was conscious of a Christian
culture stretching from the patristic age to the present. Thus, to the
ancients, he was able to counterpose the Christian moderns: Dante and
the great poets of the Italian Counter-Reformation, Vida and Sannazaro. Not only did Valier inculcate a certain attitude of detachment
with regard to classical culture, but also he placed a relatively low
estimate upon literary cultivation, which was one of the primary
objectives of a humanist education based upon the classics. The graces
of antique poetry he compared to sweetmeats which undoubtedly gave
delight but appealed more to the juvenile mentality. Oratorical fluency
was not an attainment which he rated particularly highly and ornate
rhetoric he condemned as contrary to the traditions of the Venetian
patriciate. In any case, power of rhetoric was something learnt quickly
or not at all, by 'imitation' rather than by rules; here Valier appears to
have rejected many of the assumptions that lay behind the studious
efforts of many Renaissance educationalists. He was probably not
devoid of aesthetic sensitivity. He was perhaps looking for something
more profound in literature than mere stylistic elegance. Ultimately,
however, his interests were more philosophical than literary. His preference for Dante over Petrarch is significant. The latter he criticised for
conceit in his preoccupation with his own emotional processes. He was,
he said, a fine lyric poet; *sed quid tum?*—'what of that?' Dante appealed
to men of knowledge. Valier regarded him as having rare *ingegno*, a
difficult word to translate for the benefit of the modern reader; it
denotes qualities different from *elegantia* and *eloquentia*, having, perhaps,
the strongest overtones of inspiration and inventiveness. Valier goes on
to assert that Dante was profoundly versed in 'the sciences', more
particularly scholastic philosophy.

It would be crude and misleading to describe Valier as reacting against so-called 'Renaissance values'. He did sound a strong note of caution against regarding the ancients as the great masters of ethics. There was a certain contrast between Valier's outlook and Ermolao Barbaro's conviction of a profound harmony between the service of the Muses and the life of virtue, although with Barbaro literary interests had in fact been substantially subsumed by philosophical ones. The strain of humanism which Valier was perhaps above all in reaction against, however, was the elegant literary humanism represented in Venice more particularly by Pietro Bembo; his criticisms of Petrarch, Bembo's great model, are significant here. For Valier, philosophy claimed precedence over literary studies in the intellectual pursuits of a Christian scholar and ultimate supremacy must be accorded to sacred science; historical studies evidently occupied a relatively high place in his hierarchy.

The views of Valier outlined above were expressed in the *Memoriale* directed to his friend Alvise Contarini. It was not, in fact, published until 1803[16] and it is not altogether certain how much was known of Valier's cultural orientations in his lifetime, although the general influence of his personality on the Venetian patriciate was considerable. At the same time, his views could not exactly be regarded as typical of Counter-Reformation thought; his was too original and sophisticated a mind to be reducible to the dimensions of the 'typical'. The *Memoriale a Luigi Contarini*, however, did perhaps represent an unusually intelligent reaction to the pressures which the Counter-Reformation was placing on Venetian culture more generally.

In declining to assume a fundamental harmony between Christianity and antique civilisation, the leaders of Counter-Reformatory thought would not have been particularly disposed to recognise those character-building qualities which many fifteenth and early sixteenth century humanists, both Italian and northern, had claimed for a classical education; thereby they must inevitably assign to it a relatively humble role. It was not that the educationalists and scholars most closely identified with the Counter-Reformation did not generally regard classical cultivation as the essential mark of an educated man, but it was a cultivation of limited aims, deprived of its ultimate *raison d'être*, as Vittorino da Feltre or Erasmus would have conceived it. In a substantial measure it was to be precisely the Jesuit schools that were to be responsible for maintaining the dominance of classical studies in Italian education for over two centuries, but these—not unlike the Calvinist academies in

Geneva and France and the Lutheran *gymnasia* that developed under Melanchthon's influence in Germany—were to treat a classical education as primarily a training in language. On the level of research and scholarship more properly speaking, the Counter-Reformation influence did perhaps have the effect of pushing classical studies in the direction of compendious accumulation of knowledge devoid of ultimate philosophical or ethical purpose. Precisely because of this, however, it may have stimulated the direction of scholarly energies into other fields of enquiry such as antiquarian studies, historiography and even science. At the same time, the climate of intellectual caution which it engendered probably tended to canalise these energies into the patient accumulation of facts; while enquiry was restricted, erudition burgeoned.

It has become common to refer to an 'erudite' movement in seventeenth-century scholarship, the roots of which can be seen in Renaissance humanism. It is extremely convenient to use the word 'erudition' in a specific and technical sense with reference to a particular historical context in this way. What it can signify is perhaps best understood by somewhat roundabout means, namely by examining eighteenth-century views of seventeenth-century scholarship. Those men of the eighteenth century, especially in France, who rejoiced in the title of *philosophes* and who believed that their own age was one of 'enlightenment', were to counterpose their own 'philosophical history', which had a strong polemical and didactic purpose, to the 'erudite' historiography and antiquarianism of the preceding age, which was essentially concerned with the accumulation of facts. While the *philosophes*, without doubt, seriously underestimated the value of seventeenth-century scholarship and depicted it in very crude terms, their understanding of its character did perhaps contain valuable insights.

The ethos of 'erudition' can be characterised as a belief that facts were in themselves things of value, worthy of being collected, and this did in fact contain certain creative possibilities. A distinction can be posited between the 'erudite' antiquarian and the Renaissance literary humanist, of whom he was in certain respects the descendant. This distinction is particularly well illustrated by differing attitudes to the study of the past. By the seventeenth century, many scholars in this field were unwilling to distinguish between 'history' and 'antiquities'. This was a distinction that had been accepted in practice by fifteenth century Italian humanist historians and by theorists, although not perhaps so much by practitioners, of the historiographical art in the sixteenth century. *Vera historia*—'true history'—had a certain literary form,

6 Titian, *Vendramin Altarpiece*, detail, mid-1540s.
In the centre, Gabriele Vendramin, the great collector (see pp. 156-7)

7 Alvise Corner (1475–1566), agriculturalist, health-enthusiast and patron of Ruzzante and Falconetto (see pp. 23–4, 150–1, 167–70). Portrait attributed to Tintoretto

usually based on classical models, it was selective, it dealt essentially with 'great events', which basically meant political and military ones, it examined the causes of events and it had, perhaps, a certain didactic purpose. It was distinguished from 'annals', the unadorned record, and again from 'antiquities', the study of 'fragments', whether archaeological remains, inscriptions or isolated documents. The essence of the study of 'antiquities' was that it dealt with the fragmentary. In point of fact the most advanced work on ancient society and institutions was conducted precisely in this field, just as some of the most valuable writing on recent history was set down in annal form. The climate of opinion which favoured a separation of genres was responsible for a severe impoverishment of Renaissance historiography and it was to be one of the great achievements of seventeenth-century scholarship that it achieved, if only in its outstanding monuments, a synthesis between them. No longer was 'true history' then regarded as a primarily literary genre. It would be hard to find such a synthesis in the work of any individual writer in late sixteenth century Italy and there is no particular reason for thinking that a fundamental change of attitudes regarding the relationship between 'history' and 'antiquities' had as yet taken place. Nevertheless, the dignity of 'antiquities' was increasingly being recognised.[17]

The development of antiquarian studies, archaeology, epigraphy (the study of inscriptions), numismatics (the study of coins and medals), and diplomatic (the study of the language, form and orthography of documents) undoubtedly grew in large measure out of the classical humanist movement and had been closely connected with it from the early fifteenth century, if not before. Antiquarian knowledge had been used to elucidate literary texts and by the turn of the sixteenth century was being increasingly used in combination with them to re-establish a picture of antique society. Initially, however, such work was largely in the hands of a small body of outstanding scholars and the vulgar herd of literary humanists tended to regard antiquarian studies with a certain air of superiority. By the mid-sixteenth century, however, antiquarian studies were already challenging the hegemony of a purely literary humanism in Italy, not least in Venice where a wide-ranging compendious erudition was emerging as one of the ruling passions of the aristocratic intelligentsia.[18]

By this time, the intellectual interests of Venetians were, it seems, becoming increasingly encyclopaedic. In any case, a primarily literary humanism has never been particularly strong among the Venetian

D

patriciate: Pietro Bembo was a somewhat idiosyncratic figure and even with him Ciceronianism and the cult of poetry was a relatively late development which has too often been allowed to eclipse his early interests in natural history. While the bulk of plebeian humanists devoted themselves primarily to the more technical aspects of classical scholarship, the interests of patrician humanist *eruditi* were, if anything, philosophical rather than literary. In any case, the cult of antiquity did not exercise an overwhelming preponderance in the intellectual pursuits of the Venetian aristocracy. For instance, there was a tradition of vernacular historiography, basically independent of classical models, which followed annal form or synthesised it with that of *vera historia*. As the sixteenth century progressed, however, the intellectual interests of the Venetian aristocracy were perhaps increasingly moving towards historiography and antiquarian studies, directed towards the examination of both antique civilisation and recent history, as well as towards political studies and natural science. Throughout the fifteenth century, the Veneto had been the main centre of the trade in antiques and already, by the 1530s, a number of major antique collections were in existence in Venice itself; by the end of the century, the passion for accumulating antique sculptures, coins and medals was becoming a veritable mania. Perhaps the most distinguished representatives of antiquarian scholarship were the numismatist Sebastiano Erizzo (1525–85) and the collector Giacomo Contarini (1536–95). The tradition of political writing extending from Gasparo Contarini to Sarpi has already been examined in some measure; that of historical writing from Sanudo to Sarpi and Nicolò Contarini will receive further attention in due course.

Antiquarian interests doubtless grew in part out of the humanist heritage and perhaps even scientific interests developed in some measure out of a philosophical-cum-philological humanism directed towards the study of antique scientific texts. Other factors, however, were forcing Venetians to look outside the boundaries of humanist studies. In particular, the need to examine and analyse the contemporary political scene could not be fulfilled by a historiography whose literary and analytic form was based on classical, or at least antique Roman models. Also, as has been suggested, the ethos of the Counter-Reformation, by stifling the development of an ideology out of classical humanism may have not only encouraged a monumental but often unreflective erudition but also stimulated the diversion of intellectual energies into new areas.

The effects of intellectual developments on the arts will be examined in forthcoming chapters. It will be seen how study of the grammar and etymology of the classical tongues was paralleled in the field of the vernacular and how it was Venetians who, in combination precisely with a purist Latin classicism, took the lead in raising the claims of the *volgare* as a literary language in the early sixteenth century. With regard to the visual arts, it was perhaps through interest in antique literature no less than in antique art that the influence of classical scholarship made itself felt in painting in the first instance. By the mid-sixteenth century, the effects of antiquarianism were to be seen with particular clarity in architecture and sculpture, and throughout the century the history of the picture collection was closely bound up with that of the antiquarian *studio*. Finally, the intellectual interests of the ruling class made Venice the home of vital developments in one particular branch of vernacular literature: historical writing as an art form.

Notes

[1] P. O. Kristeller, *Renaissance Thought, the Classic, Scholastic and Humanist Strains,* (New York, 1951), ch. 1

[2] B. Nardi, 'Letteratura e cultura veneziana del Quattrocento', in *La Civiltà veneziana del Quattrocento,* ed. Centro di Cultura e Civiltà della Fondazione G. Cini (Florence 1957), pp. 99–145; B. Nardi, 'La Scuola di Rialto e l'Umanesimo veneziano', in *Umanesimo europeo e Umanesimo veneziano,* ed. V. Branca (Florence 1963), pp. 93–140; V. Branca, 'Late quattrocento Venetian Humanism' in *Venetian Studies,* ed. J. R. Hale (London 1972)

[3] M. Battagia, *Delle accademie veneziane. Dissertazione storica* (Venice 1826); M. Maylender, *Storia delle accademie d'Italia,* v (Bologna 1930), pp. 436–46; W. Th. Elwert, 'Pietro Bembo e la vita letteraria del suo tempo', in *La Civiltà veneziana del Rinascimento,* ed. Fondazione G. Cini (Florence 1958), pp. 129–36; Bibl. Correr, Venice, *Cod. Cicogna,* 3281, Fasc. IV, 32 'Accademia della Fama'; P. L. Rose, 'The Accademia Venetiana, Science and Culture in Renaissance Venice', *Studi Veneziani,* XI (1969); on the Morosini circle see A. Favaro, 'Un ridotto scientifico a venezia al tempo di Galileo Galilei', *N. Arch. Ven.,* IX (1893), pp. 199–209

[4] Maylender, *op. cit.* III (Bologna 1929), p. 267

[5] P. Gualdus, *Vita I. V. Pinelli* (Augsburg 1607), pp. 18–20, 45–6; A. Favaro, 'Fulgenzio Micanzi e Galileo Galilei', *N. Arch. Ven.,* v (1893), p. 43

[6] Bibl. Correr, Venice, *MSS Cicogna,* 3251, 'Memorie dell'Accademia Olympica raccolte da Bartolomeo Ziggiotti'; also Maylender, *op. cit.,* IV (Bologna 1929), p. 109

[7] John of Speyer's first publication was in 1469. Jenson's first publication bears the

date 1461, but this may have been a typographical error, the date of publication being in fact 1471

[8] Horatio Brown, *The Venetian Printing-Press,* (London 1891); *Scritti sopra Aldo Manuzio* (Florence 1955), especially the article by M. Dazzi; C. Dionisotti, 'Aldo Manuzio umanista', in *Umanesimo europeo e umanesimo veneziano,* ed. V. Branca (Florence 1963), pp. 213–43; Branca 'Late quattrocento Venetian humanism', *cit.*; D. J. Geanakoplos, *Greek Scholars in Venice* (Cambridge Mass. 1962), pp.58–9, 201–13

[9] The genealogical information in the succeeding paragraphs is available in A. S. Ven, *Barbaro Albori,* except where stated

[10] P. Paschini, 'Daniele Barbaro', etc. *Rivista di Storia della Chiesa in Italia,* XVI (1962), p. 81. There is no clue to the relationship in A. S. Ven, *Barbaro Albori*

[11] B. Nardi, 'I tre filosofi del Giorgione', *Il Mondo* (23 August 1955), pp. 11–12

[12] A. Ferriguto, *Attraverso i 'misteri' di Giorgione,* (Castelfranco Veneto 1933), pp.61–102; Ferriguto, *Almorò Barbaro, l'alta cultura del settent rione d'Italia nel '400* (Venice 1922), pp. 160–70

[13] Hermolaus Barbarus, *Epistolae, orationes et carmina,* ed. V. Branca (Florence 1943), Ep. XII

[14] A. Ferriguto, *Almorò Barbaro, l'alta cultura del settentrione nel 400, cit.*; V. Branca, 'Ermolao Barbaro e l'umanesimo veneziano', in *Umanesimo europeo e umanesimo veneziano,* pp. 193–212; idem, 'Late quattrocento Venetian humanism'

[15] P. L. Rose, 'The Accademia Venetiana' etc., pp. 9–10

[16] A. Valier, *Memoriale . . . a Luigi Contarini Cavaliere sopra gli studi ad un senatore veneziano convenienti ,* ed. G. Morelli (Venice 1803)

[17] On the theory and practice of historical writing see especially: G. Spini, 'I trattatisti dell'arte storica nella Controriforma italiana', in *Contributi alla storia del Concilio di Trento e della Controriforma,* Quaderni del Belfagor (Florence 1948), translated with certain deletions in E. Cochrane (ed.), *The Late Renaissance 1525–1630,* (London 1970); A. Momigliano, 'Ancient History and the Antiquarian', in *Contributo alla storia degli studi classici* (Rome 1955), reprinted in *Studies in Historiography* (London 1969); F. Gilbert, *Machiavelli and Guicciardini. Politics and History in Sixteenth Century Florence,* pp. 205–26

[18] On Antiquarian Studies in Venice, see especially M. Foscarini, *Della letteratura veneziana,* (Venice 1854), *passim*

six

Literature

It was through her historians and political writers that Venice made her main impact upon the European reading public. Her literature as a whole, for all its distinction, remains a relatively esoteric field of study. The portion of it that could most naturally be expected to appeal to modern taste, the tradition of dialect comedy, has never become widely appreciated outside Italy, in part, perhaps, because it loses much of its force in translation. It was, however, natives of the Veneto who were foremost in raising the claims of the vernacular as a literary language in the early sixteenth century and in defining precisely what the *volgare* was. Yet it was not this in itself that enabled Venetian literature to achieve distinction, not directly at any rate. Indeed, in Bembo's case, the defence of the *volgare* involved a linguistic antiquarianism that was not always felicitous in its stylistic applications. The attempts to define the *volgare* and to elaborate a standard vernacular usage did perhaps open the way, however, for the appreciation of dialect as a distinct linguistic form in itself with its own literary potentialities.

In the fourteenth century, the exponents of the *dolce stil nuovo* in Italy had revealed the literary potentialities of their own vernacular tongue. Its claims as a literary language had soon been challenged, however, with the rise of Latin humanism. Roman writers of the Golden Age were imitated with a skill that few, if any, mediaeval writers of Latin had hitherto been able to command and the new Latin became the goal of that training in literary arts provided by teachers of 'humane letters'. *Humanistae* with a professional axe to grind were often disposed to claim that Latin was the highest, even the sole means of polite literary expression. It is doubtful how seriously these claims were generally regarded among the Italian intelligentsia, but they found ready acceptance among northern humanists at the turn of the sixteenth century. At this time, at any rate, literary exponents of the *volgare* evidently felt that the dignity of their chosen vehicle of expression was under attack. By the middle of the century, however, the literary rights of *volgare* prose and poetry were scarcely disputed and the *favella toscana* had been given a canonical quality rather similar to that of the Ciceronian style. It should be said that 'Tuscan' as it came to be defined was not the polite parlance of contemporary Tuscany, nor even, exactly, the language of contemporary Tuscan literature, but a synthetic language based on analysis of what were regarded as the best models of literary elegance. These models were more particularly sought in the Tuscan *trecento*, above all in Petrarch and Boccaccio, from whose usages the literary language of sixteenth-century Tuscany already deviated quite substantially. Many variants employed by them were, in fact, jettisoned, but on the basis of their work it was possible to define various norms which could serve as the basis for a uniform literary usage. If 'Tuscan' became the high literary language of Italy, it was in large measure due to natives of the Veneto.

The first critical editions of Dante and Petrarch were printed in Venice in the years 1501–2. The first three works devoted to the study of the *volgare* were G. F. Fortunio's *Regole della Volgar Lingua* of 1516, Nicolo Liburnio's *Vulgari Elegantie* of 1521 and Pietro Bembo's *Prose della Volgar lingua* of which a substantial draft existed in 1512 and which was first published in 1525. The works of Fortunio and Liburnio were primarily studies of usage; with Bembo's *Prose*, examination of usage was inserted into a work of general polemic in defence of the *volgare*. A similar polemic was contained in Sperone Speroni's *Dialogo delle lingue*, which followed shortly after. Fortunio and Liburnio were Friulians having close links with Venice. Bembo was himself a Venetian and Sperone a native of Padua, as well as a professor at the University there. It may be asked why it was natives of the Veneto who took the lead in linguistic studies of the vernacular and in defending its literary merits. Venice's outstanding position as a typographical centre was evidently significant here, for publishers were the major force pressing for linguistic and stylistic uniformity, looking precisely to the writers of the Tuscan *trecento* for a canon of authority.[1] The Venetian tradition of Greek and Latin scholarship should also be noted. Here ancillary studies such as etymology and analysis of prose and verse forms had received their most notable development in the Veneto and techniques first developed in the field of classical studies came to be applied in that of the vernacular. Furthermore, Venetians, even the most educated of whom utilised a vernacular with certain regional peculiarities, may well have approached the Tuscan tongue with a measure of detachment which enabled them to observe its mechanics with a heightened degree

of consciousness; the Friulians came to it virtually as an alien language
which they had to analyse rigorously before they could write it with
fluency.[2] In the case of Pietro Bembo, however, the defence of the
volgare and the attempt to revive the style of Petrarch and Boccaccio in
his own writing was the fruit not only of a particular methodological
approach but also of an especially broad and cosmopolitan culture
which embraced a scholarly knowledge of mediaeval Provençal
literature as well as Italian literature of the *trecento*.

Bembo's life-history not only points to his wide cultural experiences
but also suggests personal ones that were as rich and profound as they
were varied and picturesque. On the threshold of manhood he had
accompanied his father to Ferrara and Rome. In 1492 he took the unusual step of journeying to Messina to study Greek under Lascaris and
in the years 1497–9 he studied Latin under Leoncineno at the great
humanist academy of Ferrara. His first work, the *De Aetna* of 1496 was,
significantly, a work of geography and natural history, suggesting that
he had absorbed certain of the naturalistic enthusiasms of his friend
Ermolao Barbaro. Bembo's interests in geography were again to be
shown in his study of Lake Benaco. In the years 1501–2, he was co-
operating with Aldus, being responsible for critical editions of Virgil,
Horace and, more significantly, Petrarch and Dante. Thus Bembo
played an active role in the process whereby the Aldine editorial enterprises emerged from the exclusive field of antique literature into that of
the *volgare* classics. In the years 1501–2, he was again at Ferrara. Ferrara
was significant for his development in a number of ways. It was the
home not only of Italy's greatest centre for education in Latin letters
but also of one of its most brilliant courts. Bembo was exposed both to
a tradition of sober classical pedagogy and to one of urbane courtly
refinement imbued with a romantic and somewhat antiquated chivalric
ethos. It may have been in Ferrara that he first began to develop his
interest in the lyric poetry of mediaeval Provence. His romantic inclinations took on a perilous form with his admiration for Lucrezia Borgia,
the Duchess-to-be, and, also at Ferrara, he cemented a liaison with
Marietta Savorgnan. Returning to the Veneto, he moved in the only
court circle it possessed, that of Caterina Corner, the dowager queen of
Cyprus, at Asolo. It is this little court that is depicted in the *Asolani*,
published in 1505 and dedicated to Lucrezia Borgia. In this work, which
relates a series of discussions on the topic of love interspersed with verse
recitations, the fruits of Bembo's studies of Petrarch were already being
revealed. It provoked something of a scandal in Venice. Bembo was

seen as having abandoned classical philology for less serious pursuits and while the work in no way infringed the rules of propriety, the subject matter was evidently considered to be lacking in dignity. The crisis of Bembo's life had now come. As has already been seen, he had failed to make progress in competition for government office and he perhaps felt himself a spiritual exile in his native city.

In 1506 he left Venice for Urbino, where he remained until 1512, attached to the exceedingly refined court of Guidobaldo di Montefeltro. Here he continued writing poetry and produced the first draft of the *Prose della volgar lingua*. The problem of a career continued to present itself and Bembo's ambitions turned towards an ecclesiastical one. Here, however, skill in writing love-lyrics was hardly an adequate qualification. Bembo evidently realised that the pursuit of Latin elegance offered the opportunities most consonant with his talents and he turned to the cult of Cicero. He acquired his first ecclesiastical benefices in 1508. These were, in fact, 'commendams', fiefs belonging to the crusading order of the Knights of Jerusalem. Up to the time of his promotion to the see of Gubbio in 1539, the bulk of Bembo's benefices were of this nature and prior to his elevation to the episcopate he was an ecclesiastic only in a purely technical sense. In 1512 he moved to Rome and in the following year was made one of the two personal secretaries to Leo x. Together with his colleague Sadoleto, he was probably now recognised as the outstanding Latin stylist in Italy. He failed to obtain the cardinalate under Leo and again with the accession of Adrian vi in 1521. Disappointed he returned to the Venetian dominions in this year and retired to his Paduan villa. He was now immensely rich. In his villa, he accumulated a magnificent collection of antiques and works of art, which included paintings by Memlinc, Mantegna, Giovanni Bellini and Raphael, for the last of whom he had developed a particular appreciation at the time of his Roman sojourn. His villa also housed a distinguished group of scholars, including the Frenchman Christophe Longueil, the Englishman Reginald Pole and Marcantonio Flaminio, perhaps the outstanding neo-Virgilian poet of his time. In Padua, Bembo lived on terms of domestic intimacy with Moresina, the great love of his life, whom he had met in Rome in 1513 and who bore him three children. She died in 1535. In 1539 Pietro was made cardinal and bishop of Gubbio by Paul iii and he now became a priest, going into residence in his diocese in 1543. In 1544, he was also made bishop of Bergamo, but he entrusted the government of the see to a coadjutor. He died in 1547 at the age of seventy-eight.

Many modern writers have evidently found it difficult to take Bembo seriously as a man. In reality, his was an extremely complex personality, by no means devoid of depth. At first sight, he was the worst type of curialist of the old school, a churchman with no particular sense of religious vocation, closely associated with the most vapid, although not altogether the most corrupt papal court of the Renaissance period, a Ciceronian and poetaster more than a Christian perhaps, who continued to pen amorous sonnets into old age and lived with mistresses for much of his life. Even his writings might seem to suggest a fundamental vacuousness. Yet there are indications that such a characterisation would be highly superficial. Even the artistic portrayals of Bembo's intense, sensitive, aquiline features come as something of a surprise, whether that of the curiously ascetic Silenus in Bellini's 'Feast of the Gods', or Titian's depiction of the dignified, almost austere 71-year-old cardinal painted in 1540, or the last portrait, again by Titian, perhaps the most moving and enigmatic he ever produced, of the frail, bird-like sage in the half-light. It is curious that the first biography of Bembo should have been written by Ludovico Beccadelli, a prelate notably imbued with the outlook of the Catholic reform movement, who obviously respected him as a man. He noted, as evidence of Bembo's integrity, the fact that, prior to the cardinalate, he only accepted ecclesiastical preferments which entailed no obligation to residence. Obviously Beccadelli was not over-exigent in his standards, but Bembo never notably sullied the priesthood, which he only entered in 1539, and as a bishop although not particularly active, he seems to have been a respected figure. His late religious poems, which have a curiously courtly tone and almost seem to address the Deity as a great lord in terms of deferential intimacy, do not, however, suggest any particularly profound religious sensitivity. His previous amours were probably not regarded with grave disfavour at the time and his relationship with Moresina appears to have been, but for the technicalities, a normal conjugal one, marked by fidelity and tenderness. The long intimacy with his 'trusted consort', this 'guide and support' enriched the emotional qualities of his poetry. We may choose to regard the writer of the *Asolani* as a vapid poetaster, but the 65 year old widower who looked back on Moresina was a very different person:

> *Che mi giova mirar donne e donzelle*
> *E prati e selve, e 'l bel governo*
> *Che fa del mondo il buon motore eterno*

Mar, terra, cielo e vaghe o ferme stelle?

Spenta colei, ch' un sol fu tra le belle
E tra le saggie, or e mio nembo interno.
Forme d'orror mi sembra quant' io scerno
Esser cieco vorrei per non vedelle.[3]

(What joy does it give me to behold ladies and maidens, meadows,
woods, banks and the beneficent Prime Mover's beautious governance
of the universe, sea, earth, sky and the moving or fixed stars, now that
she is dead who was a sun among women of beauty and of wisdom and
is now a cloud within me? They appear to me as forms of horror and I
would be blind rather than see them.)

Bembo was probably less a sensualist than a person of extreme sensitivity
and it was perhaps this, rather than mere frivolity, that made him an
exile from the Venetian patriciate.[4]

Bembo was an outstanding Ciceronian latinist as well as an exponent
of the *volgare* and it is desirable to relate these two aspects of his endeavour. It might appear surprising that a man who believed in close
imitation of Cicero as the sole key to an elegant Latin style should have
resolutely defended the literary claims of the *volgare*. Here a contrast
with Erasmus suggests itself. The latter, while attacking servile imitation
of Cicero, had little hope for the literary possibilities of the vernacular
tongues. His position apparently stemmed from a belief that Latin
could be developed as a living language, as the *lingua franca* of the international scholarly community, and that it must remain flexible if it were
to serve the needs of the contemporary world. Bembo, on the other
hand, probably saw Latin as a dead language; certainly he did not regard
it as the patrimony of Italians in any sense comparable to the *volgare*.
He defended the employment of the latter for literary purposes in the
Prose della volgar lingua. Although this was not published until 1525, it
is desirable to examine it before Bembo's other works, for he had been
working on it since 1500 and it does much to shed light on his entire
literary output.

The *Prose* purports to describe a discussion between scholars. Among
the speakers, Ercole Strozzi represents a pure Latin humanism, Giuliano
de' Medici defends the *volgare* without reserve and Carlo Bembo, the
brother of Pietro, whose thought he evidently expresses, is disposed
towards a conciliation between *volgare* tradition and classicism. It is use-

less, says Giuliano, to contend whether the *volgare* is superior or inferior to Latin; the fact is that it is our own language and to insist on perfecting the ancient language, forgetting the modern, is to resemble 'those men who build great palaces, resplendent with costly marbles and gold, in some remote and solitary place, and who live in the vilest dwellings in their own cities'. For Carlo Bembo, Latin is the 'second language' of Italians, just as Greek was the second language of the Romans. An enquiry follows into the origins and nature of the *volgare*, an enquiry which confronts the problem of different linguistic usages within the Italian peninsula. Carlo Bembo regards the *volgare* as a language of heterogeneous origins, being a mixture of Latin and Barbarian elements, and he shows, in particular, the debt of fourteenth-century Tuscan literature to Provence. The model of the *volgare* is to be sought not in any particular modern regional usages, since these, being in a state of constant flux, have no particular claim to authority, but in the best literary monuments. These are provided, above all, by Petrarch and Boccaccio, it being necessary to follow Dante only with a certain amount of caution; in some measure a synthesis of the usage of Petrarch, Boccaccio and Dante with modern practice may be necessary. But what criteria of judgement should be used if an even greater stylist than Petrarch and Boccaccio should arise? Carlo Bembo replies that: 'the elements to consider are in large measure the same as are considered with regard to Latin'. Hence the ancients constitute models which are valid also for *volgare* writers.[5]

In the *Prose* Bembo put forward Petrarch and Boccaccio as models of *volgare* style and linguistic usage rather in the same way as, in the *De Imitatione*, he set up Cicero as a model for Latinists.[6] He did so, however, not because he regarded the Italian language as necessarily static, but, because he believed that authority lay with those writers who had achieved the greatest stylistic beauty. As for Roman writers, these could set certain standards for Italian ones, just as the Greek writers had provided models for them. Bembo had no illusions as to the degree of similarity between Latin and the *volgare*. It was precisely here that his immersion in classical scholarship bore fruit, for it was in the latter field that scientific analysis of language had been first developed. At that time, perhaps only a person with the methodology of a classical grammarian and etymologist, skilled in the arts of stylistic imitation, as well as a scholar of old Provençal, could have traced the disparate origins of the *volgare*. Again, perhaps only a classical philologist of this kind could have freed the *volgare* from the latinisations of construction and vocabulary found in the studies of Fortunio and Liburnio and, furthermore, could have realised that the *volgare* had changed appreciably since the fourteenth century. Within this context of flux, the concept of a model acquired particular significance. It was Bembo's contribution to have defended the claims of the *volgare* not as a bastardised Latin but as a distinct language with its own rules and its own particular genius. By making a distinction between style and linguistic usage, Bembo left the way open for a certain imitation of ancient classical models, but he did not, like Speroni, who followed him in the defence of the *volgare* as a language, assert the supremacy of these; for his own literary practice in the vernacular, Petrarch, Boccaccio and, to a lesser degree Dante, were his guiding stars.

The *Asolani*,[7] written prior to 1502 but published in 1505, represented Bembo's first major literary exercise in the *volgare*. Here it is evident that his archaising tendencies had lead to an affected and unduly convoluted style. An atmosphere of romantic languor pervades the description of a debate on the joys and sorrows of love taking place at Caterina Corner's court. In the verdant landscape by the foothills of the Giulian Alps, the chief speakers accompany their discourses by singing Petrarchesque stanzas to the accompaniment of lutes and viols, urged on by the plaudits of handsome and splendidly dressed noble youths and maidens. On the first day, the pale, sorrowful Perottino castigates love as the cause of emotional disturbance and pain: *nulla amore senz' amaro*. On the second day, Gismondo defends love as the source of all joys. On the third day, Lavinello attempts to conciliate the two opposing theses, asserting that ills come from sensual love, joy from a spiritual rapture purged of carnality. He reports the discourse of a hermit he has encountered in the woods: the true love he describes is ultimately the love of God, awakened in the soul by the female image. In the love sonnets and laments, Bembo had substantially followed Petrarchan and Provençal models, but in the hermit's discourse he introduces a Dantesque theme whose ostensible gravity contrasts with the generally light tone of the work as a whole. It is basically a book of facile content, designed for the ladies. Its importance as a literary monument lies less in the arguments it puts forward than in the technical competence and lyric qualities of its prose and verse and in its peculiar mood of romantic languor which calls to mind the ideal world of Giorgione or Titian's *Sacred and profane love*, which may possibly have been inspired by it.

The encomia of the admired woman in the *Asolani* most obviously derive from mediaeval chivalric and courtly tradition, more particularly as represented by Petrarch and Boccaccio. Bembo's depiction of the qualities of the beloved differs in certain notable respects, however, from that of the Tuscan *trecento* poets and also from that of the modern Florentine Neoplatonist ones. The former had idealised and spiritualised earthly beauty, the latter treated it specifically as a symbol of spiritual beauty. Bembo essentially treats physical beauty and moral excellence as distinct entities. In the *rima 'Si rubella d'amor'*, of the *Asolani*, in praising his lady's grace and chastity, he suggests the tensions which, between them, these two qualities might create in the beholder, while in fact establishing a symbiosis between them and reconciling the contrary dispositions to which they give rise. As a love lyricist, Bembo may in some measure be counted as one of the group of poets, especially associated with the princely courts, who sought to celebrate the specific and more particularly feminine qualities of the lady, moving away from the formalistic rhetorical idealisation of the Tuscan *trecento* poets and the Florentine Neoplatonists' elevation of amorous sentiment to the realm of the abstract. A relatively new vocabulary of sentiment emerges in the late *rime* on the death of Morosina who is celebrated for her more specifically conjugal virtues. It cannot be said, however, that Bembo ever provides a truly concrete picture of the woman loved.

As a poet, Bembo was not a slavish imitator of Petrarch to the degree that has sometimes been supposed. Indeed in the *De Imitatione*, 'emulation' of a model was put forward ultimately as a means of attaining a personal style. Bembo's position was that the concept of style was not innate, but was developed as a result of observing other writers and that a consistent style could only be achieved by following a sole model of excellence, not by eclecticism; ultimately the model could be transcended. As a writer, Bembo looked to Petrarch for a canon of linguistic usage, he followed him in his verse forms, but his borrowings of Petrarchan themes and phrases can be easily misunderstood. These were, in some measure, points of departure for the exercise of Bembo's own poetic initiative; he developed Petrarchan themes rather in the same way as one composer will produce variants on the theme of another. Bembo may incorporate into his verse deliberate, erudite references to a Petrarchan passage, producing a variation by inversions of word order or use of synonyms, then introduce a 'counter-theme' of his own, subsequently exploiting the recurrent interplay between the two themes.[8] It cannot be denied, however, that the immediate impression conveyed by Bembo's verses is one of monotonous echoing of Petrarch and the massive formal complexity of some of them, greater perhaps than with any other Italian poet, does not make them easy reading.

Bembo, both in his defence of the *volgare* and in his elevation of Petrarch and Boccaccio as its supreme stylistic exemplars, found numerous followers in Italy; his stylistic analyses and practice were crucial for the development of Italian prose in the sixteenth century. It was probably partly under his influence that a movement arose in Tuscany of defence of the native literary tradition, with a particular stress on the *trecento*. In Venice almost every noble clan boasted a Petrarchesque poetiser; here Orsato Giustiniani, Bernardo Capello and Andrea Navagero are perhaps the most noted names. The Secretary of the Senate and great linguist Celio Magno was also a distinguished practitioner of the genre. Perhaps its finest exponent was the precocious maiden Gaspara Stampa (1523–54) who with great economy of means and with almost imprudent openness expressed her adoration for the Conte di Collaltro and her sorrow at unrequited love. There was also, in Venice, a notable tradition of Petrarchesque verse in dialect form.

While Bembo's impact on Venetian prose writing was by no means negligible, there were, nevertheless, strong reactions against Bembism in the Venetian dominions. On the one hand, the Accademia degli Infiammati of Padua, while devoted to the study and practice of *volgare* literature, looked primarily to the ancient classics as literary models rather than to the Tuscan *trecento*. Speroni, in his *Dialogo delle Lingue* asserted, through the mouth of Bembo, who figures as one of the speakers in the imaginary debate, that the *volgare* was the rising sun, but went on to suggest that the glories of antique literature should be revived in it. By making a more rigid distinction than Bembo had done between style and language, Speroni was able to assert the primacy of the ancients as models, here laying stress on the Greeks rather than the Romans. In his own tragedy *Canace* (written and first performed in 1542 but only published in 1546) he had, according to his own claims, sought to apply Aristotelian dramatic principles; it is not certain, however, whether he had really set out to write Aristotelian tragedy or whether he subsequently sought to justify himself by these claims in the face of attacks on his work.[9] A more clearly deliberate attempt to imitate Greek models had been made a quarter of a century earlier by a Vicentine humanist, the noble Giangiorgio Trissino in the *Sophonisba* (written in 1515 and published in 1524) the first regular classical tragedy in a vernacular language. A reaction against Bembism in a different direction came in the middle years of the sixteenth century with a group of writers who asserted the literary rights of Venetian dialect and denied any obligation to conform to Tuscan models. There was, in fact, already an extensive literary tradition in dialect.[10]

A species of dialect was probably used by all classes of the Venetian population. Government decrees used a relatively standard literary language, but, even here, the cadence of the prose had a certain regional flavour and a limited number of regional orthographic idiosyncrasies are to be found. These are quite common in the testaments of nobles, although less frequent in the case of the more high ranking ones: thus *x* may be substituted for *ch* or *z*,[11] *g* for *ch*, *lg* for *gl*, *d* for *t* or vice-versa; there may also be certain word variants: thus *fioli* for *figli*, *tuor* for *togliere*, *muneghe* for *monache*. Such variants are, however, inserted into periods of what is, cadence apart, basically standard Tuscan and tend to occur in particular phrases or contexts; the more barbarous orthographic variants such as *x* for *l*, *gn* for *ng* are unusual. Such barbarities can, however, be found in certain testaments of the populace which suggest not only a total ignorance of orthographic rules, but also attempts to phoneticise spoken language. While testaments may use variants of standard words, they do not, however, use a distinctive regional vocabulary. This can, on the other hand, be found in a large number of printed works, together with the most extreme linguistic and orthographic variants; there has obviously been a deliberate attempt to reproduce the spoken language of the populace.

In part, Venetian dialect was used for a *popolaresco* effect in light or comic works, for 'popular' rather than for comic effect it should be said; it is unlikely that Venetians were disposed to regard their own native dialect as being grotesque in character and where dialects were used for a grotesque comic effect, they were primarily those of the Terraferma, more particularly Bergamese patois. Venetian dialect in a pronounced form was not only used for works of light entertainment, but also for poetry and prose with elevated literary pretensions, dialect Petrarchism being a case in point. It was utilised by patrician writers among others and its literary employment was evidently relished among the better-educated sections of society in the sixteenth century. The practice was obviously conscious and deliberate, rather than due to ignorance of the rules of 'Tuscan' speech. It is probable that the taste for it came, in part, precisely as a result of Bembo's linguistic reforms rather than in spite of them. It was, perhaps, only when a clear distinction had been drawn between dialect and normative Tuscan that the former could be envisaged as an entity in itself and be relished for its *popolaresco* flavour.[12]

Popolaresco comedy had received its main initial development in Siena, but in the first half of the sixteenth century it achieved a notable efflorescence in dialect form in Venice and Padua and a number of plays in this genre have reached us in manuscripts or printed books. Here the outstanding figure was undoubtedly the Paduan Angelo Beolco, nicknamed 'Il Ruzzante' (pre-1502–42), who wrote in Paduan dialect.

He was the illegitimate son of one Francesco Beolco, who was described as a 'doctor of arts and medicine'. There is no sure foundation for the assertion that his mother was a peasant and it would be quite wrong to regard Angelo as a genius miraculously risen from the populace. He was brought up in the house of his father Francesco who moved in university circles and it is safest to regard Angelo's original social milieu as professional and academic. He became the head of a group of players, for which he wrote the pieces, himself specialising in rather unattractive burlesque peasant or valet parts. Sanudo records numerous representations by his troupe in Venetian noble houses under the auspices of certain of the noble *compagnie* which organised public festivities, between 1520 and 1526. Around 1525 he came into contact with Alvise Corner, the wealthy Venetian who, for technical reasons, had been refused inscription on the rolls of the Venetian patriciate and had settled in Padua. His fame as an agricultural theorist and health-fanatic has already been referred to. He was also a distinguished patron of the arts and had built a small theatre in his splendid town house in Padua. Beolco became a member of his household and acted on his behalf in business affairs. It seems reasonable to assume that he put on performances in Corner's house. The last mention of Beolco occurs immediately before his death in 1542, when he is found preparing a performance, surprisingly enough, of Speroni's *Canace* under the auspices of the Accademia degli Infiammati. Two points about Beolco's life are particularly worth noting. In the first place he was, despite his illegitimate birth, of relatively elevated social origins and probably a man of some education. Secondly he moved in a milieu in which anti-Venetian sentiment was strong. Many of his relatives had been exiled or imprisoned by the Venetian government for treasonable activities in 1509. Several members of Corner's circle had likewise fallen into disfavour with the Serenissima and even Corner himself had reasons for resentment against Venice. In Beolco's work, a certain anti-Venetian sentiment can be found in combination with an exuberant Paduan patriotism. His frequently expressed pride in his native speech is one aspect of the latter. While Beolco used a mixture of dialects in his work, the basis was provided by Paduan patois. Other dialects are used simply in accordance with the characters' supposed place of origin and generally, in fact, for the more unpleasant characters—Bergamese for the licentious soldier, Venetian for the roué noble—although Tuscan is used for some of the more distinguished personages.[13]

In the *Prima oratione* of 1521, Beolco presents himself in the guise of a peasant defending his brethren against the grasping *cittadini* of Padua, but it was with the latter that he belonged by origins and upbringing. It is doubtful whether a peasant could have written peasant comedy. It would be wrong, however, to describe his attitude towards the peasant as one of a patronising bourgeois; it was something more intense. It was, perhaps, less a sentiment of contempt than of hatred mingled with fascination, which ultimately gave way to a certain sympathy. The early plays of the 1520s fall into the genre of *anti-villanesco* comedy. The peasants and small townspeople are shown as sly, grasping and cowardly, with an unattractive capacity for compromise and turning a blind eye. The latter is the product of cowardice, often of cynicism, but it is also perhaps the attitude of a people who must survive somehow and are ultimately dependent upon one anothers' good will and forbearance. Between 1521 and 1528, the grim history of the Padovano repeatedly intrudes itself into Ruzzante's work. Memories of the 1509 invasion were still alive there and it was ravaged by plague and famine in the late 1520s. In the *Prima orazione* of 1521, the impudent demands made of Cardinal Corner, for all their burlesque character, were perhaps intended to represent some of the genuine grievances of the peasant in humorous guise. In the *Primo dialogo in lingua rustica*, probably of the late 1520s, the peasant soldier, who has survived the wars by judicious cowardice and pathetically struggles to terminate his wife's infidelities, emerges almost as an anti-hero. In the *Secondo dialogo* (*Bilora*) probably of the same period, the theme of the peasant who has been cuckolded by an aged Venetian noble takes on grim overtones. The *Seconda oratione* (1528) describes the miseries of the Padovano in essentially serious terms. Possibly contact with Alvise Corner was helping to lead Beolco in new directions and the disasters of the later 1520s, with which he could have come into close contact as Corner's business-factor, may have softened his vision. In the later comedies, dating from the early 1530s, the figure of the plebeian semi-hero emerges in the shape of the loyal valet, who uses his cunning, duplicity and dishonesty in the service of his master.

In Beolco's work, the figure constantly emerges of the peasant who is both block-head and fox, a coward and braggart and often a cuckold. It was in this type of part that Beolco specialised as an actor and often this figure bore the name of 'Ruzzante', hence Beolco's pseudonym. The loyal valet who will lie and cheat for his master would appear to be a development of this 'Ruzzante' figure. Beolco evidently also specialised in comic monologues, and in studying the printed text of these, the reader must imagine for himself the arts of gesture, tonal inflection and dramatic pause that must have been applied to their rendering. A particularly fine example is provided in *La Moschetta*, where Ruzzante, having been deserted by his wife Betia, declares his intention to commit suicide:

> Oh, if I had a knife on me, *they* couldn't stop me killing myself. If I haven't got a knife, I'll kill myself with my fists. There, take that you oaf! A pox on you! Take that, and that! Why not strangle myself? My eyes will pop out and I will frighten everyone . . . (Hits himself in the neck). I'm going to eat myself. Betia, come and look at me, so you can cry 'Jesus' when I leave this life for the next. Which end shall I eat first? The feet. If I started with the hands, I couldn't help myself to the rest. Betia! Say a *Pater noster* for me at least. God be with you now, I'm starting. I can't eat the whole of me, but I can eat until I die. And when I'm dead, what will you have got out of it? Oh! Drop me a wee rope Betia, so I can hang myself and put myself out of this agony.

Of Beolco's surviving works, the one in which he first showed his comic powers to the full was not a play but a jester's monologue, the *Prima oratione* (1521), delivered to Cardinal Marco Corner in his castle at Asolo. The encomium of Padua takes on burlesque tones. Beolco described its crops, its splendid broad beans, onions, cabbages and cucumbers, its livestock and women, whose fine points, like John Donne, he describes from the feet upwards. He suggests that the new bishop of Padua should grant a number of relaxations of discipline for the benefit of the peasants. It should be permissible to hunt on Sundays without attending Mass, peasants should be dispensed from fasting and be allowed to work on Sundays at harvest-time. It should not be regarded as a sin to eat more than is necessary. Priests should be either married or castrated, for they are men like the rest, often with an extra portion of virility, and are getting the peasants' women with child. As for the *cittadini* of Padua, these use the peasants harshly, treat them with opprobrium and seduce their wives. The solution is for peasant men to be allowed to take four wives and peasant women four husbands. The *cittadini* will hurry to become peasants in order to enjoy these advantages and the population of the Padovano will become one great happy family. Beolco is obviously jesting, but is also, perhaps, partly in earnest. Regulations on fasting and observance of feast days were undoubtedly widely resented at the time. A genuine anti-clericalism and resentment against the *cittadini* were doubtless being given expression under the jester's mask; the technique used is perhaps somewhat similar to that of Erasmus's *Praise of Folly*. The extraordinary impudence and obscenity of a work addressed to an eminent, although not particularly worthy prelate may cause surprise. It was perhaps the sly revenge of the under-dog, of the subjugated provincial resentful of his Venetian masters. Profiting from his jester's licence, Beolco, while intermittently caressing the Venetian prelate, was doing his best to make him feel uncomfortable.

Beolco's early comedies have a relatively free formal structure; some have a clearly defined plot, but some are simply in the nature of comic dialogues. They show Beolco at his most malicious and misanthropic and with his most fully developed powers of burlesque. In *La Betia* (1523–5), he notably exploits the device of the burlesque encomium, which had already been developed in Sienese popular comedy. Zilio addresses Betia, whom he is wooing:

> O sweet, beautiful sister, o eyes radiant as the sun,
> O cheeks more marbled than ever was salt ham,
> O rosey lips, o teeth white as turnips,
> O honeyed, angelic mouth of silver and rubies,
> O breasts whose size would rejoice the heart of any cowman,
> O lovely broad feet, fine for trampling the grape,
> O thick, well-nourished legs,
> O lovely calves, round, plump, white and smooth,
> A cask is small beside you . . .

Betia declines at first to accept Zilio, implying that he will be unable to give her the satisfaction a woman requires. His friend Nale whispers to her that if she marries Zilio, he, himself, will act as a second husband. Betia agrees to marry Zilio and prepares to elope with him, carrying off most of her mother Menega's household effects, but she is caught by the latter. With a band of armed men, Nale and Zilio attack Menega's house. The innkeeper Tazio arrives on the scene and sets out to compose the affair; he obviously stands to profit from the wedding celebrations which are to follow. Menega agrees to give her daughter to Zilio. Now follows one of the scenes of female volatility and play-acting beloved of Beolco: Menega tells her daughter never to see her again but, when Betia begs forgiveness, she plunges into an orgy of maternal sentimentality and the two women swoon. The marriage follows. Here a curious peasant rite is depicted. It is conducted by an orator, evidently the innkeeper, who makes a long speech in patois, interspersed with barbarised scholastic jargon, and hands to the bride various symbolic objects, an apple, sage, rue, mule's hide, cat's hair, a pot. This passage may well be of considerable interest as a documentation of peasant customs. Menega delivers an encomium of her daughter, praising her household skills, her thoroughness in masticating food, her strength and ferocious courage, vaunting her heroic, but unspecified services to the occupying troops; the speech is designed to cause embarrassment and uncertainty in the new husband. The married pair depart and Nale follows, indicating to Zilio that they have agreed to share Betia. Zilio strikes him, leaving him for dead. Nale's wife Tamia delivers a long lament on his supposed death, lauding him as a paragon of virtue and strength. It soon emerges, however, that she is planning to remarry quickly. Nale presents himself as a ghost, straight from Hell. Tamia soon forgets her initial fright, fascinated by Nale's highly imaginative descriptions of the place of torment and busily asking how certain noted local figures fare there. Finally she asks Nale if he ever truly loved her. 'Since I must tell the truth,' he says, 'in God's name, no!' 'And I only pretended,' she replies. She accepts the hand of Menegazo, who arrives on the scene. Nale is forced to reveal that he is alive and the pair bury the hatchet.

The 'Ruzzante' figure, already prefigured in the Nale of *La Betia*, is fully developed in *La Moschetta* (1528). Ruzzante discovers that his wife would betray him if she had the chance, but she cows him into pretending to ignore the fact. The soldier Tonin has entrusted him with money and Ruzzante tries to swindle him by claiming that he has been robbed of it, actually bludgeoning Tonin into pretending to believe him. He is cuckolded both by Tonin and his own friend Menato, but holds on to the money and gets Menato to partly reimburse the soldier out of his own pocket. After an encounter with Tonin, he is terrified of the latter's revenge and is lead back through the dark streets of Padua, quaking for his life. Abandoned there, he plunges into his own fantasy world and comes up with the old story that he has been attacked by a hundred armed men. On learning that Tonin has been seriously injured, he comes to believe that he, himself, dealt the deadly blow in his epic struggle. Fortified by illusions of his own courage, he makes his peace with his wife and Menato. The crude peasant capacity for compromise is shown particularly strongly in *La Fiorina* (of uncertain date). The idyll between Flore and Melchior is interrupted when the former is carried off by Ruzzante. Ruzzante's father quickly finds another wife for Melchior, who readily accepts her.

In the two *Dialoghi*, which have been judged on stylistic grounds to be roughly contemporaneous to *La Moschetta*, the savagery of the early plays so far examined can still be seen, but the misanthropy has perhaps been tempered by a bitter sense of the pathetic. The Ruzzante who has returned from the wars in the *Primo dialogo* is still the old Ruzzante. He has run all the way from Agnadello at a champion's pace and when he is downed by a rival, he naturally claims that he has been assaulted by the usual band of armed thugs. His wife and friend who reproach him for cowardice are the truly unattractive characters; he might at least have come home with some booty or lost a leg in order to show his courage, they say. As a coward, Ruzzante is *simpatico*, as a cuckold he is pathetic, but he has done the minimum of harm to others and he has survived. Bilora in the *Secondo dialogo* is a truly pathetic figure. Again he is a coward, he will accept a meal from his wife who refuses to leave the old roué noble, his attempts to cow the latter are hilarious in their ineptitude, but in the end the peasant takes his revenge and batters the licentious patrician to death.

In *L'Anconitana* (?1522–26) and the later plays, *La Piovana* (1533) and *La Vaccaria* (1533), Beolco employs more complex and sophisticated plots than in most of his earlier comedies. The plots are substantially based on Plautus, from whom he also borrows phrases extensively. Association with the Accademia degli Infiammati may possibly have helped to introduce this classicising vein. While Beolco's obscenity remains unabated, the burlesque element has been considerably curtailed. The author's misanthropy is now more discriminating. There are heroes and heroines, likable rogues and real villains, a division which had barely appeared in Beolco's earlier work. He has achieved a new brilliance in his portrayal of totally revolting characters, notably old roués and pimps, such as Placido in *La Vaccaria*, who tolerates and even encourages his son's liaisons in the *bas monde*, partly out of indulgence, partly out of desire to be introduced into illicit pleasures himself and partly, it seems, out of desire to spite his own wife; or Loron, again in *La Vaccaria*, who prides himself on his artistry in exploit-

ing the weakness of his masters and clients. The fortunes of bewildered
bourgeois and nobles hang on the outcome of struggles between good
and bad valets. The good are unmitigated rogues, but in an honourable
cause. Thus with the late Beolco, the valet part comes into its own,
but in a form far removed from the conventions of seventeenth-and
eighteenth-century comedy. Molière's and Beaumarchais' creations
were very restrained in comparison with Beolco's foul-mouthed,
tortuous and totally ruthless guardians of their masters' interests. In his
later works, Beolco polished his form and restrained his burlesque, but
he never lost his sense of the farcical. This perhaps reached its highest
expression at the close of *L'Anconitana*, where the old roué Ser Tomaso
prepares for a rendezvous with a courtesan in the countryside. Ruzzante,
his valet, urges him to move under a deluge of enquiries as to whether
he has brought everything needed for the night: bedroom slippers,
night-cap, socks, ointment, gloves and sabre.

Perhaps the outstanding example of *popolaresco* comedy of strictly
Venetian origin is the anonymous *La Venexiana*, probably written in
1536, or shortly afterwards.[14] Venetian dialect is used for the speeches of
the main characters, Bergamese patois for the clod-hopping porter. The
plot is simple. Julius, a smooth-tongued gentleman of fortune, woos a
married woman Valiera, but is also desired by the widow Angela.
Angela's servant obtains him for her. Julius and Angela make passionate
love and swear mutual fidelity, but the former, after some hesitation,
subsequently accepts the advances of Valiera and resigns himself to the
hard task of keeping two women happy at the same time. The manuscript of the play ends at this point and it is generally assumed to be
complete. Despite the lack of sophistication of the plot, it is evident that
the author was a man of letters of considerable learning. This is indicated
not only by the formalistic, erudite character of the prologue but also
by the refined technical strategems and arts of dramatic suggestion
employed. The dialogue is of extreme economy and succinctness. A
residue of courtly language is to be found in combination with an
extremely frank presentation of sexual passion, although, as compared
with Ruzzante, this is expressed in essentially chaste language, even
where suggestions of intimate caresses are made. The lilting, drawling
cadence and the softened consonants of Venetian dialect provide an
admirable vehicle for the expression of languorous passion. The work
is remarkable for its depiction of the mature woman consumed by
restless desire and subsequently giving outlet to it.

The best known Venetian exponent of *popolaresco* dialect comedy was Andrea Calmo (1510–70), who enjoyed a reputation as an actor even greater than Beolco's. As a writer he appears, in some measure, to have continued the latter's tradition, but is generally regarded as greatly inferior to him. Calmo used a mixture of Terraferma dialects or mongrel languages, partly composed of German and Greek elements, for comic effect; a similar effect was given to Venetian dialect by mixing it with Latinisms. The formal structure of his plays was of a classical nature, relying heavily on the conventions of the scheming valet and the licentious dotard, already developed by Beolco.[15]

La Venexiana was only discovered in the 1920s in manuscript. Alvise Corner, however, was responsible for the collection of Ruzzante's works and their transmission to the publisher. There were numerous reprintings of these between 1545, when Ruzzante's first comedy was published, and 1617 the date of the last collective edition of his works prior to this century. The bulk of Calmo's comedies were published between 1549 and 1556. Ruzzante's works in particular were obviously liable to harsh treatment by censors in the Counter-Reformation era. This was, however, the great period of his popularity. Censorship only became well-organised after 1562 and only covered newly printed works; virtually all of Ruzzante's comedies had already been published by this time. The effects of the tighter censorship that was instituted after 1596 can however be seen with subsequent editions of his works, references to churches and ecclesiastics were deleted from certain plays, often making complete nonsense of the text.

Censorship was probably in large measure responsible for the fact that relatively few new comedies were printed in Venice in the latter half of the sixteenth century and for confining the genre to the realm of oral tradition. Even here, burlesque comedy was under attack. The Jesuits conducted a systematic campaign for the suppression of comedies, finding support in the late 1570s from many distinguished nobles of the older generation. In 1577, the Senate ordered the expulsion of actors and again prohibited comedies in 1581. The passion for the theatre, frequently castigated as one of the city's great vices, had been widespread in Venice, however, especially among the city's noble youth. It is not known how effective government prohibitions were. A relaxation of these was evidently expected in 1607, after Venice's quarrel with Rome which had lead to the expulsion of the Jesuits, and there certainly seems to have been a marked revival of theatrical activity in the decade following the Interdict.[16]

At any rate, the Venetian dominions remained one of the great *foyers* of an oral tradition of popular comedy. This tradition evidently used a repertoire of stock situations and even stock speeches, which allowed for extensive improvisation by the individual actor. The importance of the Venetian dominions in the development of burlesque comedy is attested by two terms which took their origin there: 'pantomime' and 'zany'. The former derives from 'Pantaleone', a popular and distinctly regional Venetian christian name borne by the stock-figure of the crotchety dotard in traditional farce. His origins are perhaps to be seen in figures created by Calmo. 'Zane' is the Bergamese form of 'Giovanni'. The *zani* were the famous Bergamese clowns. There is doubt as to how far Ruzzante was responsible for their creation, but it would seem that the origins of the Italian improvised comedy, which was to become famous all over Europe from the late seventeenth century was in considerable measure developed in the Veneto and its origins can probably be traced there back to the sixteenth century, although it was probably only in the seventeenth that it acquired a crystallised traditional form.

★   ★   ★

Another literary field in which Venice possessed a distinctive tradition was that of historical writing. Although there was a certain tradition of Latin historiography there, the historians for whom she is best remembered were, in general, *volgare* ones. In practice, the use of the *volgare* tended to imply a distinctive approach towards the form of historical writing and in particular an independent attitude *vis-à-vis* antique Roman models. In a letter of 30 December 1495, Marino Sanudo defended his decision to write the history of the Ferrarese war in the *volgare*. He was writing, he said, for the benefit of those occupied in affairs and for nobles who did not possess erudition, and continued: 'if these diligently consider the utility of my work, not looking for ornate and elegant language, I do not doubt that they will commend my useful and honest endeavours'.[17] In passing from the question of language to that of style, Sanudo implicitly indicated his intention to depart from the oratorical traditions of the Latin historiography of his age. In the early years of the seventeenth century, when the dignity of *volgare* historiography had for long been accepted, Venetian historians were expressing intentions similar to Sanudo's. The Paduan Enrico Davila, in his *Istoria della guerre civili di Francia*, probably written in the first decade of the century, declared his utilitarian approach to the task of obtaining 'a perfect knowledge of worldly affairs': 'I shall bring neither richness of language nor brilliant concepts . . . I hope to find the due order and natural explanation of these events.'[18] Davila was evidently implying that rhetorical preoccupations would detract from the functionality of his account and his analysis. Again, Nicolò Contarini, in his *Historia Vinitiana* of the 1620s, wrote: 'I do not intend to provide entertainment for anyone by my labours nor to flaunt eloquence in my discourse, but solely to describe and document by simple narration . . . that which may be of profit in civil affairs.'[19] The disclaimers of this kind which occur in Venetian *volgare* historiography would appear to indicate a deliberate detachment from the practices of the old humanist historical writing, modelled on Livy and Sallust, which had proved manifestly inadequate for the exposition of highly complex events.

A number of the problems posed by this tradition were, in effect, examined in Paruta's *Della perfezione della vita politica*. In the debate, which it purports to describe, the Partiarch Grimani favours the insertion into the narrative of frequent reflections on the lessons of history, while the Ambassador Surian calls for bare narration of the facts. Daniele Barbaro rejects those inserted reflections that break the thread of narration, but he believes that certain reflective passages can help to knit it together, by comparing or drawing connections between certain cases and events; in this way, civil prudence can be taught. The question of the examination of causality is treated by Barbaro in conjunction with that of general reflections. He wants a historical writing which does not simply present events 'simple and naked', but 'clothed in their causes'. He praises Thucydides and Guicciardini for discretion in their use of general reflections but, while Giacomo Contarini, another speaker in the dialogue, regards Guicciardini as the model in his examination of causes, Barbaro criticises him for over-complexity in this respect; a similar qualification to a strong appreciation for Guicciardini had been made by Agostino Valier in his treatise on historical writing.

Reference has already been made to the traditional humanist distinction between 'annals', which were simply records, and *vera historia*, 'true history', which had a more developed literary form and for which annals were basically the raw material: *vera historia*, in addition to being composed in elevated style, dealt primarily with 'great actions'; it obeyed Cicero's admonition that the historian should show 'not only what was done and said but how and why'. Insofar as Livy was regarded as the great model, 'true history', as fifteenth-century humanists conceived it, tended to follow a set pattern of narration with certain

traditional points of climax, such as a battle-scene; it concentrated on
the heroic and excluded the mundane and it employed devices such as
the imaginary speech. The older humanists also tended to regard it as
an instrument for the inculcation of moral principles and patriotic
sentiment and for instruction in worldly wisdom; they were hence
disposed towards the insertion of general reflections into a narrative.[20]
The formal structure of the major Roman histories did, in practice,
have certain limitations as a model for emulation. While certainly
explaining causes, Livy and Sallust essentially described a succession of
events in the life of one particular people. What connections there were
between these events did not impose a particularly complex analytical
structure. Unity was given to the historical work by a primary concentration on the continuous stream of Roman history upon which the
doings of other nations from time to time impinged. Such a form was
unsuitable for describing an event like the Italian wars at the turn of the
sixteenth century or the situation subsequent to them. Here it was a
question of a group of peninsular states which were threatened by two
or three outside powers more or less simultaneously. A complex network of tensions between states had to be analysed by the historian.
Here the most appropriate model was provided less by any Roman
historian than by Thucydides who, in examining the breakdown of
relations between a group of states, had traced the sources of disparate
streams of events and shown how they joined together to produce
catastrophe. It was substantially the Thucydidean model that the Florentine Francesco Guicciardini had followed when in the 1520s he wrote
the history of the Italian wars and examined the breakdown of the old
diplomatic concert. Guicciardini was, however, rather more economical
than Thucydides in his literary method. He was sparing in his use of
imaginary speeches, as well as general reflections; he eschewed heroic
battle descriptions. In general, the desire to comprehend the contemporary world imposed upon historians the need for a more ascetic
technique. Where the primary aim was to examine the web of inter-
state tensions, it was difficult to make a battle the high point of a
historical work as Livy had done. Furthermore, a highly complex
analysis, such as was now required, would easily be fragmented by the
insertion of lengthy reflections.

The orientations represented in Paruta's dialogue by Grimani, Surian
and Barbaro can all be found in Venetian historiography. At its worst,
Venetian historical writing can be indiscriminate and unreflective or
pompous and stridently didactic. It was, however, the achievement of

the great Venetian historians that, while jettisoning the paraphernalia of moralisation and fictional speeches formerly regarded as adjuncts of 'true history', and rejecting servile imitation of Roman authors, they were selective and preoccupied with causation. In mid-sixteenth-century Italy, indeed, the Livian model of 'true history' while paid due homage in theoretical treatises had in practice been substantially abandoned, but historians often produced little more than polished yet indiscriminate narrations of events. By purging *vera historia* of elements which were not strictly descriptive or analytical, thereby bringing it closer to the annal form, but without descending to bald, indiscriminate narration, certain Venetian historians, more particularly in the late sixteenth and early seventeenth centuries, proved themselves in some measure Guicciardini's heirs.

Venetian historians were remarkable for their consciousness of events outside Italy. Undoubtedly the period of foreign invasion between 1494 and 1527 had imposed upon Italian historians the need to look at events beyond the Alps, but Venice's trading interests and her position as perhaps the most powerful of the independent Italian states may have helped to make her historians particularly sensitive to these events. A source of information was ready to hand in the *relazioni* of Venetian ambassadors, *comptes rendues* which they presented to the Maggior Consiglio on the expiry of their term of office; these may be regarded as a species of historical genre on their own. In the middle years of the sixteenth century, an event of European importance occurred which was liable to effect Venetian society profoundly and which in some measure posed challenges to long-standing Venetian tradition: the Council of Trent. It was a Venetian, Antonio Milledonnis, who had been secretary to Bernardo Navagero the Venetian Ambassador to the Council, who wrote what was probably its first history and it was Fra Paolo Sarpi who produced the classic study of it. The antecedents and proceedings of the Council could not be understood without an extensive knowledge of European politics. Although Italy had ceased to be a major centre of international conflict after 1527 and although peace had been made between Habsburg and Valois at Cateau Cambrésis in 1559, the possibility of a general European conflagration, centring on Habsburg-Valois rivalry, which might ultimately affect Italy, was always imminent. When, from the late 1580s, Spanish intervention in France loomed ever closer, Venetian historians examined the international scene attentively and continued to do so throughout the period of international tensions that culminated in the Thirty Years War. All this could not fail to affect the formal structure of historical writing. Bare narration of events was inadequate. The less functional forms of humanist historiography were a luxury that could not be afforded when describing a complex web of factors. Nicolò Contarini and Sarpi in particular evolved a cryptic and economical mode of expression which nevertheless kept the reader informed of cause and context. Venetian historians, above all Nicolò Contarini and Sarpi, are also particularly notable for their analysis of motivation, often tendentious and inspired by polemical considerations, but a relatively new element in Renaissance historiography.

Most of the sixteenth-century Venetian historians substantially followed the annal form. This holds true even of Pietro Bembo who, despite the high literary polish of his work, wrote annalistic history of the driest and most limited type. A series of outstanding works in annal form were, however, produced by the Younger Marino Sanudo (1466–1536). Sanudo wrote in some measure in direct reaction against the Roman Marcantonio Sabellico who had produced the first official Venetian history on the commission of the Serenissima in 1489 (*Rerum Venetiarum ab urbe condita libri XXXI*). Sabellico's history had been a grandiose work on the Livian model, concerned with 'great events' and great men, designed to buttress the mythology of Venice's greatness, her liberty, independence and civil prudence. Sanudo was undoubtedly a patriotic historian, but he evidently realised that history could not yield its lessons if its students simply concentrated on great deeds; it was necessary to examine the minute details that provided linkages between events and here due attention must be paid to the role of minor figures. In the *Vite dei Dogi* (begun 1493 and completed post-1530), the *Chronichetta* (1493) and the *Diaries*, covering the period 1496–1533, he gave a detailed picture of Venetian politics, constitutional forms and city life. The Diaries were envisaged by Sanudo as the raw material from which he would later construct a 'true' history of Venice; when he was forced to place them at the disposal of Bembo in order that the latter might produce precisely a work of this nature, Sanudo felt that his own life work had been in vain. In point of fact, Sanudo's *Diaries* are infinitely superior to Bembo's more pretentious work in the insight which they give into events at the time. Although Sanudo could hardly resist retailing juicy items of news, his recording of data is by no means indiscriminate and in certain cases is highly systematic; for instance, details of prices are furnished consistently in such a way that it would be possible to base statistical tables upon them. Sanudo reveals a wide knowledge of European and Mediterranean affairs. His presentation is such that connections between events can at least be perceived and the raw material is obviously available for a truly analytic history. The *Diaries* unfold a rich panorama of Venetian life and have constantly attracted readers by the sense of living history which they convey. Sanudo's history of Charles VIII's invasion of Italy was basically designed as a work of 'true history'. The work, except in the opening sections, tends to read as a rather laborious chronicle; the relations between events are not explored in such a way as to give a dynamic structure to the narrative. Sanudo evidently sought, however, to explain the motives of statesmen and to give an idea of the play of forces between the contending powers, here again revealing his wide understanding of Italian and European affairs. He did not really attempt to show, as Guicciardini did, why Charles VIII invaded Italy, but through examination of Charles's relations with other potentates, he showed more clearly than Guicciardini how the French king was free to do so.[21]

In the decades following the war of the league of Cambrai, a number of Venetian historians tried to narrate the turmoils that had convulsed Italy since Charles VIII's invasion, although the official historiographers were often dilatory in writing and the slowly unfolding public annals fell far behind the march of events. From about the 1570s, there appears to have been a notable awakening of interest in the art of historiography, as evidenced not only by active historical writing, but also by theoretical discussion, notable examples of which are provided in the Paduan Francesco Patrizi's *Della Historia* (1560) and Paruta's *Della Perfezione* of 1579. The renaissance of interest in history, if such it can be called, may have been partly due to a wave of patriotic enthusiasm following the victory of Lepanto in 1571 and partly also perhaps to anxieties with regard to Venice's position in a troubled Europe. The theoretical discussions of Patrizi and Paruta, however, must be attributed to quite different considerations. Patrizi's concerns were heavily philosophical with a strong orientation towards epistemological problems. In the cases of both Patrizi and Paruta, preoccupations with the status of history appear to have been substantially linked to scepticism regarding the relationship between speculative philosophy and political action. Both writers seem to support the view that history is a guide to political action while indicating, through the mouths of certain speakers, a distaste for treating historical writing as an occasion for abstract theorising. Patrizi in particular strongly attacks the concept of history as a branch of rhetoric.

Agostino Valier and, in some measure, Alvise Contarini, were the
exponents of a historiography serving patriotic and moralistic ends, but
with the two public historians Paolo Paruta and Andrea Morosini we
find a historiography that confined itself to the narration and explanation of events. The restrained admiration for Guicciardini expressed
by Barbaro in the *Della Perfezione* may well have been Paruta's own.
His *Historia Vinitiana*, left in manuscript in 1598, has been criticised,
however, for lack of organisation and for failure to evaluate and explain
the events described. Here a worthier disciple of Guicciardini was
Andrea Morosini, whose official history was completed in 1605. The
outstanding monument of Venetian official historiography, however,
is perhaps the *Historie Vinitiane* of Nicolò Contarini, the prominent
member of the Giovani party and future Doge. It was written in the
1620s but never published. This was evidently due to its acidly polemical
tone rather than to any reservations as to its value as a piece of historical
writing.

It was historiography of the most rigorously functional kind, in
accordance with Contarini's declared intentions. Truth, he declared,
was the soul of history. Contarini's accuracy can hardly be faulted,
although his fairness in judgement of persons and their motives may
well be questioned. His descriptions are starkly economical, although
embellished by epigrammatic interjections and vicious sallies against his
old political opponents and the court of Rome. His style was as polished
and incisive as it was unpretentious and the *Historie Vinitiane* was a
literary masterpiece which had all the qualities of 'true history' reduced
to its most functional elements. Contarini showed a consummate
mastery in knitting the disparate strands of his narrative together. He
did not follow a rigidly chronological scheme but described a series of
episodes, explaining the long-term antecedents of each, where necessary.
The resulting account is in no way fragmentary, since the relationship
between the episodes emerges in due course, to produce an exceedingly
complex network of cause and effect.

The work begins with a note of menace:

From this time (i.e. 1597), the state of the world changed much; in
Europe especially, there was shown in the great powers an ambition
to dominate Italy and our Republic greater than ever before. The
schemes and aims of some, for long hidden or artfully dissimulated,
now that the sails were swelled by favourable winds, revealed themselves openly. . . . Henceforth the Republic must be embroiled in

open war or in perilous circumstances generally worse than war itself.

It followed that the historian of Venice in these years must relate affairs in Europe and the Mediterranean generally. Contarini wrote:

Had I been content to confine myself to facts pertaining to our Republic alone, what I have written would be obscure and imperfect. . . . The doings of men, if narrated with regard to one single place, will always be dark or deeply puzzling, but when they are brought together with more distant ones, they will be better understood and more profitable to those who utilise them.

In the early pages, Contarini sets an opening motif rather similar to that of Guicciardini's *History of Italy*. The Florentine historian had depicted the era of Lorenzo the Magnificent as the golden age of peace and prosperity in Italy; upon this happy land, the foreign invasions had fallen, ushering in a new age marked by violence and corruption of manners and Guicciardini had sought the causes of the disaster. For Contarini, Venice in 1597 was enjoying the fruits of peace and was at the height of her prosperity, but the ambitions of other powers, as he subsequently tries to show, brought a host of troubles upon her. Contarini gives a brief description of the economic situation in general and then examines in detail the measures for liquidating the public debt that had been undertaken since 1577. Contarini, in examining this mundane topic, reveals his alienation from the tradition represented by the more grandiose type of *vera historia* and he is outstanding among historians of his age in the attention he gives to economic questions. In examining the public finances towards the very beginning of his narrative, Contarini broaches a topic that is to recur repeatedly throughout his work. In due course it is to be shown how other events and circumstances, Venice's diplomatic and military embroilments and the financial schemes of other European powers, impinged on her economic position. Having examined the progress in liquidating the public debt up to about 1597, Contarini introduces the first villains onto the stage: the Spaniards, Uskoks and Austrians. The envious great powers did not dare to attack Venice openly, but sought to undermine her slowly and by craft; the chosen weapon was piracy. Venetian shipping was attacked by the Spanish fleet and by the Uskoks, a wild piratical tribe inhabiting the island of Senj off the Dalmatian coast who had attracted many of the Serenissima's disobedient subjects into their ranks. With

Austrian connivance, the Uskoks were attacking not only Venetian ships but also those of Turkish subjects and the Ottomans were blaming Venice. An example is shown here of Contarini's analysis of motives and chess-board tactics: the Austrians, he says were encouraging the Uskoks to attack Turkish shipping with the deliberate aim of embroiling the Serenissima with the Porte. Contarini's first section on the Uskoks closes with an account of the extraordinary imbroglio surrounding the isle of Clissa, recently seized by the Uskoks, which was recaptured by the Turks while a Venetian fleet stood in the offing, apparently poised for action against the Serenissima's own disobedient subjects among the defenders of the island. Contarini then turns to examine the development of the emporium of Spalato, instituted by the Venetians, in agreement with the Turks, with the aim of attracting the trade of the hinterland into a Venetian town; the project, Contarini indicates, was to be damaged by the Clissa affair. In subsequent episodes, attention is given to the affairs of the Papacy, France, Spain, England and the United Provinces of the Netherlands and to the manner in which they impinged on Venice. The Interdict dispute of 1606 and the War of Gradisca of 1615–17 against the Austrian Archdukes in some measure provides independent climaxes to the work; descriptions of the schemes and villainies of Spain, the Papacy and Austria are here brought to their logical conclusion. A clear assessment of the European situation and what it signified for Venice is strongly implied: the ambitions of the Habsburg powers and the Papacy constitute a constant threat to Venice and her natural alignment is with France and the Protestant powers of England and the United Provinces.

In his organisation of material and capacity for causal analysis, Contarini rivalled Guicciardini and perhaps even surpassed him. The *Historie Vinitiane* was, in fact, a more complex work than the *Storia d'Italia*; Guicciardini only had to deal with Italian states, France, Spain and the Empire, without bringing in Turks, Netherlanders and Uskoks as well. Contarini, however, avoided chaos in his narrative by virtue of a more pronouncedly episodic scheme than Guicciardini's. True to Venetian tradition, he showed an infinitely deeper understanding of the internal affairs of foreign states than the great Florentine had done. His detailed knowledge of Dutch affairs and of the religious debates within the Netherlands' Reformed Church is a notable case in point. As a literary portraitist, he was in some respects Guicciardini's superior. He gives a richer, more detailed and more incisive effect than the latter, whose highly polished portraits tend to be vague and generalised, but he lacks

8   G. M. Falconetto, the Loggia Cornaro, Padua, built for Alvise Corner
and completed in 1524 (see pp. 168–9)

9   Palladio, Villa Barbaro, Maser, c. 1555–9 (see pp. 173–4)

10   J. Sansovino, the Public Library, Venice, begun 1537 (see p. 184)

Guicciardini's sense of the ultimate mystery of the human character. The energy of his descriptions is primarily motivated by spleen, their victims are neatly labelled in the most harsh and uncompromising language, but the brilliance of their effect distracts attention from the limitations of Contarini's human vision. A notable example is his portrait of Philip II. He contrasts his reputation in arms and skill in government, his caution and capacity for hiding resentment, his occasional magnanimity and his religious demeanour, with his total ruthlessness:

> He showed himself in every action most religious, so that if one regards what can be seen, words and outward acts, there was never a more pious nor religious prince than he. The inner recesses of a man one cannot penetrate; the effects of this piety, however, were of marvellous profit to the king. . . . It was most notable of all in Philip, king of Spain that, being most religious, religion never impeded him from any advancement of the State . . . and whatever he did was always put forward publicly as being in the service of God and for the aggrandisement of the Catholic faith. . . . Thus it was added to his reputation for piety to have Popes elected according to his will, to hold them in dependence by giving states to their nephews, to make plots against princes, Catholics as well as heretics, when they were not on his side, and to win by corruption the ministers of other states. . . .

Contarini's epigrammatic jibes were often no more than spiteful interjections, but in many cases they were illuminating and served a functional purpose, as in his comment that, from antiquity, 'there was no king more affluent nor more short of money than Philip II'. His ironies at their best are worthy of Gibbon.[22]

If Contarini was perhaps the most outstanding of the official historiographers writing by commission of the Serenissima, Paolo Sarpi, who wrote his histories in an essentially private capacity is the best known of all Venetian historians. Sarpi's main historical works are the *Istoria dell' Interdetto* (completed in 1610 and first published in 1624), the *Trattato delle materie beneficiarie* (completed in 1610), the *Istoria del Concilio Tridentino* (probably written *c.* 1612–15 and first published in England in 1619) and the *Aggiunta* to Minucio's *Guerra degli Uscocchi* (first published in 1633). The *Istoria dell' Interdetto* and the *Aggiunta* are fairly straightforward narrative accounts. The *Trattato delle materie beneficiarie*

E

(on ecclesiastical benefices)[23] is notable as an examination of change within the Church. It had been one of the great contributions of humanist scholars of the antique past to have appreciated that the ancient world was essentially different in character from their own. They realised that the world had changed, but an actual process of change extending over several centuries had been examined by relatively few historians before Sarpi, although the Magdeburg Centuriators, the group of German Lutheran historians writing in the latter half of the sixteenth century had tried to indicate that the Church had undergone a process of deformation from the time of the Apostles. Sarpi set out to document this process as he conceived it. He tried to show how the Church had departed from an original poverty and democratic structure and had become a hierarchical, property-owning body; how the corpus of the once equal *presbiteri* had been divided into priests and bishops and how the system of ecclesiastical benefices had evolved. Already, in the *Trattato*, Sarpi traced the growth of Papal absolutism, but the culmination of this process, as he envisaged it, was to be studied in the *History of the Council of Trent*.[24] It is upon this work that Sarpi's fame primarily rests.

The reasons for its extraordinary reputation are hard to divine. Undoubtedly it was due in part to its appeal to Protestant prejudices. It was, however, a work of stupendous erudition which organised a mass of highly complex material into a comprehensive form and successfully related the main topic to the general framework of European affairs. It can hardly be regarded as superior in these respects, however, to the work of Nicolò Contarini, although Sarpi's analysis of motivation is perhaps particularly sophisticated.

As with Contarini, the comparison with Guicciardini naturally presents itself, not only with regard to Sarpi's economical annalistic exposition, but also with regard to the way in which he presented his work as the explanation of a great historical change. Like Guicciardini, he believed that the generation prior to his own had seen in Italy an event which had ushered in a new era, in this case the Council of prelates which had sat at Trent intermittently between 1545 and 1563 in order to reform the Church and deal with the problems raised by the Protestant schism and which, in Sarpi's view, had completed the slavery of the Church:

It was conducted with a variety of different aims and its end result was quite contrary to the designs of those who brought it about and

totally belied the fears of those who made every effort to sabotage it.
. . . For this Council, desired and brought about by pious men in
order to reunite the Church which was beginning to break apart, has,
on the contrary, so confirmed the schism and hardened attitudes as
to make the disagreements irresolvable. Promoted by princes for the
reform of the ecclesiastical order, it has caused the greatest deformation in the ecclesiastical order that has ever been seen, so that the name
of Christianity is hated. Taken up by the bishops in order to restore
episcopal authority, which had fallen in large measure into the hands
of the Roman Court, it has caused them to lose it almost completely
and make them happy in their servitude. But feared and shunned by
the Roman Court as an effective means of moderating that exorbitant
power which, from small beginnings and by various means, had become monstrous and unlimited, it has so strengthened its hold over
what remains subject to it that never was anything so firmly rooted.[25]

The form of the *Istoria del Concilio tridentino* is not, in fact, notably
determined by an analytical framework. It reads basically as a straight-
forward chronological account, devoid of analytical interjections, where
the actual events of the Council or its immediate antecedents are concerned; where digressions occur, it is to explain the origins of doctrines
and practices which were under discussion at the Council. Sarpi only
explains his method of writing at an advanced stage of the work, in
Book III Chapter 1 and Book VII Chapter 1.[26] In the latter passage, he
states that he has used the annal form for the events leading up to the
Council and for the periods of its suspension, and a day-by-day diary
form for the periods during which the Council was in session. He is
aware that the diary form may be criticised, but in both passages he
expresses the belief that it is the form most appropriate to the subject-
matter, and form must be determined by matter rather than the reverse.
It may indeed be said that the diary scheme will exclude much of the
material necessary to an extensive narrative, but the great affairs of the
world are, in any case, often arcana. Sarpi did, in fact, succeed in setting
the history of the council within a European context without apparently
breaking the essentially linear form of his work.

After examining, at the very beginning of the work, the origins of the
practice of holding Church councils, Sarpi proceeds to show how the
convocation of a new Council became necessary in the sixteenth century. He relates the indulgence controversy and the subsequent emergence of Luther and Zwingli and passes to the demands of the German

Princes and the Emperor for a reforming council. The narrative of the twenty-five years before the convocation at Trent centres on the negotiations for a Council between Charles v and successive Popes, reference being made at various points to the complicating factor of Charles v's embroilments with France and to the English schism; the account is essentially focused on the Rome–Germany axis. Following the actual convocation at Trent, the doings of the Council are the central topic, examinations of Imperial–Papal relations, the affairs of Germany and, at a relatively late stage, those of France being inserted at intervals. It cannot be denied that Sarpi's account, with its primary concentration on events at Trent and on the political relations between the Papacy, the Emperor and the King of France, leaves a large amount of highly important material uncovered. For instance, virtually no attention is paid to the more general history of the Catholic church in the fifteenth and sixteenth centuries; the aspirations and programmes of Catholic reformers are left unexplained, while only oblique references are made to the painful history of conciliarism which did so much to account for papal attitudes to the Council. Nevertheless, Sarpi was remarkably successful in knitting a complex pattern of European events into his deceptively simple although highly detailed narrative.

Sarpi believed that the Council brought final disaster to the Church, yet no more than Guicciardini in the *Storia d'Italia* did he at any point clearly resume for the benefit of the reader the reasons for the tragedy; the reader must diligently search the narrative and draw his own conclusions. Obviously the descriptions of the final sessions of the Council in late 1562 and 1563 are crucial.

Throughout the proceedings of the Council, many prelates had pressed for the use in decrees of phraseology implying that the bishops received their full powers directly of God, as successors to the Apostles, and not through the intermediacy of the Pope as successor of Peter; hence the demands, somewhat distasteful to the Papacy, that the bishops' duty of residence should be declared *de jure divino*. Such demands, while corresponding to the views of many Italian prelates, were made with particular force by the Spanish bishops in the first instance, and then by the French bishops, when they arrived at Trent in 1562. Their arrival deepened the crisis in the Council, although the leader of their delegation, the ever-diplomatic Cardinal of Lorraine adopted a somewhat ambiguous stance. At the same time, far-reaching demands were being made in Germany for reform and disciplinary changes, including vernacular liturgy, the concession of the chalice to the laity and permission for priests to marry; this was leading to tension between Emperor and Pope. On all sides, calls were being made for reforms which threatened papal control over the sphere of Church discipline. The papal Legates who presided over the Council, however, brought about an outcome favourable to the Papacy. Simonetta, Sarpi suggests, bludgeoned individual Italian prelates into toeing the papal line and succeeded in dividing the Italians from their Spanish brethren. Morone paid a flying visit to Innsbruck and achieved some sort of agreement with the Emperor; what its precise nature was, Sarpi does not know, but he suggests that Morone persuaded the Emperor that reform could not be expected of the Council and that it might as well be brought to a swift conclusion. Morone then proceeded to win over Guise, by arts of flattery, Sarpi seems to hint, encouraging him to regard himself as one of the leaders of the Council alongside the Legates. The murder of Lorraine's brother, the Duke of Guise in the summer of 1563 precipitated his conversion to the papal camp: 'he saw clearly that there was no other way to support religion and his family in France than union with the Apostolic See'. The actions of Guise were obviously in Sarpi's mind crucial for the outcome of the Council. By his extreme diplomatic tact in smoothing-over differences of opinion, he had mitigated the force of the Gallican prelates' demands and, although this is not clearly stated, Sarpi probably felt that he had betrayed Gallicanism. Deprived of the support of the secular powers and urged on by the Legates, who now enjoyed the full support of Guise, the bishops at Trent rushed through the final reform decrees, certain of which were notable for the subordination of secular rulers to the Papacy in religious matters. The hurriedly drafted decrees, in Sarpi's view, failed to deal with the real problems of the Church, they left wide scope for papal initiative and they left the arbitrary powers of the Roman pontiff untouched.

Sarpi's analysis, as presented here, did not in itself give a particularly clear form to the closing sections of his work. The outcome turned on a number of relatively minor issues or ones that could not be fully clarified: the detailed machinations of the legates, the personality of Guise and his individual circumstances, the secret agreement with the Emperor. As with Guicciardini, the concentration on a host of minor issues makes for a highly detailed and superficially indiscriminate narrative, but unity is given to the work by references to a consistent papal policy, executed by the legates, of checking any attempts to subject the Papacy to a general Church Council, of ensuring that control over

Church discipline remained in papal hands, and of bringing the Council to an end as quickly as possible.

Sarpi was aware that his narrative might appear indiscriminate in its study of detail, but he felt that such detail would give a more lively effect and served a functional purpose. 'I observe,' he wrote, 'that in the *Expedition of Cyrus* Xenophon is more absorbing and informative in describing the discussions, both grave and humorous, of soldiers than the actions and deliberations of kings.'[27] The historian of the Council must show 'what tiny rivulets produced a great lake that covered Europe'.[28] Sarpi was copious in his narrative and declined to concentrate exclusively on 'great actions' because he believed that a mass of small causes produces great changes and a thesis can ultimately be extracted from his work.

★   ★   ★

Considerable attention has been devoted here to the work of Bembo, Beolco Ruzzante and Sarpi and these are probably the most noted literary lights of the Veneto in the sixteenth and early seventeenth centuries. None can be regarded as typical of a Venetian literary tradition, if such a thing ever existed, and their contribution was not altogether likely to be welcomed among certain influential sections of Venetian society. Bembo was the great spiritual exile from the Venetian aristocratic caste, whose literary pursuits were evidently regarded as somewhat frivolous in certain quarters. The high-flown oratory of his prose ran counter to sober Venetian oratorical tradition, at least as Agostino Valier defined it. As a prose-stylist and writer of Petrarchesque verse he found many followers in Venice, but his writings were also a bone of contention thrown into the Venetian literary arena and as such helped to provoke the patriotic anti-Tuscan reaction in the middle years of the sixteenth century. Ruzzante's troupe was generously patronised by the Venetian noble companies responsible for organising festivities and his works were extensively printed in Venice in the latter half of the sixteenth century. His spiritual roots, however, lay in a stubborn Paduan provincialism and his comedies may have been relished in Venice precisely for their alien quality: it is significant that Venetian writers did not generally use their own dialect for a savagely comic effect in the way that Ruzzante had done. Whatever the popularity of Ruzzante's comedies in the late sixteenth century, it can be assumed that many Venetians would have regarded their impieties and obscenities with horror. The technique of Sarpi's historical writing can undoubtedly be aligned with Venetian tradition, but his ideology was his own. Anti-clericalism, mistrust of the Papacy and a desire for a purified Church more closely approximating to that of the early centuries, were certainly strong Venetian traditions, but hardly in the extreme and splenetically combative form that Sarpi expressed them. Undoubtedly Sarpi was regarded in his lifetime as a meritorious servant of the state who deserved protection from the revenge of the Roman court, but the public expression of his more daring personal views could hardly be tolerated. His great historical masterpiece had to be printed abroad; the Serenissima could not have afforded to permit its publication in Venice and would probably not have wished to do so. Bembo found his true milieu not in Venice but in the courts of Ferrara, Urbino and Rome, Ruzzante was a resentful provincial, Sarpi an *enfant terrible* perhaps only tolerated and protected as a point of honour, but it is perhaps these three men above all who have given Venetian literature of the sixteenth and early seventeenth centuries its fame.

Notes

[1] W. Th. Elwert, *Studi di letteratura veneziana* (Venice–Rome 1956), p. 20

[2] C. Dionisotti, 'Niccolò Liburnio e la letteratura cortigiana' in *Rinascimento europeo e Rinascimento veneziano*, ed. V. Branca (Florence 1967), pp. 26–37

[3] Rima CLXI, in P. Bembo, *Prose e rime*, ed. C. Dionisotti (Turin 1960), p. 602

[4] On Bembo generally, see: introduction by Dionisotti to Bembo, *Prose e rime*, cit.; Dionisotti, 'Pietro Bembo e la nuova letteratura' in *Rinascimento europeo e Rinascimento veneziano*, cit., pp. 47–60; Elwert, *Studi di letteratura veneziana*, cit., pp. 111–46; G. Toffanin, *Il Cinquecento, Storia letteraria d'Italia*, IV (2nd. ed. Milan 1941), pp. 82–107

[5] In *Prose e rime*, cit., pp. 73–309

[6] Translation in Izora Scott (ed.), *Controversies over Cicero as a model for style*, etc. (New York 1910)

[7] In *Prose e rime*, pp. 311–504

[8] On Bembo as imitator, see Elwert, *Studi*, pp. 111–46

[9] See Toffanin, *Il Cinquecento*, pp. 105–7, 467–9

[10] See Elwert, 'Pietro Bembo e la vita letteraria', in *La Civiltà veneziana del Rinascimento*, ed. Centro Cultura e Civiltà Fond. G. Cini (Florence 1958), pp. 161 and seq.

[11] The *x* can obviously be identified with the phonetic ȝ still found in Venetian dialect

[12] Elwert, 'Pietro Bembo' etc., pp. 157–66

[13] A. Mortier, *Un dramaturge populaire de la Renaissance italienne: Ruzzante (1502–42)*, T. I *Introduction*, T. II *Oeuvres* (Paris 1925); G. Carnazzi,' Posizione storica del

Ruzzante: i suoi rapporti con Alvise Cornaro e gli influssi della satira rusticale', *Ateneo Veneto*, N.S., v (1967), pp. 45–65; L. Zorzi, introduction to Ruzzante, *Teatro. Prima edizione completa* (Turin 1967). The latter provides the first complete collected edition of Beolco-Ruzzante's works. The dating of the works utilised below is taken from Professor Zorzi's introduction

[14] G. Padoan, 'La veneixiana: "non fabula non comedia ma vera historia" ', *Lettere Italiane*, XIX (1967), pp. 1–54; see pp. 13–19 on dating

[15] For Calmo and Venetian comedy generally, see D. Valeri, 'Caratteri e valori del teatro comico', in *La Civiltà veneziana del Rinascimento*, pp. 1–25

[16] G. Cozzi, 'Appunti sul teatro e i teatri a Venezia agli inizi del Seicento', *Boll. Ist. Stor. Soc. & Stat. Ven.*, I (1959), pp. 187–92

[17] *Diarii di M. Sanudo. Prefazione* by G. Berchet (Venice 1902), p. 24, cf. p. 36

[18] Arrigo Caterino Davila, *Dell'Istoria della guerra civile di Francia* (Milan 1807 ed.), I, p. 4

[19] Reprod. in Cozzi, *Il Doge Nicolò Contarini* at p. 310

[20] See especially F. Gilbert, *Machiavelli and Guicciardini. Politics and History in Sixteenth Century Florence* (Princeton 1965), pp. 205–26

[21] See especially: Berchet, *Diarii di M. Sanudo. Prefazione*; G. Cozzi, 'Cultura politica e religione nella "pubblica storiografia" veneziana del '500', *Boll. Ist. Stor. Soc. & Stat. Ven.*, v (1965), pp. 13–14, 19–20; Cozzi, 'Marino Sanudo il Giovane: dalla cronaca alla storia', *Riv. Stor. It.*, LXXX (1968), pp. 297–314

[22] The text of the *Historie Viniziane* normally cited is in A. S. Ven, *Fondo Codici ex Vienna*. This is probably the earliest surviving text. There is, however, a fine example in the British Museum (Kings MSS 151, 152). Portions of the work are reproduced in the Appendix to Cozzi, *Il Doge Nicolò Contarini*

[23] Reproduced in P. Sarpi, *Scritti giurisdizionalisti*, ed. G. Gambarin (Bari 1958)

[24] The edition to be cited here will be P. Sarpi, *Istoria del Concilio Tridentino*, 2 vols introd. Pecchioli (Florence 1966). This reproduces the text of the three volume edition ed. G. Gambarin (Bari 1935)

[25] *ed. cit.* I, pp. 3–4

[26] *ed. cit.* I, p. 337; II, p. 739

[27] *ed. cit.* I, p. 337

[28] *ed. cit.* I, p. 145

seven

Artistic Theory and Propaganda for the Artist

Venetian painters of the sixteenth century, like Tuscan ones, enjoyed the support of a body of writers and artistic theorists who vaunted their merits. Not surprisingly, colouristic richness and, in some measure, freedom of handling were among the elements they stressed, but they certainly did not lay a dominant emphasis upon them. They portrayed Venetian artists not so much as representing a distinctive tradition as uniting in their work all the major elements of good painting. Here their apologetic was carried on in large measure within the traditional framework of the artistic treatise.

Early Italian art theory was substantially bound up with the defence of painting as a liberal art. Theorists raised the claims of the painter by means very similar to those employed in the defence of humane letters. Partly as a result of this, the elements into which Italian theorists, from the mid-fifteenth century, divided the art of painting were substantially derived from the traditional division of the art of rhetoric into *inventio, dispositio* and *elocutio*, which can perhaps best be translated as 'conception', 'form' and 'elegance of expression'. Alberti transposed these categories into pictorial terms as *compositio, circumscriptio* and *lumina*— 'composition', 'delineation' and 'illumination'. Within this framework, Alberti in fact laid particular stress on the element of mathematics, which was central to his defence of painting as a liberal art. In the sixteenth century, the art of painting was commonly envisaged in terms of the categories of *invenzione, disegno* and *colore*. It is generally believed to have been the Venetian Paolo Pino who first made a rigid categorisation along these lines in his *Dialogo della pittura* published in 1548, although elements of it can be seen with theorists writing before him and it was given extensive publicity with Vasari's *Lives,* first published in 1550. Among artistic theorists in general, *invenzione* comprised both the conception of a subject and the accommodation of pictorial representation to it: the devising of suitable attitudes and gestures for the figures, the portrayal in them of appropriate emotions and the conferment upon them of distinctive dramatic roles. *Disegno* comprised not merely draughtsmanship but the plastic or formal elements of a painting in general, including composition. *Colore* included tone and chiaroscuro. The division between *disegno* and *colore* would naturally seem rather artificial to the modern outlook, which has been conditioned, not least, by the experience of the works of the great Venetian colourists: with these, colour is an indispensable element in the presentation of three dimensional form in all its solidity and it is the brush-stroke as much as the contour that is the essential element of delineation. It is perhaps to be reckoned to the credit of Titian's early champion, Pietro Aretino, that he realised this.

Among the other concepts interwoven with the categories of *invenzione*, *disegno* and *colore* were those of *naturalezza*, *bellezza* and *grazia*. *Naturalezza* meant truth to life in the most literal sense, not merely what we would call 'photographic realism', but a rendering of the living object in all its spontaneity. In discussing 'beauty', artistic theorists could seldom forbid themselves a mention of the story of Zeuxis retailed by Pliny: Zeuxis, when he sought to represent a Venus of surpassing beauty, unable to find a single model, chose five maidens of Croton 'for the purpose of reproducing in the picture the most admirable points in the form of each'. This story was to be taken as the foundation of the theory that the artist should 'surpass nature': in order to achieve an ideal of perfect beauty, he should seek out the best elements in nature and combine them together. This 'idealist' notion only became fully crystallised, with strong Platonist overtones, among the Roman theorists of the seventeenth century, but elements of it can be found with many sixteenth-century writers. In general, sixteenth-century theorists handled the story of Zeuxis with considerable freedom, some using it to show that the artist should surpass nature, others to indicate that it was nature rather than an abstract canon that was the artist's source for the notion of beauty. The concept of *bellezza* tended, however, to have strong intellectualist overtones; 'beauty' was something that the artist must discover and this, it usually seems to have been implied, by some sort of rational process. *Grazia* or *venustà* seems to have been treated as a quality more strictly intrinsic to the artist's style and the concept of it was more diffuse and less intellectualist in its overtones. In some measure it derived from the concept of *charis*—'grace' or 'charm'—the quality for which, on Pliny's authority, Apelles had been particularly admired and on account of which praise had recently been bestowed on 'the new Apelles', Botticelli. In the middle years of the sixteenth century, the concepts of *grazia* and *venustà* made their triumphant entry into artistic criticism, with Vasari and Pino among others. It is probably true to say that the term *bellezza* tended to be applied more particularly to the formal elements of a painting, whereas *grazia* and *venustà* were more general in their application.

In the seventeenth century, a division was to develop between the Roman theorists of 'classical idealism' who, in exalting the essentially intellectual task of the artist to discover the canon of ideal beauty, laid the dominant stress on *disegno*, and theorists sympathetic to the Venetian *maniera* who defended the claims of colour and spontaneity. In the sixteenth century, the issues were not so clearly defined, although a certain divergence along these lines as between Venetian and central Italian theorists can perhaps be seen in embryo. The earliest propaganda for Venetian artists, in the middle years of the sixteenth century, came at a time when central Italian artistic influences were exercising attraction on both artists and patrons in Venice. Only in part did such propaganda represent a reaction to these influences: in part it was conditioned by them. While Aretino had not indulged in theorisation within a framework of rigid conceptual categories, Pino and Dolce, who, unlike Aretino, were both in fact Venetians, substantially conducted their defence within the critical framework used by central Italian writers and essentially accepted its criteria. It is also worth noting that with Dolce, the defence of Titian was closely associated with that of Raphael. In the seventeenth century, Raphael was to be the hero of the 'classical idealists' who, in boosting the claims of Annibale Carracci and Guido Reni, were disposed to treat the great Venetian colourists as lacking the fullness of artistic perfection in as far as they appealed to the eye rather than to the intellect. In sixteenth-century Venice, however, the taste for Raphael was strong and Dolce evidently regarded him and Titian as very similar sorts of artist. In general, in examining Venetian taste, it is illuminating to observe reactions to non-Venetian artists; this casts considerable light on the way in which Venetian painters were regarded by their admirers.

One of the earliest documents of Venetian taste is the so-called *Anonimo Morelliano*, discovered in 1800, which gives details of works of art and collections of antiques to be found in Venice and other north Italian towns around the second quarter of the sixteenth century. The common ascription of the work to the historian Marcantonio Michiel is open to some criticism and it is unlikely, certainly, that he was the author of the document in its entirety. The anonymous author has been hailed as a pioneer of the science of picture-notation and cataloguing. The document is filled with critical comments on the works described. Particular appreciation is shown for paintings by Rogier van der Weyden, Antonello da Messina, Leonardo, Raphael and Giorgione. Respect for Antonello, who probably exercised an important influence on Giovanni Bellini, was not unnatural in a Venetian of the period, but the author looked beyond fifteenth-century tradition. His appreciation for Giovanni Bellini was mingled with criticism. Speaking of a Madonna by the latter, he wrote: 'it is clearly outlined, with the bold reflections badly united with the half-tones, but it is an admirable work on account of the graciousness of the atmosphere and the draperies and other parts'. Evidently, as an admirer of Giorgione, he could not tolerate lack of tonal fusion. In combining his admiration for Venetian works with that of the fifteenth-century Flemings and Raphael, the author seems to mirror the taste shown in the very Venetian collections he describes.

Among the earliest propaganda for Venetian artists was that provided in poems, most notably those by Pietro Bembo, Bernardo Tasso and Pietro Aretino, which referred to portraits by Titian, although these poems were designed to praise the person portrayed as much as the artist and the encomia of the latter did little more than speak in generalised terms of the appropriateness with which the sitter was rendered. Aretino, who settled in Venice in 1527 and remained there until his death in 1556 devoted much of his energies to conducting propaganda for his artist friends through his letters, a portion of which were published by him in 1535. Their recipients included Charles v and his ministers, Italian princes and cardinals. Aretino evidently expected artists to pay for these services by gifts of their work and he built up a substantial collection. He was a close friend of the sculptors Jacopo Sansovino and Danese Cattaneo, both of whom spent the bulk of their working lives in Venice, and was particularly intimate with Titian. He conducted propaganda on behalf of all three artists, but above all for the latter. Although Vasari's story that he first brought Titian to the notice of Charles v is apocryphal, Aretino did much to promote the reputation of Titian in Italian and European courts, as well as sending dunning letters to the ministers of crowned heads on his behalf.

Probably the bulk of Aretino's propaganda was devoid of serious critical intent. This was only to be expected where his letters were

directed to patrons with money to dispose of rather than to *cognoscenti*.
For the most part, he praised artists in the most vague and generalised
terms, without any notable indication of where their peculiar excellence
lay, although truth to nature was a constantly reiterated theme; only on
rare occasions did the vocabulary of his encomia take on particular
significance. On these occasions, however, the reader has cause to bear
with the looseness of his vocabulary; one has the impression that
Aretino was trying to say precisely what could not be expressed within
the rigid categories beloved of contemporary theorists.

Despite his partisanship of Titian, his most natural allegiance was
perhaps to central Italian tradition. Titian apart, the artists on whom he
lavished the most extensive praise were Michelangelo, Raphael, Sansovino, Danese Cattaneo and Leone Leoni. His attitude towards Michelangelo is hard to define. It was relatively seldom that he coupled his
name with that of Titian. He perhaps felt that Michelangelo, 'more
divine than human', simply could not be discussed in the same terms as
other artists; thus he wrote that Jacopo Sansovino 'being second to
Buonarotti is held first among sculptors'.[1] He constantly coupled the
names of Sansovino and Titian, 'the former unique in marble, the latter
outstanding in colours'.[2] There is an obvious contrast between the
great Venetian colourist and the Florentine who, as a sculptor, trans-
ported to Venice the polished, idealising, formalistic tradition of
cinquecento central Italy. It is possible that, to Aretino's mind, the
standards of excellence in painting and sculpture were of a different
order, but his placing of Sansovino alongside Titian should deter us
from concluding too readily that his ultimate allegiance was to the
distinctive qualities of the Venetian painterly tradition, such as they are
now commonly envisaged, or that he laid a particularly heavy stress
upon spontaneity of handling. Certainly he defended his refusal to give
a laborious polish to his own literary works on the grounds of the value
of spontaneity, and here used comparisons drawn from the visual arts:

> I attempt to depict the nature of others with the vivacity with which
> the miraculous Titian depicts a face, and since good painters greatly
> appreciate a sketch of a fine group of figures, I have my works
> printed as they are and do not trouble about detailed limning with
> words (*di miniar parole*), because the effort lies in *disegno*.[3]

Undoubtedly Aretino showed himself one of the more discerning
cognoscenti of his time in his appreciation of the value of the sketch, but
this did not withhold him from a particular admiration for artists who

gave a high polish to their work and he was to criticise Tintoretto for
his rapid handling.

How did Aretino view Titian? In 1553, à propos of the Vargas
portrait he wrote:

> *Divino in venustà fu Rafaello*
> *E Michel Agnol più divin che umano*
> *Nel disegno stupendo; e Tiziano*
> *Il senso delle cose ha nel penello*[4]

('Raphael was divine on account of his grace; Michelangelo, more
divine than human, is wondrous in his *disegno*; Titian has the sense
of things in his brush.')

With regard to Titian, this perhaps implied two things: firstly that he
portrayed nature in all its living qualities and secondly that the art of
the brush was something different from *disegno*. Aretino constantly
stressed Titian's capacity for portraying the essential qualities of the
person or object depicted, for producing not merely a likeness but a
living likeness and a revelation of the spirit. He also perhaps appreciated
that in representing the human figure, technical achievement consisted
not merely of rendering surfaces but also of conveying the peculiar
qualities of flesh. Of the Vargas portrait he wrote: 'the spirit is in him,
clothed in bone and flesh'.[5] Of an *Ecce homo* he wrote:

> The crown that pierces him is of thorns and it is blood that their
> points shed; in no other way can a scourge make flesh swollen and
> bruised than that in which your divine brush has made the flesh of
> the holy limbs swollen and bruised in this sacred picture; the suffering
> with which the figure of Jesus is consumed moves to penitence who-
> ever regards in Christian spirit the arms bitten by the rope. . . .[6]

At no point did Aretino state that Titian's peculiar excellence lay in
his qualities as a colourist. Where he refers to Titian's colour, this is
usually a rhetorical device with a purpose quite extrinsic to discussion
of the artist's work. Indeed, Aretino believed that colour, unaccom-
panied by qualities of *disegno*, was nothing. Ultimately he does not
appear to have regarded colour and *disegno* as distinct entities in a
painting; he did perhaps see the art of painting as involving a particular
fusion of the two in the very brush-strokes. Thus he wrote: 'What
distinction lies in attractive colours which are expended in painting
trifles without *disegno*?' Their splendour lies in the touches with which

Michelangelo distributes them ('*nei tratti con che li distende Michelagnolo*').[7] Evidently he realised that for Titian colouring was not simply an adjunct to a previously worked-out *disegno*: he referred to his use of 'those colours which he puts down before the *disegno*'.[8] Aretino apparently appreciated the specifically 'painterly' characteristics of Titian's work, but the qualities which he generally stressed were vivacity, truth to life and *vaghezza*; the concept of *vaghezza* appears to have been rather similar to that of *venustà*, which Aretino applied to Raphael and Paris Bordone,[9] but was perhaps rather more appropriate to effects of colour, lighting and atmosphere.

Tintoretto he also praised for his truth to life. He apparently admired him more for his academic qualities than for his spontaneity. Of Tintoretto's *Miracle of the Slave*, he wrote in 1548:

> There is no man so little instructed in the virtues of *disegno* that he will not be astonished at the solidity (*rilievo*) of the figure which, totally naked and extended on the ground, is subjected to the cruel torture. His colours, his flesh, his rounded form and, I swear . . . the complexions, the manner and the faces of the crowd which surround him are so appropriate to their place in such a work that the scene appears more real than imaginary.

Aretino warned the painter not to yield to pride if he aspired to higher achievements and advised him to 'reduce rapidity of execution in the direction of patience'.[10] In point of fact, Tintoretto's handling in the painting in question was not as free as in many of his other works.

In Aretino's writings there can perhaps be seen in embryo the vision, which was to find its full expression with Boschini a century later of the qualities of vivacity, spontaneity and 'painterly' use of colouristic effects in the work of Titian and Tintoretto. There is a severe danger, however, of reading too much of the seventeenth-century outlook back into Aretino's comments, just as there is danger of reading into them too much of the position adopted by the fictional Aretino in Dolce's *Dialogo*. Ultimately, Aretino's importance in the history of artistic criticism lies perhaps less in his remarks on painters than in his realisation of the pictorial qualities of Venetian light, air and water. In 1544, he wrote to Titian of his impressions of a scene on the Grand Canal:

> The air was such that those who envy you, for not being you, would desire to show it. Imagine, as I relate this to you, in the first place the buildings which, although they are truly of stone, appeared to be of

artificial matter. And then regard the air, which I perceived in some places to be pure and fresh, in others cloudy and dull. Consider also my wonder at the clouds composed of condensed moisture which partly lay close to the roofs of the buildings and partly in the background, the foreground being in a haze inclining towards dark grey. I was astonished at the varied colours they revealed; the nearest shone with the flames of the sun; the distant ones were incarnadine with the brightness of red lead not quite fully burnt. Oh, with what lovely strokes the brushes of nature laid out the air, distinguishing it from the palaces in the way that Vercellio does in his landscapes! There appeared in certain quarters a greenish blue and in others a bluish green, truly composed of the fantasy of nature, master of masters. She, with light and shade, gave depth and brought out solid forms, so that I cried out three or four times: 'Titian, where are you?'[11]

It was here perhaps more than in his critical comments that Aretino revealed his understanding of Titian and showed himself a pioneer in the literary appreciation of the colouristic painterly tradition.

In the *Dialogo della pittura* (1548) of the Venetian painter Paolo Pino,[12] the defence of Venetian artists at first sight appears peripheral to the main lines of the work; on closer examination, however, the encomium of Giorgione can be seen as closely related to the main argument. In the introduction, Pino says that no one has fully explained what painting is. Previous artistic treatises, it is indicated, have not really been about painting as such: Alberti's treatise is 'more on mathematics than on paintings' and evidently for Pino that of Dürer fell into the same category; Gaurico wrote as a sculptor. Pino himself would 'discuss painting as a painter'. The body of the work consists of a dialogue between the Venetian Lauro and the *forestiero* (i.e. non-Venetian) Fabio. It is, in fact, the latter who dominates the dialogue. Fabio's discourse is in substantial measure indebted to fifteenth-century Tuscan theory, although the new division is made of the art of painting into the elements of *invenzione*, *disegno* and *colore* and the subdivision of these categories indicates a rather more 'painterly' outlook than that of, say, Alberti. Pino accepts the Albertian *circonscrizione* as one element of *disegno*, but specifies that the latter includes chiaroscuro as well as contour and ultimately brings in the alternative term *schizzo* which carries strong overtones of rapidity and freedom in handling. The attributes of colouring are designated as *proprietà*, *prontezza* and *lume*: appropriateness, sureness and luminosity. The introduction into a discussion of colour of the concept of

Titian, *Cain and Abel*, originally in S. Spirito in Isola, 1543–9 (see p. 235)

12   Titian, *Diana and Callisto*, late 1550s (see pp. 135–6)

13   Titian, *Diana and Actaeon*, late 1550s (see pp. 235–6)

14 Paolo Veronese, *The Triumph of Mordecai*, ceiling painting,
church of S. Sebastian, Venice, 1555–6, (see p. 237)

prontezza or *ispedizione* indicating decisiveness in the actual manipulation of the pigments is indicative of a particularly 'painterly' approach
to the question. With regard to the medium employed, Fabio regards
oils as 'the most perfect manner and the true practice', since the colouristic range they bestow is best suited to the imitation of nature, although
he indicates a particular predilection for fresco, since it necessitates
greater rapidity and sureness of hand. Lauro appears to assent to all this.
Towards the end of the dialogue, however, he abandons his hitherto
quiescent role in a discussion of Venetian painters. Fabio has already
made certain remarks about these in his discussion of 'economy'
(*brevità*) and *ispedizione*. It was undesirable, he said, 'to draw pictures
with too extreme a diligence, composing all in light and shade as
Giovanni Bellini did; it is wasted effort, since the whole has to be
covered with colours'. Venetian *cognoscenti* of the time would probably
not have dissented from this judgement. Fabio has blamed Andrea
Schiavone for carelessness in his excessive rapidity. Further on he has
indicated Michelangelo and Titian as the princes of painting. Lauro
follows with a long list of distinguished painters, putting Giovanni
Bellini, Giorgione, Jacopo Palma, Pordenone, Sebastiano del Piombo,
Tintoretto and Paris Bordone alongside Mantegna, Dürer, Leonardo,
Raphael and Bronzino, among others, but stating his ultimate reverence
for Michelangelo and Titian and being most insistent in placing the
latter above Bronzino. He follows with the sentence that was to be so
pregnant for the development of Italian art criticism and that was to
form the basis of the seventeenth-century Tintoretto myth: 'if Titian
and Michelangelo were of one body or if, to the *disegno* of Michelangelo
were to be joined the colouring of Titian, he could be called the god of
painting'. Fabio's assertion of the superiority of painting over sculpture,
on the grounds that it makes possible the depiction of all natural effects,
gives Lauro the opportunity to sing the praises of Giorgione, whom he
refers to as 'our celebrated painter, no less worthy than the ancients'.
Giorgione put sculptors to shame by his picture of St George reflected
in a rippling pool of water and by mirrors on either side. Evidently
Lauro wishes to indicate that Giorgione achieved effects quite peculiar
to painting. The work in question was 'perfectly executed in all the
three parts of painting, that is *disegno*, *invenzione* and *colore*'. By
dividing the art of painting into these three categories and by putting
forward Giorgione as a painter who had excelled in all of them together,
Pino laid the basis for Dolce's defence of Titian.

    Before turning to Dolce, it is necessary to examine the first edition of Vasari's *Lives*, the *Torrentina* edition of 1550, which was in part the occasion of Dolce's *Dialogue*. This work was strongly imbued with a tone of Tuscan patriotism. Tuscany, more than any other region, abounded in great artists and Tuscan painters, sculptors and architects, from the time of Giotto, had taken the lead in raising the state of art and bringing in 'the modern manner'. It cannot be denied that Vasari bestowed accolades upon Venetian painters. Giorgione 'acquired the renown . . . of competing with those who worked in Tuscany and were authors of the modern manner'. Titian's works were 'truly worthy evidence that, if Tuscany abounded in artists at all times, the regions by the mountains were not always abandoned and forgotten by heaven'.[13] Vasari's compliments towards Venetian artists, for all their fulsomeness, implied a somewhat patronising attitude towards the Venetian school as a whole. Titian was only briefly dealt with on the grounds that he was still alive. Those who wished to raise the claims of Venetian artists could not accept in silence Vasari's assessment of Michelangelo. As the culmination of a long history of progressive development, Buonarotti had brought art to perfection. 'Painters need not trouble,' wrote Vasari, 'to seek out and invent new postures and ways of draping figures, new styles of expression and awesomeness . . . since all the perfection that can be attained . . . he has attained.'[14] The elements which he praised in Michelangelo's work were, in fact, mainly formal and plastic ones: skill in portraying the human figure and in foreshortenings, solidity of form, proportion, grace and elegance.

'Whoever has once seen the picture of the divine Michelangelo truly need not trouble, one may say, to open his eyes to see the work of any other painter.' So speaks Fabrini, obviously intended to represent the Vasarian viewpoint taken *à l'outrance*, in Ludovico Dolce's *Dialogo della pittura*. In the *Dialogo*,[15] published in 1557, the attack on the excessive worship of Michelangelo and the defence not only of Venetian tradition but also of a broader Italian one is entrusted to the figure of Aretino. He puts forward Raphael and Titian as equal to and even superior to Michelangelo: the defence of Raphael lays the basis for the elevation of Titian. He makes the now standard division of the art of painting into *disegno*, *invenzione* and *colore*. Here, in fact, he substantially follows Vasari's *Introduzione alle tre arti del disegno*, which prefaced the *Lives*. He avoids, however, Vasari's intellectualist definition of *disegno* as the expression of the concept of universal forms in the artist's mind, while asserting that the artist should not merely imitate nature but surpass it, in the manner of Zeuxis. In general, he lays a greater stress on the imitation of nature than Vasari. Certain of Aretino's observations on the marks of good painting suggest that Dolce was likely to be appreciative of precisely the kind of style that Giorgione and Titian had developed. He criticises the use of bright colours in portraying flesh-tints, stating a liking for the use of brown, allegedly much used by Apelles, who was in fact praised for the purity of his colours. Aretino agrees with Fabrini that the artist should show a certain *sprezzatura*. This term had been applied by Castiglione to the demeanour of the perfect courtier who should show in his actions a certain studied negligence, not appearing to put painful effort or thought into what he did; it suggests ease of manner with a certain element of panache. Aretino asserts that the painter should 'above all avoid excessive diligence, which is always harmful': he should know when to leave off work.

Aretino proceeds to defend Raphael on the grounds that he combined all the elements of good painting in his work: *disegno, invenzione* and *colore*. Here Michelangelo is compared unfavourably with him. Michelangelo was supreme in sculpture, but Raphael surpassed him in painting. In *disegno*, Michelangelo was stupendous, but he put little care into his colouring. Even with regard to *disegno*, he had his limitations. He excelled only in the portrayal of the muscular nude in its most awe-inspiring and fantastic aspects (*la forma più terribile e ricercata*). Raphael, on the other hand, knew how to portray all kinds of nude, in their most pleasing and graceful aspects, and also excelled in the clothed figure. All Michelangelo's figures are the same, whereas Raphael was marvellous in his observations of age and sex and thus fitted form to subject matter. Hence Raphael was superior in one particular branch of *invenzione*, that is *convenevolezza*, and here Dolce has exploited precisely the definition elaborated by Vasari. Thus he asserts the superiority of Raphael on the grounds not only of colouristic mastery but also of *invenzione* and, in some measure, *disegno* as well. The groundwork has now been laid for asserting the supremacy of Titian among the moderns:

In him alone, we truly see combined and perfected all the excellent parts, which, with many, have been divided, for in invention and *disegno* no one ever surpassed him. With regard to colouring no one ever equalled him. To Titian alone we must accord the glory of perfect colouring, which none of the ancients had, or, if he did, his work is lost, and which is more or less lacking in all the moderns; for . . . he equals nature, his figures are alive and moving and their flesh palpitates. In his works, Titian has shown not mere charm but also

propriety in his colours, not affected ornamentation but the sobriety of
a master, not harshness, but the mellow softness (*pastoso*) of nature;
in his works, light and shade strive playfully with one another
(*combattono e scherzano*); they obscure forms and give them depth
(*perdono e diminuiscono*) in the same way as nature.

Dolce, it should be noted, asserted not merely that Titian showed all
the elements of good painting in his work but that he *combined* what
other artists had kept separate.

In the *Dialogo*, Dolce attenuated the intellectualist element in art-
appreciation. Fabrini suggests that just as learning and letters are necessary
in order to distinguish good from evil, so also, in order to distinguish
beauty from ugliness, there is need for 'subtle insight' and a distinct
skill which belongs to the painter alone. Aretino replies that the
intellect can be deceived but not, as a rule, the eye; thus he implies that
appreciation of painting is a matter of the eye rather than of the intellect.
All men have a sense of beauty and ugliness and Apelles, he notes,
submitted his works to common judgement. He admits that he himself
is thinking primarily of certain *belli ingegni* who, having refined their
judgement with the study of letters and by practice, can surely judge a
variety of things and especially painting which pertains to 'the less
fallible instrument of the eye'. He considers that 'any man of talent,
combining this with practical experience, can judge painting, and all
the more so if he takes pleasure in regarding antique works and works
of good masters, for, having a certain image of perfection in his mind,
it is easy for him to judge how far things painted approximate to it or
are removed from it'. Later on in the discussion, he indicated that
Michelangelo appealed only to the erudite. Dolce, through the mouth
of Aretino, did not deny that art appreciation is *in part* an intellectual
activity; he even used the intellectualist concept of the 'idea of the
beautiful'. What he appears to have denied is that art appreciation is a
predominantly intellectual activity and that it is the exclusive province of
painters: he left scope for the educated amateur. This is perhaps connected with the fact that, while employing the somewhat intellectualist
concept of *bellezza*, he laid heavy stress on 'imitation of nature', which
can be understood by the many, and in general used less the concept of
bellezza than the more sensualist ones of *grazia* and *venustà*. In some
measure Dolce anticipated the arguments to be used around the 1680s
by French critics such as Dufresnoy and De Piles who gave a more
'popularist' orientation to art theory by stressing that art, as the imita-

tion of nature, appeals primarily to the eye, and who, within this framework, laid a particular stress on the element of colour.

Dolce's *Dialogo*, evidently intended as a challenge to Vasari, induced the latter to modify and develop his critical position in the 1568 edition of the *Lives*, published by the Giunta firm in Venice.[16] Two years earlier, Vasari himself had visited Venice and met Dolce and Titian personally, as well as obtaining a deeper first-hand knowledge of the Venetian school. In the 1568 edition of the *Lives*, the Tuscans retained their heroic role as the pioneers of the 'modern style', but the critical examination of Raphael was now very much more developed and Venetian painters were examined in more detail, an entire chapter being devoted to Titian. The latter was treated as an outstanding artist, but weak in *disegno*. Vasari criticised him for not making preliminary drawings and here the contrast between Vasari and Aretino is noteworthy. He retailed the views of Sebastiano del Piombo and Michelangelo that if Titian had devoted more attention to *disegno*, he would be unsurpassed, for in Sebastiano's view he was 'the best master of our day in the imitation of natural tints'. The suggestion that Titian's excellence lay primarily in his colouring had perhaps been implicit in Pino's work, but it took a critic with a somewhat patronising attitude towards the Venetian school to make the suggestion with full force in the first instance. Extensive propaganda for Venetian artists was provided in the guide-book *Tutte le cose notabili e belle che sono in Venezia*, first published in Venice in 1556. It appeared under the pseudonym of Anselmo Guisconi, but the author is generally believed to have been Francesco Sansovino, a rather plodding *erudito* of encyclopaedic interests, the son of the sculptor and architect Jacopo. It ran through seven editions in the sixteenth century and eight in the seventeenth, appearing under various pseudonyms and with various additions. The original core-section describes a dialogue between a Venetian and a *forestiero*. The former makes the now traditional criticism of the Bellini: 'their manner was very diligent and they almost painted like miniaturists, but if anything they erred in their diligence, since their figures were lacking in softness and relief'. Giorgione, on the other hand, had 'a most lively manner' and Titian rivalled Michelangelo, while Pordenone had 'a sound manner, lively in the attitudes and excellent in foreshortenings'. Sansovino at first sight appears as a prophet of the seventeenth-century outlook in his description of Tintoretto's work as '*tutto spirito, tutto prontezza*'—all spirit and dash—but he makes the standard criticism of Tintoretto, which was not really to be reversed until Boschini: 'he is fertile in *invenzione*, but he is lacking in patience, which is necessary to bring everything to a conclusion and he certainly takes on too much'.

A rather more 'modern' attitude towards Tintoretto is, however, expressed in the *Osservazioni della pittura* of the Veronese painter and stage-designer Cristoforo Sorte, published in 1580.[17] Tintoretto is cited as one of the painters who have accompanied 'a certain liveliness of spirit with graceful and perfect imitation': 'with perfect judgement in the painting and portraits which he does from nature, he rapidly puts in their place the contrasts, shadows and half-tones, the reliefs and well-imitated flesh and it is a marvel to watch him work with such bold application, speed and promptness'.

In Sorte's *Osservazioni* and in the attached letter from a patron, considerable feeling is shown for effects of light and atmosphere, with particular application to landscape painting. In his letter to Sorte, the patron Vitale writes:

> I am greatly pleased by the artifice which you have shown in accommodating the colours to the quality of the landscape, so that it is easy to discern which are the fertile places and which the sterile ones. This is the secret and excellence of painting, whence you have learnt what should be the true green of meadows, the variety of flowers, the diversity of grasses, the denseness of woods, the grimness of mountains, the transparency of water, the colour of flesh, the black and the blue of eyes, the colour of clothes, the depth of perspectives, the effects of the lovely dawn, the serenity of night, sea-tempests, fires and all that nature embraces in her store of infinite artifice.

Here, perhaps, Vitale reveals a certain Tassoesque, romantic sensibility.

In response to Vitale's request, Sorte explains his method of depicting nature, describing in detail his choice and manipulation of pigments in depicting earth and rock, flesh, sky-effects, tempests, fires and snow-scenes, devoting considerable attention to his use of colour in creating an illusion of aerial perspective. The painters whom Sorte holds up as examples of good technique are predominantly from the Venetian dominions but mostly rather obscure ones, Tintoretto being the main exception. Vitale and Sorte, the former as a *cognoscente*, the latter as a painter writing on the techniques of his craft, both show an awareness of the potentialities of colourism, but within the context of land-scape painting rather than in that of a classicising figurative tradition, as with Dolce; *disegno* and *invenzione* are nowhere mentioned. It should be said that although both men were evidently Venetian subjects—

Vitale wrote from Desenzano on Lake Garda—and although the work was published in Venice, neither was Venetian and did not apparently have close connections with the Venetian milieu,[18] in which the artistic treatise tended to have a rather more erudite and theoretical character.

Nevertheless, Venetian art-criticism of the sixteenth century tended to be less theoretical and rationalising in character and perhaps revealed a greater sensibility to actual painterly practice than that of Tuscany. At the same time, the canons of excellence recognised by Venetian theorists were fundamentally the same as those put forward by Tuscan ones; although there was a less dominant stress on *disegno*, there was not, correspondingly, a dominant stress on colour. As has been suggested, it was Vasari rather than any Venetian theorist of the sixteenth century who indicated that Titian's excellence lay primarily in his colouring. The seventeenth century debate on *disegno* or *dessein* versus colour, which was in any case rather more a French than an Italian affair, would probably have been meaningless to sixteenth-century Venetian theorists and practitioners of painting.

Treatises on the art of painting were as a rule not merely discussions of aesthetics, but also in some measure pieces of propaganda designed to raise the artist's position in society. In the first instance, Renaissance theorists had tried to show that painting was a liberal art rather than a mechanical craft, a position, incidentally, which no *cognoscente* from the time of Giotto had denied. Curiously enough, the defence of the artist's position was conducted for the benefit of the painter rather than the sculptor, although propaganda for the architect was developed in a rather similar manner. As has already been indicated, propaganda for the painter was conducted on lines very similar to those followed by humanists in their defence of the orator or man of letters, the ultimate models being Cicero's *De oratore* and Quintilian's *Institutio oratoriae*. This meant that, with fifteenth-century art-theorists, there was a strong stress on the intellectual nature of the painter's activity, this being reinforced, particularly in Alberti's case, by the preoccupation with mathematics. With many sixteenth-century theorists, notably central Italian ones, the intellectualist element was maintained with the notion of the 'idea of the beautiful'. Ultimately, the stress on *disegno* and *invenzione* was integral to the intellectualist conception of the art of painting, for it was within these categories of the art that knowledge of mathematics and proportion, the discernment of ideal beauty and general erudition were employed. Furthermore, if *invenzione* and *disegno* corresponded in pictorial terms to the position occupied by conception and form in the art of literature, while colour corresponded to elegance of expression, there would be a tendency to regard colour as being in the nature of an ornamental adjunct to the basic structure of a painting. How was the artist's position to be buttressed when the stress on *disegno* was attenuated and the concept of beauty, rather than being a notion of ideal forms, became merged with the concepts of *grazia* and *venustà*? Above all, how was it to be maintained when, as in the case of Dolce, the concept of painting as an arcane, erudite discipline was rejected?

It is not perhaps without significance that Pino and Dolce laid considerable stress on the role of the artist as a social figure. In Pino's dialogue, Fabrini attempts to describe a perfect painter. In addition to his professional skills, the painter should possess soundness of moral character and have worthwhile relaxations, such as poetry or music, he should be versed in letters and may distinguish himself in arms or in athletic pursuits. These demands are superficially rather similar to those made by Alberti, but while Alberti's models appear to be ultimately the portraits of the perfect orator by Cicero and Quintilian, Pino's model is perhaps rather more Castiglione's *Courtier*. Just as, in the traditional treatise on the art of oratory or humane letters, encyclopaedic knowledge and graces of person are ultimately ancillary virtues, related to the central exercise of the pursuit of oratory or letters which subsumes them all, so also for Alberti, erudition and personal possession of a fine body are clearly made out to be ancillary to the art of painting. With Castiglione, on the other hand, a variety of skills are simply a galaxy of graces adorning the person of the courtier and not related to any central discipline. Likewise with Pino, civilised pursuits seem to be simply adornments to the artist's person rather than necessary adjuncts to his professional skill. The tone of his description of the perfect painter is courtly rather than erudite, social rather than professional in its preoccupations. In Dolce's *Dialogue*, Aretino, following his denial of the mysterious nature of artistic appreciation, discusses the dignity of the art of painting. After the traditional argument from the example of great men in antiquity who appreciated painting or practiced it, he turns to Venetian nobles of his own time who themselves drew and painted. At the conclusion of the dialogue, considerable attention is given to Titian's social position and to his social graces. No one has brought a greater reputation to the art of painting, for he only paints great men and distinguished personages who find themselves in Venice always visit him. Not only is he unequalled as a painter, but among his many other great qualities, he is a good speaker and has fine manners. Vasari, in the 1550 edition of the *Lives*, had already laid some stress on Raphael's urbanity and his position in Roman society, but his references to Titian's good manners and distinguished connections only came in the Giuntine edition of 1568 and were obviously based on Dolce. Contemporary assertions about an artist's circle of acquaintances and social graces should be treated with caution and be regarded, in the first instance, as propaganda designed to raise the status of the artist. Taken at this level, however, such assertions are of great interest and may perhaps be symptomatic of the partial abandonment, more particularly by Venetian theorists, of the more extreme intellectualist conception of the artist's activity.

A model for the Renaissance architectural treatise existed in Vitruvius's *Ten Books of Architecture*. This contained a certain basis upon which the defence of architecture as a liberal art could be erected. Vitruvius had said that the architect should have a knowledge of other intellectual disciplines: letters, mathematics, philosophy, music, medicine, law and history. Here he had evidently based himself on the antique portrait of the orator—probably Cicero's—which was also in part the ultimate model for a number of Renaissance treatises on painting. In certain Renaissance treatises on architecture, the affinities with ones on the art of letters was likewise marked. It was only natural that Renaissance theorists who sought to raise the claims of architecture as a liberal profession should elaborate Vitruvius's comments on the education of the architect. Furthermore, a number of them lent force to the picture of the architect as an *erudito*, by detailed examination of theories of proportion, a subject which Vitruvius had barely touched. Here there was not only a large mathematical element but also, in a number of cases, a stress on the affinities between architectural proportion and musical harmony; Platonic–Pythagorean number-mysticism was often present.

Among writers on architecture in the Veneto, Alvise Corner and Palladio in no way discussed the position of architecture as a liberal art and concentrated on practical problems. Daniele Barbaro, however, showed a highly philosophical approach in the commentaries to his Vitruvius edition of 1556. By grafting Aristotelian and Platonist theory onto the core of Vitruvius's introduction, he conferred a particularly intellectualist character upon the concept of architecture as a liberal art. Barbaro indulged in lengthy discussions as to which branch of knowledge architecture pertained, whether *scientia*, *intellectus* or *sapientia*, coming down in favour of the latter as the sphere of '*il vero contingente*', relative truth and applied knowledge. He then set out to show that the architect was not an artisan but rather a 'head of artisans'. He seemed to imply that the architect's special quality resided in the fact that he alone understood the 'end' to which the artisans' activities were directed; this teleological concept was perhaps the fruit of the Patriarch of Aquilea Elect's Aristotelian enthusiasms. With regard to Vitruvius's remarks on the architect's need to be versed in many branches of knowledge, Barbaro pointed out that rhetoric and medicine, no less than architecture, were 'adorned' by other arts, but that the architect was in a peculiar position since he alone applied the faculty of judgement to the end-products of those arts ancillary to his profession. For Barbaro, architecture was not simply a craft or skill: 'art', he wrote, 'resides in the intellect'. Throughout the treatise, there was a strong stress on mathematics, corresponding to Barbaro's concentration on proportion as the essential element of architecture. Vincenzo Scamozzi's *Idea dell' architettura* (1615) was likewise highly scholastic in tone and he devoted extensive space to claiming for it a position at the summit of the sciences and liberal arts, alongside ethics, natural science and mathematics; in no sense was it a 'mechanical art'. Scamozzi expatiated at some length on the architect's need for knowledge of all the liberal arts, but the reasons he gives are for the most part highly unconvincing.

The contrast between Scamozzi's treatise and Palladio's essentially untheoretical *Quattro libri* is marked. The latter architect's development can only be fully understood, however, against the background of a climate of opinion which regarded the architect as the practitioner of a liberal art. His education had been taken in hand by the great Vicentine humanist Giangiorgio Trissino and Palladio. although obviously not a *uomo universale* of the type of Alberti, was one of the most erudite of all Renaissance architects. By contrast, Venetian painters, although certain of them belonged to learned academies, were hardly members of the erudite milieu in any genuine sense. Titian was, by all accounts, a social figure of some note and the detail of his iconography suggests that he at least had access to a store of erudite knowledge, although whether he acquired this knowledge on his own account is by no means certain. Alberti's ideal of the learned painter does not seem however to have been realised in Venice and it was one to which even artistic theorists there paid relatively little tribute; rather the 'perfect artist' was envisaged as a man who could conduct himself with dignity in polite society.

Notes

1 P. Aretino, *Lettere sull' arte*, comment. F. Pertile, ed. E. Camasasca, 3 vols. in 4 (Milan 1957), doc. DCVIII

2 *Ibid.*, doc. CDXIII

3 *Ibid.*, doc. LXVI

4 *Ibid.*, doc. DCLXIII

5 As above

6 *Ibid.*, CCCLXXXIII

7 *Ibid.*, XXXII

8 *Ibid.*, doc. DXII

9 *Ibid.*, doc. CDLXXV

10 *Ibid.*, doc. CDII, cf. doc. CCX

11 *Ibid.*, doc. CLXXIX

12 Reproduced in P. Barocchi (ed.), *Trattati d'arte del Cinquecento fra manierismo e controriforma*, I (Bari 1960)

13 *Le vite de' piu eccelenti pittori scultori e architetti*, III (Florence 1550), pp. 578, 580, cf. pp. 947–8

14 *Ibid.*, p. 965

15 Reproduced in Barocchi, *Trattati d'arte del Cinquecento*, I. English trans. in M. W. Roskill, *Dolce's Aretino and Venetian Art-Theory of the Cinquecento*, (New York 1968)

16 This is the version normally reproduced or translated in modern editions of the *Lives*

17 Reproduced in Barocchi, *Trattati d'Arte del Cinquecento*, I

18 Sorte did, however, design the *stucchi* for the Maggior Consiglio, Scrutinio and Senate in the Ducal Palace

eight

Patronage and Collecting of Art

Statesmen and patrician writers, who regarded themselves as the guardians of true Venetian tradition, complained intermittently, of the growth of luxury and extravagance in Venice. Such complaints are particularly evident in the early sixteenth century and at the turn of the seventeenth. In the late sixteenth century, heavy financial commitments to the arts may well have been connected with a more general trend of opulent expenditure. Only to a limited degree, however, was art patronage an aspect of conspicuous expenditure in our period. The collection of easel pictures was closely connected with the collection of antique statues, coins and cameos and hence had a certain erudite character. Furthermore, the *studio*, the collection of small antique pieces and modern works of art in the study of a wealthy man or scholar, was essentially intimate in character and would not as a rule have been formed out of desire for ostentation. Moralistic disapproval of luxury and opulence may, indeed, have done something to divert financial resources into works of art and buildings. Expenditure on weddings, funerals and female dress, as well as public celebrations was obviously vast, but Venetian nobles were evidently disposed, in many cases, to regard expenditure on the impermanent as frivolous, while treating that on permanent objects as being of a different order. At the same time they were seemingly inclined to devote resources more to the adornment of their public face than to their personal comfort. They spent heavily on buildings, but by comparison with the nobilities of northern Europe, they seem to have been relatively modest in their expenditure on clothing, domestic service and hospitality.[1] Undoubtedly there was often a certain element of insincerity in attacks on extravagance, but it is not, perhaps, altogether surprising that certain testators should insist in their wills that they wished to be buried 'without any pomp whatsoever' and then go on to make elaborate provisions for an imposing tomb;[2] this, after all, would be a permanent monument to the distinction of a noble house.

Expenditure on buildings and works of art did not necessarily follow the same pattern as other forms of expenditure and was not even necessarily related to the vigour of the economy. Venetians may have been inclined to put their money into buildings and works of art not least when commercial activity was risky or offered limited returns. Contemporaries certainly believed that opulent expenditure grew with the retreat from the sea. The lavish artistic patronage of the middle and latter years of the sixteenth century may have been connected in some measure with the Mediterranean trade-boom of the 1550s and '60s, but it is hardly surprising that patronage did not undergo any notable restrictions after the boom had weakened or that certain forms of artistic expenditure continued to be prominent throughout the economic crises of the seventeenth century. It is perhaps to be expected, however, that at times of economic stagnation, the strongest tendency would be to invest in *objets d'art* which could be easily disposed of rather than in buildings or murals.

It is extremely difficult to plot the development of artistic expenditure in the sixteenth and early seventeenth centuries. Our information on art collections, especially in the middle years of the sixteenth century is fragmentary. Palaces and villas were often erected over several decades and in many cases little is known about the different stages of their construction. The first three decades of the sixteenth century do appear to have been a relatively barren period for palace building. While work on a number of outstanding late fifteenth-century projects was continued, it seems that relatively few new palaces of major importance were begun. On the other hand, a number of important art and antique collections, probably not in themselves the fruit of outstandingly heavy expenditures, were in existence by about 1530. From the 1530s, new palace projects did, perhaps, become more numerous and at the end of this decade the Grimani family of S. Maria Formosa helped to initiate a new fashion for grandiose mural decorations in domestic buildings. Again, Falconetto's Villa dei Vescovi at Luvigliano, built between 1529 and 1535 set a new standard of sumptuousness in country residences and between the 1540s and the end of the century, a series of magnificent villas spread over the Veneto, a testimony to the increased interest of Venetians in landed property. While construction of public works had continued fairly steadily in the first three decades of the sixteenth century, the main enterprises were basically continuations of the late fifteenth century projects. With the late 1530s, however, an ambitious scheme of buildings on the Piazza S. Marco was undertaken and the

period from the mid 1550s to the late 1580s was the great era for decorations in the buildings of the Piazza and the Ducal Palace, partly
initiated, it is true, as a result of fires of 1574 and 1577. In the seventeenth century, work on state projects became restricted. There was
some impressive investment in heavy masonry with palaces and villas,
most notably those designed by Longhena, but it has been observed that
there was a marked fall in commissions for ceiling decorations: at least
28 ceiling projects had been executed in the last quarter of the sixteenth
century, but only eight are known to have been executed in the first
quarter of the seventeenth.[3] It would seem, however, that in the seventeenth century the mania for collecting pictures and antiques became
more widely diffused than ever before, this perhaps being in part a
reflection precisely of Venice's economic stagnation. It should be noted,
however, that if the character of the work of art as a financial investment ever weighed at all heavily with Venetian collectors, it never did
so to the extent that they concentrated on highly finished works of
cabinet size which could be easily stored and disposed of.

There was no genuine court-culture in the Veneto. The doges did
not possess a court and as far as artistic projects were concerned their
personal patronage was very limited in extent, being basically confined
to the adornment of their private apartments; they would at the most
exercise only an indirect influence over commissions for the Ducal
Palace as a whole. Perhaps the nearest thing to a court that the Venetian
dominions ever possessed was the circle of Caterina Corner at Altivole
near Asolo. Caterina, daughter of an immensely wealthy Venetian
noble house, had been the wife of Jacques de Lusignan, the last King of
Cyprus. Upon his death, the Serenissima had forced her to abdicate in
its own favour. She was pensioned off and granted the territory of Altivole. There she provided extensive hospitality and put on a continuous
series of lavish entertainments, the life of her 'court' being portrayed in
an idealised form by Pietro Bembo in the *Asolani*. A number of major
artists visited it, Caterina herself being painted by Giovanni Bellini and
Giorgione.[4]

Certain nobles or persons of equivalent status in the Veneto also kept
households in which hospitality and even permanent residence was
granted to scholars and artists. The most notable examples from the
point of view of art patronage were those of Alvise Corner in Padua and
Giangiorgio Trissino at Cricoli near Vicenza and that of the Grimani
di S. Maria Formosa in Venice. An obvious comparison can be made
between the households of Corner and Trissino and the permanent

'academy' which Pietro Bembo kept in his Paduan villa, although the membership of the latter did not apparently extend to Bembo's various artist friends. While these households were maintained in abodes of considerable elegance and even sumptuousness, they were probably relatively modest domestic establishments quite different in character from the households of great nobles of the northern European type. The relationship of patron and artists could be one of considerable intimacy. Corner's household around the 1530s included the painter and architect Giacomo Falconetto and the playwright Beolco Ruzzante. In Padua, Corner possessed a fine house in the present Via del Santo and in his gardens on the other side of the road he had a 'guest house'. Falconetto, together with his sons and his son-in-law, the stuccoist Ottaviano Ridolfi, lived with his patron in the main house. The guest house, in addition to Corner's daughter and her husband, contained Ruzzante and his theatrical company and other artists who worked for Corner, stuccoists and decorators for the most part. Ruzzante's company probably gave performances in Corner's house.[5] Trissino took a number of young Vicentine nobles into his house and along with them he accepted the young Andrea Palladio, with whom he appears to have been on terms of friendship and whom he took to Rome to study antique remains. All the evidence suggests that Corner and Trissino treated their main protégés as friends and not as domestics. Corner, indeed, was prepared to share his tomb with Falconetto and Ruzzante, a remarkable gesture of friendship and intimacy. On the other hand, he probably treated Ruzzante's company and the subsidiary artist who worked for him more as simple employees. The Grimani of S. Maria Formosa appear to have kept resident artists essentially as dependants. According to Vasari, the miniaturist Giulio Clovio, when he came to Italy from his native Croatia, 'put himself in the service of cardinal Marino Grimani, with whom he stayed three years occupied in drawing'. His functions included the relatively unelevated task of making copies from medals.[6] This would have been around 1539. Again, evidently speaking this time of the early 1550s, Vasari refers to the painter G. B. Ponchino known as 'Il Bazzacco' as a 'dependant' (*creato*) of the Grimani.[7] In his testament of 1592, the patriarch Giovanni Grimani referred to 'Titian, painter and sculptor (i.e. Tiziano Aspetti) and Uberto of Flanders, members of my household, my friends and servants'.[8]

In general, there is little evidence of artists in the Venetian dominions working under the institution of *servitù particolare* whereby a single patron monopolised an artist's activities or at least controlled who he worked for. In point of fact, notwithstanding a few notable examples to the contrary, few artists of real calibre in Europe as a whole accepted such an arrangement. The relationship with a patron that it involved tended to be a menial one, the artist or craftsman being treated somewhat as a domestic servant. The Grimani probably retained their artists under conditions of this kind, but, as far as the Venetian dominions are concerned, their case appears to have been an unusual one.

While Venice had no court culture, there was an extensive state patronage, controlled by various magistracies or specially delegated groups of superintendents. Patronage in Venice had two other particularly notable features: the wide dissemination of private art collections and the important role of large charitable confraternities (the *Scuole Grandi*) whose resources were very much greater than those of any normal guild or religious sodality.

Here attention will be devoted to patronage as exercised by private individuals, the State, ecclesiastical bodies and lay confraternities. With regard to private patronage, it is usually known at least who commissioned buildings and mural decorations. On the other hand, information on actual commissions of easel-paintings is scarce. With regard to small-scale works, the concentration here will be upon collection and possession of paintings and sculptures rather than on commissions. The collection of modern works of art cannot be treated in isolation from that of antique objects and the latter will be discussed in its own right as an example of Venetian taste and for the light it sheds on the phenomenon of collecting mania.

Private patronage and collecting

'Collezionismo'

Undoubtedly the greatest diffusion of the non-princely art and antiquarian collection in the sixteenth century, outside the orbit of the papal court, was in Venice and, Rome apart, Venice probably held the lead in the number of its private collections in the seventeenth century when collecting mania was becoming fairly generalised throughout Italy. It is possible to recognise a specific phenomenon of collecting in sixteenth- and seventeenth-century Venice. There is a certain difference between forming a collection and simply amassing works of art in a dwelling. A collection may be regarded as having a particular value as a totality. Its

15 Paolo Veronese, *Feast in the House of Levi*, 1573, painted for the Dominicans of SS Giovanni e Paolo (see p. 201)

16   Jacopo Tintoretto, *Miracle of the Slave*, detail, originally in the Scuola di S. Marco, 1548
(see pp. 207, 240)

owner may not wish it to be dispersed, even among heirs, after his death. It may be housed in a special part of a building. It may be intended as a representative assemblage of works by leading artists, thus having an illustrative as well as a decorative function. Certain Venetian collectors, in their testaments, not only subjected their collections to *fidecommesse* but also specified that under no circumstances, or only the most pressing ones, were they to be broken up.[9] Venetian guide-books of the late sixteenth and early seventeenth centuries commonly referred to collections of antiques and other *objets d'art* as *studi*. The term *studio*, indicating an intimate study rather than a large gallery, was probably used fairly loosely. Inventories of great collections, where they exist, suggest however that *objets d'art* tended to be concentrated in certain parts of a house which were not necessarily the main state rooms. Assemblages of pictures, bronzes, small pieces of sculpture, vases and cabinets of cameos, medals and coins are most often described as being either in a *studio*, or where pieces of cabinet size were not involved, in a *portego* (probably either a vestibule or an arcaded gallery): large pieces of sculpture or marble fragments would tend to go in a courtyard. Antique pieces were obviously kept as objects of interest as well as ornamental sources of pleasure and there is reason to suppose that the same was often true of modern paintings.

Two possible ancestors of the Renaissance art collection are the collection of family relics and memorials and the antiquarian collection. The first Venetian family museums in the fifteenth century were it has been suggested of the former kind—collections of arms and banners and other family relics[10]—and doubtless in such shrines to the family *lares* and *penates* many sixteenth-century portraits found a natural place. The evidence suggests, however, that the systematic collection of works of art tended to be more closely associated with the collection of antique objects.

The passion for collecting antiques seems to have developed in Italy quite early in the fifteenth century and was in full flood by the middle of it. The collections of the Po valley region were probably the most advanced initially, but the mania was well established in Florence and at the papal court. The earliest collectors seem to have been mainly persons of humanist interests—Poggio, Niccoli and Marsuppini had major collections in Florence—plus a few artists, including Donatello, Ghiberti and Mantegna. There is no evidence to suggest that anti-quarian collections in fifteenth-century Italy normally contained any appreciable number of modern paintings, the collections of Piero di

F

Cosimo de Medici and Lorenzo the Magnificent being evidently major exceptions which may well mark an important stage in the evolution of the art collection.[11]

Information on collections in fifteenth-century Venice is scarce, although there appear to have been some collections of coins, medals and inscriptions there and Mantegna's master, Squarcione, formed a small archaeological museum in Padua. There were, however, a number of major antique collections in Venice in the second and third decades of the sixteenth century and in many Venetian collections of the first half of the sixteenth century, antique fragments and modern paintings were kept together.

Our sources of information regarding sixteenth-century Venetian collections are fragmentary but tantalising, those for the seventeenth century very good indeed. For the earlier period there is firstly the famous *Anonimo Morelliano*, usually attributed to the Venetian scholar Marcantonio Michiel, containing descriptions of works of art in houses, churches and private buildings in various north Italian towns, including Venice and Padua; the catalogues of Venetian collections are dated and they were mostly seen in the period 1525–43.[12] In the *Anonimo Morelliano*, the very precise descriptions of certain paintings make clear identification possible. The development of three of the collections catalogued there is further clarified by inventories.[13] Certain fragmentary details of works in private houses in the middle years of the century can be gathered from Vasari's *Lives*. The occasional inventory of value exists from the turn of the seventeenth century, and an inventory was also made in 1714 of the collection of Giacomo Contarini (*d.* 1595) when it passed into the hands of the State. There are in addition a fair number of inventories covering the sixteenth century as a whole in the Archive of the *Magistrato alla Petizion* but these were for purely legal purposes and only described precious objects in detail, being silent on the authorship of pictures. From the late sixteenth century, guide books began to list who were the main collectors of antiques and works of art. There were two main series of guide books. Firstly there was the *Delle cose notabili della città de Venezia* (or variants on this title), which first appeared in 1556 under the name of Anselmo Guisconi, generally assumed to be a pseudonym of Francesco Sansovino; it went through no less than nineteen editions between 1556 and 1692, appearing under the names of the different authors who made additions to it (Bardi and Goldioni). The second main guide was Francesco Sansovino's *Venetia città nobilissima et singolare*, first published in 1581. It was republished with substantial additions by Giovanni Stringa in 1604 and with further additions by Giustiniano Martinoni in 1663. Vincenzo Scamozzi's *Idea dell' Architettura* of 1615 also gave certain details of collections. Sansovino in the *Venetia città nobilissima* of 1581 had only really been interested in antique collections and the references to ownership of paintings in the 1592 and 1601 Bardi editions of the *Cose notabili* were very fragmentary. Stringa in the 1604 edition of the *Venetia città nobilissima* showed considerable interest in works of the great Venetian masters and gave lists of those represented in a few collections. Scamozzi in 1615, while observing that the use of 'galleries' had not become common in Venice in the same way as in Rome and Genoa, or in France and Spain, noted the spread in Venice 'for some time past' of collections (*raccolte*) of antiques and paintings. He listed certain major collections, indicating their general shape—whether they possessed antiques, marble pieces, bronzes, numismata or paintings–but only noted authorship of paintings in a desultory manner. The Stringa and Scamozzi editions perhaps indicate an increased consciousness of the significance of picture collections, but the first standard guide book to give substantial lists of paintings was the Martinoni edition of 1663. For the mid-seventeenth century, we are very well informed. Ridolfi's *Meraviglie dell' Arte* of 1648, devoted to painters of the Venetian school, is a valuable source for the location of works at the time and also gives extensive details of locations in the sixteenth century, considerably supplementing Vasari. Also the curious rhymed critical guide, Marco Boschini's *Carta del navegar pittoresco* (1660) gives details and information on the contents of many private collections. From these sources Dr Savini-Branca has been able to construct a very extensive picture of collections of works by Venetian masters in the seventeenth century.[14] It is not possible to build up a similar picture for the sixteenth century, except for the period covered by the *Anonimo Morelliano*.

Apart from references to houses which contained the odd work of interest the *Anonimo* lists about sixteen collections of some significance in Venice and Padua, the Venetian ones, as already indicated, being mostly seen between 1512 and 1543. Perhaps the most interesting collections described were those of Pietro Bembo, Cardinal Domenico Grimani and Gabriele Vendramin.

Domenico Grimani was the son of Doge Antonio Grimani, who had himself made a considerable fortune by trade from small beginnings. With the aid of his family wealth, Domenico had purchased the cardinalate and used the position thus acquired to obtain a truly monstrous number of ecclesiastical preferments for himself and his nephews. But withal he was reckoned by Erasmus as one of the most learned prelates of the Roman court and he possessed a magnificent collection of codices. His museum included one of the most important collections of antiquities of the age. The marbles, which he bequeathed to the state and which included some particularly fine Pergamene works formed perhaps the most precious element of the Venetian public collection of antiquities (now the Museo d'Antichità). He also possessed large numbers of antique engraved jewels, cameos, coins and precious objects. With regard to modern paintings, in addition to works by Titian and Giorgione, he possessed four Memlincs, three Patenirs, three Boschs (two *Temptations of St Anthony* and *the Beatific Vision*) works (presumably prints) by Dürer, a Raphael cartoon, books of drawings by Raphael and probably also Leonardo and Michelangelo drawings. He also owned one of the world's most famous illuminated codices, the Grimani Breviary which contains fine floral illuminations on virtually every page and a number of major illuminated tableaux, some of which were allegedly by Memlinc and Hugo van der Goes; when Giovanni Grimani presented it to the Serenissima in 1593 it is evident that even then it was regarded as a priceless work. Doubtless the commercial contacts of the Grimani family and Domenico's residence in Rome at a time of major excavations (some in fact on his own property) facilitated the formation of a collection of such wide scope.[15]

Pietro Bembo's central position in Italian letters and scholarship has already been examined. He was obviously sensitive to the visual arts and understood artists. It was he who excused Giovanni Bellini's uncooperativeness to Isabella d'Este on the grounds that 'few precise limitations can be imposed on his style, he is accustomed to follow his own whim in his pictures'. He was an admirer and patron of Raphael and referred in his sonnets to Titian's success in painting his beloved. In addition to a large collection of antique marbles, bronzes, vases, engraved gems and other precious objects, he possessed, in his Paduan villa, several portraits and drawings by his favourite Raphael, a Memlinc, two Mantegnas and works by Titian and Giovanni Bellini.[16]

The combination of interests in antiques, modern Venetian works and fifteenth century Flemish ones was again found in the massive collection of Gabriele Vendramin (*d.* 1552), which was described by the *Anonimo* in 1530 and of which an inventory was finally made in 1567. In his testament of 1547, Gabriele expressed great pride in the collection which, he said, 'has given me a little repose and peace of soul in the many labours of body and mind I have undergone in family affairs'. He ordered that it should be maintained intact and kept closed until an heir might present himself who showed an interest in objects and studies of this kind. Vendramin was described as a merchant, and appears from his testament to have been a man of great wealth. His exhortation to his heirs was redolent of merchant prudhommerie: they should devote themselves to trade and learn the arts of navigation and maritime warfare, but also not abandon the study of letters; they should regard the family business as a gift of God and 'not offend him by extremes, always keeping to moderation'. The spirit of Vendramin's testament almost seems to breathe in the sober splendour of Titian's votive portrait of the Vendramin family, gathered round the reserved, patriarchal figure of Gabriele in adoration of the crucifix. Gabriele was not perhaps particularly typical of Venetian patrons. There is no evidence that, like many of the more important ones, he was either himself an *erudito* or belonged to the nobility of high government office. On the other hand, there are indications that he was friendly with or related to certain of the most outstanding humanists of the previous generation.[17]

Among the collectors whose possessions were described in the *Anonimo Morelliano*, we find a group of men apparently connected by personal links. Vendramin had in 1504 been sponsored for entry to the Great Council by Pietro Bembo's father Bernardo, himself a distinquished *erudito*. The latter had also sponsored Gerolamo Marcello another quite interesting collector. Both the elder Bembo and the humanist Gerolamo Donà, who was a co-sponsor of Marcello, had been friends of the great scholar Ermolao Barbaro to whom Gabriele Vendramin was also related. Gabriele and Gerolamo Marcello possessed and had probably commissioned two of Giorgione's most important works, the *Tempestà* and the *Sleeping Venus*, and it has been suggested that the subject matter of these two paintings drew its inspiration from the currents of Aristotelian and Plinian scholarship which Ermolao Barbaro helped to initiate.[18]

Turning to the contents of the *Anonimo* more generally, of the 16 or so owners of works of art or antiques in Venice and Padua who can be described as collectors in any meaningful sense, 11 lived in Venice and five in Padua. Of the former, nine were probably nobles. Of the latter, one, Pietro Bembo, was a Venetian noble, one, Leonico Tomeo, was a distinquished philosopher and one, Marco da Mantova, possessed a university doctorate. The great Alvise Corner has here been left out of the account since his paintings and sculptures were adornments to an architectural scheme, there being no evidence that he possessed a museum.

Out of the 16 collectors, 10 apparently possessed antiques in consider-able quantity (that is they can be assumed to have had over ten statues or fragments of statues, or, where the number of these was rather fewer, they had appreciable numbers of vases, numismata or engraved jewels). Two others possessed at least some antiques. Three-quarters of the total number possessed works by painters not belonging to Veneto schools, fifteenth-century Flemish works here being in the lead; among Italian artists from outside the Venetian dominions, Raphael predominated. There was absolutely no division between enthusiasts for Flemish on the one hand and antiquarians or, for that matter, admirers of Raphael on the other. The larger the collection, the more catholic its taste. It was the larger collection which was the most likely to contain works by fifteenth-century Flemings or other non-Venetian artists and in practice the number of Flemish works tended to be in proportion to the size of the antique collection. Out of the nine collections which included Flemish works, eight had appreciable numbers of antiques and of the six collectors who possessed works by Raphael, five also possessed Flemish works. Four collectors were indicated as possessing drawings: Grimani, Bembo and Vendramin owned ones by Raphael, Vendramin also possessed drawings by Jacopo Bellini and another collector (Michele Contarini) had two by Giorgione. The implication seems to be that it was the large-scale erudite collector who treasured drawings.[19]

The interest in Flemish works was not peculiar to Venice, being also marked in late fifteenth century Florence, as well as in various princely collections. The interest which manifested itself in Venice, however, may well be symptomatic of an appreciation of paintings of rich and subtle colouring with a strong orientation towards landscape. The fact that Flemish works and substantial numbers of antiques tended to be found together may be explained in part by facilities for acquisition. These, as in the case of the Grimani, may have been favoured by family trading links with both Flanders and the Levant. It should be said, how-ever, that it was probably fairly easy to acquire Flemish works on the Italian market—the Grimani Breviary was purchased in Rome—and we do not know how many antiques were acquired in the Eastern Mediterranean as against north Italian markets, where there was probably an extensive residue of Greek as well as Roman pieces formed as a result of importations from the East over several centuries. It is probable, however, that large marble pieces from the East, as distinct from small precious objects, tended to be of fairly recent importation and Domenico Grimani certainly obtained some pieces directly from the Morea. Availability, was perhaps not the only determining factor. It is hard to escape the impression that it was scholars and antiquarians who had the widest collecting interests and this is suggested by other Venetian and non-Venetian collections. The interest in Raphael among non-Venetian artists is significant. Ludovico Dolce, in his *Dialogo della pittura* of 1557 was to use the defence of Raphael as the ground work for his encomium of Titian, evidently regarding the two as very similar sorts of artist. Perhaps Dolce reflected an attitude towards Raphael that had already become established among Venetian connoisseurs.

Although we possess the names of a substantial number of collectors around the turn of the seventeenth century, information on the actual shape of collections in the latter half of the sixteenth century and the first decade of the seventeenth is scarce. The four of which we have a particularly good idea, however, reveal a combination of learned interests with the collection of modern works of art. These were the collections of Giacomo Contarini of S. Samuele (1536–95), the Patriarch of Aquilea Giovanni Grimani (1506–94), the Procurator Federigo Contarini (1538–1609) and Ottaviano Fabri, whose collection was mentioned by Stringa in 1604.[20]

Giacomo Contarini was the most interesting both as a collector and as a man. A patrician with a fairly distinguished government career, he was a *virtuoso* of encyclopaedic interests, being learned in history, philosophy and science, with a particular emphasis on mathematics and mechanics. His circle of friends reflected his artistic, erudite and scientific interests. They included his mentor, Daniele Barbaro, the Paduan *erudito* and antiquarian G. V. Pinelli, Galileo, for whom he obtained state patronage, Palladio, who bequeathed his drawings to him and Francesco Bassano, of whom he was the special protector. His house was a meeting place for men of letters and artists, of whom Tintoretto was one. He evidently also gave support to Palma Giovane. His library of books and manuscripts, especially rich in copies of chronicles and ambassadorial reports is one of the more valuable collections in the Marciana Library. In addition, his palace housed paintings and antique marbles, bronzes and vases and an outstanding collection of mathematical and cosmographical instruments, together with various objects —minerals and fossils—indicative of an interest in natural history. In his testament of 1595, he referred to his studio with great pride as 'one of the dearest things I have, from which all my honours have proceeded'.

He specified that no part of the collection was to be alienated under any circumstances, remaining in the family under *fidecommesso*; if the male line of descent died out, the collections were to go to the state.

They did, in fact, pass into the hands of the state in 1713; in 1714 an inventory was made of the collection with the exception of Veronese's *Rape of Europa* and Jacopo Bassano's *Return of Jacob from Canaan*, which had probably been transferred to the Ducal Palace the previous year. The inventory was cautious in its attributions of paintings, generally ascribing them to the 'schools' of Giorgione, Titian, Tintoretto or Palma Giovane, or noting them as copies of works by these artists, while definitely ascribing certain works to Tintoretto, Veronese and 'Il Bassano'. Where ascriptions of paintings are made to specific artists or to their schools, they were predominantly of the Venetian school, with the odd Flemish work. It is conceivable that the collection which passed into the hands of the state in 1713 had been added to by Contarini's heirs in the seventeenth century. Ridolfi, in his *Meraviglie* of 1648 referred to over seventeen paintings as being in the palace of Ca Contarini of S. Samuele or as being in the hands of Contarini's heirs Gerolamo and Francesco (his great nephews). It is only Veronese's *Rape of Europa* and Francesco Bassano's *SS. Anthony and Sebastian* that he clearly indicates as having been commissioned by Giacomo. Where, however, paintings are coupled with the names of Gerolamo and Francesco and where these works are clearly described, it is impossible to identify them in the 1714 inventory. It is not unlikely, especially bearing in mind Giacomo Contarini's anxiety that the identity of his collection should be preserved, that the 1714 inventory substantially represents the shape of his original collection. Unfortunately, nothing is known of the drawings left to him by Palladio.[21] His role in decorative projects for the Ducal Palace will be examined in due course.

Giovanni Grimani was known as a learned prelate, but was hardly of the cream of the Venetian intelligentsia. His wider artistic patronage will be examined more fully later. With regard to the movable contents of his collections, the bulk seems to have consisted of antique works, notably medals, cameos and marbles. His antique collection was regarded as the most important of its time in Venice and it forms the larger part of the present Museo d'Antichità. It included large numbers of classical Greek as well as Graeco-Roman works. Part of the collection, probably more the smaller pieces, came from that of Giovanni's brother the Cardinal Marino, but evidently many of the larger pieces were acquired by Giovanni himself. He also possessed some paintings, including works by Giorgione and Flemish works and, as we have seen, he kept a resident Dutch painter along with the sculptor Tiziano Aspetti.[22]

The collections of Federigo Contarini and Ottaviano Fabri were very similar to that of Giacomo Contarini. Federigo Contarini, whose affluence had early set him on the road to high government office, enjoyed a great reputation as an antiquarian, and his antique collection was considered as having succeeded in importance that of Giovanni Grimani, which he was, in fact, responsible for putting in order. He also possessed a substantial number of paintings. When an inventory was made of his collection in 1613, only the subject matter of paintings was described, no reference being made to authorship. However, descriptions of the mid-seventeenth century collection of Domenico Ruzzini, into whose hands that of Federigo ultimately passed along with additional works, makes it possible to suggest authorship for certain of the latter's pictures. It is probable that he possessed several works by Titian and Tintoretto and at least one by Veronese. Various landscapes and Flemish works are also listed in the 1613 inventory. Like Giacomo Contarini, the Procurator Federigo not only possessed antiques and paintings of the great Venetian colourists, but also objects indicating interests in natural history, such as fossils and birds' eggs.[23] Ottaviano Fabri, in addition to paintings of the great Venetian masters and Raphael and sculptures by Sansovino and Giambologna, possessed a large number of mathematical and cosmographical instruments and was said to have extensive knowledge in the relevant fields.

The six collections mentioned by Scamozzi in 1615 as including paintings and which were evidently in existence at the time probably all contained antiques as well.[24] The collector of whom we have the best record is the antiquarian Andrea Vendramin, of whose museum we have an inventory dating from around 1627.[25] Vendramin was another erudite collector of the type of Giacomo Contarini, Federigo Contarini and Ottaviano Fabri. He not only possessed the usual antique bric-à-brac—sculptures, urns, coins and engraved gems—but also a natural history museum.

The catalogue of the collection was obviously made by the owner's hand and contains pen-sketches of the more important paintings which has made identification of certain of them possible. The section devoted to paintings is prefaced by a historical and critical introduction in Latin which raises fascinating suggestions as to the owner's motivations. It amounts to a defence of painting. Painting, he says, preceded the art of sculpture historically and paintings were greatly admired in antiquity, although none have survived. There follows a disquisition on the development of the art, which amounts to an analysis of its component parts, line, symmetry, colour, etc. Here Vendramin follows Pliny closely, but amplies his aesthetics somewhat, not least in his treatment of colour, light, shade and tone, laying particular stress on their subtle modulation. Following Pliny again, he gives a list of the painters of antiquity concluding: 'there flourished also in our most fortunate age Michelangelo, Raphael of Urbino, Salviati, Polidoro of Parma, Titian, Giovanni Bellini and others'. The catalogue of the collection then follows. It was predominantly composed of works by the great six-teenth century Venetian masters and contemporary Venetian ones, but also contains the odd recent non-Venetian work and panels by fifteenth-century Flemings. Apparently Vendramin saw the great painters of the sixteenth century as worthy successors to Apelles and Zeuxis. It is conceivable that his paintings were intended as companions to his antique sculptures, replacing the lost works of the ancient painters.[26]

Enthusiasm for museums of antiques was also widespread in sixteenth-century Vicenza and in these collections, modern paintings often seem to have found a place.[27] The most splendid Vicentine collection was evidently that of the Canon Gerolamo Gualdo (1492–1566), who had passed his youth in Rome, attached to Cardinal Pompeo Colonna. His collection of antiques and paintings bore many similarities to Venetian ones of the period; artists of the Venetian school were well represented but so also were native Vicentine painters, together with mid-sixteenth century Roman sculptures. The collection was further developed by the Gualdus family in the seventeenth century to become one of the most outstanding in the Venetian dominions.[28]

As the seventeenth century progressed, the link between art collec-tions and antiquarian museums in Venice appears to have become less marked. By the mid-seventeenth century, a large body of Venetian collections seem to have mirrored the tastes inculcated by the critics Ridolfi and Boschini and which had been prefigured in some measure by Dolce. The evidence available suggests that these collections were overwhelmingly orientated towards works of the Venetian school or ones which were regarded as being in 'the Venetian manner'; since the sixteenth century the Bellini had apparently declined in favour while Tintoretto had attained a new popularity. By this time, a clear current of artistic taste had emerged. The same cannot be said of the Venetian cinquecento.

Certain problems of motivation are raised by the actual form of many Venetian collections of the sixteenth and very early seventeenth centuries. A typical *studio* of a Venetian noble or *erudito* of the early to mid-sixteenth century might contain the following elements: works by contemporary or very late fifteenth century Venetian masters; the odd Flemish work; perhaps a drawing by Raphael; antique bronzes and marble statues or fragments and vases; antique and modern cameos and engraved gems; gold-work and cups of semi-precious stones; medals and antique coins. In the early seventeenth century it might contain a few fossils and birds' eggs as well. Was such a collection simply the fruit of an indiscriminate magpie mania, or was there some rationale behind it? And what was the relationship in the mind of the collector between the modern painting and the antique statuette, cameo or gem?

According to Dr Savini-Branca, there was not any clearly defined aim in Venetian picture collections of the sixteenth century and, except with the outstanding connoisseur like the author of the *Anonimo Morelliano*, pictures were valued primarily for decorative purposes and the dignity of antiques was not attributed to them.[29] It is not altogether certain that this is fair. Such a view might appear, at first sight, to be confirmed by most of the existing inventories of the sixteenth century and the first two decades of the seventeenth which did not list the names of artists and which usually described precious effects in considerably more detail than pictures; there are not infrequent references to 'Flemish paintings', but this, while it casts interesting light on the cultural resources and outlook of those who made the inventories, was probably simply a convenient way of describing paintings, particularly useful where, as in the case of landscapes, the absence of clearly defined subject matter made precise notation difficult. Under normal circumstances, testaments which refer to collections at some length do not give details of authorship either.[30] On the other hand, there is no reason why inventories made essentially for legal purposes, even though with the aid of distinguished artists like Tintoretto, Battista Franco, Palma Giovane and Alessandro Vittoria, should do anything else. The inventory of Gabriele Vendramin's collection, made in 1567 for the benefit of some future heir who should show a clear interest in the museum, was on the other hand very precise on the question of authorship. Likewise the two great inventories of the first half of the seventeenth century which give detailed ascriptions of authorship, the Andrea Vendramin catalogue (*c.* 1627) and the Gualdus inventory of 1650 were probably made essentially for intimate family purposes.

Furthermore, it must be asked whether the antiquarian art collectors simply purchased any rare and precious object that came to hand or whether they were trying to found *museums* - representative collections. The latter possibility is at least suggested by the fact that catholicity of taste was often proportionate to erudite interests. In general, it seems to have been the antiquarian collectors who showed the broadest taste; in particular it was antiquarians who seem to have been foremost in collecting Flemish works in the period covered by the *Anonimo Morelliano* and, at the turn of the seventeenth century, it is not least in the collections of antiquarians—about which we are, admittedly, the best informed in any case—that we have records of Netherlandish works.[31]

The combination of works by late fifteenth century and sixteenth century Venetian masters with fifteenth-century Flemings and Raphael found in a number of collections does perhaps indicate a certain orientation of taste towards painters who could be conceived as having certain affinities with Venetian tradition. At the same time, it would suggest that a distinction between 'classicising' and 'non-classicising' artists was alien to most Venetian collectors—just as it was apparently alien to Venetian artistic theorists—or at least that it was irrelevant to artistic purchasing. Here, however, a distinction must be made between the collection of works in a *studio* or gallery and artistic patronage in general.

Isabella d'Este in the ordering of her collection at Mantua had evidently wished to indicate a parallelism between the antique and a modern work of art by placing a Michelangelo cupid, previously mistaken for an antique work, alongside an *amorino* attributed to Praxiteles. There is no particular indication of like aspirations among Venetian collectors, although some of Vittoria's marbles and bronzes may well have found a natural place in the company of antique works. On the other hand, readers of Pliny would have realised that in Greek antiquity a distinguished tradition of painting existed alongside that in sculpture. The attention which Pliny devoted to the element of colour, lighting and tone and his reference to Apelles' depiction of 'things which cannot be represented' such as lightning and thunderbolts, would suggest that the antique painterly tradition was substantially different in character from the sculptural one. Venetian collectors, among others, may well have been inspired to put works of modern painters alongside antique sculptures in order to fill the hiatus left by the complete destruction, as it then appeared, of antique paintings; if this was the case, there was little cause for collectors to be disturbed by the stylistic differences between modern Venetian works and antique sculptures.

It is possible that Andrea Vendramin intended a juxtaposition between antique and modern works of the type indicated. It is significant that the *Tempestà*, which was in Gabriele Vendramin's collection, was very probably inspired by the description of Apelles' painting of thunder and lightning in Pliny, in the same way as Botticelli's *Birth of Venus* and his *Calumny* were probably based on descriptions of works by Apelles. Furthermore, readers of Pliny would have been aware that a Venus had been the chef d'oeuvre of Apelles and Zeuxis and Giorgione's reclining Venus, indicated by the *Anonimo* as being in the house of Gerolamo Marcello (i.e. the *Dresden Venus*) may have been deliberately intended to emulate a lost antique work, although it should be said that Marcello is not mentioned as having antiques in his collection.

It is possible that some early sixteenth century collections were designed to evoke a lost ideal world in which antique remains were surrounded by paintings suggestive of the legendary Golden Age or containing allegorical subjects.[32] It should be said, however, that in Venice the production of paintings of the 'Golden Age' genre or with allegories of a mythological type—as distinct from patriotic allegories or personifications of the virtues and sciences—was more particularly an affair of the first two decades of the sixteenth century.

It would be dangerous to assume that, in the early sixteenth century art was primarily collected for art's sake, as we would understand it. Subject matter was probably a major consideration with patrons, especially in the first two decades of the sixteenth century when there was evidently a fashion, both in Venice and elsewhere in Italy and for which Giorgione and the early Titian notably catered, for paintings with esoteric subject matter, possibly of philosophical significance or relating to mystery cults. For much of the sixteenth century, however, the subject matter of Venetian paintings tended to be relatively un-recondite. With regard to aesthetic appreciation of works of art, Venetian collections of the sixteenth century do not appear to have mirrored any strongly defined currents of taste such as were to emerge in seventeenth-century Italy. The question of taste must, however, be examined within the wider context of artistic patronage as a whole.

Private architectural commissions

The last two decades of the fifteenth century had seen the commencement in Venice of a number of fine palaces in the curious regional style with which the names of Mauro Coducci and the Lombardi are particularly associated. This style of obscure antecedents, which used the Renaissance architectural vocabulary with considerable freedom to achieve a refined sensuousness of decorative effect, was unerudite in character: it was devoid of archaeologising tendencies or preoccupations with the niceties of antique classical norms. The Palazzo Vendramin-Calergi and the Palazzo Corner-Spinelli, probably both by Coducci, had a number of unusual features as compared with contemporary palaces elsewhere in Italy; they had no fortified characteristics, the *piano nobile* was of particular importance and the window-openings were large, but these features were essentially inherited from the more outstanding Venetian palaces in the Gothic style and the introduction of Renaissance architectural forms in the late fifteenth century was not accompanied by novel solutions to the problems of domestic architecture as such. It took the new decorative forms of the late Sanmicheli and of Sansovino to exploit fully the opportunities for lightness of effect offered by large window-openings and to finally drive out of fashion the rather irrational groupings of relatively small window-openings that dominated in most Venetian palaces of the early sixteenth century.

A number of attractive villas had been built in the Veneto in the fifteenth century, the more outstanding ones mostly by provincial nobles and landowners. By and large these were picturesque creations rather than monuments of rational architectural planning and were often badly executed. In many cases, the mediaeval roots of their style can be clearly seen—sometimes they were even semi-castellated—and concessions to Renaissance architectural practice were limited. Where, as was often the case, colonnades were used, the proportions were seldom in the modern style—the ratio of height of column to height of arch often being very low—and the capitals primarily recall Romanesque models. With the villa, even more than with the city palace, it is evident that an architectural revolution occurred in the Veneto towards the middle years of the sixteenth century.

The new style, whose outstanding exponents were Falconetto, Sanmicheli, Sansovino and Palladio, was more erudite and more cosmopolitan than that of Coducci and his contemporaries. While it showed from the first a highly distinctive regional character and even, in its plans, continued in some measure the older tradition of the Veneto villa, it also drew its inspiration, especially in its treatment of façades, from Roman palace architecture of the early sixteenth century, more particularly that of Raphael, Bramante, Peruzzi and the younger Antonio

Sangallo; it followed the Vitruvian orders with nicety, as far as proportions were concerned, although in totally novel contexts and combinations, and it also evidently utilised the fruits of archaeological research. Despite its learned and archaeologising character, the buildings in the new style were designed with strong functional considerations in mind; indeed, knowledge of ancient building practice was employed in substantial measure in the service of utilitarian ends and not for the establishment of models to be slavishly imitated. An erudite outlook and informed connoisseurship is particularly evident among patrons who took the lead in promoting the new style.

The revolution in domestic architecture in the Veneto was more particularly associated in its origins with country villas and with palaces in provincial cities rather than with private palaces in the metropolis. Here the most notable provincial cities were Vicenza and, to a lesser extent, Verona. The regions most important for the development of the new type of villa were the Vicentino countryside, where many Vicentine nobles held estates, and the main area of Venetian landed property, stretching from the Polesine, through the Padovano, to the Trevigiano. The architectural revolution can be related in some measure to the acquisition and exploitation of estates in the Terraferma by Venetian nobles or, perhaps more precisely, to a new attitude towards the countryside that ensued upon the spread of Venetian landholding. Venetian nobles had been building villas in the Terraferma from the late fifteenth century, but these appear to have been unambitious projects in the main. The development of the new type of villa, of which the Palladian form is the best known, was perhaps related to a realisation that the countryside was not merely a terrain for exploitation but also a pleasant place to live in. Such a realisation was forcibly expressed by Alvise Corner. Corner, who had taken the lead in stressing the necessity for exploiting the economic resources of the mainland, also extolled the virtue and joys of country life in the *Vita sobria* (1558), his manifesto for healthy regimen and diet.

The country villa, as developed by Venetian nobles, was both a place of recreation and the centre of an economic unit, designed to facilitate the oversight of estates and often, in its very building structure, integrated into the life of the farm. Venetian villas often had *barchesse*, long arcades in which produce and agricultural implements could be stored, although in several villas of the Vicentino region the originally planned outbuildings were not executed, or only partially so. There is no reason for supposing that Vicentine nobles in general neglected their estates, but certain of their villas, notably the Rotunda and the Villa Cricoli, were less centres for estate management than places for dignified leisure.

If there was a seminal figure in the revolution in domestic architecture, it was Alvise Corner the agriculturalist and health-fanatic who, having been refused inscription in the Golden Book of the Venetian nobility, settled in Padua to manage his estates. In the very first sentence of his *Trattato dell' architettua*, he mentioned convenience, durability and beauty as the important qualities of architecture and throughout the treatise the stress was on commodiousness and soundness of construction; the fact that he lived in a well-designed building, he asserted, had enabled him to retain his health and survive to an advanced age. Corner declared his intention to examine a branch of architecture to which Vitruvius had devoted little attention: houses for 'citizens'. Vitruvius was of limited utility, in part because of the problems raised by the text of his treatise, which was now corrupted and used a vocabulary that was no longer understood, but also because what he wrote related essentially to public buildings and was not really applicable to domestic architecture. Corner claimed that he had learnt more from the study of actual antique buildings than from Vitruvius. He would not discuss the components of the classical orders of architecture: 'I do not hold it as a necessary conclusion,' he wrote, 'that a building cannot be beautiful if it does not have any of these elements. The Church of S. Antonio in Padua and other buildings are extremely beautiful and yet they are not adorned with any Doric, Ionic or Corinthian orders. These orders and adornments are very expensive and hence not for all citizens and they do not make buildings more commodious or durable, but only more beautiful.' Corner's treatise was novel in its concern with financial economy, ease of maintenance, salubriousness and functional relationships between building structure and domestic life. For example, Corner indicated that door and window openings should be related to the positions in which furniture must be located; he even examined the construction of chimneys and lavatories in some detail. In his remarks on general design, Corner showed evidence of a rationalising taste, totally unsympathetic to the kind of picturesque jumble that had characterised many villas of the fifteenth century. He laid particular emphasis on symmetry, both in elevations and plans; thus back-doors should correspond to front-doors. There should be no overhanging upper storeys. In his treatise à propos of the reconstruction of Padua Cathedral, Corner attempted to show that the work could be done at a third of the cost originally estimated. For instance, sculptured friezes were unnecessary, for the Santo of Padua which was without them was more beautiful than S. Giustina which had them.[33] Corner's enthusiasm for the basilica of the Santo, which overlooked his house, was unusual to say the least.

In point of fact, the loggia and odeon, which his protégé Falconetto designed for him in his town house, are works of exquisite elegance. They were completed in 1524. The loggia, strongly reminiscent of Sangallo's courtyard in the Palazzo Farnese, was probably the first building in the Veneto to introduce the architectural vocabulary of the Roman late Renaissance. This can be seen in the alternating curved and triangular window-pediments, but above all in the arcading system: between the pilaster-piers that support the arches are set doric columns which extend above the arcade to the entablature which marks the division of the storeys, the line of the columns being extended by the pilasters on the second storey, thus giving a monumental unity to the composition. This, with its delicacy and exploitation of subtly fragmented light and shade effects, was the first true precursor in the Veneto of the style of Sansovino and Palladio. Significantly, it was the only domestic building referred to in the *Anonimo Morelliano*. The stuccoes and grotesques in the odeon by Giovanni da Udine, Bartolomeo Ridolfi and probably Domenico Campagnola were also revolutionary, for they marked the introduction into the Veneto of the style of decoration modelled on Nero's baths, recently developed in Rome under the aegis of Raphael by Giovanni da Udine himself. Falconetto also executed work for Corner on his villa at Codevigo, the centre of one of the latter's successful agricultural experiments. It is believed that Corner also had Falconetto design around 1529 his Villa dei Vescovi at Luvigliano for another patron; this imposing yet delicate building set upon a massive stone platform among the Eugenean hills was Falconetto's *chef d'oeuvre*. 'When wishing to know how to build in town, a gentleman should come to the Casa Cornara in Padua . . . should he wish to build a villa instead, he should go to Codevigo and Campagna . . . and if he wishes to build a princely palace he should then go to Luvigliano,' the painter Francesco Marcolini wrote to Corner. Falconetto may well have exercised a crucial influence on the young Palladio, and at all events he pointed towards the future. Corner's patronage of him was no less inspired than that extended to Beolco Ruzzante. Falconetto left a number of buildings of major importance in the Padua region, all executed when he was past the age of fifty. Hitherto he had revealed himself only as a rather timid painter in the style of his master Melozzo da Forli. It is perhaps significant that he embarked on his impressive architectural career in the 1520s precisely at the time when he moved into Corner's orbit, the loggia and odeon probably being his first buildings.[34]

It was Giangiorgio Trissino who discovered Palladio.[35] Trissino was a truly cosmopolitan figure who, though a married layman, served the Papacy in a number of diplomatic missions. He was the most distinguished Vicentine humanist and man of letters of the sixteenth century and, as the founder and superintendent of the Cricoli Academy, he was the mentor of the younger generation of Vicentine humanists. As a writer, he sought to revive antique literary forms in an eclectic Italian which would be the quintessence of the various usages of the Peninsula. His tragedy, the *Sophonisba*, was the first regular classical tragedy of the Renaissance, but although highly regarded at the time, it is now mainly of specialist interest. His ponderous *Italia liberata dai Goti*, which sought to revive the forms of the Homeric and Virgilian epic in a tale of the exploits of Belisaurus's Christian army, never really caught the wind of sixteenth-century fashion. In the words of Professor Wittkower: 'Trissino's brand of humanism was aristocratic and in a way anachronistic; he advanced a formal, esoteric and dogmatic classicism free from any popular tendencies.'[36] His unappealing literary productions were more the fruit of a rigid theoretical programme than of poetic vision. They were the work of a cold and exceedingly unpleasant man whose cultured refinement contrasted notably with the anarchy of his family relationships. In Trissino's life, the savagery and the precious quasi-courtly refinement of Vicentine society met.

Trissino possessed one of the earliest recorded Vicentine museums, comprising medals, cameos and other unspecified *objets d'art*, and he was a passionate enthusiast for architecture. In his writings in general, he tried to fill what he regarded as the serious gap in contemporary literature and he aspired to do the same for the architectural treatise. In the preface to his fragmentary treatise, he declared that the art of architecture was in need of illumination. Vitruvius was now ill-understood or uninformative; he had only dealt superficially with facts that were then common knowledge but were now unknown, he had referred to buildings that had since disappeared and he had written primarily for professionals in the art. Alberti had written at excessive length and left serious gaps, while dealing with many superfluities. Trissino in fact went no further than a section on fortifications and the beginnings of a section on domestic architecture.[37] Whatever the arrogance of its tone, his treatise was significant for the realisation that Vitruvius could not be regarded as the comprehensive authority on antique architecture. It would seem that he intended to integrate the Vitruvian text into a broader picture of antique building practice rather than regarding him, in the manner of Corner, as a writer who was now of limited relevance. Various pieces of evidence suggest that his interest in Vitruvius was strong. In particular, the *Italia liberata* contains a description by Belisaurus's guardian-angel of an enchanted palace which while fantastic in places reads at some points like a poetic paraphrase of Vitruvius:

> *E quel cortile e circondato interno*
> *Di large logge, con colonne tonde*
> *Che son tant' alte, quanto è grosso la larghezza*
> *Del pavimento e sono grosse anchora*
> *L'ottava parte, e più di quella altezza*
> *Et han sovr'esse capitei d'argento*
> *Tant' alti quanto la colonna e grossa*
> *E sotto han spine di metal, che sono*
> *Per la metà del capitello in alto.*
> *Queste sustengon li epistili immensi*
> *Sopra cui si riposa il palco d'oro.*[38]

(The courtyard is surrounded by spacious arcades with round columns whose height is equal to the width of the pavement and whose thickness is rather more than an eighth part of their height. They bear silver capitals as high as the column is thick, and they rest upon metal bases whose height is half that of the capitals. These sustain the great architraves upon which the golden roof rests.)

The palace is built of gold, silver and diamonds, but its proportions are Vitruvian.

Certainly Trissino was interested in the form of the antique house. In his treatise, he reproduced a plan of one, prior to a description of his own project for a house in Vicenza. As it happened, Trissino's villa at Cricoli, probably a late fifteenth century work, like many Veneto villas of that period followed a form very similar to that of the Roman country house which may well have survived in the region from late antiquity: it consists of a central loggia of three bays, flanked by projecting tower-like structures. Trissino decided to remodel the central loggia, possibly intending to give a rather more antique form to the villa, which was to be the home of his academy and a meeting-place for men of letters. The project is reminiscent of Peruzzi's Villa Farnesina which Trissino might well have seen on his visits to Rome. It is generally believed that the design was by Trissino himself. The construction took place in the years 1530–8.

Around 1537 Trissino picked out one of the masons working on the building, Andrea di Pietro, and took him under his protection. He subsequently took the name of Belisaurus's guardian angel in the *Italia liberata*—Palladio. Andrea was then aged about 30 and probably well on the way to being a master builder of modest standing. He evidently joined the life of Trissino's academy and the latter took him to Rome, together with the painter Maganza, to study ancient remains at first hand. Palladio related in the preface to his own *Quattro libri dell' Achitettura* that Trissino had taught him the principles of military science. According to Palladio's early biographer Giuseppe Gualdus: 'when Trissino first noticed that Palladio was a very spirited young man with much inclination for mathematics, he decided, in order to encourage his abilities, to explain Vitruvius to him'. In view, however, of what we know about Trissino's attitude to Vitruvius, it would be dangerous to assume that he treated his work as the 'open sesame' to the world of erudite architectural study; Trissino's real gift to Palladio may well have been to have carried his architectural studies beyond Vitruvius. It was also probably due to Trissino, with his encyclopaedic interests, that Palladio was led to extend his interests outside the field of architecture and to become the most erudite and coherent writer among the architects of his age.

The bulk of Palladio's domestic buildings from 1538 to 1552 were in the Vicenza region and he continued to work there extensively up to the time of his settlement in Venice in 1570 although many of his ambitious projects for Vicentine patrons were never in fact executed. His Vicentine patrons were mostly of the nobility. In the *Quattro libri* Palladio specifically recorded the names of a number of them. His encounters with certain of his earlier patrons were probably in the first instance fortuitous; some of them lived in the same parish. When, in the years 1545–9, the projects for the re-building of the 'Basilica' (Palazzo della Ragione) were being discussed, a group of nobles gave strong backing to Palladio's designs. Several of these had already commissioned buildings from him and others were evidently inspired by Palladio's achievements with the Basilica to do so subsequently, most notably Gerolamo Chierigato, who was among the first supporters of Palladio's design and presided over the construction of the building and who, in 1551, commissioned the most outstanding of all Vicentine palaces from Andrea. Subsequently a number of Palladio's patrons held the posts of *Provveditori* for the Basilica and their villas and palaces were constructed precisely during their periods of office.[39]

In the 1550s and '60s, Palladio designed a number of villas for Venetian nobles, perhaps the most outstanding being the Villa Foscari, or 'La Malcontenta', at Gambara (1550–60), the Villa Barbaro at Maser (1555–9) and the Villa Cornaro at Piombino Dese (1560–5). Since it is often difficult to provide a precise identification of the Venetians who commissioned villas from Palladio, it is undesirable to attempt any general statement about the position within the aristocracy of his Venetian patrons. Those who commissioned the three villas mentioned above were, however, apparently drawn from the nobility of high office[40] and we are particularly well informed about Daniele and Marcantonio Barbaro, the masters of Maser.

The intellectual role of Daniele Barbaro Patriarch of Aquilea Elect and his architectural theories have already been examined in some detail. According to the critic Dolce, he was a good draughtsman and painter [41] and according to Ridolfi, writing a century later, he designed the palace of Camillo Trevisan at Murano;[42] it is possible that he also worked out the iconography of the frescoes executed by Veronese there, for, in engravings of these, motifs appear which were later repeated at Maser. Palladio had been with Barbaro in Rome in 1554 and had provided the drawings of ancient monuments in the latter's 1556 edition of Vitruvius, the first which truly utilised recent architectural research.[43] Daniele's brother the Procurator Marcantonio (1518–95) was one of the relatively few Venetian nobles who actually held a Paduan doctorate, but his life was devoted primarily to the service of the state, in which he followed an extremely distinguished career, chiefly of a diplomatic character. In a letter addressed to him in 1546, however, Pietro Aretino referred to his skill as a painter, engraver and stuccoist and in the art of perspective.[44] It is, indeed, possible that one or other of the Barbaro brothers executed certain stuccoes in the grotto at Maser.

At first sight, the Villa Maser is not a particularly lavish building. The relatively small central loggia and the arcaded *barchesse* flanking it form an extended line of fairly low buildings, the impression being of length rather than massiveness. Inside, however, the rooms are richly decorated with stuccoes and statues by Alessandro Vittoria and his assistants and with murals by Veronese. Daniele may have had particularly close links with Veronese and, at the least, he would presumably have had good knowledge of his works in the Palazzo Trevisan and in the rooms of the Council of Ten; he had allegedly provided the scheme for the decoration of the latter.[45] The Veronese cycle at Maser, with its picturesque landscapes, perspective balcony scenes, military trophies, allegories of the virtues and muses bearing the instrument of music and architecture—perhaps a reference to the intellectual interests of the Barbaro family—was the most ambitious he ever executed for a private patron. The nymphaeum in the garden with its fantastic yet delicate stuccoes is likewise of exquisite lavishness and the small church at Maser, perhaps Palladio's richest piece of ecclesiastical architecture, although not an outstandingly original piece of design, was built entirely at the expense of Marcantonio.

Palladio only accounted for a small proportion of the villas constructed in the Veneto in the sixteenth century. Together with Falconetto's works, a seminal role in the development of the villa had been played by Sansovino's Villa Garzoni at Pontecasale. There were a number of masters in the Vicenza region working in a style very difficult to distinguish from Palladio's.[46] A few projects were executed by Sanmichele, primarily in the Veronese region[47] and a large number either executed or projected in the Veneto as a whole by the Vicentine architect Vincenzo Scamozzi (1531–1616).[48] The latter two architects, together with Sansovino, also designed several palaces in Venice[49] which never, in fact, saw a piece of domestic architecture of Palladio's. Scamozzi in his *Idea dell' Architettura* of 1615, gave the names of a large number of patrons for whom he produced designs, but none of these appear to have been of particular note as connoisseurs or intellectuals.

In the country villa, the requirements of patrons made new demands upon architects. If the nobilities of Venice and the Terraferma in any way shared Alvise Corner's attitude towards the countryside, it was desirable that the villa should exploit its position in the landscape or be artistically integrated into it. To place an imposing block of masonry on top of an eminence, as was done with Falconetto's Villa dei Vescovi, Palladio's Rotonda and Scamozzi's rather similar edifice, the 'Rocca Pisani' (appropriately christened 'La Fortezza') at Lonigo, was only one solution. The Villa Maser exemplifies a very different approach. Here the long, relatively low line of buildings emerge from slightly sloping ground and is set against the line of the Prealps. In contrast to the hilltop villas, which challenge their natural surroundings, the Villa Barbaro almost seems to grow out of them. The relationship of farm buildings to the main loggia of a building also posed problems which were related in some measure to that of integrating a building into its surrounding landscape. Arcaded *barchesse* for storage purposes were an ingenious solution, but their placing in itself involved difficulties. A courtyard, with the *barchesse* at right-angles to the main loggia was the most obvious solution, but it was one that was seldom adopted. Only two sixteenth-century villas of major importance, the Villa della Torre at Fumane (Giulio Romano or Sanmicheli) and Palladio's rather similar Villa Sarego, both in the Verona region, were built on plans with a square or deep rectangular courtyard. For aesthetic reasons, a right-angled courtyard must either be square or at least have the façade of the main loggia forming the longer side of the rectangle, and this was only practicable where a large area of *barchesse* was not required. Furthermore, the setting of one of the main loggia façades in a deep courtyard meant that it was not open to the surrounding landscape. At Luvigliano, Falconetto adopted the ingenious device, admirable in a hill-top villa, of setting his *barchesse* in the great rusticated stone platform on which the main loggia rests. Palladio positively exploited long wings of arcade *barchesse*. In a number of projects, few of which were in fact executed, the arcades flanking the central loggia were to extend forwards at their extremities, like arms, as if embracing the terrain. This solution was given classic form with the Villa Badoer at Fratta Polesine where the colonnades are curved, giving an effect, in small-scale, rather similar to Bernini's Piazza S. Pietro. In certain other villas, notably the Villa Emo, Fanzolo and the Villa Barbaro, the *barchesse* form a straight line, foiling the temple-front of the main loggia; at Maser, the problem of their great length was resolved by placing 'punctuation-marks' at their extremities in the shape of decorative pavillions.

Architecture is a branch of the visual arts in which the amateur has traditionally been able to exercise a creative role. The Veneto evidently produced its minor Lord Burlingtons. Giangiorgio Trissino and Daniele Barbaro are both believed to have designed buildings and there is a tradition that the Patriarch Giovanni Grimani designed the palace at S. Maria Formosa, although it is likely that he received considerable help from professionals in this; on the other hand, suggestions that Alvise Corner collaborated with Falconetto are now treated with scepticism. The creative role of the amateur should not be overestimated, but he could exercise an important influence on the artist's development in the semi-erudite art of architecture. Alvise Corner may well have played a crucial part in encouraging Falconetto, hitherto a painter, to enter the field of architecture. The Cardinal Marino Grimani may well have played a similar role with regard to Giovanni da Udine (1487–1564), the Friulian architect par excellence; up to 1539, Giovanni had been chiefly known as a painter and stuccoist and it was when he came under Grimani patronage at this time that he began to develop as an architect. It is possible that Corner's theories helped to inspire Falconetto in the rationality and symmetry of his compositions, although the works that he commissioned from him—or at least those that have survived—were hardly 'houses for citizens' in the obvious sense of the term and did not exemplify Corner's preoccupations with economy. It was perhaps Palladio, through the intermediacy of Falconetto, who was the true heir to Corner's ideological heritage. It is uncertain how far Trissino influenced Palladio as an artist, although he certainly introduced him to antique remains. It is tempting to imagine that he conceived Andrea in a part similar to the one in which he cast himself, of filling a serious gap in contemporary culture by the revival of a lost art of antiquity, in this case domestic architecture. Certainly it is not unreasonable to suppose that it was in substantial measure due to Trissino that Palladio became a learned architect although perhaps not exactly the *erudito* of all-embracing culture that Daniele Barbaro demanded in his treatise on Vitruvius. Patrons would seem to have played a greater role in the development of architecture than any of the other visual arts.

The great patrons and currents of taste

Clear divisions of taste of the type that were to emerge in seventeenth-century Italy can hardly be seen in sixteenth-century Venice. This is particularly evident where collections are concerned. Connoisseurs, however, may purchase widely for their collections but show more narrowly defined orientations in their actual commissions. The latter phenomenon can be seen to a limited degree with certain sixteenth-century Venetian patrons. A division can be seen between those who primarily patronised Venetian artists and enthusiasts for central Italian traditions, although it should be said that artists reared in central Italian schools were liable to accommodate themselves to native traditions when they settled in Venice, Battista Franco being a notable case in point. It would be unwise to envisage the division in terms of contrasting traditions of colourism and plastic values, and the ambiguous term 'classicism' would be best avoided in this context. What taste for central Italian tradition seems to have implied more than anything was a liking for a particular kind of large-scale decorative scheme, grandiose yet elegant, precious even, with a certain chromatic lightness. With the Grimani of S. Maria Formosa, there was a certain rapport between such a predilection and the collection of large-scale antiques, but in general the passion for antique remnants seems to have implied no particular orientation of taste and indeed it was often allied to an extreme catholicity of taste. In examining currents of taste, it is also tempting to enquire what kind of patrons were particularly inclined towards Paolo Veronese, an artist who, it might be said, stood between the more strictly Venetian tradition represented by the heritage of Giorgione and the tradition of the school of Verona, less chromatically sonorous, with its strong debt to Giulio Romano. It might be expected that he would have appealed especially to patrons of the supremely elegant styles of Palladio and Vittoria. Certainly this can be seen with the Barbaro and artists of Paolo's circle often worked on Palladian villas.

In sixteenth-century Venice, two families particularly represented the Roman connection from the ecclesiastico-political point of view, the Corner of S. Polo and S. Maurizio and the Grimani of S. Maria Formosa. Both were immensely affluent families who manipulated the ecclesiastical beneficiary system to their own massive advantage. Admittedly, after the death of the Cardinal Marino Grimani in 1546, his family ceased to have an entrenched Roman base and his brother Giovanni the Patriarch of Aquilea was not highly regarded by the Papacy, but since he had to make intermittent visits to Rome in attempts to establish his religious orthodoxy, it can be said that he was quite well-acquainted with the city.

In the case of the Corner, contacts with the Roman Court do not appear to have affected their taste in the sixteenth century, although they undoubtedly played an important role in the Venetian patronage system by virtue of their commissions over a century and a half from the time of Queen Caterina. The family, it may be said, was not noted for its intellectual distinction, even in its numerous prelates. It was judicious in its patronage, but substantially confining itself to artists with an established Venetian clientèle and choosing the most prominent ones to hand: Giovanni Bellini, Sanmicheli, Sansovino, Palladio and Scamozzi. The employment of Vasari on the decorations of the newly re-modelled palazzo at S. Angelo was probably due primarily to the good offices on his behalf of the architect, Sanmicheli, rather than to any consciousness on the part of the Corner of artistic developments elsewhere in Italy. In the important collection of pictures which the S.

Maurizio branch possessed in the mid-seventeenth century, works by Venetian painters bulked large; there were some works by non-Venetian painters but these were only evidence of offices held by members of the family outside the Republic and contacts with the Roman Court and were not necessarily suggestive of taste open to new currents.[50, 51]

The Grimani, by contrast, were the main propagators of central Italian artistic taste in the mid-sixteenth century. The brothers Marino (1488–1546), Vettore (d. 1558) and Giovanni (1506–94) extensively employed or favoured central Italian artists with Roman training such as Jacopo Sansovino, Francesco de' Rossi (called 'Il Salviati'), Giuseppe della Porta and Federico Zuccari, or Veneto artists who were Roman-trained, such as Giovanni Ricamatori da Udine, Sanmicheli, G. B. Ponchino and Battista Franco; of the home-grown artists to whom they gave commissions, Pordenone developed strong inclinations towards the Roman manner and Tiziano Aspetti represented in some measure, a continuation of the Sansovino tradition. In the cases of Sansovino, Francesco de' Rossi, Giovanni da Udine, Ponchino and Battista Franco, the artists were employed in the early stages of their settlement or re-settlement in Venetian territory.[52] The Grimani commissions were mainly executed in the family palace of S. Maria Formosa and in the family tomb at S. Francesco della Vigna, a number of projects also being planned in the bishoprics held by members of the family.

Marino Grimani, whose antique collections have already been referred to, became a cardinal in 1538 and was a frequent visitor to Rome. He was responsible for bringing Rossi, together with his pupil Giuseppe della Porta and probably also Giovanni da Udine, from Rome to Venice in 1529. Rossi and Giovanni da Udine, together with Battista Franco and others were employed on the decoration of the palace of S. Maria Formosa primarily, it would seem, at the behest of Giovanni Grimani. The paintings of mythological subjects and the stuccoes, with their exploitation of white and gold, were works of a precious refinement. The paintings were described by Vasari, at a time when he was not particularly sensitive to the achievements of the Venetian school, as 'the finest work of painting in Venice'. The Cardinal Marino evidently had a particular predilection for Giovanni da Udine and, as has been suggested, may well have encouraged him to engage in architecture. For the Cardinal, Giovanni designed projects, never in fact executed, for a chapel in Marino's cathedral church at Aquilea and for the choir of the collegiate church at Udine (in practice the seat of the patriarchate of Aquilea). Marino was also Bishop of Ceneda and as such exercised temporal jurisdiction over the town and district. Marino is said to have commissioned Pordenone to paint the Loggia della Ragione there, although the frescoes are usually attributed to the painter's son-in-law, Pompeo Amalteo. According to Vasari, when Sansovino was passing through Venice in 1529, 'Cardinal Domenico Grimani told Doge Gritti that he was just the man to repair the cupola of St Mark's. This must, in fact, have been Marino, for Domenico had died in 1523. Sansovino had, however, established contact with Domenico in Rome in the first decade of the century. Subsequently Marino's brother Vettore revealed himself as a great admirer and promoter of Sansovino, being responsible for the erection of the campanile-loggia in the Piazza S. Marco. Sansovino designed the Grimani chapel in S. Francesco della Vigna, commissioned by Giovanni, then Patriarch of Aquilea. All the artists who were successively employed on it had at least a second-hand training in central Italian traditions. It was decorated by Battista Franco, who had already executed lunettes in the palace at S. Maria Formosa, and after him Federico Zuccari, the final statues being entrusted to the younger Tiziano Aspetti. There is also a tradition that Giovanni Grimani commissioned the notable façade of the Vigna church from Palladio.[53]

If this was, in fact, the case, Giovanni Grimani's patronage overlapped in some measure with that of his coadjutor Daniele Barbaro who was probably also his kinsman; Barbaro was a major patron of Palladio and his mortuary chapel, close to that of the Grimani in S. Francesco della Vigna, was likewise decorated by Battista Franco. In contrast to the Grimani however, the Barbaro brothers mainly patronised artists with strong roots in the Veneto. The preferences of the Barbaro were evidently for the more refined and intellectual strains in Venetian artistic tradition. The lightness and rationality of the internal decoration at Maser contrasts notably with, say, the exuberance and heavy opulence of much of the decoration in the Ducal Palace. Vittoria's stuccoes, with their archaising neoclassicism, exploitation of delicate light and shade effects and occasional bursts of fancy were natural companions to Palladio's architecture The same can be said of Veronese's Maser frescoes, with their restrained colour and crispness.

Daniele Barbaro's protégé, Giacomo Contarini, likewise showed a marked allegiance to Venetian tradition, but in its broader aspects. In addition to his close links with Palladio, he commissioned works from or gave support to Veronese, Jacopo and Francesco Bassano and probably

Palma Giovane, being also allegedly associated with Tintoretto; he was the special protector of Francesco Bassano, who appears to have received little in the way of important commissions from Venetian nobles. Contarini's patronage of the Bassani suggests a taste for the *tenebroso* manner which it is difficult to detect in any other major Venetian patron of the sixteenth century. His links with Francesco Bassano on the one hand and Veronese and Palladio on the other was perhaps indicative of a catholic taste unusual at the time.

How far can particular orientations of taste be seen among patrons more generally? Here it may be asked, while bearing in mind the factor of established working-partnerships, how far particular groups of architects, painters and stuccoists were to be found working together on private commissions? In the adornment of Palladio's villas, a remarkably clear pattern emerges. As might be expected, Vittoria, or artists working in a similar style such as Ottaviano Ridolfi, were normally chosen as stuccoists; by contrast Cristoforo Sorte, whose heavy, quasi-baroque scroll-work was more obviously attuned to the pompous official style of the Ducal Palace, does not seem to have been employed at all. Sculptures were frequently by members of Vittoria's school. Murals in the new type of villa tended to be executed by artists who either had Roman training or who showed allegiances to the tradition of Giulio Romano or who were associated with Paolo Veronese; the most notable examples were perhaps Battista Franco, Battista Zelotti, Antonio Fasolo, and Giovan Battista Maganza. One factor, of course, was the distinct preference for frescoes in villa-decoration and here it was artists of the Veronese school or ones with Roman training who had most to offer. Also the personal preferences of the artists themselves must certainly have operated not least in Palladio's working partnerships with Maganza, a fellow-member of the Olympica, and Franco, whom he described as 'the greatest painter of our time'. The Palladio-Vittoria- Ridolfi- Veronese- Zelotti- Fasolo combination was undoubtedly, however, a remarkably harmonious one from the stylistic point of view. Grimani patronage apart, the pattern of private decorative commissions in Venice itself does not present the same clear lines as in the country villa.

A number of artists had their own special patrons and promoters, Alvise Corner for Falconetto, Trissino and the Barbaro for Palladio, Daniele Barbaro again, in some measure, for Veronese, the Grimani for Giovanni da Udine, Ponchino and Sansovino, Giacomo Contarini for Francesco Bassano. Titian, although he had an energetic promoter

in Aretino and had a circle of Venetian friends, some of whom purchased his work, cannot be said to have had any particular Venetian
patron. Vasari lists five doges among his friends. Vasari's assertions
should probably be treated with a certain amount of scepticism, however, and, Andrea Gritti apart, all that can be definitely said is that
Titian painted portraits of most of the doges mentioned. Andrea Gritti,
who was referred to by Vasari, admittedly prone to exaggeration, as 'a
patron of genius' and as a patron of Sansovino, did, according to the
Florentine writer's account, help Titian to obtain state commissions in
addition to commissioning works from him on a private basis. Titian
was, however, a figure of European stature whose works were readily
accepted, if not always paid for, by monarchs. He might need a public
relations man like Aretino, but he did not require special patrons in
Venice and he was probably too expensive for the individual Venetian
to acquire many of his works. Tintoretto again does not appear to have
had a major Venetian patron although he evidently had a group of
partisans—and enemies—among the *cittadini* of the *scuole grandi*. As we
shall see in the forthcoming section, a number of major private patrons
and connoisseurs helped artists to obtain state commissions or played a
role in state patronage.

State patronage

A large number of magistracies were in fact responsible for building
projects. It was, however, the *Procuratori di S. Marco de Supra*, the
Council of Ten, the *Provveditori sopra la fabrica del Palazzo* and the
Senate, together with certain *ad hoc* commissions, who initiated the
most ambitious building projects and decorative schemes. The office of
Procuratore, together with the grade of the *Cavaleriato*, was the highest
honour open to Venetian nobles. It was either awarded to statesmen
who had reached the summit of the *cursus honorum* or sold, naturally at
a price which only the most affluent could afford. Since the *Procurazia*
tended to be the province of the richest families, by the law of averages
it not infrequently happened that the post was held by nobles who were
major connoisseurs or patrons of the arts in their own right. The Procurators of St Mark's were, in their origins, the wardens of the Ducal
Chapel. In our period, however, the *Procurazia* was divided into three
branches, *de sopra*, *de citra* and *de ultra*; the latter two were concerned

with the execution of testaments, and it was the *Procurazia de Supra* that dealt with the Basilica. It was also responsible for the main buildings in the Piazza, the offices of the *Procurazia*, the public library and the Campanile. Its activities with respect to music in the Ducal Chapel will be examined in another chapter. The initial decisions that certain portions of the Ducal Palace were to be developed or adorned were normally taken by the Council of Ten, and it was the latter that authorised payments to artists for work executed in the Palace. In the sixteenth century it also granted pensions to artists in the shape of a *sansaria* or broker's patent of the Fondaco dei Tedeschi.[54] Direct control over work on the Palace was exercised by the *Provveditori alla fabbrica*, of which there was a regular series from 1533. They appear to have acted in some measure as a committee ancillary to the Council of Ten, but they were elected by the Senate and could be chosen from the membership of the Great Council at large. The *Protho* (*protomaestro*), or superintendent of public works, was elected by the Senate. Actual payment for the costs of the Ducal Palace and many other buildings was made by the *Magistrato al Sal* which superintended the state salt-monopoly. It evidently exercised this function simply because it was an administrative organ with funds to dispose of and there is no reason for thinking that its officers, as such, played any role in commissions, although individual ones might also be among the *Provveditori alla fabrica*. The Senate played a distinguished role in state patronage through projects for the votive churches of the Redentore and the Salute. Among the many organs responsible for building projects, two magistracies deserve particular mention: the *Provveditori* who supervised the building of the Rialto bridge and the *Provveditori alle fortezze*. A number of fortifications in the region of the Lagoon, as well as town gates in provincial cities, for which the local *rettori* were responsible, were works of considerable architectural merit, especially those designed by Sanmichele.

As has been seen, the Serenissima had its own official architect, the *Protho*. This did not prevent other architects being employed for designs as well as the execution of projects in the Palazzo, while the *Protho* himself might work on outside commissions. An artist who held one of the *sansarie* of the Fondaco dei Tedeschi enjoyed a quasi-official status as painter of the Serenissima. The post had been granted to Gentile and Giovanni Bellini respectively in 1474 and 1479. Titian was given the expectation of it in 1513 and finally obtained it in 1516. The office was again granted to Tintoretto in 1574.[55] Titian and Tintoretto obtained it, on their own petition, by offering to execute certain large-scale projects in the Palace. Its tenure also involved painting a portrait and votive picture of each new Doge. Much of the Bellini's work for the state was on restoration of paintings, while Titian persistently failed to fulfil the obligations incurred when he took the *sansaria* and accounted for relatively little work on state projects although, like the *Protho* Sansovino, he did give advice on the employment of other artists. Tintoretto was the first artist-incumbent of the *sansaria* to execute truly extensive state projects.

Reconstruction of portions of the Ducal Palace in the Renaissance style commenced after the fire of 1483. The east façade overlooking the canal by the Bridge of Sighs and the east face of the main courtyard were constructed by the *Protho* Antonio Rizzo, the decoration of the courtyard being continued by Pietro Lombardo, who succeeded as *Protho* in 1498.[56] Rizzo's flat façades and Lombardo's decorations are deficient in plastic values and are generally uninspiring, but they were among the first harbingers of the Renaissance architectural style in Venice. On account of the fires of 1574 and 1577, little of the internal decoration of the Palace prior to the 1570s survives. Among the works destroyed were paintings by Carpaccio, Giovanni and Gentile Bellini, Titian, Pordenone, Veronese, and Tintoretto. Of particular importance were the *Submission of Frederick Barbarossa to Pope Alexander III in Venice*, begun by Giovanni Bellini and finished by Titian, and Titian's battle-scene, usually known as the *Battle of Cadore*, both in the Maggior Consiglio.[57] It was Titian's offer to paint the latter picture that had gained him the *sansaria* in 1513, but he only completed it in 1538 after his dilatoriness had lead to suspension of salary.[58] It was the first painting of its kind to appear in Venice and the evidence from engravings indicates that it marked an important stage in the evolution of the battle-scene genre.

Work on the *Procurazie vecchie* on the north side of the Piazza was begun in the 1490s; they had been carried by Coducci up to the first floor in 1500, the work being continued by the *Protho* Bartolomeo Bon after a great fire in 1512. The lower end was completed by Sansovino in 1532.[59]

According to Vasari's account, Sansovino, when passing through Venice after the Sack of Rome of 1527, was sent for by Doge Andrea Gritti, the latter having been informed by Cardinal Grimani that the Florentine architect was just the man to repair the cupola of St Mark's. He was commissioned to do the work, and its excellence induced the Senate to appoint him *Protho* in 1529.[60] In 1537, he was commissioned

by the Great Council to rebuild the *Zecca* or Mint and this was completed in 1545. This edifice now houses the Marciana Library, the
present main reading-room being in the original courtyard. It is hidden
from the Piazza by the extension to the colonnade of the original Public
Library, a quite different project of Sansovino's, but one façade is
visible from the water-front.[61] This austere, imposing building, with
its strongly defined, semi-rusticated stone blocks, is reminiscent in its
spirit, although not precisely its architectural detail, more of the
fifteenth-century Florentine fortress-palace than of the early sixteenth-
century Roman palace, which in some respects provided the point of
departure for Sansovino's library project.

In addition to being *Protho* of the Ducal Palace, Sansovino also became *Protho* of the Procurators. According to Vasari, 'the Procurators
did nothing without his help or advice and were always employing him
for their friends and relations as well as for themselves'. Vasari mentioned among his special admirers Vettore Grimani and Giovanni da
Legge,[62] who were both *Procuratori di sopra*. Vettore was the brother of
the Patriarchs of Aquilea Marino and Giovanni and the promotion of
central Italian artistic currents by the Grimani brothers has already
been noted. In 1537, under the aegis of the *Procuratori di sopra*, Sansovino undertook the projects of the public library and the *loggietta* of the
campanile. According to the Guisconi guide of 1563 (probably by
Jacopo Sansovino's son Francesco), the Loggia was 'proposed by the
Clarissimo M. Antonio Capello, Procurator, who took great pleasure in
adorning the city'. Guisconi adds that 'this building was the special care
of the Clarissimo Vettore Grimani, Proc.'.[63] When in 1557 the Senate
and Collegio took over responsibility for the façade of the Church of
S. Geminian on the Piazza, it was Grimani and Capello who judged
Sansovino's project.[64] In December 1545, the vault of the library had
collapsed and Sansovino was thrown into prison. It was, allegedly, the
good offices of the Imperial ambassador, solicited by Titian and Aretino
that obtained his release. There is no information as to the role played
by his noble protectors in all this, but the Procurators were disposed to
be accommodating. In order to regain his post as *Protho*, Sansovino was
obliged to replace the vault at his own expense, the cost being reckoned
at between 800 and 1,000 ducats. It so happened that Sansovino, without
a prior contract, had made four bronze figures for the loggia of the
Campanile and certain tableaux for the tribune of St Mark's, and he
agreed to allow the Procurators to pay him for them according to their
discretion. The Procurators Michiel Antonio Capello, Giovanni da

7 Jacopo Tintoretto, *Presentation of the Virgin*, church of S. Maria dell 'Horto,
Venice, 1556 (see p. 240)

18 Jacopo Tintoretto, *Transportation of the Body of St Mark*, originally in the
Scuola di S. Marco, 1562+

Legge, Vettore Grimani and two others, in the absence of their remaining colleagues, voted him 900 ducats.[65]

In the years 1553–6, an ambitious programme of decorations was undertaken in the rooms of the Council of Ten.[66] The commission for the Hall was initially entrusted to Ponchino who, in the event, worked alongside Zelotti and Veronese. According to Vasari, Ponchino, who was a 'dependant' of the Grimani, received the commission 'through favour',[67] presumably that of his aforementioned patrons. Vettore Grimani had in fact been one of the *Provveditori alla Fabrica* in the years 1550–3.[68] According to Stringa (1604), the allegories were the *invenzione* of Daniele Barbaro,[69] that is to say he worked out the subject matter and probably the iconography as well. The *Sala dei Capi del Consiglio dei Dieci* and the Sala della Bussola were decorated by Veronese and Zelotti.

In the 1550s another ambitious scheme of decorations was undertaken under the auspices of the *Procuratori di Sopra* in the Sansovino Library and the *Procurazie Vecchie*. Between 1556 and 1557, payments were made to Giuseppe della Porta ('Il Salviati'), Paolo Veronese, Battista Zelotti, Giovanni da Mio, Giulio Licinio, Battista Franco and Andrea Schiavone for the magnificent series of roundels in the ceiling of the Library hall, the golden chain offered as a prize for the best work being given to Veronese.[70] As we have seen, della Porta and Franco were Grimani protégés, and the Procurator Vettore Grimani was still alive at the time. The artists were allegedly selected, however, by Titian and Sansovino. At first sight the list of artists might seem to suggest a balance between native Veneto traditions, as represented especially by Veronese, Zelotti and Giulio Licinio and the central Italian tradition as represented by della Porto and Franco, and it might be thought that this corresponded to the respective inclinations of Titian and Sansovino. It is doubtful, however, whether the two friends would have regarded themselves as representing different artistic traditions. Besides, Titian, who could not tolerate rivals, was probably ill-disposed to favour artists in a style which could be conceived of as similar to his own. It is likely that on this, as on other occasions, he kept a commission out of Tintoretto's hands[71] and it was only around 1571–2 that the latter executed the series of philosophers on the walls of the Hall. Veronese, on the other hand, was probably too dissimilar an artist to arouse Titian's antipathy in the same way. If Titian now gave a hand to younger Venetian artists, it was probably because he now felt that he could afford to do so after the death of his great rival Pordenone. In the

G

event, the ceiling of the Library can in no way be seen as a battleground
of schools—Franco in particular had moved towards a more 'Venetian'
style by this time—and the great cycle forms a remarkable harmonious
whole. The Procurators obviously relied extensively upon the judgement of Titian and Sansovino. They were, it is believed, the judges of
the competition for the golden chain. The 1559 contract of the Procurators with Cristoforo Rossi of Brescia for the architectural perspective scenes on the ceiling of the Library vestibule stated that Titian
and Sansovino were to estimate the value of the work.[72] Titian's active
role in the project was confined to the 'Truth' on the vestibule ceiling.
The great staircase of the Library possessed in its decoration the classic
combination, seen in a number of Venetian villas, of stuccoes by
Vittoria and paintings by Battista Franco. The former had executed the
gigantic caryatides on the doorway of the Library in the colonnade and
also executed the stuccoes in the great Hall (contract 1560).[73] The group
of painters who decorated the great Hall, with the addition of Tintoretto, were also being paid for decorations in the *Procurazie Vecchie* in
the years 1555–6.[74]

   In July 1574, Henry III of France stayed in Venice for a few days. A
series of magnificent public festivities was put on and a number of
temporary buildings were erected, most notably a triumphal arch by
Palladio on the Lido, the form of which was later substantially followed
in the portal of the Sala del Scrutinio in the Ducal Palace. The three
patricians deputed to organise the festivities were Federigo Contarini,
Giacomo Contarini and Leonardo Emo. The record of the two Contarini's as connoisseurs has already been examined; the Leonardo Emo
in question is presumably identifiable with the patrician who had
commissioned the Villa Emo at Fanzolo, built in the late 1550s on
designs by Palladio and decorated by Veronese and Zelotti. Thus when
Palladio designed the triumphal arch he was, with Emo and Giacomo
Contarini, working under the aegis of two *deputati* who were also his
patrons.

   In May 1574, two months before Henry III's visit, a fire had destroyed
the halls of the Collegio and the Senate in the Ducal Palace. The fire of
December 1577 destroyed the upper floors facing the Piazza and the
waterfront, including the hall of the Maggior Consiglio. These disasters came at a time when the victory of Lepanto had given rise to a
wave of patriotic sentiment. This perhaps revealed itself in the literary
field in the shape of renewed interest in the Venetian past. It was to be
expected that ambitious mural decorations would be in demand, cele-

brating both Lepanto and Venice's other great victories. The climate of opinion was perhaps also favourable to allegories celebrating the justice and power of the Venetian state.

Of the three new *Provveditori alla Fabrica* appointed after the 1574 fire, none was apparently of any note as a promoter of the arts, but in 1575 one of their number was replaced by Marcantonio Barbaro, the master of Maser.[75] There is no direct evidence that he was responsible for Veronese's employment on the massive project of the ceiling and tribune in the *Sala del Collegio* or for the fact that the constructions and ornament of the *Sala del Collegio* and the *Antepregadi* (Room of the Four Doors) was in the Palladian style. It is significant, however, that the Veronese cycle was the artist's most ambitious project to date in the Ducal Palace and that this was the first occasion on which decorations in the Palladian style appeared there. The *Sala del Collegio* and *Antepregadi* were in fact constructed by the *Protho* Antonio da Ponte, apparently on the designs of Palladio and Rusconi.[76] It was also at this time that Tintoretto received his first large-scale commission in the Ducal Palace; in September 1574, he had been given the expectation of a *sansaria* of the Fondaco dei Tedeschi. Probably much of the work in the aforementioned rooms and halls was executed after the 1577 fire, and this was certainly the case with the extensive decorations of the *Sala del Senato* by Tintoretto and others.

In February 1578, four new *Provveditori* were elected.[77] Again, none of these appears to have been of any note as a patron of the arts. At some stage, however, a commission was formed to advise on the decorations of the Maggior Consiglio and *Sala del Scrutinio*. According to Ridolfi, the Senate appointed the Procurator Giacomo Soranzo, Francesco Bernardo, Giacomo Marcello and the Procurator Giacomo Contarini.[78] There is no confirmation of this from known documentary sources. Out of the group mentioned, only the names of Contarini and Marcello are attached to the memorandum on the decorative scheme later presented. Bernardo and Soranzo were, however, elected *Provveditori alla Fabrica* in February 1579. Contarini was the great scholar and collector. He may have recently gained some architectural experience as *Provveditore alle Fortezze* and he was subsequently elected *Provveditore alla Fabrica* in 1582 and 1584. Bernardo was also to possess an important antique collection; according to his testament of 1589, he had been building this up for over twelve years and it included antique sculptures and Greek and Roman medals, although he made no mention of paintings.[79] Marcello owned a major library.[80] Soranzo was a fairly important political figure. There is no evidence that he had notable artistic or erudite interests, but he was made *Provveditore alla Fabrica* with unusual frequency.

A programme for the decoration of the Maggior Consiglio and Scrutinio and for the statues on the four doors of the *Antepregadi* was presented by Contarini and Marcello, assisted by the Camaldolese monk Gerolamo Bardi, to whose authorship the memorandum is sometimes ascribed. He was described in the document as a 'celebrated historian' and it was he who wrote the appendix on the history cycles in the Maggior Consiglio attached to the Guisconi guide-book in the 1592 and subsequent editions. Francesco Sansovino, the architect Jacopo's son, is also believed to have been associated with the project; he was a learned but not particularly brilliant *erudito*, with interests in history and antiquities, and a compiler of guide-books. The memorandum referred merely to the subject-matter and symbolism of the proposed decorative cycles. For the walls of the Scrutinio and Maggior Consiglio, historical subjects were indicated: for the Scrutinio, scenes of naval battles; for the Maggior Consiglio, episodes of the Fourth Crusade and other wars and the history of Venice's mediation between Pope Alexander III and the Emperor Barbarossa in the years 1176–7. Thus the themes, which in some measure followed the examples set by the lost works of Bellini and Titian, were to be Venice's military glories and her record as defender of the Church. In the lengthy descriptions of the proposed scenes, the memorandum was essentially devoted to explaining the historical circumstances of each occasion; the painters would have learned little more than what standards and emblems to depict. For the ceiling of the Scrutinio, allegories of religion and the virtues were indicated, and for that of the Maggior Consiglio, apotheoses of Venice. Here the artists had very detailed regulations to follow. With regard to the apotheoses, it was specified how the allegorical figure of Venice was to be adorned and how she was to be seated, whether on spoils of war, thrones and sceptres or the rudder of a ship. In some pictures views of Venice and the symbolic lion were to be introduced. It was specified what the ancillary figures were to be, whether nymphs, chained slaves, personifications of the subject provinces, or personifications of victory, peace and abundance. The iconography of the figures of religion and the virtues in the Scrutinio was described in great detail, the insignia and dress of each being prescribed. By contrast, nothing was laid down regarding the iconography of the *Paradise* over the tribune of the Maggior Consiglio: various *invenzioni* were to be made and the best chosen.[81] The *deputati* may have been reluctant to restrict the freedom of artists in what would be the major painting of the hall and, besides, religious iconography was probably not the *forte* of either Contarini or Bardi. Where iconography was prescribed in the greatest detail of all was with regard to the figures over the four doors in the *Antepregadi*. It must have been realised at the time that these figures would be, as they are now, relatively small and unobtrusive. The author of this section of the memorandum was obviously anxious that the figure of Justice, Authority, Fidelity, Secrecy and Diligence should be, as far as was appropriate, in accordance with the norms of iconography and symbolism found in antique sculpture; frequent references are made to antique sculptures of the deities and allegories of virtues and skills.[82]

Why were Contarini, Marcello and Bardi chosen to devise the scheme? Probably their erudition was a major consideration. Contarini as a collector of chronicles would doubtless have been well-versed in Venetian history. As a collector of antique sculptures, medals and cameos he could well have had authoritative knowledge of antique iconography and symbolism. It was clearly indicated that Bardi was valued as a historian[83] and it is probable that Sansovino was taken on as the author of works on universal history rather than as the son of the great architect. Of Marcello's erudite interests we know nothing. It is doubtful whether Contarini's reputation as a connoisseur of painting was a substantial consideration in his selection as *deputato*. If, however, the intention had indeed been to appoint an antiquarian with first-hand knowledge of ancient sculpture and craft-work, there was an appreciable chance that such a person would be a connoisseur of modern paintings, given the patterns of the collecting enthusiasm in late sixteenth-century Venice. In the event, it was one of the most outstanding Venetian connoisseurs of the age that was brought in on the project. He evidently made good use of his position. According to Ridolfi, when Veronese failed to put himself forward for the new commissions in the Palace, Contarini persuaded him to do so. Again, according to Ridolfi, when Tintoretto and Veronese were unable to cope with all the work, Contarini's favour was used to obtain commissions for his special protégé Francesco Bassano.[84] As has already been indicated, Contarini's taste was probably unusually catholic.

The decoration of the Maggior Consiglio, executed between 1578 and 1585 was entrusted to Jacopo Tintoretto, Paolo Veronese, Palma Giovane, Francesco Bassano and Andrea Vicentino, the dominant works being undoubtedly the three apotheoses on the ceiling by Veronese, Tintoretto and Palma and Tintoretto's *Paradise* over the tribune. For the *Paradise*, projects had been requested from Veronese and Francesco Bassano, and it was decided that the two artists should work together. The enterprise collapsed, however, with the sudden death of Veronese in 1588, and the work was executed by Jacopo Tintoretto, assisted by his son Domenico and Palma among others.[85] A co-operative effort was obviously essential for such a large picture-space, but it meant that the mural did not fulfil the promise of Tinto-retto's sketch for the project (now in the Louvre). The discordances produced by the work of different hands are perhaps less, however, than would have been the case with the original Veronese–Bassano project. The proposal for a co-operative effort by these two artists seems an astonishing one. It can possibly be explained by pressures brought by Giacomo Contarini on behalf of his protégés. If so, it can be ques-tioned whether Contarini's catholic taste was altogether beneficial. By comparison with the *Libreria*, admittedly a smaller project, the decora-tion of the Maggior Consiglio, with its medley of styles, lacks unity; in particular, the juxtaposition of the Tintoretto and Veronese apotheoses on the ceiling is unfortunate. At the same time it cannot be said that a unified effect is altogether achieved in the *Sala del Scrutinio*, where the work was basically entrusted to pupils of Veronese.[86] The iconographi-cal detail of the figures on the doors of the *Antepregadi* is not easily observable. It was fitting, however, that the work should be entrusted to Alessandro Vittoria and his pupils, for Vittoria among Venetian sculptors perhaps best reflected the contemporary current of erudite antiquarianism.

Titian, who had allegedly endeavoured to keep commissions from Tintoretto, had died in 1576. Another potential rival had been removed with Veronese's death in 1588. Between the late seventies and the late eighties, Tintoretto and his pupils emerged as the dominant team in the decoration of the Ducal Palace, occupying a position that had been in some measure held by the Veronese *studio* rather earlier. The four mythological pictures by Jacopo in the anteroom between Collegio and Ducal Chancery (*Vulcan's Workshop*, *Mercury and the Graces*, *Pallas and Mars* and *Bacchus and Ariadne*, all now in the Antecollegio) were completed in 1579.[87] The ceilings in the Senate were decorated by Tintoretto and his pupils, probably immediately after the completion of the stuccoes in 1587, and the paintings on the walls were executed by the Tintoretto studio and Palma Giovane between 1585 and 1595.[88] While the four allegories were among Tintoretto's *chefs d'oeuvre*, the decorations in the Senate have all the qualities of studio work.

In the years 1575–6, Venice was ravaged by plague and on 8 September 1576, the Doge made a vow on behalf of the Serenissima to construct a church in commemoration of the city's deliverance from the epidemic. It was into the hands of the Senate that the affair passed in the first instance. After some debate, the latter decided to build a church for the Capuchins, The Capuchins were a rigorist off-shoot of the Franciscan order, vowed to total poverty, particularly noted for their pastoral and charitable work among the lower classes. Hitherto the Venetian members of the order had lived under very austere conditions and they were apparently somewhat embarrassed by the offer of a fine new church. It was evident that it would have to be decent but in no way ostentatious. The decision of the Senate of 4 September 1577 stated that the 'temple' should be built 'without ornamentation (*non facendo nella fabrica sudetta lavori*) nor with marbles, but making a sober building, such as is appropriate to a church destined for devotion'. Some Senators, principally the great Marcantonio Barbaro, wanted a round church in imitation of antique votive temples, for 'the buildings decreed by the munificent Senate should be magnificent and show forth the dignity of the Republic'. Barbaro perhaps had in mind something rather similar to his own *tempietto* at Maser which was to be built in the years 1579–80. This, however, was obviously not quite what was required under the circumstances. The majority of Senators preferred a longitudinal church. It was decided that alternative models for round and longitudinal churches should be submitted in the first instance. The shape of the original models may be preserved in the medals cast to celebrate the foundation of the Redentore. One shows a façade similar to that of the present church, the second a casket-shaped building rather similar to the Miracoli, and the third a domed octagonal building, rather on the lines of the traditional 'Jerusalem Temple'. The longitudinal form was chosen by the Senate and the project was submitted for approval to the Collegio, which exercised tutelage over the Venetian Church. It was indicated that the expense should not exceed 12,000 ducats, a modest sum. (The dowry of a high-ranking noble's daughter at that time would have been between 20,000 and 30,000 ducats.) The *Protho* Da Ponte, Ruscone, Scamozzi and Palladio were asked to submit designs and that of Palladio was chosen. Palladio had already revealed his capacities as an ecclesiastical architect with S. Giorgio Maggiore and the façade of S. Francesco della Vigna. Together with the *tempietto* at Maser, the church of the Redentore was his last work and, unlike many of his later works, it was one whose construction he substantially supervised. The building, which cost very much more than the originally estimated 12,000 ducats, was austere only by comparison with S. Giorgio Maggiore. The plain brick shell was fronted by an imposing stone façade of a modified temple-form and, inside, the barrel vault was borne on a classical arcade of considerable elegance. Attempts were made to reduce the expense of the internal decoration. Palladio's project for sculptural decoration was abandoned and instead a project by one of the Capuchin fathers, the former painter Paolo Piazza, was adopted of chiaroscuro decorations in the niches designed for status. Nevertheless, the *tempio* acquired a relatively fine collection of paintings in due course.[89]

In 1582, the *Procuratori di Sopra* accepted Scamozzi' splan, out of several others, for the new offices of the *Procurazia* on the south side of the Piazza. The design substantially represented a continuation of the scheme of the Sansovino Library. One of the Procurators involved in the decision was Marcantonio Barbaro. He was probably regarded by his colleagues as having competence in the oversight of building-work, for in 1586 he tied with Giacomo Foscarini, a former *Provveditore alla Fabrica del Palazzo*, when the Procurators tried to elect a *deputato* from among their number to supervise the project. It appears, however, to have been the great antiquarian Federigo Contarini who played the most active role in the erection of the *Procurazie Nuove*. His recorded interventions in discussion, like those of Barbaro, were substantially concerned with technicalities of construction. In fact, this great Maecenas, when faced with the possibility that construction would be delayed by difficulties in obtaining Istrian stone, not only indicated that stonework could be reduced on the façade which did not face the Piazza but also suggested that the courtyards could do without pillars, which he described as 'adornments for theatres rather than houses'.[90] It was not, however, a judgement from which the great Alvise Corner would have dissented.

The major piece of state patronage in the early seventeenth century was undoubtedly the building of the Salute. In October 1630, Doge Nicolò Contarini vowed that the state would erect a new votive church in thanksgiving for the city's recent deliverance from the plague. As in the case of the Redentore, the arrangements were entrusted to the Senate. Out of the eleven models presented, the one chosen was that of Baldassare Longhena, then aged only 26. The building, which was only completed in 1686, occupied most of his lifetime and was undoubtedly his *chef d'oeuvre*. As in the case of the alternative project for a votive church submitted in 1576, the Salute was a domed octagonal church.

The new temple, with its lavish opulence was however a very different affair from the 'sober building' presented to the barefoot Capuchin friars. The Redentore was constructed at the highwater-mark of the Catholic reform movement, the Salute in a less severe age when the Papacy itself had jettisoned the ascetic outlook of the earlier period and had embarked on a policy of artistic patronage of almost unprecedented extravagance. It was perhaps ironical that the puritanical Nicolò Contarini should have made the vow to erect the Salute. The Salute, however, like Monteverdi's Mass of 1631, was an exuberant act of thanksgiving for deliverance. It was a monument to state munifi-cence, perhaps deliberately intended to rival the artistic projects of the contemporary Roman Court. As the slow process of its erection per-haps testified, it was an act to munificence which the Venetian govern-ment could ill-afford. The tragedy which had been the occasion of Contarini's vow, the devastating plague of 1630, was perhaps the main trigger of Venice's economic difficulties in the ensuing decades. In these years, while private patronage continued to be lavish, the prudent Serenissima must restrict the scope of its commissions.

The Church

Although a number of Venetian bishops were major patrons of the arts in their own right, the role of such men in ecclesiastical patronage of the arts properly speaking was negligible. This was true even in the case of Marino Grimani, since his projects for work at Aquilea and Udine were never in fact executed. In general, it cannot be said that the many Venetians who held sees in the dominions of the Serenissima played a particularly distinguished role in church patronage of the arts. In the latter half of the sixteenth century and early decades of the seventeenth, new cathedrals were built in Venice, Padua and Brescia. Notwith-standing a certain element of pomposity and floridity in the architecture and ornament of the latter two, they were basically utilitarian structures designed to hold large congregations. None of them had notable artistic pretensions, not even S. Pietro di Castello in Venice, where Palladio's original designs were substantially altered by Francesco Smeraldi and the building, obviously a cheap effort and completed inside two years, was badly executed.

By contrast, a number of ambitious and tasteful building projects and decorative schemes were associated with the male religious orders who had some forty houses in Venice and the surrounding islands. The male orders enjoyed a social and intellectual cachet not possessed by the parochial clergy. While hardly any Venetian nobles entered the ranks of the latter, an appreciable number, although perhaps only one or two per cent of the total body of the patriciate, joined religious orders, more particularly the stricter ones and above all, it would seem, the Capuchins, Jesuits and Theatines.[91] It should be said, however, that those who entered these new orders probably seldom remained in Venice. Certain of the stricter orders, notably the three just mentioned, had followings of devotees among the nobility and high citizenry. Little is known about the wealth of individual monasteries and convents. The landed property of Venetian houses, as distinct from those of the Terraferma was in any case small.[92] The pattern of testamentary bequests to houses of male religious, in themselves inconsiderable, suggests that the volume of charitable gifts to them may have tended to be in inverse proportion to their established wealth, orders with a reputation for apostolic poverty or rigorous piety normally receiving the most generous treatment.[93] In any case, it is evident that the Jesuits and Theatines, who were presented with old churches and buildings in the first instance, found the wherewithal to expand and remodel them on a lavish scale. The Capuchins, as we have seen, were provided with a new church and convent by the state.

The houses of orders vowed to strict poverty normally had lay procurators, who handled their finances, and a number of other houses had lay protectors. It is probable that these gave advice on building programmes in many cases. It would certainly be dangerous to assume that the effective choice regarding them was normally exercised by the religious themselves.

An outstanding example of discretion exercised by members of a religious house had, however, been provided with the erection between about 1468 and 1499 of the Church of S. Michele in Isola, one of Mauro Coducci's finest works and probably his first in the region of the Lagoon. The Camaldolese house of S. Michele was one of the monasteries which a significant number of nobles were prepared to enter, it enjoyed a considerable reputation for scholarship and at this time it had a number of important lay devotees. One of its monks, the noble Pietro Delfin was to emerge as a distinguished humanist and a great prelate; he became Minister-General of his order in 1480, being subsequently deposed by the reformers within the order headed by Giustiniani and Querini. It was he who encouraged the Abbot Pietro Donà, a fellow-

patrician, to undertake the ambitious building-project and he supervised the work during Donà's absences in the years after 1475. Delfin's
letters reveal the esteem in which Coducci was held by the Camaldolese,
who entrusted him with certain confidential business. In August 1477,
Delfin wrote to Donà pressing him to come and view the splendid
building for himself:

> Exception made for the Church of St Marks, I prefer it to all others. . . .
> All marvel that this great pile has been erected in so short a time, yet
> with such great art. It not merely recalls the antique, but has truly
> restored antiquity (*non modum antiquum redolet, verum etiam maximam
> refert antiquitatem.*) You will realise that you have never seen anything
> better than this temple and it is impossible to conceive its elegance.

Delfin continued to interest himself in the project after he had become
Minister-General in 1480 and moved to Camaldoli. Coducci's idiosyncratic and highly personal style can hardly be called 'antique'. The
interior does in fact have certain affinities with early Christian architecture and Delfin's remarks may have had a particular significance for
Donà, who was at that time in Ravenna. There can be no doubt, however, that S. Michele initiated an architectural revolution in the Lagoon.
    There is no evidence that the great benefactor of the monastery
Andrea Loredan, a patron of Coducci, was in any way responsible for
his employment by the Camaldolese. His great Palazzo Non Nobis
Domine, the most ambitious of the domestic projects attributed to
Coducci, was not commenced until 1480. It is probable, therefore, that
he encountered Coducci at S. Michele rather than introduced him
there. On the other hand, the Camaldolese were heavily dependant on
their lay benefactors, not least because Delfin's optimism regarding the
total cost of the building was shown to be ill-founded. A number of
these benefactors were consulted on the project and paid for the various
chapels, most notably the fine octagonal Capella della Croce, probably
the work of P. Lombardo.[94]
    There was relatively little ecclesiastical building in Venice in the first
half of the sixteenth century. Perhaps the most important new church
belonging to male Regulars was that of the Hieronymites of S.
Sebastian, a modest but tasteful work built between 1506 and 1548 on
the designs of Antonio Abbondi (Lo Scarpagnino).[95] A number of
major projects were executed for male orders, both old and new,
around the second half of the century.
    In the building of S. Francesco della Vigna, the main house of the

Franciscan Observants in Venice, the initiative was substantially taken by the patrons of the monastery. The Observants were naturally particularly dependent on these, being vowed to strict poverty and obliged to leave the management of their finances in the hands of lay procurators. The original *modello* for the church was commissioned from Jacopo Sansovino by Doge Andrea Gritti in 1534 or shortly before. Gritti, who was to be buried in the church, was obviously acting in the capacity of a private lay patron. When, however, differences arose as to the proportions of the church, Gritti turned to one of the friars, Francesco di Giorgi or Groppi, who was an authority on theories of number and proportion. In 1525 he had published a lengthy tome on the harmony of the universe in which he had maintained, with a combination of Neoplatonist and Christian theories, the mysterious efficacy of certain numbers and ratios. It was not altogether surprising that S. Francesco, which had a strong tradition of erudite studies, should produce a theoretician of Groppi's type. After the advice of Titian, the architect Serlio and the humanist Fortunato Spira had been taken, Groppi's suggestion for the plan were substantially accepted. Sansovino's project for the façade was eventually abandoned and replaced by a design of Palladio made in 1565, apparently on the instructions of Giovanni Grimani Patriarch of Aquilea.[96] The Grimani, who had been closely associated with Doge Gritti, likewise had their tomb in the Church and the Patriarch Giovanni was responsible for the ambitious project of the family chapel there.[97]

The Benedictines of S. Giorgio Maggiore definitely appear to have commissioned Palladio's works there, the refectory (1560–2) and the magnificent church (1565). Palladio's work was continued by Simon Sorella, *Protho* of the Serenissima, whose name may have been suggested by the great Leonardo Donà, the protector of the monastery. S. Giorgio does not seem to have been particularly notable from the social point of view, but it had a certain scholarly record. It was at the turn of the seventeenth century that a monk emerged who took a close interest in building projects, Fortunato Olmo, a man distinguished for letters and for historical studies who, among other projects, helped to bring Palladio's façade to completion in 1629.[98]

Apart from the Capuchin church of the Redentore, which we have examined under the heading of state patronage, the other most noteworthy building designed for a male religious order was undoubtedly the new convent of the Lateran Canons of the Carità. This was built on Palladio's designs, probably between 1559 and 1560.[99] The austere cloister is one of the less well-known of Palladio's works, although it was one of the ones most admired by Goethe. The Jesuit church of S. Maria dell' Umiltà (1550–89) and the Theatine church of S. Nicolò dei Tolentini, begun in 1591 on the designs of Vincenzo Scamozzi, were evidently major projects. Nothing now remains of the Umiltà, however, and the Tolentini was never properly finished.[100]

There were some 2,500 nuns in Venice in 1581, as against rather over 1,000 male regulars, and by 1642 there were some 2,900.[101] The tradition that patrician girls whom their fathers could not afford to marry-off were put in nunneries is amply confirmed by the evidence of testaments. The vast and evidently swelling number of their occupants, which put heavy strains upon their resources, explains in part why the 50-odd nunneries in Venice and the nearby islands, while constantly obliged to extend their living quarters, did not play a significant role in building commissions of note. The two outstanding projects for nuns' churches in the Renaissance period were fifteenth-century ones: the *tempietto* of the Madonna dei Miracoli built, probably by P. Lombardo, between 1483 and 1489 and the façade of S. Zaccaria, built mostly by Coducci between 1480 and 1500. Significantly S. Zaccaria was, by all accounts, one of the wealthiest Venetian nunneries and its choir-nuns were by tradition exclusively noble. The church and convent of the Miracoli was not in fact commissioned by nuns but by lay procurators appointed by the people of the parish who wished to erect a shrine to house a much-revered image of the Virgin.[102] The Catholic Reformation did not involve movements within the female religious orders in any way comparable to those among the male orders and the new nunneries in Venice were of minor importance, with the notable exception of the *Convertite*, the house for reformed prostitutes following the Augustinian rule. The Venetian nunneries were, for the most part, in a difficult financial position in the late sixteenth and early seventeenth centuries and from the 1590s they were under orders both from the state and from the Patriarch of Venice to limit the size of the dowries they required of entrants. Any funds available for building had to be substantially devoted to the utilitarian purpose of expanding accommodation.[103]

The lay procurators or wardens of parish churches would probably have taken a major initiative in commissions for their rebuilding or improvement. There is little evidence that the parochial clergy played a particularly active role, although business might be carried out in the name of the parish-priest and the latter would certainly have to petition

the Senate for the permit necessary for any extension or major development of premises. In general, it is unclear what role private patrons
played. A major exception is provided by the activities of Tomaso di
Ravenna, better known as Il Rangone, who had accumulated substantial wealth through his medical practice and who was a noted
philologist. In the story of S. Geminian, Rangone, the parish priest and
the state all played notable roles. The church of S. Geminian on the
Piazza S. Marco had been largely rebuilt in the first two decades of the
sixteenth century with substantial state subsidies granted by the Council
of Ten, but it lacked a façade. In 1552, Rangone asked his friend Jacopo
Sansovino to design a façade which was to include a monument to
himself. He obtained approval for the project from the parish-priest
Benedetto Manzino and the chapter of the Church, obliging himself to
meet all the expenses of construction. Notwithstanding Manzino's
support for the project, however, the Senate rejected it, evidently taking
exception to the idea of having a monument to a single individual on
the Piazza. In the event, the Senate and Collegio took over responsibility
for the scheme in 1557, both providing funds and reserving the right to
approve the design, the Procurators Grimani and Capello, together with
the parish-priest, being responsible for supervising the project. According to Bardi's guide, Manzino was 'promoter and backer of the work'.
In fact, however, the only documentary records of his activity with
respect to the actual building relate to his support of the Rangone
project and his requests to the Senate for funds, although he did have an
outstanding organ with panels painted by Veronese constructed at his
own expense. S. Geminian, destroyed at the beginning of the nineteenth
century to make way for the present 'Napoleonic wing' of the Piazza,
figures in many old depictions of the great square; with its fine façade
by Sansovino it was perhaps the most outstanding Venetian parish
church to be built in the sixteenth century. Meanwhile, Rangone was
not to be outdone. In 1553, he obliged himself to give 1,000 ducats for
the façade and general refurbishment of the parish church of S. Giulian
on condition that a bronze sculpture of himself could be put on the
façade. This time the Senate gave permission and the façade was built
by Jacopo Sansovino probably aided by Alessandro Vittoria, who certainly made the bronze statue.[104] Thus it was a private patron who had
taken the initiative in Sansovino's two most important parish-church
projects, but the organization of patronage of parish-church projects in
general remains unclear.

With regard to the many paintings in Venetian parish churches or

churches of religious orders, only in a few cases is it certain that these
were commissioned by clergy or, as was most often the case, by religious
orders. Many were certainly ordered by lay persons who had chapels
or tombs in churches or by guilds and religious confraternities for their
chapels. On certain occasions, however, members of religious orders
showed enterprise in their choice of artists. Thus in the years 1554–5,
Paolo Veronese was commissioned to paint the ceilings first of the
sacristy and then of the church of S. Sebastian by his friend and fellow
native of Verona Fra Bernardo Torlone, Prior of the Hieronymite
monastery. These were among Paolo's first works in Venice, immediately
following his works in the chambers of the Council of Ten. The project
on the church ceiling was the great *Esther and Ahasuerus* cycle. In 1570,
Paolo was commissioned to paint a *Last Supper* (now in the Brera) for
the convent refectory. According to Ridolfi, he received 'friendship
and protection' from the friars.[105] A number of artists in fact had close
connections with particular religious houses and executed work for
them. It is not certain how far Titian's personal connections with the
Friars Minor had developed when he painted the great Assumption in
the *Frari* church in 1516 at the behest of the Prior Marco Zerman.[106] By
1549, however, he had a confessor in the convent (shared with Aretino)[107] and he was buried in the church. Palma Giovane allegedly had
a particular devotion to the *Crociferi* (Crutched Friars), having been
protected by them since childhood[108] and he produced a large number
of paintings for their hospital. Again he carried out extensive work for
the Theatines at S. Nicolò where one of the fathers, Francesco Savioni,
was a supporter of his.[109]

Opulent, large-scale religious paintings were, of course, relatively
few in number. Here the canvases that have found their way into the
world's great galleries can give a misleading impression, while at the
same time Venetian churches, as we now know them, have been
despoiled of some of their largest altarpieces. It must also be remembered
that some of the most imposing paintings now in churches, particularly
those that are broad in relation to their height, were originally in
sacristies or in monastic refectories. Where paintings for churches were
concerned, artists often worked on canvases whose shape did not offer
much scope for compositional experiment and subject-matter was
relatively restricted. Altarpieces in side-chapels were normally tall and
narrow, having, in most cases, semicircular heads, although there was
more variety in pieces for high altars. Crucifixions and depositions,
groups of the Madonna and Child with saints and groups of saints were

especially common. Subjects of the joyful and glorious mysteries—the Annunciation, the Visitation, the Adorations of the Shepherds and the Magi, the Assumption—were certainly often to be found, but these did not predominate over grave christocentric subjects such as the Baptism of Christ and scenes of the Passion. The latter, in particular, were well-suited to narrow canvases. Martyrdoms of saints were not very common and apotheoses of saints were to be more a seventeenth-century genre. Paintings on organ-doors (a distinctive Venetian genre it would seem) offered a certain scope for inventiveness and so also of course did ceiling-paintings. At least 24 churches out of the 140 or so in the dioceses of Venice and Torcello are known to have acquired ceiling-paintings in the sixteenth century. Significantly, 13 of these belonged to male religious orders, while only five belonged to nunneries and six were parish-churches. In the late fifteenth and early sixteenth centuries, painted ceilings had been divided into a large number of very small square panels. From the 1540s, however, the practice spread of having large square, oblong or oval panels, usually single or three in number in the centre of a ceiling; the true *soffitto veneziano*. The most remarkable projects were, perhaps, Titian's Old Testament scenes painted for the Canons Regular of S. Spirito in Isola (1542–4), Veronese's *Esther and Ahasuerus* cycle in S. Sebastian, his *Assumption, Annunciation* and *Adoration of the Shepherds* done for the Jesuits in the Umiltà (1566) (now in the Capella del Rosario of SS. Giovanni e Paolo) and his work done for the Friars Minor at S. Nicolò ai Frari (the *Adoration of the Magi, et al.*) (c. 1581).[110] In general, however, Venetian churches were not remarkable for their ceiling-paintings; it was in state buildings and in the Scuole Grandi that the *soffitto veneziano* was to find its most ambitious and brilliant development. In most cases, the panels on the ceilings of Venetian churches were not of outstanding size and their shape often limited the artist's freedom. In refectory paintings, on the other hand, where large oblong canvases were the rule and subject-matter could be provided by any biblical reference to a feast or a meal, there could be considerable opportunities for the exercise of artistic fancy in large figure compositions, as evidenced by Paolo Veronese's *Marriage at Cana*, painted in 1560 for the Benedictines of S. Giorgio Maggiore (now in the Louvre), his *Feast in the House of Levi*, painted in 1573 for the 'conventual' Dominicans of SS. Giovanni e Paolo (now in the Accademia), or Jacopo Tintoretto's *Manna* and *Last Supper* painted in 1591 for S. Giorgio Maggiore (now in the chancel of the Church). Commissions for churches taken as a whole, however, did not offer much scope for

19   Illustration to Francesco Colonna's *Hypnerotomachia Polifili* published in Venice
in 1499 (see pp. 245–6)

20   Palazzo Vendramin-Calergi, Venice, attributed to Mauro Coducci, ordered by
Andrea Loredan in 1481 (see pp. 246–8)

21   J. Sansovino, Palazzo Corner di S. Maurizio, Venice, begun 1537 (see pp. 247–8)

22 M. Sanmicheli, Palazzo Bevilacqua, Verona, designed before 1537 (see p. 248)

the development of religious art as a genre of large scale figure-composition which would tax the inventiveness of the artist. In paintings for the Scuole Grandi, where novel types of religious subject-matter were acceptable and where artists had vast and conveniently shaped canvases to work on, the opportunities were very much greater.

In the latter half of the sixteenth century, there was probably more construction, remodelling and adornment of churches than in any other region of Italy. These enterprises can be regarded in some measure as an aspect of the more general efflorescence of artistic expenditure in the period. In part they drew their impetus from the Catholic reform movement. There were new orders, particularly preoccupied with preaching who required churches to hold large congregations. The Cathedral of S. Pietro di Castello in Venice and the new cathedrals in the Terraferma had to serve the same function. Movements in the field of the religious confraternities, which had gained momentum in the latter half of the fifteenth century, expanded still further in the sixteenth; the smaller devotional confraternities, which did not possess their own buildings, would need their own chapels in churches and would wish to adorn them. Furthermore, the ecclesiastical authorities endeavoured to activate the Scuole di Sacramento established in each parish, whose function was to ensure that the sacraments were administered under fitting conditions and which had particular responsibilities for the high altars and *capelle maggiori*.

While, however, the Catholic reform movement doubtless brought increased opportunities for artists and craftsmen to work upon ecclesiastical projects, their freedom of action was substantially curtailed. The diocesan authorities and the new religious orders were liable, in their commissions for sacred art, to have rather different predilections from lay patrons and probably many of the older religious orders as well. Italian churchmen who prescribed the qualities required of religious figurative art laid stress on sobriety, didactic effect and appropriateness of treatment to subject-matter. An artist who did not observe these requirements in religious painting could find himself in trouble. Thus Veronese was summoned before the Inquisition in 1574 on account of the *Feast in the House of Levi* painted for the refectory of SS. Giovanni e Paolo; the charge was that unseemly incidents and bizarre objects were portrayed.[111] Bishops, in the course of their pastoral visitations, frequently ordered the removal of 'unseemly' pictures from churches. Pillars of the Church would be disposed to patronise obedient artists rather than distinguished ones. The cautious Palma Giovane, who worked extensively for the Capuchins and Theatines was perhaps more the sort of artist who would be preferred. Together with the Hieronymites of S. Sebastian and the Dominicans of SS. Giovanni e Paolo it was the Benedictines of S. Giorgio Maggiore and S. Giustina Padua and Praglia, doubtless estimable men, living on the heritage of a great early fifteenth-century reform, but not notably touched by the latest reforming currents and without particular pastoral preoccupations, who commissioned the most ambitious and lavish ecclesiastical works of Paolo Veronese and Jacopo Tintoretto. In any case, these monasteries, and particularly S. Giustina and S. Maria di Praglia, which were enriched by ambitious programmes of land-development, could probably afford such luxuries. The diocesan authorities could hardly do so. The bishops of the post-Tridentine era were extremely anxious that the sacraments should be administered in fitting circumstances, but their preoccupations in the first instance were with decency rather than beauty of surroundings. The funds at their disposal must be devoted to providing capacious buildings which had a certain impressiveness, befitting temples of God, rather than gems of exquisite taste. Where adornment could be afforded, it was the high altar and *capella maggiore* that claimed precedence. Overall designs which required high craftsmanship and costly materials in the architectural detail could hardly be afforded. The great age of stucco was now beginning.

The outlook of the post-Tridentine bishops and the exigencies they faced were such that they were not likely to be outstanding patrons of the arts. The initiative lay with the superiors of religious houses and with lay patrons. In the event, it is often difficult to distinguish ecclesiastical patronage properly speaking from lay patronage of church projects, but where commissions appear to have originated with ecclesiastics, it was the religious orders who stood out. This was still to be the case in the eighteenth century.[112]

Lay Confraternities

The life of the lay religious and charitable confraternities in Italy was extremely vigorous and perhaps nowhere more than in Venice. Some of the confraternities there had been founded as early as the mid-thirteenth century. In the latter half of the fifteenth century, although there were few new foundations in Venice itself, there had been a revival of enthusiasm for devotional sodalities in Italy as a whole and well over 30 new confraternities were founded in Venice between 1500 and 1630.

Ranking first in importance were the six charitable confraternities known as the Scuole Grandi: S. Teodoro, the Carità, S. Giovanni Evangelista and S. Marco, all apparently mid-thirteenth-century foundations, the Misericordia (1308) and the late fifteenth-century foundation of S. Rocco; S. Teodoro only gained the title of Scuola Grande in 1552 and was considerably less important than the rest. The Scuole Grandi had been founded as religious confraternities and in the sixteenth century they clearly retained this character, but in the course of time they had become primarily philanthropic rather than primarily religious bodies. In addition to distributing alms to the sick and indigent in Venice as a whole, they helped to support their own poor brethren in cases of need. The Scuole Grandi appeared on certain state ceremonial occasions, notably the great Corpus Domini procession in the Piazza S. Marco, and they accompanied their dead brethren to burial.

The direction of each of these bodies lay theoretically in the Chapter General which was normally in the sixteenth century a relatively restricted body. Government in routine matters and during the intervals between the meetings of the Chapter General lay, however, in the hands of a still smaller board of sixteen 'guardians', usually known as the *Banca* and by the sixteenth century the *banche* had substantially become the effective directorates of the Scuole.

The Scuole Grandi contained both rich and poor. The poor members could earn gifts of alms by walking in funeral processions and could expect charitable aid in cases of necessity. At the other extreme there were those who were accepted into the scuola for what they could give in the way of money and administrative expertise. Such persons might be exempted from the 'discipline' of the scuola and from the normal obligations to take part in processions. Many nobles joined the Scuole Grandi, but mainly, it would seem, simply in order to participate in their spiritual benefits by virtue of mere aggregation. They were excluded from the *banche* and Chapters General. These were the province of the citizens, either *cittadini originarii* or at least *cittadini* who had been members for 20 years. The post of *Guardian Grande* of one of the great scuole was an extremely honorific one. As has been seen, Gasparo Contarini, as one of his proofs that Venice was a 'mixed' state, adduced the fact that the guardianships were open to citizens, who could thereby imitate the nobility. Botero evidently regarded it as an ingenious stratagem of the ruling caste designed to keep the citizens content and compensate them for their exclusion from political power. Certainly office in the Scuole gave them major responsibilities and an opportunity to dress in scarlet robes.[113]

The Scuole Grandi put on lavish ceremonies and they were major patrons of the arts and music. There were in fact complaints of a discrepancy between their heavy expenditure on 'pomps' and their function of succouring the poor. In the mid-sixteenth century attempts were in fact made, both by the State and by the scuole themselves, to curtail their expenditure on superfluities. They were attacked in the dialect poem the *Sogno di Caravia*, published in 1541 and evidently written by the jeweller Alessandro Caravia. In this poem, St Peter, while saying that many virtues are to be found in the Scuole Grandi, castigates their members for having succumbed to the sin of pride:

> I wish to tell you of the many errors
> Of some who wear proud habits,
> Although I do not tell you their names.
> Some follow the saint of the plague (i.e. S. Rocco)
> And these are they who have produced such fine works
> With foliage, harpies and all those fine heads,
> Fantastic columns in new styles,
> For each one wants to prove himself a master mason.
> The truth is that every time there is a new chapter,
> Everyone wants to prove himself a great deviser of schemes,
> Changing now this staircase and now the other,
> Doing away with former doors and windows,
> All quarreling with one another, saying:
> 'Such and such a man did not know how to do things.'[114]

The Scuola di S. Rocco, to which St Peter is referring, has spent 80,000 ducats on buildings, while it is failing to fulfil its obligations towards the poor. Similar criticisms are made of the Misericordia, the Carità and S. Giovanni Evangelista: the members of the latter, 'finding their purses over-heavy', have built a new hospice 'where one could hold a ball if necessary'.

Caravia, doubtless, was not an unbiased observer, for he had his own ideological axe to grind (he was summoned before the Inquisition for his views on Justification), but the chaos and petty rivalries he describes would certainly help to explain the bad relations between the guardians of certain scuole and their architects: Bartolomeo Bon and Sante

Lombardo had successively abandoned the post of *protomaestro* of S. Rocco in 1524[115] and Pietro Lombardo's relations with S. Marco were far from happy.[116] Caravia's allegations may also cast some light on the difficulties experienced by Tintoretto with these two scuole.

The other scuole ranged from relatively large confraternities, which bore the title of 'so-called Scuole Grandi', to small religious sodalities. Guilds were normally a combination of two overlapping institutions: an *arte* or craft association, and a scuola or religious association. Certain foreign communities living in Venice, most notably the Greeks and Dalmatians, also had their own scuole. The smaller confraternities had no more than a chapel or altar in some church, but many of the larger ones had their own buildings. Scuola buildings were normally of two storeys, the main hall being on the upper floor. Often the ceilings of the halls were richly decorated. In S. Rocco, S. Marco, and S. Giovanni Evangelista, among others, there was, leading off the upper hall, an *albergo* or board-room for the *banca*.

Perhaps the most important artistic projects of scuole were as follows:

a Scuola Grande di S. Giovanni Evangelista. The fine marble screen at the entrance to the courtyard, attributed to P. Lombardo, was built around 1481. Mauro Coducci, who became a member of the scuola in 1498, built the hall and great stairway around that time and probably designed the great doorway. The great hall, Hall of the Cross and *albergo* were decorated with paintings by Gentile Bellini, Vittore Carpaccio, Titian, Palma Giovane and Domenico Tintoretto. The cycle of *Miracles of the Fragment of the True Cross* by Gentile Bellini and Carpaccio, formerly in the Hall of the Cross, are now in the Accademia, Venice. Titian's paintings in the *albergo* are now partly dispersed and part lost, his central panel, the *St John on Patmos* being in the National Gallery in Washington.[117]

b Scuola Grande di S. Marco.[118] The imposing building, now the Ospedale Civile, next to SS. Giovanni e Paolo, was commenced in 1485. The façade is basically the work of P. Lombardo, who was assisted by his son and by Giovanni Buora. The work was subsequently taken over by Coducci, who added the curious circular pediments.[119] A fine ground-floor hall was built by Coducci in 1495 but was destroyed in the early nineteenth century. The back-premises were extended and enlarged on designs of Jacopo Sansovino between 1533 and 1543. Giovanni Bellini had been one of the chiefs of the scuola in 1492 and in 1500 Gentile Bellini and Ludovico and Bartolomeo Vivarini were also mentioned as members.[120] In addition to paintings by the

Bellini, Paris Bordone and Palma Vecchio,[121] the scuola was particularly remarkable for a cycle of pictures by Jacopo Tintoretto depicting miracles of St Mark and the events surrounding the transportation of his body. The *Miracle of the Slave* (Accademia) was painted as a result of a commission from the scuola of 1548. In 1562, the Guardian Tomaso di Ravenna received permission from the Scuola to have three pictures painted at his own expense. These were the *Invention of the Body of St Mark* (Brera), the *Transportation of the body of St Mark* (Accademia) and *St Mark Saving a Saracen at Sea* (Accademia). Eighty ducats were promised by Ser Tomaso for the latter work in 1568.[122] Tomaso di Ravenna, better known as 'Il Rangone', the famous philologist and scholar of medicine was, as we have seen, a notable patron of the arts, being the principal promoter of the reconstruction of the Church of S. Giulian by Sansovino, and Alessandro Vittoria.[123] He was furthermore a particularly close friend of the latter, who became a member of the scuola in 1562 during Tomaso's guardianship[124] although he does not appear to have executed any work in the building.

c Scuola di S. Orsola. The cycle of scenes from the life of St Ursula (1490–5) by Carpaccio (now in the Accademia) was originally here. They were probably commissioned under the auspices of the Barbaro family.[125]

d Scuola di S. Giorgio dei Schiavoni (the Confraternity of the Dalmatians). This contains the outstanding Carpaccio cycle (*c.* 1502–4), which includes *St George killing the dragon* and *St Jerome in his study*.[126]

e Scuola Grande della Carità. The richly decorated *albergo* with its fine gilded ceiling and Titian's *Presentation of the Virgin* is now in room XXIV of the Accademia Gallery.[127]

f Scuola Grande di S. Rocco. The new building was begun in 1515, but not completed for nearly 50 years. It was commenced by the *Protho* of the Serenissima, Bartolomeo Bon, who was dismissed in 1524, and in 1529 Scarpagnino took over. The work bears the marks of the eccentric local style which developed out of the work of Coducci and his contemporaries. The interior contains the monumental cycles by Tintoretto, executed between 1564 and about 1588. It also contains important works by Titian among other artists. In September 1553, Titian had in fact been asked to provide a cycle of paintings for the walls, but the project fell through; possibly its failure was connected with a decision made the previous April to cut down on superfluous expenditure in view of the pressing needs of charity.[128]

g Scuola Grande della Misericordia. The new building was begun on the designs of Jacopo Sansovino in 1532 and never completely finished; a grandiose interior is still in existence, but the building is not faced on the outside.[129]

h *Scuola di S. Maria del Rosario in SS. Giovanni e Paolo.* The Confraternity acquired a chapel in the Dominican Church in 1582. This was perhaps the most outstanding chapel to be possessed by any confraternity in a Venetian church. It was probably commenced shortly after 1582 and a large number of artists worked on it. Alessandro Vittoria was probably the artist mainly responsible for the general architectural scheme and the pictures were by artists of the circle closely associated with him, the two Tintorettos, Palma Giovane, Francesco Bassano and Andrea Vicentino among others. The chapel was destroyed by fire in 1867.[130]

i *Compagnia dell Giustizia* or *Della Buona Morte* by S. Fantin. Following a fire of 1562, the new scuola was built between 1592 and 1600. Alessandro Vittoria probably played a general consultative role on the entire project and he helped to select the architect (Contin), but probably entrusted the entire stucco decorations to others. The commission for the painted decorations was given to Palma Giovane.

Where guardians were jostling for eminence, pressures on behalf of or in opposition to particular artists might well have been expected. Pressures of both kinds can be surmised in the case of Tintoretto, who was, indeed, a controversial artist. Ridolfi and Boschini indicate that, after the Scuola di S. Marco had commissioned Tintoretto to paint the series of the Miracles of St Mark in 1548, there was disagreement among the brethren regarding acceptance of the *Miracle of the Slave* and the then Guardian was opposed to it, although the work was ultimately taken.[131] The slight to Tintoretto was later repaired by the great Tomaso Rangone, but he had to pay for three paintings out of his own pocket. Again, Tintoretto's work for the Scuola di S. Rocco was a cause of strong dissension. On 22 May 1564, 30 members of the *banca* and *zonta* committed themselves to paying for the decorations of the confraternity's building out of their personal resources. One of their number, however, Giovanni di Zignioni, specified that he would only contribute if a painter other than Tintoretto was given the commission. The proposal to employ Tintoretto, which must obviously have already been made, evidently encountered wider opposition, for on 31 May it was decided to hold a competition for the project. According to Vasari, sketches were prepared by Paolo Veronese, Giuseppe Salviati and Federico Zuccari; Ridolfi adds the name of Andrea Schiavone. These artists may well have been considered as possibilities, but in fact the competition never took place. On 22 June, it was announced that Tintoretto had presented, as a gift, a painted canvas for the central panel of the ceiling of the *albergo*, apparently offering to put the finishing touches to it. Tintoretto would probably only have attempted this *fait accompli* if he was assured of the connivance of supporters on the *banca*. On 29 June, following a motion made four days earlier by the Guardian Grande and two other members of the *banca*, the Chapter General annulled the decision of 31 May to hold a competition and accepted Tintoretto's painting, at the same time empowering the *banca* and *zonta* to commission him to proceed with further work. The motion was passed by 31 votes to 20; which in fact indicated a sharp division of opinion; by contrast the Council of Ten's grant of the *Sansaria* of the *Fondaco dei Tedeschi* to Tintoretto in 1574 was passed by 25 votes to three, with two abstensions.[132] Tintoretto was accepted as a member of the scuola in March 1565 (by 85 votes to 19), but this did not altogether save him from further trouble. In July 1575, his offer to paint the central panel of the ceiling in the great hall was apparently accepted without much opposition and the same was true of his offer of June 1577 to execute two further paintings there leaving payment to the discretion of the scuola. On 27 November 1577, Tintoretto offered to devote himself, for the remainder of his life, to the decoration of the scuola and the church of S. Rocco, producing three pictures yearly, in return for a modest annuity of 100 ducats per year. The following day, the members of the *banca* and *zonta*, by 16 votes to four, obliged themselves and their successors in office to pay the sum annually, and the Chapter General approved this decision by 45 votes to three. It is evident, however, that the small defeated minorities continued their opposition. On 16 February 1578, the *banca* and *zonta* reiterated that the 100 ducats annuity was to be paid out of the pockets of their members and not out of the funds of the scuola and it was decided that the issue should again be put to the vote. This time Tintoretto's supporters had not diminished, but his opponents must have brought in their friends, for the vote in the *banca* and *zonta* was 16 to 12 and in the Chapter General 45 to 25.[133] In the event, Tintoretto went on to complete a series of works with which, among Italian Renaissance picture cycles by a sole artist, only Michelangelos' Sistine Chapel and Giulio Romano's works in the ducal palaces at Mantua can be compared.

There is no clear indication as to why Tintoretto's opponents had been so persistent. His controversial style may not have appealed to certain solid citizens of the *banca* or they may have felt that it ill-befitted a confraternity with sober religious and philanthropic aims. The *Apotheosis of S. Rocco*, the instrument of his *coup* of June 1564, for all its daring foreshortenings, was not particularly liable to bruise conservative sensibilities and may have helped to reconcile the members of the scuola towards his employment. On the other hand, the *Brazen serpent*, painted for the ceiling of the great hall in 1575, with its mass of sprawling, contorted figures, may have reawakened hostility. It should also be said that Jacopo Robusti was unusual among the artists who worked in Venice in being a *cittadino originario* of the city and may have been known personally to several members of the *banca*, possessing enemies there as well as friends.

Nevertheless, the fact that Tintoretto was a local man, quite apart from his sharp practice and willingness to do work cheaply or for nothing, may explain in part why work for scuole bulked so large in the commissions he received in his thirties and forties at a time when he was still struggling for the heights. The fact that Palma Giovane was likewise Venetian born, although not apparently a *cittadino*, may also help to account for the large number of scuole commissions he received. Palma, however, was evidently well-blessed with friends who helped him to obtain employment, most notably the sculptor Alessandro Vittoria. Ridolfi indicates that it was personal links, whether direct or through the mediacy of Vittoria it is not quite clear, which accounted for the insistence of the *Guardian Grande* of the Compagnia della Giustizia, Francesco Tedaldo, that the decoration of the upper hall of the scuola should be exclusively entrusted to Palma.[134]

The paintings commissioned by scuole invariably had some sort of religious subject-matter. In many cases, however, it was a question of history painting which was only technically within the religious genre and allowed greater scope for the artist's fancy than most ecclesiastical commissions. He was also afforded extensive scope by the broad and varied areas he had to work on. Thus at S. Rocco Tintoretto was able to give a totally novel treatment to the Annunciation and Crucifixion. Magnificent opportunities were offered for artistic fantasy by lives or posthumous miracles of saints such as St Ursula, St George or St Mark, to whom scuole were dedicated, or St Jerome, a favourite patron of religious confraternities, whose deeds were depicted by Carpaccio at S. Giorgio dei Schiavoni, not to mention the story of the theft and transportation of St Mark's body from Alexandria to Venice. In the St Ursula and St Jerome cycles and in the cycle of the *Miracles of the Frag-*

ment of the Cross, Carpaccio and Gentile Bellini were able to indulge in what was, in many respects, secular history painting. Furthermore, while paintings of Old Testament subjects were rare in churches, the ceiling of the upper hall of the Scuola di S. Rocco contained no less than twelve, and these allowed Tintoretto to indulge in daring experiments with massed figure compositions, most notably in the *Brazen serpent*, the *Gathering of manna* and *Moses striking water from the rock*. It was perhaps their scuola commissions that gave Gentile Bellini, Carpaccio and Tintoretto their fullest opportunities to experiment in the genre of history painting.

Conclusion

With regard to employment of individual artists, there were certain differences between private, state, ecclesiastical and scuola patronage. Giorgione catered extensively and perhaps primarily for private connoisseurs. Veronese appears to have been very much a protégé of the aristocracy, taking both his state and his private commissions into account, and his studio executed scarcely any works for scuole. Palladio, who had begun as the protégé of private patrons from the Vicentine and Venetian aristocracies, only won state commissions in the last decade of his life. Jacopo and Domenico Tintoretto and their studio had especially heavy commitments on state and scuola projects. This is not to be taken as necessarily showing that the citizenry of the scuole were particularly broadminded in accepting, with Jacopo, an artist who had to struggle for recognition in the first instance and whose style was in marked contrast to the classicism favoured by many patrician *cognoscenti*: nowhere was the lack of appreciation of his work more evident than among certain minorities in the scuole. It would be dangerous to regard him as being in any sense a 'popular' artist. It must be remembered that the citizenry contained a number of highly educated men and Jacopo Tintoretto's great supporter in the Scuola di S. Marco, Tomaso Rangone, was a distinguished humanist. Palma Giovane, evidently aided by his personal connections, appears to have been particularly favoured by ecclesiastical bodies and lay confraternities. There were, of course, certain artists who had a particular flair for mural decorations in villas, notably Zelotti, Fasolo and other members of the Veronese and Vicentine groups.

With both state and scuola commissions, friends and protectors used their good offices on behalf of artists. If strong pressures were brought at government level, however, they have been covered with a discreet veil of silence: evidence of favours exercised on behalf of artists comes from writers like Vasari and Ridolfi, not from the records of government organs. Even in the communal council of Vicenza, where Palladio had strong backers for his Basilica plans, there is no evidence of a tug-of-war over the project. It is with regard to scuola patronage that the pressures on behalf of and in opposition to a particular artist are most apparent and the evidence for these can be gathered from scuola records. Doubtless the citizens of the *banche* and chapters general were less likely to be discreet than patricians of the ruling caste. Furthermore, the guardians who supported Jacopo Tintoretto and Palma Giovane may have done so in part as friends, and friends of an equivalent social rank. The Procurators Vettore Grimani, Michiel Antonio Capello, Giacomo Contarini and others like the Barbaro, who may have helped artists to obtain state commissions, may have been friends of the artists after a fashion, but ultimately they were patrons bestowing graces from above. They were connoisseurs in the fullest sense and, even where they had preferences for a particular style, they were unlikely to give violently partisan support to their protégés to the detriment of other artists of proven excellence. Where selection of artists was involved, the *amour propre* of the Procurators of St Mark and other leading statesmen would not have been at stake in the same way as it was with guardians of scuole: they played for higher stakes than the demonstration of the excellence of their own artistic taste and flagrant jobbery would only have damaged their own political prospects. The Grimani had artists dependent on them and their favour might be crucial to the advancement of a relatively obscure painter such as Ponchino, but there is nothing to suggest that Sansovino, Battista Franco, Paolo Veronese or Francesco Bassano were in any sense 'creatures' of the Grimani, or the Barbaro brothers or Giacomo Contarini. There was little reason why pressurising and jobbery should give a clear direction to state patronage, although discreet favours on behalf of certain artists may well have lead to some rather bizarre combinations of collaborators on certain decorative projects in the Ducal Palace. In contrast to scuola commissions, where a remarkably unified policy was followed in certain projects, the choice of artists for state commissions was catholic in the extreme and often appears devoid of conscious coordination. While the scuole may have shown a certain preference for Venetian-born artists this was certainly not so with state commissions, where there was in any case a problem of recruiting a vast work-force. While those responsible for state commissions did not actually import painters, sculptors and architects into the Venetian dominions, they were quite prepared to employ artists who were not even Venetian subjects, Sansovino and Vittoria being notable cases in point.

Venetian artistic patronage was undoubtedly orientated primarily towards artists of the Venetian and Terraferma schools, but Venetian taste was not closed to outside currents. Records of collections and art criticism suggest a particular enthusiasm for Raphael in the first half of the sixteenth century and in the middle years of the century there was an invasion of central Italian artists, principally encouraged by the Grimani of S. Maria Formosa. The development of the Venetian school of painting can only be fully understood within the context of a current of taste which, while strongly appreciative of native schools, was in some measure sympathetic to developments elsewhere in Italy. The nature of artistic patronage also casts light on the development of Venetian art in another way. The collection of pictures was closely related to that of antiques and antiquarianism made its impact on art, not so much in painting as in architecture and sculpture, the most distinguished interpreters of the antiquarian and archaising current being Palladio and a sculptor now often forgotten but the arbiter of taste in late sixteenth-century Venice—Alessandro Vittoria.

It is difficult to assess the contribution in bulk made by individual artists to adorning the city of Venice, since so many works were removed by foreign collectors in the seventeenth and eighteenth centuries, although Ridolfi and Boschini obviously provide valuable guides to the artistic riches of Venice prior to the mid-seventeenth century. The loss of works by Titian appears to have been particularly heavy. Titian, in any case, worked for non-Venetian patrons both in Italy and abroad and it is unlikely that his contribution to the adornment of Venice itself was comparable to Tintoretto's. The artists who perhaps above all left their mark upon Venice were the Florentine Jacopo Sansovino, the Venetian Jacopo Tintoretto and the Trentino Alessandro Vittoria, a testimony to the strong contrasts within an artistic tradition that was created by Venetian, Veneto and central Italian artists.

Notes

[1] For the diarist Gerolamo Priuli's belief in the spread of extravagance around the turn of the sixteenth century, see the text cited in A. Fanfani, *Storia del lavoro in Italia* (Milan 1943), pp. 26–7; for observations and moralistic attitudes around the turn of the seventeenth century, see G. Cozzi, 'Federigo Contarini: un antiquario veneziano tra Rinascimento e Controriforma', *Boll. Ist. Stor. Soc. & Stat. Ven.*, III (1961), pp. 208–11; for observations on the ways in which nobles spent or economised, made by Thomas Coryat, who visited Venice in 1608 see *Coryat's Crudities*, vol. I (Glasgow 1905 ed.), pp. 397–8, 415

[2] An outstanding example is the testament of the Procurator Marcantonio Grimani of 1558. (A. S. Ven, *Notarile, Testamenti*, B. 1262 ff., 18r and seq.). For the testament of the Procurator Federigo Contarini (1609) see Cozzi, 'Federigo Contarini', pp.2 07–8

[3] Juergen Schulz, *Venetian Painted Ceilings of the Renaissance* (California 1968), pp. 39–40

[4] See Appendix

[5] G. Fiocco, *Alvise Cornaro, il suo tempo e le sue opere* (Venice 1965), pp. 42–58; Fiocco, 'La Casa di Alvise Cornaro', *Misc. in Onore di R. Cessi* (Rome 1958), vol. II, p. 70

[6] G. Vasari, *Lives of the Painters, Sculptors and Architects*, IV (London 1950), p. 244

[7] *Ibid.*, IV, p. 26

[8] A. S. Ven, *Notarile, Testamenti*, B. 68 no. 396

[9] Testament Gabriele Vendramin, 1547 (A. S. Ven, *Notarile, Testamenti*, B. 1217, Protocol VIII seq. f. 21. Testament Giacomo Contarini 1595 (*Ibid.* B. 1194, Prot. V seq. f. 4). For Federigo Contarini's 1609 testament see Cozzi, 'Federigo Contarini', p. 221. Collections are entailed by the testament of Francesco Bernardo, 1589 (A. S. Ven. *Notarile, Testamenti*, B. 194 no. 432) and Cristoforo Barbarigo (*Ibid.* 1194 VI, seq. f. 57e)

[10] This assertion was made in the ms. Fapanni, *Elenco dei musei* etc. (1877–89), p. 2 (Bibl. Marciana, Ven., *Cod. it.* Ser VII 10479). Fapanni evidently based himself on a reference by Maria Soranzo in 1461 to the Venetian practice of collecting and display-ing arms, cited in F. Mutinelli, *Lessico veneto* (Venice 1851), p. 32

[11] See especially: R. Weiss, 'Lineamenti per una storia degli studi antiquari in Italia dal dodesimo secolo al sacco di Roma di 1527', *Rinascimento*, IX (1958), pp. 141–99; Weiss, *The Renaissance Discovery of Classical Antiquity* (Oxford 1969). On Florence see: A. Chastel, *Art et humanisme à Florence au temps de Laurent le Magnifique*, pp. 31–5; E. Gombrich, *Norm and Form. Studies in the Art of the Renaissance* (London 1966) Ch. 'The early Medici as patrons of art'. On Florentine collecting and patronage more generally, see M. Wackernagel, *Der Lebensraum des Kunstlers des Florentinischen Renaissance* (Leipzig 1938), esp. pp. 232–82

[12] *Der Anonimo Morelliano—Marcantonio Michiels Notizia d'opere del disegno*, ed. T.

Frimmel (Vienna 1888). There is an English edition, published as *The Anonimo*, ed. G. C. Williamson (London 1903)

[13] Domenico Grimani (1528), Andrea Odoni (1558), Gabriele Vendramin (1567–9). See Appendix

[14] S. Savini-Branca, *Il collezionismo veneziano del Seicento* (Padua 1964)

[15] See Appendix

[16] See Appendix

[17] See Appendix

[18] A. Ferriguto, *Attraverso i 'misteri' di Giorgione* (Castelfranco Veneto 1933), pp. 183–97

[19] These remarks are based on the surviving inventories of the effects of collections mentioned in the *Anonimo*, as well as on the *Anonimo* itself

[20] The lack of information about Andrea Loredan and Cristoforo Barbarigo is particularly unfortunate. Loredan's studio was referred to by Scamozzi as one of the particularly fine ones seen by him in his youth. Loredan acquired some of Gabriele Vendramin's medals in 1565. The only references to his collection relate to antiques. It is uncertain whether he had any responsibility for the adornment of the magnificent Palazzo Non Nobis Domine which he inherited, or even whether he personally acquired the Titian *Flight into Egypt* mentioned as being in the palace. Cristoforo Barbarigo (*b*. 1544—testated 1600) certainly bought a number of works from the studio of the deceased Titian and his heirs possessed a fine collection of works by Venetian masters but it is uncertain how many of them had been acquired by Cristoforo. (See Appendix)

[21] For Giacomo Contarini, see Appendix

[22] See Appendix

[23] See Appendix

[24] The collections listed at pp. 305–6 (excluding the Gabriele Vendramin inheritance) were those of Carlo Ruzzini, Andrea Vendramin, Giovanni Mocenigo, Pietro Pellegrini, Bortolomeo della Nave and the Fleming Daniele Nis. Carlo Ruzzini in fact inherited the collection of Federigo Contarini but himself added paintings to it. Scamozzi did not generally specify whether the statues, busts, etc. were antique, except in the case of Ruzzini. We know from other sources, however, that Vendramin and Mocenigo possessed antiques. Scamozzi specified that Della Nave and Nis had bought statues from the collections of Pietro Bembo and Simon Zeno respectively, both of whom certainly possessed numbers of antiques

[25] The collection was obviously distinct from that of Gabriele Vendramin mentioned earlier, although Andrea and Gabriele probably belonged to the same branch of the family

[26] See Appendix

[27] B. Morsolin, *Le collezioni di cose d'arte nel secolo decimo sesto a Vicenza* (Vicenza 1881)

[28] See Appendix

[29] Savini-Branca, *Il Collezionismo veneziano*, p. 16

[30] An exception is that of Cristoforo Barbarigo who had purchased a number of works from the studio of the deceased Titian and specifically mentioned in his will that he had a number of works by that artist's hand

[31] Giacomo Contarini, Giovanni Grimani and Federigo Contarini as above. Seven Flemish works are also mentioned, in the Alessandro Ram inventory (1592). It is not altogether clear whether Ram's marble pieces were antique. (See Appendix)

[32] C.p. Isabella d'Este's collections and pictorial cycles at Mantua. See E. Wind, *Bellini's Feast of the Gods: a Study in Venetian Humanism* (Harvard 1948)

[33] Corner's treatises are reproduced in G. Fiocco, *Alvise Cornaro, il suo tempo e le sue opere* (Venice 1965)

[34] See Fiocco, *Alvise Cornaro,* pp. 42–66; G. Mazzotti, *Palladian and other Venetianaro Villas* (London–Rome 1966), pp. 103–9

[35] On Trissino and his relations with Palladio, see especially G. Piovene, 'Trissino e Palladio nell' Umanesimo vicentino', *Boll. Centr. Internaz. di Studi di Architettura A. Palladio,* v (1963); pp. 13–23, R.Wittkower, *Architectural Principles in the Age of Humanism* (London 1952), pp. 51–7. See also Appendix below

[36] *Op. cit.*, p. 51

[37] Copy in Bibl. Marciana, Venice, *Mss. italici*, Cl iv n. 190 (5159)

[38] G. G. Trissino, *Italia liberata dai Goti* (Rome 1547), Bk. v. at p. 80v, cf. p. 93r

[39] G. G. Zorzi, 'La problematica palladiana in relazione alle più recenti scoperte', *Boll. Centr. Internaz di Studi di Arch. A. Palladio*, v (1963), pp. 93–5

See Appendix under Giuseppe da Porto, Marcantonio Thiene, Francesco and Ludovico Trissino, Giovan Alvise Valmarana, Orazio Thiene, Giuliano and Guido Piovene

[40] The Nicolò and Alvise Foscari (Palladio, *Quattro Libri*, p. 48) who commissioned the Villa Malcontenta were presumably Nicolò (1518–60) and Alvise (1521–98), the sons of Federigo, son of Nicolò. Nicolò was a member of the Council of Ten and Alvise Savio del Consiglio. In 1574, he lodged Henry iii of France in his house

The Villa Cornaro (Dese, Piombino Castelfranco) contains statues of Caterina Queen of Cyprus and her husband. This suggests that the Giorgio Corner who commissioned it (*Quattro libri* p. 51) belonged either to the branch of S. Maurizio or to that of S. Polo and was presumably Giorgio (1533–86) the son of Giacomo Proc., son of Giorgio. He was a member of the Consiglio and the Council of Ten

[41] See in P. Barocchi (ed.), *Trattati d'arte del Cinquecento*, i (Bari 1960), p. 159

[42] Ridolfi, *Meraviglie*, i, p. 332

[43] See Appendix

[44] See Appendix

[45] See p. 185

[46] For example Giovan Domenico Scamozzi (Vincenzo's father), Pietro da Nanto and Domenico Groppino

[47] Most notably the Villa della Torre, Fumane (Veronese) (alternatively attrib. to G. Romano) and the Villa Soranza, Treville (Trevigiano) (1544–51), now destroyed

[48] Perhaps the most remarkable projects actually executed by him, or attributed to

him, are the Villa Pisani, Lonigo (1576), Villa Duodo, Monselice (1593), Villa Contarini, Este (attrib.), Villa Nani-Mocenigo, Scanda (Rovigo) (attrib.), Villa Molin, Mandriola (Padua) (1597)

⁴⁹ Especially noteworthy are Sanmicheli's Pal. Grimani, S. Luca and Sansovino's Pal. Corner, S. Maurizio and Pal. Dolfin-Manin. Scamozzi was mainly engaged on extensions to existing palaces. Perhaps his most extensive complete work in the Pal. Contarini ai Scrigni (1609)

⁵⁰ Savini-Branca, *op. cit.*, pp. 26–7

⁵¹ For Corner patronage generally see Appendix

⁵² The observation that the Grimani were primarily responsible for the promotion of mannerist currents in Venice is chiefly due to L. Coletti, 'La crisi manieristica della pittura veneziana', *Convivium* (1941), p. 118

⁵³ For Grimani patronage generally, see Appendix

⁵⁴ The grants to Gentile and Giovanni Bellini of 1474 and 1479 had, however, been made by Senate and Maggior Consiglio respectively

⁵⁵ G. B. Lorenzi, *Monumenti per servire alla storia del Palazzo Ducale*, I (Venice 1868), pp. 85, 88, 157, 391

⁵⁶ G. Lorenzetti, *Venice and its Lagoon* (Rome 1961), p. 246; Lorenzi, *op. cit.*

⁵⁷ Lorenzetti, *op. cit.*, p. 237; C. Ridolfi, *Le meraviglie dell' arte* (1648), ed. D. von Hadeln (Rome 1965), I, pp. 45, 64–7, 106, 123, 157, 165–6; II, pp. 23–5

⁵⁸ Lorenzi, *op. cit.,* pp. 157–61, 219

⁵⁹ Lorenzetti, *op. cit.*, p. 140

⁶⁰ Vasari, *Lives* (London 1950), IV, p. 221. The commission may in fact have been given on the occasion of an earlier visit to Venice

⁶¹ Lorenzetti, *op. cit.*, p. 158

⁶² Vasari, *op. cit.*, p. 225

⁶³ *Dialogo di tutte le cose notabili etc.*

⁶⁴ R. Gallo, 'Contributi su Jacopo Sansovino', *Saggi e Memorie della storia dell' Arte*, I (1957), pp. 96–8

⁶⁵ A. S. Ven, *Proc. di Supra*, B. 68, *processo* 151, fasc. III, under dates 5 Feb. 1545 (i.e. 1546) (with report of 22 Dec. 1545) and 10 Feb. 1545 (1546)

⁶⁶ Lorenzetti, *op. cit.*, p. 599

⁶⁷ *Lives*, IV, p. 26, under 'Bazzacco'

⁶⁸ Lorenzi, *op. cit.*, p. 599

⁶⁹ Sansovino-Stringa, *Venetia città*, etc., p. 123v

⁷⁰ A. S. Ven, *Proc. di Supra*, B. 58, proc. 151, fasc. II; Lorenzetti, *op. cit.*, pp. 153–4; Schulz, *op. cit.*, pp. 93–6

⁷¹ Ridolfi, *Meraviglie*, ed. cit. II, p. 26

⁷² *Proc. di Supra*, B. 68, proc. 151, fasc. II under date 1559, 9 September

⁷³ Lorenzetti, *op. cit.*, pp. 151–2; Schulz, *op. cit.*, pp. 95–6

⁷⁴ *Proc. di Supra*, B. 68, proc. 151, fasc. II

⁷⁵ Lorenzi, *op. cit.*, p. 599

⁷⁶ Lorenzetti, *op. cit.*, pp. 253–5, 257–8; Schulz, *op. cit.*, pp. 104–7

23 Palladio, church of the Redentore, Venice, 1576–7 (see pp. 191–2, 249–50)

24   A. Vittoria, bust of Nicolò da Ponte, Doge 1578–85 (see p. 252)

[77] For this and future references to *Provveditori* see Lorenzi, *op. cit.*, pp. 599–600

[78] Ridolfi, *Meraviglie*, I (Rome 1965 ed.), p. 326

[79] See Appendix

[80] Sansovino, *Venetia città* (1581 ed.), p. 138

[81] The *Last Judgement* above the tribune in the Scrutinio was to be the same as before the fire

[82] Copy in Bibl. Marciana, Ven, *MSS. Italiani*, Cl. IV. n. 22, 5361, and published by W. Wolters in *Mitteilungen des Kunsthistorischen Institut in Florenz*, XII (1965–6), pp. 271 ff

[83] In 1584 Bardi was to publish a history of Venice's relations with Alexander III and Barbarossa

[84] Ridolfi, *ed. cit.*, I, pp. 326, 404

[85] Lorenzetti, *op. cit.*, pp. 272–9; Schulz, *op. cit.*, pp. 107–11

[86] Lorenzetti, *op. cit.*, pp. 279–83; Schulz, *op. cit.*, pp, 114–16

[87] Lorenzi, *op. cit.*, p. 499

[88] Lorenzetti, *op. cit.*, p. 260

[89] Davide da Portogruaro, 'Il Tempio e il Convento del Redentore', *Rivista di Venezia*, April–May 1930, pp. 141–233

[90] A. S. Ven, *Proc. di Supra*, B. 65 ff, 19r–74r

[91] These remarks are based upon an examination of genealogies: A. S. Ven, *Barbaro Albori*; Bibl. Mariana, Ven., Capellari-Vivaro, *Il Campidoglio veneto*. The information that these give on patrician members of orders is incomplete and it is possible that they tend to give particular attention to orders with a high reputation

[92] Details of revenues from religious houses from immoveable property in Venice alone are given in D. Beltrami, *Storia della popolazione di Venezia dalla fine del secolo XVI all fine della Repubblica* (Padua 1954), table 23

[93] These remarks are based on a study of about 110 testaments in which bequests, other than burial fees or stipends for masses, are made to male religious houses, out of a total sample of some 1,500 testaments of the period 1540–1630 in A. S. Ven, *Notarile, Testamenti*

[94] P. Vittorio Meneghin, *S. Michele in Isola di Venezia* (Venice 1962), pp. 295–323; P. Paoletti, *L'architettura e scultura del Rinascimento in Venezia*, II (Venice 1893), pp. 163–72

[95] E. A. Cicogna, *Delle iscrizioni veneziane* (Venice 1824–53) IV, pp. 134–53

[96] Lorenzetti, *op. cit.*, pp. 377; G. Mariacher, *Il Sansovino* (Milan 1962), pp. 111–13; for Francesco di Giorgi and his proposals see Wittkower, *Architectural Principles*, pp. 90–94

[97] See above

[98] G. Damerini, *L'Isola e il Cenobio di San Giorgio Maggiore* (Venice 1956), pp. 64–82

[99] Pane, *Andrea Palladio*, pp. 293–5

[100] For S. M. dell'Umiltà see A. de Mosto, *L'Archivio di Stato di Venezia*, I (Rome 1940), pp. 142–3; Schulz, *Venetian Painted Ceilings*, pp. 71–2. The Umiltà is not to be confused with S. Maria Assunta, the former church of the *Crociferi* taken over by the

H

Jesuits in 1657. For the Tolentini: Lorenzetti, *op. cit.*, pp. 485–6; F. Barbieri, *Vincenzo Scamozzi* (Vicenza 1962), pp. 144–5

[101] Beltrami, *Stori della popolazione di Venezia*, p. 79

[102] For S. Zaccaria see Paoletti, *op. cit.*, I, pp. 173–5; for the Miracoli, *ibid.*, pp. 205–16

[103] My points on the social and economic position of the nunneries are argued at length in my thesis, *Studies in the Religious Life of Venice in the Sixteenth and Early Seventeenth Centuries*, Univ. of Cambridge, Faculty of History, 1967, in University Library, Cambridge

[104] R. Gallo, 'Contributi su Jacopo Sansovino', *Saggi e Memorie della Storia dell'Arte*, I (1957), pp. 83–105; *cf.* Bardi, *Delle cose notabili* (1592), pp. 41–2

[105] Ridolfi, *ed. cit.*, I, p. 390 et seq.; Schulz, *Venetian Painted Ceilings*, pp. 75–7

[106] E. Cheyney, *Original Documents Relating to Venetian Painters and their Pictures in the Sixteenth Century. Miscellanies of the Philobiblion Society*, XIV (1872–6), pp. 13–20

[107] P. Aretino, *Lettere sull' arte*, comment F. Pertile, ed. E. Camasasca (Milan 1957), II doc. DXXX

[108] Ridolfi, *ed. cit.*, I, pp. 179–83

[109] *Ibid.*, pp. 184–6

[110] See Schulz, *Venetian Painted Ceilings*, esp. pp. 63–80, 130–5

[111] E. G. Holt (ed.), *A Documentary History of Art*, II, pp. 65–70

[112] See Francis Haskell, *Patrons and Painters. A Study in the Relations Between Italian Art and Society in the Age of the Baroque* (London 1963), pp. 267–75

[113] B. S. Pullan, *Rich and Poor in Renaissance Venice, the social institutions of a Catholic state to 1620* (Oxford 1970). For Botero's comments see *Relatione della Repubblica Veneziana* (Venice 1605), pp. 97r–v

[114] *Il sogno di Caravia* (Venice 1541), pages un-numbered

[115] Paoletti, *op. cit.*, II, pp. 280–1, 289–90

[116] *Ibid.*, p. 176

[117] Lorenzetti, *op. cit.*, pp. 612–15, 687–9. For the building, see Paoletti, *op. cit.*, II, pp. 181–3, 221–2; for the paintings see also Ridolfi, *ed. cit.*, II, pp. 175–6, Schulz, *Venetian Painted Ceilings*, pp. 84–5

[118] Lorenzetti, pp. 340–3; U. Stefanutti, *La Scuola Grande di S. Marco* (Venice undated), pp. 9–28

[119] Paoletti, *op. cit.*, II, pp. 174–7, 222–6

[120] *Ibid.*, pp. 176, 177

[121] The *St Mark Preaching in Alexandria* by Gentile and Giovanni Bellini (Ridolfi, *ed. cit.*, I, p. 60 and note) is now in the Brera. Paris Bordone's *Fisherman presenting the Ring to the Signory* (Vasari, *Lives*, IV (London 1950)) is now in the Accademia. The *Storm during the Transportation of the Body of St Mark* (now in the Accademia) is variously attributed, but according to Vasari (*ed. cit.*, IV) it was commissioned from Palma Vecchio as the result of a competition

[122] Cheyney, *Original documents*, pp. 21–3; Ridolfi, *ed. cit.*, II, pp. 21–3 and notes

[123] See above p. 198

[124] F. Cessi, *Alessandro Vittoria, Bronzista* (Trent 1967), p. 28

[125] Lorenzetti, *op. cit.*, pp. 689–91; Savini-Branca, p. 13

[126] Lorenzetti, *op. cit.*, pp. 373–6

[127] *Ibid.*, pp. 665, 693–4

[128] *Ibid.*, pp. 604–12; Paoletti, *op. cit.*, II, pp. 280–1, 289–90; R. Berliner, 'Die Tatigkeit Tintorettos in der Scuola di San Rocco', *Kunstchronik u. Kunstmarkt*, LV (1919–20), pp. 469–70, 492–7; E. Huttinger, *Die Bilderzyklen Tintorettos in der Scuola di S. Rocco zu Venedig* (Zurich 1962)

[129] Lorenzetti, *op. cit.*, p. 407; Mariacher, *Il Sansovino*, pp. 96–110

[130] F. Z. Boccazzi, *La Basilica dei Santi Giovanni e Paolo in Venezia* (Padua 1965), pp. 194–8; F. Cessi, *Alessandro Vittoria, architetto e stuccatore* (Trent 1961), pp. 60–3; Schulz, *Venetian Painted Ceilings*, pp. 131–2

[131] Ridolfi, *ed. cit.*, II, pp. 21–3 and notes; M. Boschini, *Carta del navegar pittoresco* (Venice 1660), p. 480

[132] Lorenzi, *op. cit.*, p. 391

[133] Berliner, 'Die Tatigkeit Tintorettos' etc.

[134] Ridolfi, *ed. cit.*, II, p. 177

nine

The Visual Arts

As early as the mid-sixteenth century, Venetian painters had found their apologists and propagandists. The first comprehensive history of the Venetian school of painting came with the Veronese Carlo Ridolfi's *Meraviglie dell' Arte* of 1648 and in his writings shortly afterwards the Venetian Mario Boschini showed a profound consciousness of a distinct Venetian *maniera*. It was not however until 1778, with the Vicentine Tomaso Temanza's *Vite dei più celebri architetti e scultori veneziani* that the first history of Renaissance architecture in the Veneto appeared; here it should be said that the area of study was the Veneto as a whole and not Venice specifically, but, quite apart from the aesthetic orientations of Temanza's generation, the reasons for this are fully comprehensible, given the fact that architectural developments in the metropolis often followed those in the Provinces. By contrast with the vast wealth of studies devoted to Venetian painting, relatively little attention has been paid to Renaissance architecture and sculpture in Venice and the Veneto. Palladio was always the major exception. The intensive study which P. Paoletti devoted to Coducci and his contemporaries in his *Architettura e scultura del Rinascimento in Venezia* of 1893 found little emulation before the end of the last war. Sanmicheli was always a name to be conjured with, but close interest in the work of Gian Maria Falconetto, Giovanni Ricamatori da Udine, Alessandro Vittoria and Vincenzo Scamozzi has been a relatively recent affair.

A detailed study of the development of the Venetian school of painting is obviously superfluous here. The present examination will concentrate upon certain limited questions: what connections did painting have with movements in scholarship, literature and thought; what was the impact upon it of antiquarianism and what lessons did it take from antique art; how far was painting in Venice related to artistic movements in the Terraferma and elsewhere in Italy? Here it will be seen that the Venetian tradition was by no means an isolated regional one. Turning to architecture, where an outline study is more obviously necessary, a curious pattern emerges. Venice was heavily dependent upon outside skills, but architects working in Venice, from Coducci to Sansovino, adapted themselves to a surprising degree to idiosyncratic local idioms. This is barely perceptible in sculpture, where imported traditions were dominant, although it will be suggested that Alessandro Vittoria may have profited from contact with Venetian painters.

If we enquire into the nature of the lessons that Venetian painters drew from the antique, it is evident that none of them was a 'neo-classicist'. They did not, as Vittoria evidently did in many of his works, seek an erudite recreation of the typical genres or of the manner of antique art. Their naturalism was never engulfed by antiquarianism. At the same time, they did not pursue the cultivated eclecticism of the true neo-classicist who seeks, in the recreation of an antique style, to emancipate himself from the motifs of individual ancient models. Furthermore, it was only with the greatest freedom that they would have been disposed to take lessons from antique *sculpture*. For them, quite obviously, the qualities of painting were totally different from those of sculpture and readers of Pliny might well have felt that this had been accepted in antiquity.[1] The fact that the impact of the ancient world upon Venetian artists came through literary descriptions of antique paintings and through the classics themselves, as well as through visual exemplars, also compelled them to use imagination. Giovanni Bellini, in his late work the *Feast of the Gods*, was evidently inspired by Lucian and throughout his life Titian was occupied with scenes from Ovid. Antique marbles, even reliefs, could seldom in themselves offer a key to the recreation of the Ovidian mood or of Lucian's ironic fantasy.[2] They had relatively little to offer to the ageing Titian who, going beyond the Ovidian presentations, was seized by the pathos and sinister drama of certain mythological themes such as the seduction of Danäe and the vindictiveness of Diana; even the lessons of Pergamene art, while certainly significant for Titian, were not truly appropriate to these particular contexts.

In what senses, then, did Venetian painters take antique sculptural pieces as models, as lessons in form and as vehicles of dramatic content, that is, and not simply as sources of motifs for erudite quotation? As keys to the understanding of the human body, almost certainly, and this perhaps especially around the first decade of the sixteenth century. On the other hand they obviously did not, in the long run, take them as models of an ultimate ideal of human beauty. They would hardly seem indeed to have a preoccupation with this as an absolute norm; such a preoccupation has in fact been one of the hallmarks of the neo-classicist artistic outlook properly speaking. What they evidently did see in antique art were lessons in bodily posture, in elegant *contraposto* poses and on the human body in movement, although it was more with the examples of Tuscan and Roman contemporaries that they nourished the taste for marked bodily contortions and for violent action. In the study of posture, inspiration must have come primarily from reliefs (more particularly those on Hellenistic and Roman sarcophagi) and where it was a question of antique free-standing sculptures it perhaps more particularly works in the Pergamene style that would have been of significance. Certainly the detailed studies that have been made of Titian's borrowings from the antique point in these directions. As well as showing figures in movement, sarcophagus reliefs may also have given artists ideas about the compositional linkage of figures. As for Pergamene art or Graeco-Roman art in the Pergamene tradition, this exercised particular fascination upon the post-Michelangelesque gene-rations of Italian artists. It was an art of pathos, often preoccupied with human suffering and with the tortured human body, exploring its movement in contortion. It was strongly sensitive to the surface qualities of form, exploiting in particular the ripple of muscles, and giving to marble the illusory quality of a malleable substance. Thereby it was a sculptural tradition that painters were particularly liable to appreciate.

Renaissance art did, of course, receive extensive stimulus from small-scale antique pieces: bronzes, coins, medallions, cameos and even en-graved jewels. Certainly Venetian collections were rich in such objects and they may well have been crucial when the Renaissance style was first developing in Venice; even later, Titian seems to have taken motifs from cameos, coins and medals. Inevitably, however, where Renaissance artists appear to have made use of small antique pieces, it was more a question of borrowing motifs than of direct absorption of ancient formal ideals, although one often feels that in such cases, just as when they were working from indifferent late-antique copies, artists were seeking to intuit the forms of original prototypes by true masters. The importance for artists of small-scale pieces probably diminished with the High Renaissance. If, in the *quattrocento*, artists had revealed their interests in the antique primarily by the 'quotation' of motifs and had been generally unselective in their choice of exemplars, in the *cinquecento* the search for more truly aesthetic lessons went hand-in-hand with a greater selectivity in the choice of models.[3]

Bearing in mind the types of antique piece that Venetian sixteenth-century painters would have found most artistically stimulating, enquiries as to how far they were indebted to works in Venetian collections are unlikely to yield very gratifying results. In many cases, of course, the contents of these collections cannot now be identified. When we come, however, to the large-scale pieces that are known to have been in sixteenth-century Venetian collections, basically those that passed into the state patrimony and form the basis of the present Museo d' Antichità, the general impression is that their importance for Venetian artists was limited, although by no means negligible. Leaving out of account the very late sixteenth-century collection of Federigo Contarini, the most important is that of the Patriarch Giovanni Grimani. Here, among the large free-standing statues there was a predominance of monolithic, highly frontalised ones, works which might well have inspired sculptors in the city but which would probably not have been deeply interesting to painters from Titian onwards. Again, Giovanni Grimani had a poor collection of reliefs, a major exception being the *Ara Grimani*, one tableau of which may have partly inspired the figure of the goddess in Titian's *Venus and Adonis*.[4] On the other hand, Giovanni's uncle Domenico possessed three very fine statues in the Pergamene idiom and two of these, the sprawling *Wounded Gaul* and the more heroic *Kneeling Gaul*, did evidently inspire Titian on a number of occasions.[5] In general, however, Venetian painters seem to have been more particularly indebted to antique works that were to be found outside their own city. Often they must have been introduced to their forms through engravings and drawings and sometimes even through the compositions of other artists. Their access to engravings may, however, have been facilitated by the current of antiquarian enthusiasm in Venice which received support from the great collectors.

Painting

In the fifteenth century, the antiquarian movement, which had one of its main centres in Padua, had only an ephemeral impact upon Venetian painters. It can certainly be seen in the sketch-books of Jacopo Bellini, whose antiquarian interests appear to have been closely allied to those of his son-in-law Andrea Mantegna, perhaps the most authentic artistic representative of Paduan antiquarianism. In Jacopo's sketch-books there are two sheets covered with painstaking studies of ancient monuments and numismata. In other drawings, antique ornamental details are inserted into renderings of what are basically Gothic buildings. Again, in playful renderings of satyrs and of the triumph of Bacchus, there are free fantasies upon antique ornamental forms.[6] Certainly there is not the consistent archaising tendency found with Mantegna and contact with the antique did not fundamentally transform Jacopo's style. The generation following Jacopo was hardly concerned with the antique directly, although undoubtedly fascinated by Mantegna. Giovanni Bellini's revolution was basically independent of classical inspiration.

Giovanni firmly broke with a provincial tradition hitherto primarily linked to that of the Marches. Together with his father Jacopo, he was among Venetian fifteenth-century painters the most direct heir of Tuscan traditions, while in his works of the 1450s and 1460s, he showed strong affinities with Mantegna. Furthermore, it is hard not to believe that he was inspired by Flemish painting or at the least encouraged in his natural penchant by a current of taste sympathetic to northern art. Indeed it seems reasonable to suppose that such a current, which was evident at the time when the *Anonimo Morelliano* was compiled, was already established in Bellini's lifetime when Flemish works were, without doubt, avidly collected elsewhere in Italy. While echoes of Rogier van der Weyden may be discerned in Giovanni's emotive treatment of the pathetic, angular figures of his dead Christs in the 1450s and 1460s, it is in certain of his works from around the turn of the sixteenth century that reminiscences of Memlinc are most strongly suggested in the Madonnas and in the female nudes and of the Van Eyck in his richly detailed landscapes.

There is also the question of Giovanni's technical procedures. Ridolfi's story that he turned from tempera to oils as a result of contact with Antonello da Messina who had in turn learnt the art from Jan van Eyck[7] can be faulted on a number of points. Quite apart from the fact that Antonello was too young to have encountered Van Eyck personally, the latter painted not in oils but with egg-tempera. Furthermore, it is not true that Italian masters of the early fifteenth century were ignorant of oil technique; the Venetians themselves early showed a preference for it, long before the visit of Antonello to their city in 1475.[8] On the other hand, the oil technique employed by Giovanni from about the 1470s, which treated pigment as a semi-transparent medium applied by an accumulation of small brush-strokes, did have closer affinities with the Van Eyck's tempera technique than with the practice of most fifteenth-century Italian masters in the mediums either of tempera or of oils. One notable difference, however, lay in the fact that while the Flemings achieved shade-effects by an intensification of colour, Bellini, like Antonello, employed admixtures of burnt umber or similar colours which tended, except in his later works to be rather dead in hue. Here it was Cima da Conegliano who more closely followed Flemish practice. Whether Giovanni's abandonment of his early method, which primarily recalls Italian tempera technique, for his new method really followed Antonello's visit to Venice to paint the S. Cassian altarpiece in the years 1475–6 is not altogether certain, since there is dispute as to the dating of the S. Giobbe altarpiece and the Pesaro *Coronation of the Virgin* which marked a crucial stage in Bellini's evolution.

In the 65 odd years of his working life from around 1450 until 1516, Giovanni constantly engaged in novel experiments in which the elements of a cosmopolitan artistic culture were synthesised into a succession of original styles. In the 1470s he abandoned the harsh, sculptural Mantegnesque figures and boldly contoured landscapes of his earlier period for a new softness of plastic form and a new subtlety and luminosity of colouristic effect. In the works of his last decade or so, the *Baptism of Christ* in S. Corona Vicenza, the *SS. Jerome, Christopher and Augustine* at S. Giovanni Crisostomo in Venice, the *Feast of the Gods* and the *Lady at her toilet*, the richness of luminous colour and shadow, the exploration of tonal subtleties and the presentation of the confident, supple human figure, now firmly detached from both Gothic and Mantegnesque traditions, pointed towards the art of both Giorgione and Titian, who may in fact have collaborated on these works.

At the turn of the sixteenth century Venetian painting became subject to a new, although limited antique wave and to the impact of German painting and graphic art. With regard to the latter, there was between Venice and Nuremberg in particular a mutually profitable interchange. Albrecht Dürer, who had already been in Venice in 1494, stayed there in the years 1505–7, coming on this occasion as an artist of established reputation with a commission from the German merchants of the Fondaco to paint the *Feast of the Rose-Garlands* in the church of S. Bartolomeo. His work must also have been widely known through engravings. Dürer himself believed that Venetian artists were fascinated by his work, even if he referred to the body of them as alternately criticising it and shamelessly plagiarising it. It was of Giovanni Bellini alone that he spoke with profound respect.[9] It is possible that the latter was influenced by the Nuremberg painter in his late works, but Dürer's fullest impact was upon the painters of the younger generation, that of

Giorgione, Lotto and Titian, perhaps precisely those to whom he referred as spiteful rivals and as thieves. Germanic influence may be perceived in a new realism in both landscape and portraiture and in a more dynamic treatment of the human figure. It is even possible that Titian was indebted to Dürer when he came to tackle the problems of the human body's structure and proportions.[10]

'It is not antique and therefore no good.'[11] This, according to Dürer, writing in 1506, was how Venetian rivals cast aspersions on his own work. Evidently the antique had now become an object of cult. In point of fact, the antiquarianising strain was most obtrusive in sculpture and metal-work and more particularly with artists such as Andrea Riccio and the younger Lombardi, Tullio and Antonio, who worked extensively in Padua. It is indeed possible that it was less the antique itself than the work of contemporary sculptors that provided the stimulus to Venetian painters in the first decade of the sixteenth century.[12] In paintings of this period, the influence of the antique manifested itself in a variety of strange forms. In Carpaccio's *Martyrdom of the Ten Thousand*, with its tortured bodies, antique motifs had undergone a bizarre translation into the local idiom. In Titian's first Pesaro altarpiece, on the other hand, there is a brilliant and sensitive pastiche of an antique relief adorning the marble block upon which St Peter stands; there seems little doubt that it is indeed a pastiche and not a copy. Let into a picture which is otherwise in the traditional Venetian manner, it has all the qualities of an archaeological relic, the remnant of a decayed civilisation over which the church has triumphed.[13] Again certain figures in Giorgione's surviving works have an aura of the antique, most notably the Dresden *Venus*—although here, in the small breasts and somewhat full belly and in the ogival contours there are reminiscences of the Flemish nude—and again in the frescoes of the Fondaco dei Tedeschi in which, to judge from eighteenth-century copies, he had moved towards a more statuesque and heroic treatment of the human figure than is found among his surviving easel-paintings. It has been impossible, however, to trace ancient prototypes. In general, Giorgione's links with antiquity were perhaps more through literary and poetic sources than through sculptural remnants.

It would seem that 'Giorgionesque' art had close links with the literary and scholarly currents of the time. That Giorgione himself catered extensively for an erudite public is suggested both by the limited circumstantial evidence on his patrons[14] and by the fact that the number of his allegories and mythological subjects was extensive,[15] although many of the works in question have been lost. In examining the erudite character of *Giorgionismo*, however, it is desirable not to confine ourselves to works that can be securely attributed to Giorgione da Castelfranco but to look more broadly at the group of paintings recognised as being 'in the Giorgionesque style' dating from around the first decade of the sixteenth century; some of these were probably executed by Andrea Previtale, Sebastiano del Piombo and Titian, but they form together a remarkably coherent corpus with regard to both style and atmosphere. Out of the paintings of this group, scholarly curiosity has been aroused in particular by the 'idylls' and the 'mystery' paintings.

The 'idylls',[16] paintings of figures in landscapes are evocative of the Golden Age or of Arcadia, although the treatment of landscape does not differ notably from that in religious paintings by the 'Giorgionesque' group. The terms 'lyrical' or 'idyllic', conventionally applied to them by modern criticism, did not belong to the critical vocabulary of the sixteenth century and there is no direct evidence that contemporaries appreciated their elegaic-romantic qualities. It seems reasonable, however, to relate the genre to the contemporary pastoral movement in literature as well as to the antique elegaic tradition of Theocritus and Virgil. Sannazaro's *Arcadia* was extremely popular at the time. The subject of the *Damon and Thyrsis* has been directly identified with one in Tebaldeo's *Poemi volgari* published in Venice in 1502. Bembo's *Asolani* also comes to mind with regard to the genre as a whole. Although there is no evidence of direct links between Giorgione and Bembo (the latter did not apparently possess any of his pictures), it is probable that Giorgione visited Queen Caterina's court where the scene of the *Asolani* was set.[17] Appreciation of the pastoral landscape can perhaps be related in some measure to the growing involvement of Venetians with the countryside, which now offered the hope of economic security in a period of trade-depression. The treatment of landscape in the idylls, it should be said, was naturalistic but not realistic and there was perhaps an escapist element in the fashion for the idyll. The 'Giorgionesque' works were painted in the black first decade of the sixteenth century and it is probable that the *Concerto campestre* was painted shortly after Agnadello. Far from reflecting the confidence and serenity of Venetian society, the *Concerto* can perhaps best be compared to Watteau's *Fêtes galantes* painted in the grim years during and immediately following the War of the Spanish Succession.

Two paintings ascribed to Giorgione in the *Anonimo Morelliano*, the *Three Philosophers* (Vienna) and the *Tempestà* (Venice Accademia) have been regarded by certain modern critics as containing recondite symbolism. It should be said that their mystery resides primarily in the fact that no one is quite sure what they represent; they do not flaunt recondite symbolism in the same way as Cossa's frescoes in the Schifanoia Palace at Ferrara or those by Mantegna and Costa in Isabella d'Este's *Grotto* at Mantua. G. F. Hartlaub suggested that the *Three Philosophers* and the *Tempestà* contain alchemistic-hermetic allegories. Hermeticism, a mystery cult combining Hellenistic and Egyptian elements, flourished in Alexandria in the early centuries of the Christian era and enjoyed a fashionable revival in the Renaissance period in connection with Neoplatonist currents. Hartlaub believed that Giorgione was associated with a humanist *cenacolo* devoted to the ancient mysteries, a kind of forerunner of the Masonic lodges.[18] There is no evidence, however, to suggest that Hermeticism, or, for that matter, enthusiasm for Neoplatonist 'mysteries' had any currency in Venice and knowing what we do of Gabriele Vendramin, who owned and probably commissioned the *Tempestà*, it is unlikely that he would have had any truck with them.[19] Arnaldo Ferriguto believed that the two paintings reflected the Aristotelian interests of the Venetian intellectual milieu. His theory that the *Three Philosophers* represented three generations of Paduan Aristotelianism has already been referred to.[20] He considered that the *Tempestà* illustrated the Aristotelian theme of change and mutability.[21] Professor Edgar Wind, while accepting that Giorgione's paintings included elaborate symbolism, evidently eschews attempts to link his iconography to any particular intellectual current.[22]

Ferriguto's theories in particular raise interesting speculations as to the rapport between the programmes of the subject matter and the actual pictorial treatment. For him, the symbolic portrayal of the three Aristotelian schools in the *Philosophers* is linked with an allegory of the 'three ages of man', a subject particularly sympathetic to Giorgione's genius as a portraitist. Ferriguto suggests that the theme of the picture exploits the contrast between the shaded trees—a symbol of seclusion—against which the two older philosophers are set, and the world of sunlight, which the younger philosopher is contemplating, or towards the contemplation of which he is at least moving. Professor Wind's totally contrary suggestion that the hooded elder is in fact the contemplator of the celestial regions and the youth the 'philosopher of the earth' does not in fact substantially diminish the role with respect to subject-matter of the lovingly-executed landscape. It is Professor Wind who suggests that the three philosophers stand at the entrance to a cave.

This idea has particular relevance to Giorgione's pictorial treatment. The depiction of a cave would have involved severe compositional problems under any circumstances and in fact Giorgione here employed a revolutionary form of composition. It is asymmetrical, the figures being grouped to the right, and it resolves the problem of a large area of dark and basically uneventful picture space; the area of half-tone formed by the rock face on the left is balanced by the strong colour and *chiaroscuro* contrasts on the right-hand side of the picture, where the figures, illuminated by a strong light from the side, are set against dark foliage. The picture marks an important stage in the development of *chiaroscuro* treatment and Giorgione may have been obliged to engage in novel experiments in design by the nature of his subject-matter. The 'mutability' theme which Ferriguto suggests for the *Tempestà* can be substantially reconciled with that indicated by Ridolfi in 1648. Ridolfi believed that the picture referred to the lines of Lucretius describing the pitiful condition of man, exposed at birth to the elements.[23] The themes of mutability and inhospitable nature offered magnificent opportunities for the treatment of landscape and meteorological phenomena. The woman and the child she is suckling, symbolical perhaps of birth and growth, are set in a landscape in which decaying ruins contrast with burgeoning foliage, while the ruffled surface of the water behind indicates the constantly changing nature of the element. In the sky above, the vapours are in flux and here, perhaps, Giorgione had sought to emulate the lost work of Apelles portraying lightning and thunder-clouds. The *Tempestà* explored new ways of portraying vapour and atmosphere and again Giorgione may have been partly inspired by his erudite subject-matter.

While the 'Aristotelian' interpretation of Giorgione links him to intellectual strains which were particularly strong in Venice and Padua, none of the modern interpretations of Titian's iconology do so to any notable extent. Discussions of the *Sacred and Profane Love*, perhaps better christened *Celestial and Terrestrial Venus*, painted probably towards 1515, do however suggest possible links between Titian's iconology and the world of his friend Pietro Bembo, the supreme Venetian practitioner of the treatise on love, and exponent of a modified Neo-platonism. The picture was in fact painted for Bembo's close friend Niccolo Aurelio, secretary of the Senate. It shows two female figures, one clothed and one nude, seated upon a *cassone* or a well-head. While there has been controversy over the meaning of the picture, modern critics tend to accept that it is the nude figure holding a lamp that is the loftier goddess, while there is good reason for thinking that they are complementary sister-deities and not rivals. It has been suggested that the subjects of the relief on the side of the *cassone*—the horse, a traditional symbol of unreason and unbridled passion, and the scourging-scene—signify bestial appetite that must be purged by chastisement. An interpretation directly along the lines of the 'bitter love', 'joyful love' and 'transcendent love' of the *Asolani* is a possibility but an interpretation which looks rather towards the Neoplatonism of the Florentines Ficino and Pico seems more convincing.[24] Nevertheless, the *Asolani* may well have provided a stimulus to a theme on differing kinds of love.

In general, modern researches into Titian's iconology suggest that the sources of the erudition which he utilised in both his secular and his sacred subjects were remarkably catholic: the classics themselves, which he often interpreted with considerable sensitivity to the text, although sometimes taking imaginative liberties, Neoplatonism, antiquarian studies and repertories of symbols and emblems, the writings of the Church Fathers and even obscure Christian traditions.[25] He had in fact well-authenticated links with scholars and men of letters, including Bembo, Aretino, Ariosto and Andrea Navagero;[26] he must also have known Jacopo Sansovino's erudite son Francesco.

It is only in the very occasional work such as the *Sacred and Profane Love* and the late *Allegory of Prudence* (*Serapis*) that the 'literary' element in Titian's work takes on the form of a deliberate occultism relating to ancient 'mysteries'. The literary element was evident rather in the *poesie*—the term was Titian's own—evocative improvisations upon antique literary themes. Examples of this genre are paintings of episodes from Ovid or—as in the *Bacchanal of the Andrians* and the *Erotes* (*Homage to Venus*)—ones based upon the ancient Greek writer Philostratus's descriptions of paintings. The *poesia*, however, would seem to have had little popularity in Venice after the middle of the second decade of the sixteenth century and Titian's *poesie* of a later date were mostly painted for Alfonso of Ferrara and Philip II of Spain. While those produced for Alfonso around 1520, the *Bacchus and Ariadne* and the two Philostratus themes, are joyous in tone, the later ones among those done for Philip, notably the *Diana and Callisto* and *Diana and Actaeon*, are dramatic and even tragic. In exploring the dramatic possibilities of the Actaeon myth, Titian had abandoned the playful treatment of it generally found in the fifteenth and early sixteenth centuries. In the *Diana and Actaeon* it is made clear that the divine beauty which the huntsman sees in the dark woodland means his own doom and the story of his destruction by his own hounds is illustrated in another picture, probably also painted for Philip. The theme of the danger of beauty, beloved of Bembo, is given sinister overtones. Actaeon and Callisto were both punished for breach of the *clausura* enclosing the goddess and her retinue: 'it seems,' wrote Professor Waterhouse, 'as if Titian were seeking to justify the creation of these intensely sensuous inventions by instilling into them a moral lesson'. Titian's later *poesie* may perhaps reflect developments in literary theory in Paduan humanist circles. The theme of the moral responsibility of the writer was put forward in the *Naugerius* written between 1540 and 1550 by the Veronese Gerolamo Fracastoro who taught medicine at Padua and who was himself painted by Titian. Titian had perhaps come to share the view, put forward in Fracastoro's dialogue by his own friend Andrea Navagero that 'if the poet has no aim beyond giving delight to himself and to others . . . he must seem . . . to be merely a frivolous and absurd person'.[27]

Titian showed his debt to the antique in a different way from his Tuscan and Roman contemporaries. Michelangelo, Raphael and their heirs were masters of the antique vocabulary and syntax to the point of being able to create figures which evoked the antique while individually having no single antique prototype. It cannot be said that Titian did this in his figures. At the same time, he showed himself more directly indebted to the antique repertoire of postures and bodily movements.[28] In his work from the second decade of the sixteenth century onwards, specific antique motifs constantly recurred.[29] This was obviously not because his power of *disegno* was weak. Had he been genuinely *dependent* on the antique, he would have left more studies from it and would indeed have been incapable of confronting the canvas without a long travail of preliminary drawings. According however to his last great pupil, Palma Giovane, he worked out his ideas with colours directly on the canvas.[30] It is perhaps precisely Titian's working method that best explain his 'borrowings' from the antique. It would seem that with him antique forms were less objects to be studied, copied and imitated than images, retained perhaps by some feat of eidetic memory, of postures and patterns of movement reduced to their most elemental characteristics. Paradoxically, it may have been thus that he was more tied to the overall forms of the individual antique prototype than the artist who engaged in painstaking academic study of the antique and sought, by passing from imitation to emulation, to transcend his models.

Titian was not engaged in mere erudite 'quotation' from the antique but in an activity more related to a comprehension of the human body's dynamism. Ultimately, however, more significant than his 'borrow-ings' from the antique in themselves are the ways in which he trans-formed motifs and integrated them into his compositions. For example, the nude figure in the *Sacred and Profane Love* appears to have been based upon an antique Nereid type commonly recurring in reliefs and on engraved gems;[31] the known exemplars are uninspiring and indiffer-ently executed and it required a feat of vision to transform the un-remarkable Nereid into a true Venus. Again, Titian probably took the figure of the leaping god in *Bacchus and Ariadne* (1522–3) from that of a warrior on the *Orestes Sarcophagus*.[32] Not only did Titian slightly modify the posture and give the figure a stronger quality of movement, but he also devised a dynamic compositional context: the line of force of Bacchus' 'swift bound' cuts across the arc of the pathway around which his chariot and brain have been moving, while the movements of his body are complimented in and foiled by the posture of Ariadne.

The *cassone* relief in the *Sacred and Profane Love* had marked the end in Titian's work of the period of mere pastiches from the antique inserted into paintings as emotive archaeological fragments, while the figure of the naked Venus in the same picture marked the beginning of the era in which he was learning formal lessons from antique reliefs; these were revealed further in the *Feast of Venus* and *Bacchanal of the Andrians* (both 1518–19).[33] The Averoldi Tryptych (SS. Nazaro and Celso, Brescia), completed in 1520, suggests significantly that his first interest in the *Laocöon* was linked to a study of Michelangelo's fettered slaves.[34] Up to the mid 1540s, Titian's debt was primarily to antique pieces outside Venice, more particularly ones in Rome and Pisa, which he could not have seen at first hand. Apart from drawings, engravings and casts available in Venice, he may well have seen Giulio Romano's sketch-books in Mantua. His first recorded visit to Rome came in the winter of 1545–6. In the previous 15 years he seems to have made little use of the antique, but the Roman visit evidently stimulated a new interest in it. Ironically, he now began to look more to pieces in Vene-tian collections. His use of the Grimani *Gauls* was symptomatic of a renewed preoccupation with the dramatic lessons of ancient art. Between about 1560 and his death in 1576, Titian made few new explorations of the antique world and where echoes of his favourite pieces occur, his increased preoccupation with dramatic expression lead him to modify them very freely.[35] Ultimately, Titian's debt to the antique cannot be viewed in isolation from a debt to Tuscan and Roman art of the High Renaissance. The example of Michelangelo may have helped to awaken him to the power of *Laocöon* and the *Belvedere Torso*. Giulio Romano may again have helped to reveal the majesty of antique forms to him. Also, it is in many cases uncertain whether Titian came to antique motifs directly, if only by means of drawings and engravings done from the original, or through the compositions of central Italian artists. This is even more the case with Veronese. The debt of the Venice to central Italian art must now be examined.

In the second and even in the third decade of the sixteenth century, the heritage of Giorgione lay heavily upon Venetian painting, but the challenge of central Italian art became increasingly insistent, a climax perhaps being reached in the late 1530s and early 1540s. Already in the second decade of the century, Pordenone had emerged as a major representative of central Italian traditions in the Veneto, although he remained the great provincial, working mainly in his native Friuli. Again, Titian in the period 1515–30 showed a strong awareness of artistic developments elsewhere in Italy. Marked reminiscences of Michelangelo and Raphael can be seen in his works of this period, recollections of the latter being not least evident in the Frari *Assumption* (?1516–18). In 1524, Giulio Romano settled in Mantua and he stayed there until 1546. The ambitious mural cycles which he executed there in the Ducal Palace and the Palazzo del Tè were to be of crucial import-ance for Venetian painting, especially mural and ceiling decoration, with regard in particular to the depiction of the heroic human figure and also to the introduction of illusionistic devices. The years following 1539 were the great period of invasion by central Italian artists. This had been presaged in some measure by the wave of exiles following the Sack of Rome of 1527 which had brought Sansovino, Aretino and Bartolomeo Ammanati. It has been suggested that Aretino, despite his partisanship of Titian, was one of the great promoters of central Italian influence. He had built up a collection of works, more particu-larly drawings and *modelli*, by central Italian masters and he gave hospitality and encouragement to fellow-Tuscans staying in Venice, including Rosso Fiorentino, Leone Leoni and Giorgio Vasari and also extending his friendship to the Ligurian sculptor Danese Cattaneo whose training was mainly Roman and Tuscan; Aretino was, of course, the great friend of Jacopo Sansovino. His expressions of enthusiasm for the work of central Italian artists, notably Michelangelo and Giulio Romano seem to have been more particularly marked in the years 1538–42. From 1539, the Grimani of S. Maria Formosa were bringing numbers of central Italian artists or Veneto artists trained in central

Italian ateliers to Venice for the decoration of their palace and in 1541 Vasari came to Venice to execute scenery and festive apparatus, staying on to execute a number of murals in palaces. It is significant that Pordenone received a spate of Venetian commissions around this time. The artists of central Italian schools who came to Venice around 1540 were mainly engaged in murals and here, as in the case of Giulio Romano, the impact was perhaps preeminently in the field of grandiose decorative schemes with large-scale figure-compositions.[36]

For Venetian artists, the challenge was posed by sixteenth-century central Italian art in the full variety of its many aspects, but perhaps rather more in its aspirations towards the grandiose and heroic and in its tendency towards rhetoric than in its 'mannered' and artificial features. *Maniera*, or 'stylishness' in the more complimentary sense, *ricercatezza*, perhaps best translated as 'stylish refinement', were certainly not insignificent elements. In the first instance, however, the impact was less of polish and *ricercatezza*, of the preciously elegant, elongated forms which we especially associate with Parmigianino and the Ammanati, than of the penchant towards the heroic, oratorical human figure, as outstandingly exemplified in very different ways in the works of Michelangelo, Raphael and Giulio Romano, and of the stress on movement. The elongated human figure can of course be seen with Tintoretto and Jacopo Bassano, who were developing their styles in the early 1540s. Tintoretto, however, was responding more generally to the tradition of figure-painting in the 'grand manner', particularly as represented by Michelangelo, and not merely to the more 'mannered' aspects of this tradition. Paolo Veronese, by contrast, in his aspirations towards the grandiose and heroic, showed a stronger disposition towards the crisp rounded forms of Giulio Romano than towards either the elongations of Parmigianinesque tradition or towards the titanic muscularity of Michelangelo. Titian only came to paint crowded canvases with hyper-elegant, elongated figures in the 1550s and here suggestions of direct central Italian influence need to be treated with caution. On the other hand, his debt to Giulio Romano is well-authenticated.

In his surviving works of the 1530s, Titian's emulation of central Italian masters might seem to have receded, but this was evidently not the case with certain works now lost but known respectively from engravings and a copy: the twelve *Roman Caesars* done for the Palazzo del Tè, and the *Battle of Cadore* promised for the Venetian Ducal Palace in 1513 and finally completed in 1538. The grandiose, multi-figured battle-scene was evidently indebted to a considerable degree to the *Battle of Constantine* in the Vatican *Stanze*, executed by Giulio Romano from Raphael's designs. From 1529 onwards, Titian made frequent visits to Mantua and in the years 1536–8 he collaborated with Giulio in the Gabinetto dei Cesari. Evidence for Giulio's influence upon Titian's figure-compositions becomes extensive from this time, while new lessons were drawn from Michelangelo.[37]

Titian in the 1540s showed a marked preoccupation with the strongly modelled human figure in violent action and in marked *contraposto* attitudes. There is even an element of brutality in his works of this period. Compositions are based on receding diagonals, something relatively rare in Titian's work, this being more reminiscent of the late Raphael than of Giulio's own design. The striking actions of the figures often seem to have been directly based on those of the latter artist, but Titian, perhaps partly by virtue of his brushwork, created an impression of true movement which is often curiously lacking in Giulio's work. The features described are particularly evident in the Louvre *Crowning with Thorns* (1540–2) and the series of Old Testament scenes painted in the years 1543–9 for the ceiling of S. Spirito in Isola and now in the Salute: *Cain and Abel*, *Abraham's Sacrifice* and *David and Goliath*. In the S. Spirito scenes and the ceiling panel *St John on Patmos* (now in Washington), executed for the Scuola di S. Giovanni Evangelista around 1544, there is also a notable exploitation of illusionist perspective.

Reference is sometimes made to Titian's 'second Mannerist crisis' following his visit to Rome of 1545–6. This designation is prompted in particular by the works of the Diana series painted in the late 1550s, notably the Ellesmere *Diana and Callisto* and *Diana and Actaeon*. It has been suggested that these may have been inspired by Parmigianino's *Diana at her bath*. In these crowded compositions we find seemingly elongated female figures in marked contortions of posture. Furthermore, the compositional system is no longer that of the High Renaissance: there is an absence of clearly defined axes, the elements being held together rather by a 'complex rhythmical concatenation'.[38] The seemingly deliberate renunciation of any bold compositional fusion and the uneasiness of rhythm—again seemingly cultivated—undoubtedly evoke the appellation 'Mannerist'. In speaking of 'elongation', however, certain qualifications must be made. The effect is achieved not through the adoption of a 'Mannerist' vocabulary of proportions and of contour, such as is found with Parmigianino and the Ammanati, and indeed only in part by the modification of Titian's own earlier formal vocabulary, but more by specifically painterly means: by penetration beyond the surface forms of the nude to an exploration of subcutaneous pressures and tensions and by the gently quivering rhythm of light and shade patterns which mould the muscles, sinews and fat deposits. This is particularly exemplified by the figure of Diana in the Ellesmere *Callisto*. In the London *Andromeda* of 1555 and even in the Diana of the Vienna *Callisto*, probably a studio work, there is a quite marked elongation of bodily form, but in the Ellesmere picture it is more a question of powerful illusion.

During his so-called 'Mannerist crisis' of the 1550s, in fact, Titian positively accentuated the most personal aspects of his art. While brushwork became freer and the contrast between shimmering translucent colour and heavy shadow moved towards its climax, more than ever the human body was portrayed as flesh rather than simply as sculptural form. At the same time, sympathy with the more effete, 'mannered' aspects of central Italian tradition may have been partly responsible for impelling Titian beyond his aspirations to paint heroic figures in emulation of Michelangelo and Raphael, thus allowing him to develop both the flickering movement and the stillness that alternately appeared in his later works. In the last fifteen years of his life he had emancipated himself more fully than ever from his models both classical and contemporary.[39]

In a number of ways Paolo Caliari, better known as 'il Veronese', represented a very different painterly tradition from that of the Venetian school deriving from Giorgione. While in part the pupil of Titian, his links with Terraferma tradition are clear. It is possible to speak of an 'urbane *maniera*' with regard to the schools of Verona and Vicenza as exemplified by the Veronese painter Battista Zelotti and the Caliari family as a whole, by the Vicentine G. B. Maganza and by Antonio Fasolo who, although of Lombard birth, likewise worked primarily in the Vicenza region; it was above all members of this group who left their mark upon the villas of the Veneto. 'Stylishness' was achieved not with precious, tapering, artificial forms, but with full, rounded ones and magnificent draperies. There was a taste for theatrical antique dress and armour, obviously inspired in part by the example of Giulio Romano's Mantuan frescoes and perhaps also appealing to the sentimental philo-Imperialism which was marked in the region; a comparison with Trissino's *Italia liberata* suggests itself. It was an aristocratic style par excellence which perhaps responded to the anachronistic aristocratic-

courtly ethos of the Terraferma nobilities. Fasolo and Zelotti in particular exploited the pictorial possibilities of modish masculine fashions
and these fashions appear to have been Terraferma rather than Venetian
ones. It is likely that the dashing opulence of Veronese's figures in
contemporary garb reflected Terraferma rather more than Venetian
taste.

Verona had particularly strong artistic links with Mantua, and the
influence of the decorations in the ducal palaces there is evident not only
in the work of Paolo Veronese but also in the frescoes of Bernardo
India and Anselmo Canera, the grotesques of Eliodoro Forbicini and
the stuccoes of Bartolomeo Ridolfi. An obvious comparison can be
made between one of Veronese's early Venetian projects, the *Esther and
Ahasuerus* cycle on the ceiling of S. Sebastian (*c.* 1555) and Giulio
Romano's *Trojan War* cycle in the Sala di Troia. Echoes of Giulio's
rearing white stallions and theatrical Roman costume are evident in
the *Triumph of Mordecai*. A debt to Giulio's Mantuan cycles can also be
seen in the concise, rounded treatment of the human figures and horses
and in the illusionist perspective. In general, however, Paolo's debt to
Giulio cannot be readily disengaged from that to the latter's master,
Raphael. Paolo was also obviously well-acquainted with the works of
the Parman school. He was evidently inspired by the light palettes of
Coreggio and Parmigianino, with their delicate cerulean blues and pale
sulphurous yellows as well as by the more sonorous colours of Titian.

The lessons Paolo took from Giulio must have been reinforced by
his Roman journey. According to Ridolfi, 'Paolo went to Rome with
the Procurator Gerolamo Grimani . . . ambassador designate to the
Pope . . . to see . . . the magnificent buildings, the pictures of Raphael,
the sculptures of Michelangelo and, in particular, the great statues,
precious relics of Roman greatness to which he devoted some study. . . .'
It is not clear whether this was in 1555, in 1560 or in 1566, when Paolo
was aged 36, for Grimani was ambassador to Rome on three occasions.[40]
The Maser frescoes, completed in 1559, in which there are reminiscences of Raphael, Michelangelo and the antique, do however strongly
suggest the impact of a previous Roman journey. With regard to
Veronese's debt to ancient art, however, the antique motifs that occur
in his work had for the most part already passed into the repertoire of
Italian painters and it is possible that in many cases he came to them
through recent paintings as well as through engravings of original
pieces. Certainly Raphael's interpretation of the antique was all-
important for him.[41]

'Tintoretto . . . having natural gifts for *disegno*, applied himself with great diligence to drawing all the fine pieces in Venice; he made close studies of Jacopo Sansovino's statues representing Mars and Neptune (i.e. those on the Scala dei Giganti in the Ducal Palace) and the works of his supreme master the divine Michelangelo, sparing no expense to have forms of his figures from the sacristy of S. Lorenzo and likewise all the good models of the best statues in Florence. Thus he himself gives testimony of recognising none other than the Florentine artists as masters in matters pertaining to *disegno*. In colour, however, he says that he has imitated nature and then, in particular, Titian.' So wrote Tintoretto's friend the Florentine Rafaello Borghini in 1583.[42] According to Ridolfi, writing 65 years later, Tintoretto's motto, inscribed on the walls of his studio was: 'the *disegno* of Michelangelo and the colour of Titian'. Borghini appears to have made the typically Tuscan assumption of a contrast between Tuscan *disegno*, or more precisely sense of form, and Titianesque *colore*; this may well have tinted his account of Tintoretto and even the way in which he presented the artist's own statements. It is doubtful how far Venetians would have made a similar assumption. It was certainly quite alien to Dolce and a strict dichotomy along Vasarian lines was not necessarily implied even by Pino who had stated that an artist who was master of Michelangelo's power of *disegno* and Titian's power of colour would be 'the god of painting'. Ridolfi, who obviously regarded Tintoretto as being little short of this, may even have been guilty of invention; his statement about Tintoretto's motto is uncorroborated from other sources. There can be no doubt that Tintoretto closely studied Michelangelo. He left many drawings of the S. Lorenzo figures[43] and while he probably only obtained casts of these after 1557, influences of Michelangelo can be detected in his works of an earlier date. At the same time he does appear to have been fascinated by Titian and developments in his own style can be closely linked to those in the work of his great rival whose studio he had apparently left under a cloud. What can hardly be accepted is that Tintoretto followed an eclectic programme of adding Titianesque colouring to Michelangelesque forms. If any Venetian artist followed such a programme, it was Sebastiano del Piombo, who left Venice for Rome.

What, in any case, did the distinction between *disegno* and *colore* imply? Those Tuscan critics who asserted that Titian, while a great master of colour, was weak in *disegno*, were evidently bound to an aesthetic outlook that approximated painting to sculpture and which regarded sheer plastic form as the basis of painting, relegating colour to the role of an adjunct. They conceived of the creation of pictorial form essentially in terms of *modelling*. With Venetian sixteenth-century painters, on the other hand, modelling, even when it was aided by subtle chromatic contrasts, was only one factor in the creation of three-dimensional illusion. They also worked with a pictorial space whose depth was created by atmospheric illusion or by *chiaroscuro* and out of which forms emerged. Here it must be remembered that the sixteenth-century concept of *colore* could embrace tone and *chiaroscuro*. The distinction between *disegno* and *colore* is not very meaningful when applied to Titian, Jacopo Bassano and Tintoretto.

In much of Titian's mature work, the atmospheric application of colour, the colouristic suggestions of the body's subcutaneous structure and the all-important role of the brush-stroke as a means of conveying an effect of luminosity and a sense of movement undoubtedly ran counter to the 'sculpturesque' conception of form. Tintoretto's distinctly sculpturesque phase of the mid-1550s seemed to mark his most determined revolt against Titian. This is particularly shown in the *Presentation of the Virgin* in S. Maria del Horto, which came at the high point of his 'Michelangelism'. It could even be said that colour was simply an adjunct to form. Progressively, Tintoretto achieved a new synthesis of *disegno* and *colore*, but the latter was not the colour of Titian. It was not the rich chromaticism of the young and middle-aged Titian, nor was it colour combined with *sfumato* to achieve effects of aerial perspective. Rather, lighting-effects, a function of both colour and *chiaroscuro*, were used to give a strong illusion of recession. In Tintoretto's work from the 1560s, figures are given three-dimensional quality in varying degrees by modelling and by the way in which they emerge from the receding picture-space that the painter has excavated with his shadows, and from which they are drawn out in the direction of the spectator by means of lighting. In certain pictures, the one or the other technique may predominate: in some cases there is a positive dissolution of forms into patterns of *chiaroscuro* and impressionistic brush-strokes, but as late as 1577, in the four mythological scenes painted for the Ducal Palace, a strikingly sculpturesque conception could re-emerge. Neither in these extreme cases nor where the two methods are balanced is it possible to speak of eclecticism.

In his juvenile works, which are probably to be ascribed to the early 1540s, while showing an apparent interest in the more 'mannered' aspects of central Italian figurative and compositional traditions, Tintoretto displayed in his colour and in his painterly technique, often quite impressionistic, an allegiance to Venetian traditions, although perhaps more those that cannot be identified specifically with Titian; it is Andrea Schiavone and Paris Bordone who most obviously come to mind as likely teachers. After this hesitant early period, he suddenly revealed himself as a fully accomplished master in the *Miracle of the Slave* of 1548. This has a rich chromatic range with an exploitation of complimentary colours that is if anything more reminiscent of Venetian painting of the first three decades of the sixteenth century than of recent developments. Simply as a large-scale, multi-figured composition, however, it was something relatively new in Venetian painting and was indeed the first example in Venice of the type of composition, notably developed by Raphael in the Stanza del Incendio and the Stanza di Eliodoro, which related the axes of figures in strong action to an all-enclosing, 'scenographic' architectural framework, although in contrast to Raphael's open perspectives, the central vista is here substantially blocked by the mass of figures. Certain of the elegant *contraposto* figures are curiously reminiscent of the late Raphael, although it is similarities with Michelangelo's Paolina frescoes that have been most often observed. In his works of the 1550s, most notably the *Cain and Abel* (probably 1550–53) and the *Presentation of the Virgin* (completed in 1556), Tintoretto appears to have been fully confronting the challenge of central Italian figurative tradition, particularly with regard to the human body in movement; a response to Michelangelo in particular has been suggested, although specific Michelangelesque motifs cannot be traced. It is probable, however, that it was Titian's style of the 1540s, above all as exemplified by the S. Spirito scenes, that prepared Jacopo for the lessons of central Italian art. The *Cain and Abel* was almost certainly painted in emulation—although not imitation—of the S. Spirito picture of the same subject, while the *Miracle of the Slave* may even have been a counterblast to Titian's *Sacrifice of Isaac*, a very different composition, but likewise a scene of a gruesome tragedy cut short by miraculous intervention, With the supremely Michelangelesque *Presentation*, which, significantly, was even praised by Vasari, Jacopo had clearly emancipated himself from Titian. On the other hand, the *Last Judgement* in the same church of S. Maria del Horto (of uncertain date but probably *c.* 1560), precisely because it was painted in emulation of the Sistine fresco, indicates particularly clearly the limits of Tintoretto's debt to Michelangelo. The technique by which strongly illuminated forms emerge from shadow was already developing and the oblique compositional arrangement is highly personal.[44]

Reference has often been made to the possible influence upon Tintoretto of central Italian and Parmese 'Mannerist' painters. Any Italian painter of this time who was occupied with large-scale figure-compositions was liable to be concerned with them in some measure. However, the compositional schemes of those mid-sixteenth-century Italian painters to whom the term 'Mannerist' is most often applied, tended to be constructed in planes and to lack clearly defined axes. This certainly applies to Tintoretto's earlier works, but among the distinctive features of his mature style is precisely the exploitation of powerful axes in recession; this reveals him essentially as a continuator and developer of those traditions of the High Renaissance which had been notably exemplified by the late Raphael. With regard to Tintoretto's figures, his male nudes have none of the bulging muscularity beloved of Michelangelo's central Italian *epigoni*. His tapering, elongated figures are, on the other hand, reminiscent of Parmigianinesque forms but, as will be suggested in due course, Tintoretto's use of such figures was closely related to the solution of the pictorial problems he set himself.

Veronese and Tintoretto both confronted the challenge of the large-scale figure-composition set by central Italian artists and met it in rather different ways. Both were strongly preoccupied with spatial recession and with movement. Their differing conceptions of movement were closely linked to the fact that Veronese's compositions tend to be constructed in planes while those of Tintoretto particularly exploit oblique lines of recession. With Tintoretto, bodily movement was of course generally stronger and bodily *contraposto* more extreme. Here it is tempting to suggest that Tintoretto was more truly the heir of the late Raphael than was Veronese, the most obtrusively 'Raphaelesque' artist of the two, more truly perhaps even than Giulio Romano; Veronese's 'Raphaelism' was if anything more closely linked to the earlier Vatican *stanze*. Furthermore, Paolo's and Jacopo's concepts of *compositional movement* were different. In Veronese's work, the use of 'counter-movement' and 'figurative inversion' is all-important. At intervals in a picture, bodily postures complement and foil one another: the forward movement of one body may be answered by the backward movement of another in a different direction but at a similar angle, the response of *saillie* and *retraite* helping to reinforce the sense of recession. This is one of the means by which rhythms of form are created. Unity is given to a composition by means of a carefully orchestrated counterpoint of rhythms, both of lines and forms through which the eye is lead to a central point of interest. The process may be reinforced by architectural backgrounds, as in the *Feast in the House of Levi*. The device of receding 'scenographic' wings formed by buildings and the strident spatial rhythms created by series of columns force the eye into the depths of the picture. Veronese was able to create an illusion of recession and link his figures to each other with only the most restrained use of *contraposto* and rhetoric of gesture. By contrast, in Tintoretto's compositions, which were substantially based upon receding axes, strong bodily movement was all-important. Linear rhythms and rhythms created by *chiaroscuro* patterns played a much greater role. It is within this context that his figurative types can be best understood. It can perhaps be said that his adoption of the elongated, tapering human form was not merely, if at all, a response to current fashions, but was an instrument enabling him to solve the problems of the dramatic large-scale figure-composition by imparting a movement which would link its elements together. Elongation and the delineation of sinewy muscularity were also crucial elements in the creation of a heroic human figure that was chaste and devoid of pagan self-confidence.

Venetian painters' treatment of the nude in the Catholic reform era raises interesting questions about the relationship between art and spiritual currents. The Fathers at the Council of Trent and a number of other Catholic reformers expressed strong mistrust of the nude as a potential incitement to lasciviousness. Furthermore, a glorification of the human body ill-accorded with the pitiful state of fallen man, of which many Catholic reformers and leading churchmen, in Venice as in Italy as a whole, were profoundly conscious. The impact of the Counter-Reformatory ethos upon the production of nudes in Venetian studios was perhaps rather less marked than elsewhere in Italy. It should be said, however, that the spate of female nudes which Titian painted in his early sixties were produced in the years when the Council of Trent had only just got under way and scarcely any of them were done for Venetian patrons, the *Venus with Organist* executed for Francesco Assonica—itself a variant on a picture originally sent to Granvelle—being a notable exception; the main purchasers of them appear to have been the Imperial Court and the Most Catholic Monarch Philip II, who evidently had a taste for erotica in his youth. Yet even in Titian's works painted for Philip in the 1550s, changes may be seen. A contrast may be observed between the *Danäe* done for Ottaviano Farnese in the years 1545–6 (Naples), with its air of luxurious relaxation and placid sur-render to the divine favours, and the more pathetic *Danäe* done for Philip in 1553 upon whom the golden rain falls like a presage of doom.

Again, it has been seen how in the *Diana and Actaeon* the theme of human beauty is mingled with bitter tragedy. Tintoretto painted some quite appealing nudes throughout his life, some in fact for the Ducal Palace. Yet he did perhaps face the problem of painting the heroic nude without paying undue homage to the glories of the flesh. Here an obvious model was the heroic-pathetic nude of the late Michelangelo who, significantly, probably shared the particularly strong conviction of the tragic state of fallen man held by the 'evangelical' Catholic reformers. When in 1574 Veronese sought to buttress his defence before the Holy Office by suggesting the unsuitability of nudes in the Sistine Chapel, the inquisitor indicated that Michelangelo had observed the rules of propriety.[45] Tintoretto's nudes can be seen as poised in varying degrees between the muscular, sinewy, almost unappealing Michel-angelesque nude and the more sensuous, lissom, Parmigianinesque figure. Even in the female nudes of his late period, such as the *Graces* and the *Venus and Ariadne* in the Ducal Palace (1577), the elongated, rippling forms somewhat attenuate the sensuousness. In the *Deliverance of the Slave* (1548) and the *Transportation of the body of St Mark* (1562–6), the human body, hard as well as elegant, is shown in all its splendour and dignity but in a manner fully befitting a religious subject.

The complex iconology of Veronese's allegorical pieces, particularly those associated with Daniele Barbaro (the decorations of the halls of the Council of Ten and the Maser frescoes)[46] and also the programme for the decorations of the Ducal Palace developed by Giacomo Contarini and his associates in 1577, indicate that in the latter half of the sixteenth century links still existed between art and the world of erudition. Icono-logy was concerned, however, with conventional allegorical figures rather than with occult allegorical subjects. In the first two decades of the century, the subject matter of works such as the *Three Philosophers* and *Sacred and Profane Love* could only have been understood by an erudite clique and it should be said that even then paintings of this kind were rare in Venice. Allegorical painting in the second half of the cen-tury evidently sought to employ a vocabulary of symbolism whose correctness would be universally accepted. Perhaps it could only be fully understood by men with a good grounding in the classics and a measure of antiquarian erudition, but it was propagandist and openly didactic to the exclusion of any deliberately esoteric element. The Maser frescoes, which probably related to the theme of the harmony of the spheres, one which closely accorded with Daniele Barbaro's per-sonal intellectual enthusiasms,[47] were in some measure an exception.

In general, except where it related to theories of the virtues and of the arts and sciences, it may be said that the erudite quality of painting was less philosophical than antiquarian.

It has been suggested above that Venetian painting was probably stimulated by Flemish and German art in the period between about 1450 and 1510 and was definitely influenced by central Italian art from the second decade of the sixteenth century onwards, a climax perhaps being reached in the 1540s. Here references to a 'Mannerist crisis' have tended to confuse the issue. It would seem to have been the examples of Michelangelo, Raphael and Giulio Romano that were crucial rather than those more effete traditions patronised by the Grimani. Vasari and the artists who worked for the Grimani doubtless helped to create a fashion for grandiose mural decorations and here Venetian artists had to emulate them, but when Titian, Tintoretto and Veronese did so, they turned more to the recognised masters of the central Italian High Renaissance as their models. Out of the central Italian artists close at hand, it was Giulio Romano whose impact was greatest. He obviously helped to acquaint Venetian painters with Raphael's heritage and it was he who had completed Raphael's last work, the Vatican *Transfiguration*, which was so strangely prophetic of developments in Venetian painting from the 1540s. Titian and Tintoretto, however, in fact came closer than did Giulio in his Mantuan period to the late Raphael with his use of strong axial movement and rhythmic *chiaroscuro* and with his sense of drama.

The influences of non-Venetian upon Venetian artists are often unobtrusive. What, then, was so distinctive in Venetian painting? We can speak of 'naturalism' only if we bear in mind that sixteenth-century Venetian landscape was idyllic rather than realistic and that Venetian painters of this period normally idealised the human form; this even holds good in some measure of the fleshy, sometimes matronly nudes of the late Titian. Venetian landscape-painting, however, did reveal a novel awareness of the effects upon vision of atmosphere and diffused light and Titian's treatment of the human body was indeed naturalistic in the sense that it was conceived of as a biological organism and not merely in terms of surface-form. Again, it is not enough to speak of 'colour'. Those critics of the sixteenth and seventeenth centuries who suggested that the excellence of Venetian painters lay primarily in their colour in fact took a rather patronising attitude towards them. Such critics tended to assume a clear distinction between form and colour, while it was peculiarly distinctive of the great Venetians that they did not treat them as separate elements in their work: with Titian, Tintoretto and Jacopo and Francesco Bassano in particular, mastery of colour and *chiaroscuro* and mastery of three-dimensional space were one. Furthermore it must be remembered that *colore*, as understood by Venetian critics, could include brushwork. Daring and rapidity of touch were essential elements in conveying an impression of movement as well as a sense of life in figures. It was precisely the peculiarly 'painterly' mastery of form and space possessed by Titian and Tintoretto that enabled them to give new meaning to the lessons provided by Michelangelo, Raphael and Giulio in recessional composition and in the movement of figures.

Architecture and Sculpture

If the early developments of the Renaissance architectural style in Tuscany had represented a return less to ancient Roman models than to local Romanesque ones, the first Renaissance architectural style that emerged in Venice in the last four decades of the fifteenth century contained strong echoes of the Byzantine-Gothic style in which St Mark's was built. This is somewhat surprising since most of the masters of the art of building working in Venice at that time were non-Venetians, Lombards and natives of the Ticino being predominant. The reminiscences of Byzantine-Gothic are particularly evident in the decorative use of insets of coloured marbles and in the use of the semicircular pediment. The plan of St Mark's was in some measure adopted in a number of domed cruciform churches, including S. Maria Formosa (1492), S. Giovanni Crisostomo (1497–1504), probably both by Mauro Coducci, and in S. Salvador (1507–12), usually attributed to Giorgio Spavento. Pietro Lombardo's S. Maria dei Miracoli (1481+) even has domes rather similar to those of St Mark's. Similarities to Early Christian architecture have also been suggested with regard to the general layout of the Miracoli and Coducci's S. Michele in Isola (1466).

The age of Antonio Rizzo, Pietro Lombardo, Mauro Coducci and Bartolomeo Bon was one of fantasy and inventive experiment in architecture, decoration and monumental sculpture. The element of fantasy was especially marked in the woodcuts illustrating the romance *Hypnoteromachia Polifili* (*The Dream of Polyphilus*) written by Francesco Colonna, a Dominican of SS. Giovanni e Paolo in Venice. It was published in Venice in 1499. These fanciful illustrations depict classical buildings and ruins, pyramids and obelisks; they even include the obelisk borne on the back of an elephant which was later to be employed by Bernini. The artist, often identified with Colonna himself, was once seen as an erudite antiquarian, who must have made first-hand studies of antique remnants in Rome, the Levant and Egypt. He was believed to have played a crucial role in the introduction of the more picturesque antique forms into Venice. It is now considered, however, that he took his inspiration not merely from contemporary engravings but also from ornamental carvings and details of tombs already in Venetian churches.[48]

Authorship of buildings in this period is often uncertain, but a specific 'Coducci style' has been isolated, although the buildings that can be attributed on documentary grounds to Mauro Coducci (c. 1440–1504) are few in number. It is difficult to trace the origins of this style among fifteenth-century buildings elsewhere in Italy and even the debts to Michelozzo, who had worked in Venice in the 1440s, seem to be limited. There are certain similarities between the façade of S. Michele in Isola and Alberti's Tempio Malatestiano in Rimini. Ultimately, however, the 'Coducci style' is one of outstanding originality in combination with a curious allegiance to the Venetian past. This can be seen in the way in which, at S. Michele, the curved pediment, inherited from St Mark's, is given a new elegance and integrated into the composition by curved flutings. It can also be seen in a relatively unobtrusive point, the form and spacing of windows. In the Palazzo Corner-Spinelli, as in many Venetian Gothic palaces, the windows are not evenly spaced, the central ones being set close together. This irregularity is also to be found, although to a less marked degree, in the Palazzo Vendramin-Calergi and does in fact subtly reinforce the monumentality of the façade. The individual windows in both buildings superficially follow a form found in many fifteenth-century Florentine palaces. The semicircular tympana are subdivided into two semicircular arches, surmounting the main lights, and a circular lunette. In the Florentine buildings, however, the effect is of a pierced solid tympanum, while in Coducci's buildings the more specifically Gothic technique of groin tracery is used. Hence an impression of extreme lightness is produced in the windows which are, in any case, unusually large for the period.

In the first three decades of the sixteenth century, Venetian architecture remained extraordinarily conservative. This is particularly illustrated by the Scuola di San Rocco, begun by Bartolomeo Bon in 1517 and not completed until 1560. It is probable that the upper storey represented a certain departure from Bon's original plan, but a substantial stylistic unity was nevertheless preserved. In sculpture, in the first three decades of the sixteenth century a fairly continuous development can be seen from the style introduced into Venice by Pietro Lombardo and Antonio Rizzo in the 1470s.

Gian Maria Falconetto can be seen as the pioneer of the architectural revolution in the Veneto with his works executed in the Padua region in the 1520s. It was, however, the Florentine Jacopo Tatti di Sansovino who introduced the architectural revolution into Venice itself. He settled there in 1527 or shortly afterwards and remained there for the rest of his life. As the exponent of early sixteenth-century Tuscan practice, Sansovino undoubtedly diverted the course of Venetian sculptural tradition, but the patrimony he bequeathed was limited in extent. His outstanding contribution in integrating sculpture into its architectural frame was never really comprehended by his successors in Venice. At the same time, as a sculptor he remained wedded to the polished, 'closed' forms of sixteenth-century Tuscan tradition. He did not attain a 'painterly' exploitation of light-and-shade effects in the same way as Danese Cattaneo and Alessandro Vittoria. As an architect, on the other hand, he did exploit to an outstanding degree the play of light and shade upon buildings.

This is not particularly noticeable in his Roman buildings, the Palazzo Lante and the Church of S. Giovanni dei Fiorentini. It appears to have been primarily a feature of his Venetian period, although it was undoubtedly achieved in large measure by subtle modifications of the architectural vocabulary of the Roman Renaissance. In the Zecca (begun in 1537) the effect is primarily one of monumental solidity, with the boldly stated contrast between void and heavily rusticated surfaces. In the roughly contemporaneous façade of the Public Library, however, the eye is prepared for the dark recesses by the complex columniated forms of the piers and by the play of light and shade on the sculpted spandrels of the arches. Sansovino was evidently inspired by the previous traditions of Venetian palace architecture at its best, with its large area of window-space and deep, open ground-floor porticos, but he achieved an even greater lightness of effect than Coducci. Here a fruitful comparison can be made between Sansovino's Palazzo Corner di S. Maurizio (1533) and Coducci's Palazzo Vendramin-Calergi. In Sansovino's work, the effect of progressive subdivision on the façade, so marked with Coducci, has been modified. In both the Palazzo Vendramin-Calergi and the Palazzo Corner, each storey is divided into bays by columns, in the former case by single free-standing columns, in the latter by double half-columns, whose total effect is rather less assertive. In Coducci's work, the main arches of the windows are supported again by columns, in Sansovino's by pilasters which appear as reinforcements to the coupled half-columns rather than as distinct elements. In the Palazzo Corner, the columns give the effect of dividing the storey only to a relative degree. They are, in a sense, elements of a larger pier-system and the transition from them to the architectural surround of the windows is less abrupt than in Coducci's work where both retain strongly distinct identities. Hence Sansovino achieved a greater lightness of effect, notwithstanding the fact that the window-space is if anything relatively smaller. With respect to Venetian tradition, Sansovino also rationalised the subdivision of the façade. In his Palazzo Dolfin-Manin the irregular disposition of the windows with a close grouping of the central ones was still to be found, but in the Palazzo Corner, probably in fact a rather earlier work, this is diminished to the point where it is barely noticeable and serves merely to give a subtly reinforced stress to the areas immediately above the portico.

With the works of the Veronese architect Michele Sanmicheli (1485–1559), the effect of progressive subdivision of façades is very much more marked and the monumentality is not combined with the same lightness. Sanmicheli spent much of his working career as a military architect in the service of the Serenissima, designing imposing, heavily rusticated city-gates and fortifications. This left its impress in the massive quality of his work. His Veronese palaces are edifices of exquisite sumptuousness, especially the Palazzo Bevilacqua, with its rusticated lower storey, Corinthian columns with twisted flutes, sculpted spandrels, festoons and frieze adorned with grotesques. In his first Venetian work, the Palazzo Corner di S. Polo, he leaned heavily on Venetian tradition. This is in fact very similar to the project for a Venetian palace in Serlio's *Regole generali di architettura* published in Venice in 1540. In the Palazzo Corner di S. Polo the central windows are grouped close together, a feature not found in Sanmicheli's Veronese palaces. In the Palazzo Grimani di S. Luca, designed in the late 1550s and possibly his last work, however, the spacing of bays is nearly even and he had adopted more Sansovinesque techniques, although the effect of progressive subdivision of the façade is still marked.

So far, buildings have been discussed here primarily in terms of their elevations. There is good reason for this. The nature of the sites they had to work on in Venice usually gave architects only limited opportunities

25 G. B. Tiepolo, *Allegory of Marriage*, ceiling painting, Ca Rezzonico, Venice *c.* 1758
(see p. 269)

26 Ca Rezzonico, Venice, begun by B. Longhena in the mid-seventeenth century,
upper storey by G. Massari *c.* 1745 (see p. 279)

for ambitious experiments in spatial design. This was more particularly true in the case of private buildings, but it cannot be said that public buildings showed any notable interest in respect of planning and the design of internal space. The same substantially applies to churches prior to Palladio's arrival in Venice. Coducci's and Spavento's domed cruciform churches are notable exceptions, but even Sansovino's churches were extremely conservative in their planning. It was in the country villas of the Veneto that the most ambitious experiments in spatial design were conducted in the first instance and with Palladio's Venetian churches a new sophistication was evident in the exploitation of internal space.

It is impossible to examine Palladio's vast achievement in any detail. His role as an erudite architect, his combination of a scholarly Vitruvian-ism and the fruits of archaeological research with the invention of new building-forms and his complex system of proportions are well-known. Here attention will essentially be devoted to the way in which his art developed when he came to work in Venice. When his activities com-menced there in the 1560s he already possessed a rich experience formed in working on open sites and he was particularly fortunate in the sites made available to him in the city. Contact with Venetian architectural tradition had perhaps opened up new stylistic possibilities for Sansovino and Sanmicheli. There is little reason for suggesting that Palladio's style underwent a similar transformation. On the other hand, he was presented with new opportunities in Venice. The remodelling of the Hall of the Collegio after the fire of 1574—if it was indeed Palladio who was responsible for it—called for lavish and grandiose interior decoration. Splendid interiors had indeed been produced at Maser, but aspirations towards a tasteful elegance had muted the effect of sumptu-ousness. Now something was required that was sumptuous and perhaps rather less elegant and what was produced was essentially the fore-runner of the Inigo Jones interior style. It was also in Venice that Palladio made his first major incursions into the field of ecclesiastical architecture, his earlier work on the Cathedral of Vicenza having been a relatively minor affair.

In both S. Giorgio Maggiore (1565+) and the Redentore (1576+) Palladio responded to the challenge that perplexed many sixteenth-century architects of setting a dome upon a longitudinal church. This presented the problems of preventing an undue hiatus between the vault of the nave and the pendentive supporting the dome. In both S. Giorgio and the Redentore, the vault tends towards a barrel form,

I

which in itself poses no problems of linkage with pendentives, while its potentially monotonous shape is in fact broken up: it is cut through at intervals to provide access to semicircular 'thermal' lights. At S. Giorgio this gives the effect of a series of parabolic groins. At the Redentore a parabolic longitudinal section helps to effect a transition to the arch leading onto the central domed space. As in St Peter's in Rome, the nave 'arcades' are not true arcades but rather pierced walls faced by columns which are purely decorative in function. In the Redentore there is no true thematic, still less structural link between column and vault and the latter seems to float above the strongly stressed cornice. Here, and in his transitional vault forms Palladio developed features later to be exploited by Baroque architects. Another problem faced by Renaissance architects was that of putting a classical temple-type frontage onto a building composed of nave and aisles. In S. Giorgio and S. Francesco della Vigna, Palladio used the simple expedient of half-pediments at the sides of the main block. In the Redentore he employed the novel device of setting the main pediment below the flat line of the roof and resolving the visual disequilibrium thus created by a series of side-wings with half-pediments.

The artist who dominated the architectural scene in the Veneto in the decades after Palladio's death was undoubtedly the Vicentine Vicenzo Scamozzi (1552–1616). He worked extensively both in Vicenza and Venice. He was a pupil of Palladio, but the contact between two very dissimilar minds was basically unfruitful and only to a limited degree can he be regarded as an imitator of Palladio. Superficially he appears as an architect of fantasy in contrast to the relative austerity and apparent Vitruvian propriety of Palladio, a sort of Gibbs to Palladio's Kent. On closer examination, however, it will be seen that it was Palladio who broke the rules and handled the elements of a neoclassical vocabulary with considerable freedom while Scamozzi, who precisely condemned Palladian fantasy, was a figure of ferocious orthodoxy. The orthodoxy in this case was essentially that of Serlio, of whom his father Gian Domenico had been the principal pupil. Scamozzi accepted Serlio's basic mannerist postulates and applied them with extreme rigour. His apparent fantasy was the fruit less of spirited experiment than of a rather mechanical eclecticism which combined elements drawn from Alberti, Sanmicheli, Sansovino and, to some extent, Palladio, within a general Serlian framework.[49]

From Sansovino's studio there emerged a school of sculptors who in some measure continued Tuscan and central Italian traditions of elegance and polish upon Venetian soil. With Sansovino's successors, however, the attempt to integrate figure sculpture with architecture was abandoned. A crucial element in Sansovino's system of integration had been his attention to the receding planes formed by the lines of orientation of figures set in restrained *contraposto* poses. All this was rejected in the long run in favour of a pronounced verticality. Perhaps the two outstanding members of the Sansovino studio were Danese Cattaneo and Alessandro Vittoria. The Ligurian Danese Cattaneo (1509–73) had come to Venice from Rome together with Sansovino. His works are of great nobility, with pleasing light-and-shade effects. His portrait busts and those of Vittoria in some ways recall the portraits of Titian in their combination of reticence with a sense of presence and respect for the aristocratic reserve of the sitter. The Trentino Alessandro Vittoria (1525–1608) joined Sansovino's studio in 1543 but soon set up on his own. By the latter years of the sixteenth century, he had become the great arbiter of taste in Venice and few artists left their mark on Venice more than he did. His position was reinforced in part by a wide circle of friendships. In 1597 he was made responsible for putting in order the Grimani antique collection in the Public Library. This suggests that he was regarded as possessing some antiquarian erudition and his work can reasonably be regarded as mirroring the antique enthusiasms of his age. It would be most unjust to regard Vittoria as simply a frigid neoclassicist sculptor, rather he showed an apparent sensitivity to what his fellow-artists were creating in the realm of painting and a refined feeling for the qualities of the medium in which he worked. In fact he worked in a number of mediums and treated marble, bronze and stucco in rather different ways. His bronzes, which are generally less formal than his marble pieces, exploit the fluid qualities of the material. His stuccoes have an element of lightness and even, on occasion, of fantasy. There is a marked contrast between the ponderous, gigantesque figures at the entrance to the Libreria Sanso-viniana and the delicate stuccoes on the stairway. Here, where the painted roundels were by Battista Franco, as at Maser, where the frescoes were by Veronese, Vittoria revealed a fine capacity for pro-ducing decorations which would harmonise with the work of painters. There is a greater gravity in the marble sculptures. By contrast with the moulded forms of the bronzes and stuccoes, the marbles firmly retain the impression of having been carved. Vittoria has often been praised for his 'painterly' treatment of sculpture, but this did not in any way imply an indifference to the particular qualities of his medium or an attempt to transcend its limitations. Rather it meant that sculptures were conceived of not merely as solid form but also as patterns of light and shade. A curious luminosity is also given to the crystalline marble by the play of highlights and this is reinforced at the psychological level by the expression of mild wonder on the faces of some of his sitters. In his bronze tableau of the Annunciation, Vittoria in fact substantially followed a painterly model, Titian's late picture of the subject, with the fluttering draperies, in S. Salvador, Venice. Here Vittoria has been criticised for his failure in attempting to transpose a particularly painterly vocabulary into bronze. It was perhaps in his fully rounded sculptures, where true shadows could be cast, rather than in reliefs that Vittoria best revealed his 'painterly' qualities. These are particularly evident in the terracotta bust of Doge Nicolò da Ponte (Seminario Patriarcale, Venice), not only in the strong *chiaroscuro* effects achieved by high-relief moulding, but also in the contrasts of textures between flesh, hair and brocade, these being envisaged not merely in terms of surface texture but in terms of the overall impression of light-and-shade patterns. Vittoria's portrait busts at their best are full of psychological insight although they are unassertive, for he always respected the aristocratic reserve of his sitters. The funerary bust of Gasparo Contarini in the church of S. Maria dell' Orto almost seems to suggest a tension between this reserve on the one hand and, on the other, a sense of expansive wonderment and an almost ebullient self-assertiveness. Few visitors to Venice examine Vittoria's works with much attention but he was, together with Giambologna, perhaps the most distinguished Italian sculptor of the second half of the sixteenth century.

★　★　★

The sculptural tradition in Venice often tends to be forgotten. Those who think of Venetian art primarily in terms of the great colourists are ill-prepared for it. It conveys an immediate, if superficial, impression of austere classicism and of close allegiance to central Italian tradition. Undoubtedly the example of antique art was fundamental and sculptors may well have drawn on the repertoire of exemplars available to them in Venetian collections; they evidently found Attic and neo-Attic art, in which these collections were well-stocked, more attractive than did Venetian painters. Most of the sculptors working in Venice in the middle years of the sixteenth century had at least a second-hand training in central Italian traditions, but Cattaneo and Vittoria did in substantial measure emancipate themselves from them, partly it seems by renewed recourse to antique examples of classic art and partly by the peculiarly Venetian sensitivity to the effects of light, shade and high-light. This sensitivity subtly leavened the austerity of their neo-classicism. Venetian painters obviously effected a far more profound modification of both antique and central Italian influences. They also learnt different lessons from antique art; in particular they were more sensitive to its qualities of movement and to its lessons on complex bodily posture. Furthermore, from Giorgione onwards, they doubtless realised that they could never replace the lost world of antique painting by mere imitation of the manner of antique sculpture. The traditions of painting and sculpture in Venice were undoubtedly markedly different and the sculpture perhaps expresses with the greatest immediacy the elements of Venetian culture and the facets of the Venetian ethos that tend to be forgotten and which can only be perceived in painting after intense scrutiny; the erudite antiquarianism and the qualities of reserve and measured severity.

Notes

[1] See above, p. 164

[2] See F. Saxl, 'Jacopo Bellini and Mantegna as Antiquarians', (Warburg lecture 1935), reprinted in *A Heritage of Images* (London 1970) at pp. 68–70

[3] On the latter point and for a general discussion of the lessons drawn by Italian artists from the antique, see P. P. Bober, *Drawings after the Antique by Amico Aspertini* (London 1957), pp. 19–26

[4] See O. J. Brendel, 'Borrowings from Ancient Art in Titian', *The Art Bulletin*, XXXVII (1955), p. 122 and figs. 21, 22

[5] *Ibid.*, p. 22, figs. 20, 23, 24

[6] See Saxl, 'Jacopo Bellini and Mantegna', *ed. cit.*, pp. 62–6

[7] Ridolfi, *ed. cit.*, I, pp. 64–6; cf. Vasari, *ed. cit.*, I, p. 356

[8] On Flemish and Italian techniques and on the relationship between Italian and Flemish art, see L. van Puyvelde, 'Renaissance italienne et Renaissance flamande', in *Venezia e l'Europa. Atti XVIII Congresso Internazionale della Storia dell' Arte*, pp. 189–96; G. Hoogenwerff, 'Rapporti fra artisti fiamminghi e l'Italia: Giovanni van Eyck e Ruggiero van der Weyden', *Rinascita*, II (1960), pp. 131–45

[9] Letter to Pirckheimer, 7 February 1506, reproduced in E. G. Holt, *A Documentary History of Art* (New York 1957) at pp. 330–2

[10] T. Pignatti, 'The Relationship between German and Venetian Painting in the Early Renaissance', in *Venetian Studies*, ed. J. R. Hale (London 1972)

[11] Letter to Pirckheimer cit.

[12] Th. Hetzer, 'Studien uber Tizians Stil', *Jahrbuch fur Kunstwissenschaft*, I (1923), p. 205

[13] Brendel, *loc. cit.*, pp. 115–16; F. Saxl, 'Titian and Pietro Aretino', (Warburg lecture 1935) in *Heritage of Images*, pp. 74–5

[14] See above, p. 157

[15] See Ridolfi

[16] The following can be classed among the 'idylls': the four matching panels, *Leda, Idillo campestre, Old Man with an Hour-Glass and Viol Player* and *Venus and Cupid*, attributed to Giorgione (Padua and Washington); *History of Damon and Thyrsis* normally attributed to A. Previtale (London); *Birth of Adonis*, variously attributed (Padua); *Legend of Romulus and Remus*, attributed to Giorgione (Frankfurt); *Homage to the Poet*, attributed to Giorgione (London); the *Tempestà*, attributed to Giorgione in the *Anonimo Morelliano* (Venice Accademia); *Concerto Campestre*, with various attributions, including Titian (Louvre). Titian's *Sacred and Profane Love* can be seen in some measure as belonging to this genre.

[17] R. Wittkower, 'L'Arcadia e il Giorgionismo', in *Umanesimo europeo e umanesimo veneziano*, ed V. Branca (Florence 1963); *cf.* A. R. Turner, *The Vision of Landscape in Renaissance Italy* (Princeton 1966), pp. 94–8

[18] G. F. Hartlaub, *Giorgiones Geheimnis* (Munich 1925)

[19] See above, pp. 156–7

[20] See above, pp. 80–1

[21] A. Ferriguto, *Attraverso i 'misteri' di Giorgione* (Castelfranco Veneto 1933)

[22] E. Wind, *Giorgione's 'Tempestà'* (London 1969)

[23] Ridolfi, *ed. cit.*, I, p. 100

[24] E. Panofsky, 'The Neoplatonic Movement in Florence and Northern Italy' in *Studies in Iconology* (1st ed. New York 1939), New York 1962 ed., pp. 129–60; idem, *Problems in Titian, mostly iconographic* (London–New York 1969), pp. 110–19; E. Wind, *Pagan Mysteries of the Renaissance* (1st ed. London 1958), London 1967 ed., pp. 142–9

[25] See especially Panofsky, *Problems, passim*, also: Wind, *Pagan Mysteries*, pp. 78*ff*, 104, 142*ff*, 260, 273; Saxl, 'A Humanist Dreamland' in *Heritage of Images*, pp. 89–97

[26] Panofsky, *Problems*, p. 88; Vasari, *ed. cit.*, IV, p. 202

[27] E. K. Waterhouse, *Titian's Diana and Actaeon* (Oxford 1952), pp. 21–3

[28] Hetzer, 'Studien', p. 223

[29] On Titian and the antique, see especially: Hetzer, 'Studien', pp. 220-37; L. Curtius, 'Zum Antikenstudien Tizians', *Archiv fur Kulturgeschichte*, XXVIII (1938), pp. 233–41; Brendel, *loc. cit.*, pp. 113–25; Panofsky, *Problems, passim*; also F. Saxl, 'Titian and Pietro Aretino' (Warburg lecture 1935), reprinted in *Heritage of Images*, pp. 71–86

[30] M. Boschini, *Breve instruzione. Premessa a Le Ricche Miniere della Pittura Veneziana* (Venice 1674)

[31] Hetzer, 'Studien', p. 229; Brendel, *loc. cit.*, p. 117 and fig. 6

[32] Hetzer, 'Studien', pp. 232–3; Brendel, *loc. cit.*, pp. 118–19 and figs. 10, 11, or Panofsky, *Problems*, figs. 57, 115

[33] Hetzer, 'Studien', pp. 232–3; Brendel, *loc. cit.*, pp. 117–18

[34] Hetzer, 'Studien', p. 229; Brendel, *loc. cit.*, p. 118

[35] Brendel, *loc. cit.*, pp. 121–5

[36] On the central Italian 'invasion', see L. Coletti, 'La crisi manieristica della pittura Veneziana', *Convivium* (1941), pp. 109–26

[37] On Titian and central Italian art, see Hetzer, 'Studien', pp. 237–48 and on his relations with Giulio Romano, J. Shearman, 'Titian's portrait of Giulio Romano', *The Burlington Magazine*, cvii (April 1965), pp. 172–7, esp. p. 174

[38] Panofsky, *Problems*, p. 156

[39] On the evolution of Titian's style, see especially Th. Hetzer, *Tizian, Geschichte seiner Farbe* (Frankfurt a. M. 1935, 1948, 1969) and Panofsky, *Problems*, Ch. I

[40] Ridolfi, I, p. 310 and notes by Hadeln

[41] See especially R. Cocke, 'Veronese and Daniele Barbaro, the decoration of the Villa Maser', *Journal of the Warburg and Courtauld Institutes* (1972)

[42] R. Borghini, *Il Riposo*, etc. (Florence 1584, facsimile ed. Hildersheim 1969), p. 551

[43] D. R. Coffin, 'Tintoretto and the Medici Tombs', *Art Bulletin*, xxxiii (1951), pp. 119–25

[44] The classic statement of the thesis that Tintoretto, rather than following an eclectic programme of combining 'the *disegno* of Michelangelo with the colour of Titian', transmuted form and colour into the pictorial element of light is in M. Pittaluga, *Il Tintoretto* (Bologna 1925); most helpful analyses of his stylistic development are in J. Wilde, 'Die Mostra del Tintoretto zu Venedig', *Zeitschrift fur Kunstgeschichte*, vii (1937), pp. 140–53 and H. Tietze, *Tintoretto* (London–New York 1948)

[45] See above, p. 201

[46] See above, pp. 173–4, 205

[47] Cocke, *loc. cit.*

[48] G. Pozzi and L. A. Ciapponi, 'La cultura figurativa di Francesco Colonna e l'arte veneta', in *Umanesimo europeo e umanesimo veneziano, cit.*, pp. 317–36

[49] F. Barbieri, *Vincenzo Scamozzi* (Vicenza 1952), pp. 93–5

ten

Music and Music Patronage

The attention given to musicians and musical instruments in
Venetian paintings of the sixteenth century has often been noted.
In part, perhaps, this was an inheritance from Netherlands pictorial
tradition. It is evident, however, that Giorgione, Titian and Veronese
had observed the postures of different kinds of instrumentalist very
closely. Attempts have been made to describe the lyricism and colouristic sonority of Giorgione and Titian and the subtle exploitation of
formal rhythms by Veronese in musical terms. It appears indeed that
Giorgione and Titian, as well as Paris Bordone, Tintoretto and Jacopo
Bassano, were practicing musicians. The paintings of the great Venetian
masters do at least bear testimony to the central role of music-making
in the Venetian cultural milieu and focus attention upon the strong
attachment to instrumental music which was a distinctive feature of
Venetian tradition.

Although the appointment of Adriaan Willaert as *Maestro di Capella*
of St Mark's in 1527 is traditionally seen as the great milestone in the
development of the Venetian musical school, the fifteenth century had
not been a musical desert, a predilection for instrumental music having
already asserted itself, and there is evidence of the important role played
by music in Venetian life at the turn of the sixteenth century. Initially
Venice's great debt, as indeed that of Italy as a whole, was to the
Netherlands. Curiously enough, but perhaps not altogether surprisingly
in view of the strained relations between Greek and Latin Churches in
the Venetian dominions, Venice appears to have taken little or nothing
from the Byzantine musical tradition apart from the organ, an instrument of Byzantine origin for whose manufacture Venice was a major
centre in the sixteenth century. Netherlandish musicians on the other
hand were to be found working in the Veneto in the early fifteenth
century and towards the end of the century singers trained in the
tradition of Ockhegm and Busnois were in Venetian service. The first
three *Maestri di Capella* of St Mark's, Petrus de Fossis (Maestro 1491–

1527), Adriaan Willaert (Maestro 1527–63) and Cipriano Rore (Maestro 1563–5) were Netherlanders and Willaert, who brought with him the tradition of Josquin des Près, was the chief founder of the Venetian musical school as we basically know it from surviving scores. It is probable, however, that the sixteenth century Venetian musical tradition also had its roots in a widely diffused local practice of music-making particularly characterised by the madrigal and by the use of lute and viola, although our main information on this tradition comes primarily from literary and pictorial sources.[1] In the event, the complex, sonorous polyphony of the Gabrieli, with its exploitation of striking chromatic and orchestral effects was very different from that of Palestrina and his Roman followers who again derived in some measure from Josquin. Palestrina responded to the demands of the Counter Reformation for a more austere church-music, purged of the extreme complexities of Flemish practice and of themes derived from secular music. While one may feel that the great Venetian masters essentially respected the sacred character of church-music, they remained blissfully indifferent to these demands.

Among the centres of music-making in Venice, the Ducal Chapel of St Mark's held pride of place and helped to fertilise musical life elsewhere in Venice, for its Maestri di Capella and organists often wrote works for outside use or performed in other churches, in scuole or at private festivities. St Mark's was furthermore important as a centre for musical training. Instructions in music was also provided in the Ducal or Gregorian Seminary which was founded in 1580 to train clergy for the service of St Mark's. The state was, in addition, responsible for providing musical entertainments at public festivities, the most notable of which were perhaps those put on in 1571 to celebrate the victory of Lepanto and in 1574 to welcome Henry III of France. Here the chief musicians of the Ducal Chapel played a leading role. Information about music-making in other churches is fragmentary, although a significant number certainly possessed organs and some churches and convents acquired a high reputation in the musical field. The Scuole Grandi were in the latter years of the sixteenth century perhaps the most important employers of musicians besides St Mark's. Only S. Rocco has been studied in detail, however. Giovanni Gabrieli and the noted Giambattista Grillo (first organist of St Mark's 1619–23) both acted as organists. There were, however, signs of decay in the musical life of the scuole in the 1620s and the famine of 1630 evidently dealt a severe blow.[2] There is extensive evidence of music-making both at private festivities and in private musical circles as well as the semi-public celebrations organised by the great festive companies such as the *compagnie della calza*. Thus Monteverdi's *Combattimento di Tancredo e Clorinda* was first performed in a patrician palace, that of the Mocenigo family, in 1624. The development of Venetian opera considerably antedated the building of the first Venetian opera-house, the Teatro Nuovo S. Cassian in 1637 and appears to have taken its origin from the public festivities of the early 1570s. Little is known at present about music-making in the Terraferma, but Vicenza seems to have enjoyed a position of distinction. There was a fully-developed musical establishment in the Cathedral. Musical performances in connection with theatrical productions were given in the Accademia Olympica from 1556 and from 1582 it appears to have developed its own orchestra; Andrea Gabrieli composed the music for the performance of Oedipus on the occasion of the Teatro Olympico's opening in 1584.

Without in any way disregarding the fact that church-music was only one facet of Venice's rich musical production, the history of music there in the sixteenth and early seventeenth centuries can in substantial measure be written round the story of music in St Mark's, for the leading figures in Venetian music held posts there as Maestro di Capella or as organists, while extensively engaged in the field of secular composition, most notably with madrigals and operas. St Mark's was the Ducal Chapel. The Cathedral of S. Pietro di Castello, while a much revered church, was situated in a quarter of Venice remote from the main city centre and it was St Mark's that was the site of state religious functions and, indeed, of the most splendid religious celebrations. In the sixteenth century it had a substantial body of choristers, some of whom enjoyed outstanding individual reputations, and also appears to have employed instrumentalists on an extensive scale. It possessed the outstanding feature of the double choir, allegedly introduced by Willaert, and its opportunities for the rendering of complex contrapuntal compositions were evidently exploited by the Gabrieli and by Monteverdi. In the middle and latter years of the sixteenth century, it rivalled the Sistine Chapel as the great Italian centre of church music.[3]

The major posts in the *capella musicale* were those of Maestro di Capella and first and second organist. From 1608, there was also a vice-maestro. The Maestro, whose office was apparently first instituted with the instalment of Petrus de Fossis in 1491, was responsible for the over-all organisation of the musicians and choristers. Although not necessarily a clergyman, he enjoyed a species of semi-ecclesiastical status and was responsible for the general good order of religious services, it being declared in 1554 that even the canons were subject to his direction in this matter. The insistence that he should be a man of good character—a preoccupation that was not particularly evident where the organists were concerned—was not mere pious verbiage but reflected the Maestro's very extensive disciplinary responsibilities. According to the constitutions of the Dean Francesco Querini of 1554, he enjoyed a rung of precedence immediately below that of the canons and sub-canons and superior to that of the deacons and sub-deacons. At the time of his appointment in 1491, Petrus de Fossis was described as '*Magistrum Capellae Nostrae et puerorum nostrorum ad canticum*', that is to say he had a clearly defined teaching function. In 1562, when the Maestro Willaert was ill, there was instituted a *capella piccola* with a cadre of experienced singers under the direction of Baldassare Donati (later Maestro) with the aim of instructing the *zaghi* (i.e. the choir and altar-boys) in singing, but this came to an end with the appointment as Maestro of Giuseppe Zarlino in 1565. It was then specified that only the Maestro was to be obliged to teach the *zaghi* in future. Zarlino's functions were defined as being 'to teach *canto figurato*, counterpoint and *canto fermo* to all the *zaghi* of the church'. The Maestro was also evidently expected to compose pieces for state occasions, civil as well as religious. What the wardens of the Basilica required in a Maestro di Capella was an accomplished composer who could organise. Monteverdi, on his own testimony, was consulted by the wardens on all appointments of organists and vice-maestri and only his reports on singers were accepted.[4] Monteverdi, however, evidently enjoyed in general an unusual position of respect.

From 1490 there were two organists, each with his own separate instrument. While they often received the same salaries, there was a distinct order of precedence, for a second organist might subsequently become first organist. While there appears to have been no standard procedure for the appointment of the Maestro, from 1541 at least the two organists were appointed by means of a competition. A document in the archive of the *Procuratori di Sopra*, in an italic hand suggestive of seventeenth-century origins, describes the 'customary examination of candidates for a post as organist'. Firstly a line is to be taken at random from the choir book and presented to the candidate who 'on the same organ which is vacant must play a fantasia on that subject in a regular fashion, not confusing the parts, as if four voices were singing'. Secondly, a piece of plain-chant is to be chosen, again at random, and the aspirant must 'play this in three parts, giving the plainsong first in base, then in tenor, then in contralto and soprano, as regular fugues and not as simple accompaniments'. Thirdly it was stated: 'the choir shall sing some verse of a composition not used too frequently, which he must transpose and reply to, in the same and different scales and this by improvisation'. The musical milieu of the time was, of course, one in which performers were expected to be capable of improvisation but it is hardly surprising that organists appointed by an examination of this kind were not infrequently capable composers. No organist, however, graduated to the post of Maestro before Francesco Cavalli in 1668.

The Maestro di Capella, the organists and the singers were appointed by the wardens of the Basilica, the *Procuratori di S. Marco di Sopra.* Certain important appointments were made by precisely those men who were responsible for the magnificent building projects of the Public Library, the Loggia of the Campanile and the Procurazie Nuove. The Procurators' rights in the matter of appointments did not prevent interventions by Doges who fancied themselves as connoisseurs of music. This was seen on the occasions of Willaert's appointment in 1527. The respective spheres jurisdiction of Doge and Procurators with regard to appointments in the Ducal Chapel were defined by the Maggior Consiglio in 1577, but this did not prevent what appears to have been a ducal intervention in the appointment of the Maestro in 1603.

We possess records of the official salaries of Maestri di Capella and organists, but these do not give a complete picture of their incomes since the organists received Christmas bonuses and both these and the Maestro might engage in outside work; intermittent attempts were made to stop the organists playing outside St Mark's, but these were not very effective and the right of the Maestro to compose works for outside functions, such as ceremonies of scuole, does not seem to have been questioned. Evidently the Maestri di Capella were fairly comfortably off at certain periods, although by the turn of the seventeenth century the value of their office had become severely depreciated as a result of inflation. Willaert had begun at 70 ducats per annum in 1527, but by 1556 his salary had risen to 200 ducats per annum. By comparison the *Amiral al Arsenal*, the overseer of the great state shipyard had a wage of 150 ducats with a house provided in 1560. If we take a working year as consisting of 300 days, 200 ducats per annum works out at 83 *soldi* per day. At this time, the average daily wage of a master artisan, which was paid on a daily and not an annual basis, was about 30 *soldi*. Willaert probably had good reason for not accepting the numerous offers of employment elsewhere. The salary of the Maestro di Capella did not rise again until 1613, however. At that time a master artisan's daily wage was about 63 *soldi*. Obviously the guaranteed annual salary of the Maestro di Capella cannot be directly compared with the wage of an artisan who was probably employed irregularly, but the salary in the first decade of the seventeenth century was, to say the least, demeaning. Nuns were supposed to be able to live off 60 ducats per annum, but it apparently took something like 120 ducats per annum to keep them in comfort. It is hardly surprising that there had been a rapid turnover of Maestri in the years immediately prior to Monteverdi's appointment. Monteverdi's salary was 300 ducats per annum at the time of his appointment in 1613 and it was raised to 400 in 1616.[5] In 1620, Monteverdi spoke of his salary in terms which indicated that he was satisfied with it—he was particularly delighted that it was paid regularly—and he added that he earned about 200 ducats per annum on outside work, evidently composition.[6] It is worth noting the increasing disparity between salaries of Maestri and those of organists. Between 1491 and 1530, they were 70 ducats and 60 ducats respectively, in the mid-1530s, 120 ducats and 80 ducats, in 1536, 200 ducats and 80 ducats. Between 1563 and 1613, they were respectively 200 ducats and 100 ducats. After Monteverdi's rise to 400 ducats in 1616 the salaries of the organists varied between 120 ducats and 140 ducats, and they did not rise above the latter sum until 1642. It can hardly be said that the organists received generous official salaries and it is hardly surprising that they took on outside work. Jaches Buus left in 1551 for Vienna, evidently finding his salary of 80 ducats per annum inadequate.

Twenty-six Maestri di Capella and organists were appointed between 1490 and 1630. The succession of Maestri is as follows:

1491   Petrus de Fossis (Flemish)
1527   Adriaan Willaert of Bruges
1563   Ciprian Rore (Flemish)
1565   Giuseppe Zarlino of Chioggia
1590   Baldassare Donati
1603   Giovanni della Croce of Chioggia
1609   Giulio Cesare Martinengo (his name suggests Brescian origin)
1613   Claudio Monteverdi of Cremona

As we have seen, the first three Maestri were Flemings. It should be said that Willaert was appointed as the result of a direct ducal intervention and there is evidence suggesting divisions of opinion or at least uncertainty among the Procurators over the appointment of another Fleming, Jaches Buus, as organist in 1540. The Italian Maestri and organists were of disparate origins. Only four are known with a high degree of certainty to have been Venetians, the organists Alvise Arciero, Andrea and Giovanni Gabrieli and Paolo Giusto. At least six of the Italians were not even Venetian subjects and it is perhaps a significant pointer to the distribution of musical centres in Italy that three of these came from the region of southern Lombardy and the Duchies: Gerolamo Parabosco from Piacenza, Claudio Merulo from the Duchy of Modena and Monteverdi from Cremona, the latter having served in Mantua before coming to Venice. It is not altogether clear what kind of apprenticeship a musician required in order to become Maestro di Capella at St Mark's. Rore and Monteverdi had already held similar posts elsewhere, the former at the court of Ferrara, the latter in the service of the Mantuan Duke. Baldassare Donati had been in charge of the temporary *scuola piccola* in St Mark's in the years 1564–5 and since 1580 had been teaching music in the Ducal Seminary. Obviously experience of choirs was essential. Petrus de Fossis, Ciprian Rore, Baldassare Donati and Giovanni della Croce had begun their careers as singers and of these all, with the exception of Rore, had performed in the Ducal Chapel. De Fossis and Donati also had high reputations as composer and organist at the time of their appointment. Zarlino had been a pupil of Willaert and was already noted as a musical theorist, but the nature of his practical experience is unclear. The Maestro could hardly hold his post unless he could turn his hand to composition and in most cases the Maestri are known to have composed works. None of the Maestri appear to have made their reputations primarily as organists and, as already noted, Cavalli was the first organist of the Ducal Chapel to graduate to the office of Maestro. It might be supposed that a musician who had passed the rigorous competitive examination for the post of organist would have at least some qualifications for handling a choir and Fra Armonio, Gerolamo Parabosco, Claudio Merulo, the two Gabrieli and G. B. Grillo were musicians of outstanding reputation. The post of Maestro did not, however, fall vacant during the periods in which Parabosco, Andrea Gabrieli and Grillo held office. Had they presented themselves as candidates, Fra Armonio, Merulo and Giovanni Gabrieli would probably have been rejected on grounds of personal unsuitability. Furthermore, however, an organist was probably in a weak position when faced with a competitor who had intimate experience of choral practice and the Maestro had to be a man who could impose his will upon the musicians and choristers and, if necessary, the clergy of the Basilica. The demands with regard to both musical knowledge and personal character made of the Maestro di Capella seem to have become increasingly insistent as time went on.

When the post of Maestro fell vacant in 1527, Fra Armonio the first organist, although a noted singer, was not apparently even considered, probably for good reason, for he lived a Bohemian existence and was frequently engaged in outside work. Rather, the choice of the Procurators seems to have fallen upon the singer Pietro Lupato, but in deference to the expressed will of Doge Andrea Gritti they elected Adriaan Willaert. Gritti, as we have already seen, was a great admirer of Titian and Jacopo Sansovino and also appears to have had strong musical interests; he had passed some time at the French court and had formed a taste for the polyphony of the school of Jean Mouton. Willaert's appointment may be indicative of Venetian appreciation of northern European music. Willaert had in fact come directly from Rome, being, like Aretino and Sansovino, one of the group of outstanding men who moved to Venice after the Sack of Rome in 1527. He was a musician of wide experience, being not only a follower of the great Flemish masters but also having spent a period in France. He was an outstanding composer both of organ music and of madrigals. He appears to have done much to build up the choir of the Ducal Chapel and he trained an entire school of musicians. Both Zarlino and Ciprian Rore appear to have studied under him and it is possible that Merulo was so as well, although it is not absolutely certain that Andrea Gabrieli was his pupil. Merulo, who held the post of organist between 1557 and 1584 was an outstanding composer of motets and madrigals.

After the brief tenure of office between 1563 and 1565 by the brilliant Ciprian Rore, Giuseppe Zarlino was appointed as Maestro. The two organists Claudio Merulo and Annibale Padovano had often sought employment elsewhere and failed to fulfil their duties in St Mark's at a time when the control of the ageing Willaert appears to have been lax. At the time of Zarlino's appointment, the Procurators made the rather pointed statement that they wanted a man who was 'not only learned and skilled in music, but also prudent and observant in performing his office, as one who is superior to other musicians must be'. The Procurators' statement probably reflected the growing preoccupation with order and decency in the Basilica which had been evidenced by the constitutions of the Dean Francesco Diedo of 1554; these had insisted that the clergy and others serving the Basilica should behave with dignity and provisions had been made to ensure that they fulfilled their statutory obligations. Such considerations may partly explain why the Procurators, notwithstanding the fact that they had an outstanding musician to hand in Merulo, chose Zarlino, although apparently possessed of limited practical experience. Zarlino, a priest, whom the people of Chioggia were later to request as their bishop, was praised for his *modestia*. Zarlino was an imposingly erudite figure, allegedly learned in Greek and Hebrew, philosophy, theology and astronomy, with strong mathematical interests which he displayed both in the contemporary discussions on the reform of the Calendar and in his treatises on harmony. His *Istituzioni harmonici* of 1558, which was followed by the *Dimostrazioni* (1571) and the *Supplementi* (1588) was probably the most comprehensive Renaissance treatise on harmony. It was the great codification of the *prima pratica*, being essentially conservative by comparison with Vicentino's *Antica musica*, although it was noteworthy for its preoccupation with the affective and mimetic qualities of music in its marriage with words. Zarlino did in fact compose a number of musical works, both ecclesiastical ones and ones for festive occasions, but few of them were printed. Under his *maestranza* the music of the Ducal Chapel reached a new splendour. Merulo was composing extensively for state functions in the 1570s. Andrea Gabrieli, who had failed in the competition for the post of organist in 1557, held the post of second organist from 1556 until his death in 1586 and his nephew Giovanni Gabrieli was first organist from 1585 until 1612. It is not clear how Andrea was appointed, but Zarlino was certainly consulted on the appointment of Giovanni.

In 1590, the post of Maestro passed to Baldassare Donati and in 1603 to Giovanni della Croce, who was noted for a number of published works. The filling of the vacancy in 1603 was the occasion of a notable intervention by the Procurator Federigo Contarini, whom we have already encountered as a prominent antiquarian collector. After the competition for the post had been publicised, Contarini presented a memorandum. The Maestro, he said, must be a man of gravity and good life. The singers, often persons of great experience, were unlikely to show respect towards young persons who hired themselves out to sing in churches and scuole and at festive banquets, appearing at the latter singing with wine-glass in hand. Previous Maestri had never incurred the blemish of having hired themselves out to festive companies and scuole or for the feasts of particular churches along with other singers and choir boys. 'The Procurators,' Contarini continued, 'have always sought to find men of respect, not only free of these blemishes but outstanding men, the leaders of their profession, with a high reputation for being not only eminently skilled in practice but also versed in theory, famous men like Master Adriaan and Master Ciprian after him, and then the most learned Zarlino, who was such a scholar in this profession and who composed profound works on theory. The truth is that such men are not to be found here on the piazza and they have to be sought out where their talents are manifest.' Contarini recommended that, 'since the only persons to be found in Venice are far from meeting these important and necessary conditions', a general survey should be made with the aid of Venice's ambassadors regarding persons of high reputation.[7] Contarini's memorandum is particularly noteworthy for its stress on the value of Maestri learned in musical theory, for its statement that qualified persons were not at that time to be found in Venice and for its advocacy of an ambitious programme of enquiries to discover the best-qualified person. A certain caution must be observed, however, in taking Contarini's statements at their face value. It is hard to resist the impression that he wanted some particular person or persons kept out of the job. Apparently only two candidates presented themselves, the Dominicans Giovanni della Croce and Costanzo Gabrieli. The latter was doubtless a relative of the then first organist. Giovanni Gabrieli did not apparently compete himself, but as a musician engaged extensively in performances for scuole and private functions he might well have fallen under Contarini's strictures. Contarini, a *dévot* and a disciple of the Jesuits may have mistrusted the Gabrieli family on account of their links with Protestant German merchants. More generally, Contarini was evidently anxious that the Maestro, as a great officer of the Basilica, should conform to the same standards of behaviour as those demanded of their clergy by the Dean of St Mark's and the Patriarch of Venice over the preceding two decades. It is of particular interest, however, that the policies advocated by Contarini were evidently adopted in the appointment of Monteverdi ten years later. In 1603, however, Contarini was overriden. On 13 July, the day that he presented his memorandum, the Procurators observed that provisions had already been made for an election and that they had been urged by the Doge and Collegio on the previous 3 April to proceed towards filling the vacancy. The same day, the Procurators elected Giovanni della Croce. The pressure put upon the Procurators to proceed to an election may well have been designed to favour the latter who was a protégé of Doge Marino Grimani, a passionate musical enthusiast. Giovanni della Croce was, at any rate, a productive composer.

In 1609 there was only one competitor for the now rather ill-paid post of Maestro, Giulio Cesare Martinengo, who was duly elected. By all accounts, this was an unsatisfactory appointment and Martinengo was of no note as a composer. In 1613, however, while Federigo Contarini was still *Procuratore di Sopra*, the kind of policy he had advocated in 1603 was adopted. The entry in the Procurators' register for 19 August notes the appointment of Claudio Monteverdi, 'letters having been written on the orders of *SS. Illustrissimi* to the *Illustrissimo* Ambassador in Rome, to all the Governors in Terraferma and the residents of the Serenissima in Milan and Mantua for information regarding persons qualified in this profession'. The appointment was made with unusual rapidity and the severe, reserved composer was doubtless all that Contarini wished for.

When he came to Venice at the age of 45, Monteverdi was already a composer of repute; the *Orfeo* and the great *Vesperi della Beata Vergine* lay behind him. The latter work had in fact been published in Venice in 1612 and may well have been crucial in securing his appointment. The *capella musicale* of St Mark's was evidently in a bad state when he took it over and it had received a severe blow with the death of Giovanni Gabrieli in 1612. Monteverdi in his early years as Maestro engaged in an extensive programme of reorganisation, persuading the Procurators to build up a repertoire of scores and strengthening the choir both in numbers and in the quality of its singers. In 1619 an organist of outstanding quality was brought in with G. B. Grillo. Again, Monteverdi brought into Venetian service the former Maestro di Capella of Ferrara Cathedral, Alessandro de Grandi. The latter was employed as a singer in the first instance, then as tutor to the choir and in 1620 he became Monteverdi's deputy as vice-maestro. The choir was evidently decimated by the plague of 1630, but Monteverdi seems to have gradually restored its strength and quality.[8] In the period prior to the plague, Monteverdi had been extensively engaged on compositions for outside performance, both in Venetian scuole and at the Mantuan court and, following the opening of the Teatro Nuovo S. Cassian in 1637, he produced at least three operas. The Procurators appear to have raised no objection to all this and probably had no reason to do so where only compositions were involved and Monteverdi was not taken away from the Basilica.

The Maestri di Capella of St Mark's were great personages, the organists not infrequently versatile Bohemians and in a number of cases they are said to have had links with the intellectual, literary and artistic circles of their times, although certain assertions to this effect should be treated with caution. Fra Armonio, a noted bohemian figure, was known as a poet, playwright and comedian and gave performances at carnival masques, being closely associated with the poet and author Antonio Molin or 'Il Burchiello'.[9] Willaert appears to have had contacts with the playwrights Andrea Calmo and Beolco Ruzzante, while again Andrea Gabriele is said to have had close links with Il Burchiello[10] and Gerolamo Parabosco, who had a reputation as a libertine poet, with Calmo and Aretino.[11] Parabosco and Merulo are both believed to have been associated with the great academician Domenico Venier, who often gave musical entertainments in his house.[12] Baldassare Donati was mentioned in 1593 as being a member of the second Accademia Veneziana, together with Tintoretto and Alessandro Vittoria.[13] Zarlino was also a friend of Tintoretto.[14] It was the erudite and revered Zarlino who most naturally belonged to the high academic milieu. A correspondent of the great Paduan *erudito* and antiquarian G. V. Pinelli,[15] he also belonged to the short-lived Accademia della Fama of Federigo Badoer, being inscribed in the musical section of the *stanza di matematica*.[16] It is fascinating to speculate whether Zarlino knew Daniele Barbaro and Palladio. All three men were immersed in the strain of Platonic-Pythagorean number-mysticism which was so fundamental both for theory of harmony and for theory of proportion in architecture at this time.[17] Certainly Daniele Barbaro and Zarlino moved in closely allied academic circles.

The personal connections of the great musicians of St Mark's are indicative of the role played by music in Venetian society. On the one hand, music, as exemplified by Zarlino, was an erudite study closely allied to mathematics, with a secure place in the world of the learned academies. On the other hand, musical performance was bound up not only with the whole framework of imposing civil and religious celebrations but also with the gay and even bohemian aspects of Venetian life, with the world of the great festive companies and of the theatre. The history of Venetian music as it now stands is one of series of great men who, after paying due attention to the lessons of the fifteenth-century Flemings developed a style of massive originality and intellectual force. We do not know how much they drew from the widely diffused, semi-popular, native tradition of music-making. It can be seen, however, that the world of Venice's musicians was one in which erudite Venice, the Venice of the Counter-Reformation and *Venezia città galante* all met.

Notes

[1] See especially G. Barblan, 'Aspetti e figure del Cinquecento musicale veneziano' in *La Civiltà veneziana del Rinascimento*, (Florence 1958), pp. 60–5

[2] D. Arnold, 'Music at the Scuola di San Rocco' in *Music and Letters*, XL (1959), pp. 229–41

[3] The forthcoming account of the history of music in the Ducal Chapel is mainly based on the following: A. S. Ven, *Procuratori di Supra Chiesa busta 90 Carica Maestro di Capella*, an un-numbered *fascicolo* containing regulations on the good order of the Ducal Chapel and *processo* 204, fasc. 1 giving details of appointments of *Maestri* and their emoluments; *ibid.*, *busta* 91 *processo* 207, *Carica di organista. Oblighi et emolumenti dal 1316 al 1767*; F. Caffi, *Storia della musica sacra nella già Capella Ducale di S. Marco in Venezia dal 1318 al 1797*, vol. II (Venice 1855)

[4] Letter to Striggio 13 March 1620, reproduced in G. F. Malipiero, *Claudio Monteverdi*, (Milan 1929), Doc. 46

[5] Details of salaries of Maestri are to be found in *Proc. di Supra Chiesa*, B. 90, and are reproduced in Caffi, *op. cit. passim*. For the *Amiral al Arsenal* see F. C. Lane, *Venetian Ships and Ship-Builders of the Renaissance* (Baltimore 1934), p. 161. For wages of artisans working in the Scuola di S. Rocco, see B. S. Pullan, 'Wage earners and the Venetian Economy, 1550–1630' in *Economic History Review*, XVI (1964), pp. 408–26. My remarks on Venetian nunneries are based on studies of state and diocesan legislation, certain monastic records and certain evidence from testaments

[6] Malipiero, *op. cit.*, Doc. 46, as above

[7] *Proc. di Supra*, B. 90, proc. 204, fasc. 1 f.8r. Memo, of 13 July 1603 cited Caffi, *op. cit.*, p. 200. My reading of this text is different from Caffi's

[8] On Monteverdi's organisational work in the Ducal Chapel see D. Arnold, *Monteverdi*, (London 1963), pp. 29–31 and 65

[9] Caffi, *op. cit.*, p. 68

[10] Barblan, *loc. cit.*, pp. 67, 72

[11] Caffi, *op. cit.*, pp. 110–11

[12] *Ibid.*, pp. 112–13, 121

[13] Bibl. Correr, Venice, *Cod. Cicogna* 2999. *Accademie letterarie etc.*, fasc. 28

[14] Caffi, *op. cit.*, p. 144

[15] *Ibid.*, pp. 160–1

[16] M. Maylender, *Storia delle Accademie d'Italia*, V (Bologna 1930), pp. 441–2. Caffi's assertion in *op. cit.*, p. 144 that Andrea Gabrieli was also a member appears to be uncorroborated by other sources.

[17] Wittkower, *Architectural Principles*, Pt. IV *passim* and esp. p. 119

eleven

Continuity and Change in Venetian Tradition

In 1745, Aurelio Rezzonico, whose forebears had been ennobled in 1687, purchased the great palace on the Grand Canal originally designed by Longhena for the Bon family and around 1758 G. B. Tiepolo executed two remarkable ceiling paintings in the state-rooms. In *Merit between Nobility and Virtue*, the noble Doctor Rezzonico is shown seated on a cloud between the two goddesses. The *Allegory of Marriage* was painted to celebrate the nuptials of Aurelio's son Ludovico with Faustina Savorgnan. The happy pair are conducted by Apollo in his car; the god had performed a similar function in carrying Beatrice of Burgundy to the Emperor Barbarossa in a painting executed by Tiepolo in the Wurzburg Residenz some six years earlier. In 1762, Tiepolo painted an even more megalomaniac apotheosis of a Venetian noble family, in this case the Pisani di S. Stefano, in the ballroom of their villa at Stra, the most magnificent of all eighteenth-century Veneto villas. By contrast with the Rezzonico, the Pisani di S. Stefano were one of the most lustrous families of the old nobility. In the Stra picture, the members of the Pisani family are presented by the figure of Venice to the Virgin, who is surrounded by the figures of Wisdom and the three Theological Virtues; Fame spreads the renown of the family to the four continents.

In both the Ca Rezzonico and the Stra paintings, the links with the past are obvious. As in so many of Tiepolo's paintings, there are reminiscences of Veronese. Apollo's horses are evidently descendants of those in Giulio Romano's frescoes in the Salone d'Apollo of the Ducal Palace at Mantua. They are perhaps relatives of the steeds who draw Mordecai the Just across the ceiling of S. Sebastian. The standard-bearer who salutes Ludovico and Faustina is not very different from the soldier who conducts Mordecai, although he is a picturesque rather than a heroic figure and his classical garb has a new touch of fantasy.

The glorifications of the Rezzonico and Pisani have obvious antecedents in traditional apotheosis compositions, more particularly seventeenth century ones of a religious nature.

In the sixteenth century, family pride had expressed itself more modestly. In Titian's second Pesaro altarpiece in the Frari, the members of the Pesaro family were shown in the presence of the Virgin and Child, but in a position clearly subordinate to that of the Holy Family, which is the central focus of attention. In Tiepolo's Stra ceiling, on the other hand, the group of figures dominated by the Virgin is no more than the most crucial of a number of different points of focus. This group on the one hand and that of the Pisani family on the other constitute complimentary poles between which the eye constantly travels. The work is indeed essentially a secular one, befitting a ballroom. The juxtaposition of the Virgin with the Virtues, let alone Fame and the Four Continents, would have been unthinkable in sixteenth or seventeenth century iconography. Quite apart, however, from the extraordinary *râgout* of religious and secular subject-matter, the Stra picture, together with the Ca Rezzonico ones, is notable simply as being an apotheosis of a Venetian family. In the sixteenth and seventeenth centuries, apotheoses of saints and apotheoses of Venice were common, but similar glorifications of Venetian families were the creation of the eighteenth century. Furthermore, in the paintings of Tintoretto, Veronese and Palma on the ceiling of the Maggior Consiglio, Venice had been a queen to whom Doge and people paid homage. In the Stra picture, she is a benevolent friend of the Pisani, perhaps even a protectress, but no more; in no way are they subordinate to her in the composition.

In the eighteenth century, the few remaining noble houses of affluence, whether ancient houses like the Pisani or relative newcomers such as the Rezzonico, could revel in the contemplation of their own splendour at a time when the aristocracy had shrunk in numbers and the polarities between rich and poor within its ranks had become perhaps more marked than ever before. In the sixteenth century, Gabriele Vendramin, whom we have examined as a collector, had, in his testamentary admonition to his heirs, firmly placed devotion to his family after devotion to the Serenissima. Now that Venice was no longer a power of European stature, however, there was perhaps less inclination among the nobility to give recognition to this hierarchy of allegiances. Now that she was no longer the defender of Italian freedom, the bastion against the Turks and the great emporium of the Christian

Mediterranean, the leaders of her society might divert themselves with extravagant but perhaps mechanical and unreflecting celebrations of the eminence of their own houses. The artists who catered for their taste did so with a vocabulary that was in some measure inherited from the traditions of two centuries, but which also contained revolutionary elements.

★ ★ ★

In the eighteenth century, Venice was constricted by economic, political and social structures that had become ossified. In the course of the seventeenth century, the shift from sea to land had continued and the wealth of the Venetian dominions resided more than ever in the natural resources and productive capacities of the Terraferma, but the Venetian government failed to accept fully the logic of the situation. The Venetian nobility failed in substantial measure to strengthen itself with new blood. Within a political structure that remained basically unchanged, the faction struggles of the eighteenth century had a curious similarity to those of the late sixteenth and early seventeenth.

The effects of Dutch exploitation of the Cape route, the superior competitiveness of northern European merchandise in Levantine markets and the decimation of Venice's labour-force during the plague of 1629–30 upon Venice's commercial position and her productive capacity have already been examined. In part perhaps as a natural reaction, the Venetian nobility, while declining in numbers, acquired an even greater proportion of the lands of the Terraferma, although Venetian landlords acted increasingly as *rentiers* rather than as active exploiters of their possessions. The agriculture of the Terraferma was undoubtedly tenacious. In the seventeenth century, the population was saved from famine by ploughing-up of marginal areas and by the extension of maize culture, although it should be said that this achievement was at the expense of agricultural diversity. In the eighteenth century, the vitality of Terraferma industrial production, especially that of cloth, was marked in certain areas, notably the Veronese and Vicentino. The eighteenth century, however, failed to bring a marked revival in the agrarian system. In the last three decades of the Republic's existence, the government devoted close attention to the agrarian issue. A certain progress was made in the direction of increased diversification. There was a mass of detailed government regulations, but a comprehensive reorganisation of the agrarian system was not promoted. This was, in substantial measure, because the government envisaged the production of the Terraferma as being primarily geared to Venetian mercantile expansion and within the framework of a balance-of-payments policy. Indeed it was directed towards a hoped-for recovery of commerce which did not materialise. Furthermore, little was done to modify the system of land tenures.[1]

Between 1550 and 1594, the number of male nobles had fallen from an estimated 2,500 to just under 2,000. After the great plague of 1629–30 there were 1,666. The nobility did not apparently recoup its numbers in the course of the seventeenth century, notwithstanding the aggregation of 127 new families between 1647 and 1718, and between 1719 and 1797 the numbers fell from some 1,700 to about 1,000. The size of the nobility thereby decreased in proportion to the population of Venice as a whole, which, by 1696, when it stood at 138,000, was nearly restored to its pre-plague level and which probably remained fairly constant throughout the eighteenth century. The reasons for the nobility's decline in numbers are not absolutely clear, but probably the nature of the Venetian family structure was one factor. As we have seen, only one or two of a group of patrician brothers normally married, although the married ones usually had quite large families. A system of this kind which clearly defined the obligation to continue the family did contain certain safeguards against the extinction of male lines, but it was an over-delicate instrument whose functioning could be easily upset by adverse biological factors.

The aggregation of 127 new families between 1647 and 1719 could not in itself have been expected to boost the actual numbers of the patrician cast at all substantially. What was involved was the ennoblement of individuals and groups of brothers together with their descendants, not of entire clans. It did, however, offer the opportunity of reinforcing the nobility as a caste of wealth and administrative expertise. Nobility was sold to the newcomers for 100,000 ducats initially. The purpose of this in the first instance, was to provide funds for the Cretan war, but there was a realisation in certain quarters that it offered a solution to the declining numbers of the nobility and to the difficulties of finding good men to fill offices. Among the 80 families aggregated in the years 1647–69, there was a notable weight of houses of the Terraferma nobilities or ones whose members had been distinguished in Venetian life for a century or more, whether in the Ducal Chancery and secretariate, or as military figures, or as merchants. Taking the entire block of ennoblements between 1647 and 1718, however, the picture was less impressive. About three-fifths of the new men were merchants or traders, one-fifth lawyers or members of the secretariat or Chancery and one-fifth Terraferma nobles. The original idea had been that only families with a distinguished record of service to the Serene Republic should be admitted and the earlier applications for aggregation had often stressed the distinguished past of the families in question, but references of this kind soon disappeared from the records and it is evident that ability to pay 100,000 ducats or more soon became the only crucial requirement. There is extensive evidence of contempt on the part of members of the old nobility for the newcomers whom they regarded as a mushroom plutocracy. Ease of access to the nobility, indeed, probably undermined its prestige in the long run. In 1775, a senatorial decree provided for the aggregation of 40 Terraferma families who could prove four generations of nobility and enjoyment of 10,000 ducats annual revenue, but only ten families presented themselves as against the 132 who had been candidates for aggregation at the time of the Cretan war. Quite apart from the strained relations between Venetian and Terraferma aristocracies that resulted from the Serenissima's shabby treatment of the provincial communes, the Terraferma nobilities were evidently reluctant to mix with that of Venice: according to one of the diplomatic representatives of the French Revolutionary Government, they regarded it as beneath them 'on account of the ease with which the dignity of patrician status has always been acquired by money'.

The degree to which ennoblements from the mid-seventeenth century onwards strengthened the patriciate as an administrative caste was limited. Undoubtedly men of the 'new' families made their way into responsible posts, but not as a rule the highest. Up until the mid-eighteenth century, governorships or a seat in the Senate were the most they could hope for. Only in the last decades of the Republic's life did any of them enter the Council of Ten or hold the main posts of the Collegio. When Ludovico Manin, whose family had been ennobled in 1648, became Doge in 1789, a contemporary remarked that it was the end of the Republic.[2]

The Venetian nobility was a legally defined order, not a class whose position rested upon any distinguishable economic base. In the sixteenth century, there had been extreme polarities of wealth as between rich and poor nobles and it is likely that the subsequent decline in numbers at least threw this polarity into sharper relief. Decline in numbers may even have meant higher per capita wealth at the upper level. Whether the number of indigent nobles really increased or their poverty deepened, it is impossible to say, but certainly from the late sixteenth century there was an increasing recognition of the fact that poor nobles were an element in the Venetian nobility. In the latter half of the sixteenth century, the problem of indigent nobles was at least receiving closer attention and by the eighteenth century the existence of a class of *Barnabotti*, impoverished nobles inhabiting the parish of S. Barnaba, was popularly recognised. At the same time, the ostentatious affluence of certain ancient noble families like the Pisani di S. Stefano was almost matched by that of 'newcomers' such as the Rezzonico, Manin and Labia who played an important role in eighteenth-century patronage of the arts.

Those newly ennobled men whose wealth had been gained through trade showed a marked tendency to abandon it once they had acquired patrician status. At the same time, they did not, for the most part, show any marked anxiety to compete for high political office. On the one hand anxious to erase the heritage of their old plebeian status, on the other showing no particular enthusiasm for shouldering the burdens of the old patriciate, it was unlikely that the men of the new families would, by and large, form a political leaven. At the same time, the tensions between poor and rich nobles did not make for the emergence of politics that can in any meaningful sense be described as radical.

The conservatism of Venetian eighteenth-century politics has often been referred to. Nowhere was this more evident than in the very programmes put forward by the chief troublemakers among the ruling caste. In their attacks on its inner oligarchy, Angelo Querini, around 1760, and Giorgio Pisani, in the 1770s, called for a return to the norms of strict constitutional legality. In particular they defended the prerogatives of the judicial magistracies such as the *Quarantie* which tended to be the province of nobles of modest or decaying fortunes. Querini wished to curb the powers of the *Inquisitori di Stato* and the Council of Ten. The latter, as in the sixteenth century, was the bastion of the families of established political influence and its members were again taking advantage of its ill-defined constitutional position to extend the Council's action into numerous areas of administration. Hence Querini's campaign against its inordinate powers had very similar objectives to that of the Giovani around 1580 and that of Renier Zeno in the 1620s. Querini's plans involved a reinforcement of the institutional system which would help to balance the powers of the Ten and the Inquisitori, but which would in no way decrease the coherence of the aristocratic order. As for Pisani, in 1774 he pointed to the deplorable situation of public finance and to the 'evils of luxury, disproportion of wealth, indigence and unwarranted exactions'; all this was to be found, he said, 'because the holy laws are spurned'. In 1779, he put forward a programme designed, among other things, to reinforce the caste structure of the patriciate by halting the decay of the lower nobility. The rates of dowries for patrician girls should be stabilised at three grades; the stipends of certain magistrates, including those of the *Quarantie*, should be raised, promotions to government office should be based on seniority and there should be a uniform for patricians. Pisani even had a secret project for state dowries to be given annually to 15 noble girls whose families were not in a position to provide adequate ones, the condition of the grant being that the maidens should marry Venetian nobles. Pisani was, strange as it may seem, regarded as a public danger and was imprisoned in 1780.[3] In no sense was he an apostle of the religion of liberty, equality and fraternity. Such apostles were certainly to be found among the citizenries of the Terraferma, but hardly among the Venetian nobility.

The ruling oligarchy was undoubtedly resistant to questionings of the Venetian political system. This, it was generally recognised, was one of the major limitations of the *libertas veneziana*. It would be misleading, however, to speak of a Venetian aristocratic conservatism pure and simple. Precisely where it was apparently most pronounced, it was a conservatism with subtle nuances. This can be seen with Andrea Tron and in his relations with his political opponents. It can be said that Tron, 'il patron', was the most distinguished of those Venetian statesmen who were hostile to experiment. He was profoundly conscious of a great Venetian heritage which he was not prepared to sacrifice to the new ideas on administration coming from across the Alps or to submit to the corrosive influence of alien elements. He aspired towards the revival of Venice's mercantile tradition, which was to be protected by a Colbertian mercantilist system. Hence he rejected the new physiocrat concept of a free economy and the demands that were being widely made in Europe for the abolition of the guild-system. Freedom of commerce would also have favoured alien elements and thereby disturbed the hierarchy of orders. His party was responsible in 1777 for measures which confined the commercial activities of the Jews to trade in second-hand articles. He had profound contempt for the ideas of his great opponent Francesco Pesaro who was the enthusiastic exponent of physiocrat ideas. Strong ideological passion in general was something he regarded with grave distaste. Yet Tron was the lover and later the husband of the noted *femme savante* Caterina Delfin, the hostess of Venice's chief 'enlightened' salon. No less than Francesco Pesaro, he was a man of broad European culture who collected the works of the Philosophes. The controversy over the Jews in the years 1775–7 represented a curious conflict: on the one hand Tron, the reader of Voltaire but also the opponent of the Jews as an element alien to Venetian mercantile traditions; on the other, as defender of the merits of the Jews, Carlo Contarini who in 1779, in a speech in support of Giorgio Pisani, was to complain of the growing promiscuity between nobles and 'low persons of the vulgar herd'.[4] Tron's interest in the writings of the French Enlightenment was an affair of taste rather than of ideology.

The Venetian cultured milieu was in no way blind to intellectual developments beyond the Alps and even writings such as those of Rousseau and Helvetius, which were prohibited by the censors, were widely known. The degree to which the actual content of French Enlightenment literature was absorbed was to all appearances limited, however. In Venice there appears to have been a certain current of enthusiasm for physiocrat ideas. There is, however, no evidence of allegiance in Venetian, as distinct from Terraferma, intellectual milieus to doctrines subversive of the existing order of society. There was in the Venetian dominions no overt enthusiasm for the atheistic, agnostic or deistic elements in transalpine thought. French writings did, however, help to mould taste, both literary and artistic.[5]

There was an astonishing element of continuity in the Venetian cultural heritage. This can be seen especially in antiquarian studies which, in the eighteenth century, remained the outstanding intellectual passion of the Venetian intelligentsia, although even here the fertilising influence of French scholarship can be seen in the compendious diocesan histories of Flaminio Corner, which followed a pattern set by the Maurist compilers of the late seventeenth century. Obvious comparisons can be drawn between G. B. Tiepolo and Paolo Veronese, between Massari and Palladio. Needless to say, great changes in taste took place in the seventeenth and eighteenth centuries. These, however, in themselves enabled different aspects of the Venetian artistic heritage to be discovered or rediscovered at different times. Even the influence of currents of taste coming from across the Alps facilitated such recoveries.

★ ★ ★

It was partly the impact of French classical tragedy from the last decades of the seventeenth century that had lead, in combination with the rejection of Baroque melodrama, to the rediscovery of sixteenth-century Italian regular tragedy, including that of the Veneto. In the second decade of the eighteenth century, the work of exhumation was undertaken by Lelio Riccoboni. The latter, although born in Modena, was of Venetian family and his main work took place in Venice. He was encouraged by the great Veronese antiquarian and man of letters Scipione Maffei. Significantly, Riccoboni's company had been performing French tragedies. The first work to be resuscitated was G. G. Trissino's *Sophonisba*, the first regular classical tragedy of the Renaissance. Revivals of works by the Venetians Orsato Giustiniani and Giovanni Delfin followed. In close connection with the Venetian patrician writer Apostolo Zeno, Scipione Maffei took the lead in a revival of the classic genre in the Veneto.[6]

In the 1730s, Goldoni wrote his first dialect comedies, although the main period of his production and the actuation of his programme of reform only began after 1748. It was Goldoni who was substantially responsible for reviving popular comedy as a written genre in the Veneto. From the time of Andrea Calmo's death, it had been essentially an affair of oral tradition whereby the *istrioni* of the Commedia dell' Arte improvised upon certain set themes. This tradition had come under heavy attack, whether because standards had, as was asserted, declined, or because taste had become unsympathetic to it, is not altogether clear. The use of traditional set themes was said to lead to monotony, and the actors were regarded as unequal to their task of invention while improvisation, by all accounts, provided occasions for obscenity.

There is no reason for thinking that Goldoni was directly inspired by Ruzzante and Calmo in his writing of comedy in the local dialect. Rather he was attempting to reform a tradition that may have in some measure derived from them in the first instance but which had ceased to be a literary genre. The most obvious inspiration was his great hero Molière who had set himself a very similar task in attempting to replace the bizarre, formless and repetitive performances of the Commedia dell' Arte by plays with varied plots, each with a duly chiselled and polished form and with a variety of fully developed character parts, while limiting the scope for licence by elimination of verbal improvisation. Ruzzante's obscenities would have horrified Goldoni. Eighteenth-century taste would have disapproved of the formlessness of Ruzzante's early plays, although it might have found his later ones based on Plautine models more congenial. Ruzzante's black comedy, with its misanthropic vision, was far removed from the urbanity and geniality of Goldoni. The latter's plays are essentially peopled by *bonhommes* and *personaggi virtuosi*: 'the man of prudence', 'the maiden of honour', the *paterfamilias*', 'the wife of good sense', 'the honourable adventurer'. They exude a Molièreque *bon sens*. Goldoni wrote bourgeois comedy, something quite different from Ruzzante's *imbrogli* of peasants and *louche* townsfolk.

The anonymous author of the sixteenth-century play *La venexiana* had used a dialect inflection perhaps partly for its 'flavour', partly for the nuances it allowed in the language of sensuous passion. Ruzzante had made use of Paduan patois to all appearances out of pride in his native soil and also, evidently, for a grotesque effect; furthermore, a mixture of dialects served to indicate the specific origins of his characters, particularly significant where the more villainous ones were concerned. Calmo had used a bizarre hybrid language composed of Venetian, Slavonic, Greek and Neo-latin elements for a grotesquely comic effect. Goldoni used dialect with a consciousness that was perhaps peculiar to the eighteenth century. No more than any writer of the sixteenth century was he disposed to use the idiom of the *Città dominante* for a grotesquely comic effect. An exception might seem to be provided in *I Rusteghi* (*The Boors*). The crotchety, pig-headed but ultimately benevolent fathers of families, who have a mortal fear of the gay world and whose idea of the highest pleasure is the occasional indulgence in gluttony among an intimate circle of friends, speak a most unrefined dialect. This undoubtedly reinforces their comic stature but it was probably not intended to be exactly comic in itself. Rather it was designed to show precisely that the men in question *are* boors, that is to say it fulfilled a dramatic purpose and was designed to create a realistic effect. For Goldoni, dialect was perhaps above all an instrument in his primary aspiration towards the natural.

In his preface to an edition of four of his plays in 1750, Goldoni wrote:

I have intended what is proper to comedy, that is the simple and the natural, not the academic or elevated. . . . The sentiments should be true and natural, not obscure and over-refined and the expression within the reach of all. . . . This is the great art of the comic poet: to attach himself entirely to nature and never depart from it.

Comparisons between Goldoni's programme and that of Boileau are obvious. More generally, Goldoni's stress on nature, simplicity and propriety was symptomatic of the rationalising taste of the eighteenth century. This led him to explore the material offered by his native surroundings and by his native idiom, although this did not essentially mean a return to the dramatic heritage of the Veneto.

With regard to architecture, it is possible to speak of a definite conservatism of taste in the seventeenth century and of an exploration of the Venetian heritage in the eighteenth. The high Baroque only had a limited impact. The church of the Salute, Longhena's *chef d'oeuvre*, was admittedly prophetic of the more advanced Roman forms of the style, but it was not typical of the architect's work as a whole. Although, in the seventeenth century, there was a new touch of fantasy in the architecture of Venice and the Terraferma, the continuing influence of Sansovino, Palladio and Scamozzi can be clearly seen in many buildings. The curious interplay of tradition and innovation can be observed in Longhena's two great Venetian palaces, Ca Pesaro and Ca Rezzonico. At first sight, they are not readily distinguishable from Sansovino's Palazzo Corner di S. Maurizio and yet there is a massiveness and a monumentality that make them unmistakeably works of the seventeenth century. The key to the difference lies in the deeper recession of Longhena's windows, which in some measure mark a return to Coducci's system, and in the treatment of the lower storeys. Here, the effect of rustication is accentuated in Longhena's works. At Ca Rezzonico, he used rusticated half-columns, in contrast to Sansovino who produced a level wall-face pierced by openings. In Ca Pesaro, where the half-columns are not used, the rustication takes on a pronounced diamond form. In a sense, Longhena had fused the elegance of the Palazzo Corner with the monumentality of Sansovino's Zecca, while at the same time introducing a richer ornamental effect. Taking his work in general, the distinctively seventeenth-century elements in Longhena's style must not be underestimated. These are revealed perhaps less significantly in the occasional fantasies in pediments than in the use of heavy rustication, the stress on the central loggia and the stress on height. With regard to the latter point, however, Longhena's links with the past can again be seen in his employment of angle towers in the villas Da Lezze and Rezzonico: here here turned to the form of the fifteenth-century Veneto villa.

In the early to middle years of the eighteenth century, the works of Massari in Venice and of Muttoni in the Vicenza region marked a revival of the lighter elements of the Palladian style after the age of the Baroque. In the latter half of the century, the Palladian revival was at its height, notably with the Venetian Tommaso Temanza and the Vicentine Ottaviano Bertotti Scamozzi: both were architects and writers and were outstanding scholars of Palladio's works. Massari and Muttoni had perhaps been reluctant Palladians whose personal inclinations were towards the Rococo. Massari gave his churches of the Gesuati and the Pietà austere unpretentious façades in the tradition of Palladio's S. Francesco della Vigna and the Cathedral of S. Pietro di Castello, while inside the Gesuati he indulged in a restrained Rococo fantasy. Massari observed that 'an artist who does not want to die of starvation must of necessity adapt himself to see and think according to the classical rules'. He bowed to a taste that was to become increasingly insistent.

Palladio's reputation emerged relatively unscathed from the eighteenth-century polemic against the irrational in architecture. Admittedly he did not escape the harsh criticism of Padre Lodoli, the eccentric Franciscan observant who was the leading campaigner for an architecture that was rigidly functional and based on rational principles derived from the nature of the material employed. Lodoli, insofar as we know his views from the account of his pupil the outstanding 'enlightened' statesman Andrea Memo, condemned both antique and modern architecture for having perpetuated in stone the proportions and building system originally created in wooden dwellings. Lodoli castigated Palladio, together with Bramante and Sansovino, for not having attained 'that philosophy which we require in this adventurous century'.[7] In fact, however, Lodoli's closest admirers, Andrea Memo himself, Andrea Querini and Filippo Farsetti all became supporters of a neo-Palladian classicism.[8] The great Venetian critic of the mid-eighteenth century, Francesco Algarotti (1712–64), while sharing certain of Lodoli's views on the functionality of architecture, was an enthusiastic admirer of Palladio. For Algarotti, writing in his *Saggio sopra l'architettura* of 1756, 'nothing must be seen in a building which does not have its proper task and is not an integral part of the building; ornament must be entirely derived from the necessary'. Here, however, he precisely quoted Palladio as an authority.[9] Like Lodoli, Algarotti had a strong distaste for the Baroque, but, with his devotion to antique art, he could never concur with the extreme rigidity of the Friar's position.[10] In his admiration for Palladio, Algarotti was not simply glorying in the Venetian past; rather it was the fruit of his broad European culture. He had been struck by the merits of the neo-Palladian style in England. Algarotti appreciated not only the rationality but also the quality of 'fantasy' in Palladio's work. In the *Saggio sopra l'architettura*, the stress was on the former element. In the *Saggio sopra la pittura* of 1762, on the other hand, where he was pointing to Palladio as an inspiration for background scenes, he stated that the latter 'did not submit himself to considerations of convenience beyond a certain measure and perhaps indulged his caprice too much in decoration'; but, he added, 'his very defects are picturesque'.[11] Love of 'fantasy' was something that progressively asserted itself in Algarotti's artistic outlook and his taste for Palladio had perhaps become increasingly involved with it in the late 1750s. In 1759, he even commissioned Canaletto to paint a *fantasia* of the Grand Canal as Palladio might have designed it,[12] a project indicative of a slightly frivolous penchant for the 'picturesque'. Basically, however, Algarotti's philo-Palladianism must ultimately be related to his ideal of a functional architecture and to his reverence for the antique. Here a valuable comparison can be made with Goethe whose profound admiration for Palladio was expressed in his *Italian Journal* of 1786. In the latter half of the eighteenth century, the search for simple and rational forms and the neo-classical reaction against Baroque and Rococo in the Veneto was substantially identified with the imitation of Palladian models.[13] This movement, however, only explored certain facets of Palladio's style: it neglected the fantasy and richness; it saw the architect of the Villa Capra, of Malcontenta and the Redentore rather than the architect of S. Giorgio Maggiore and the Tempietto of Maser.

In the seventeenth century, collectors and connoisseurs of painting had concentrated lovingly upon the great heritage of the sixteenth century. By this time, a clear orientation of taste had become evident in collections, something that had apparently been absent in the sixteenth century. The main interest was in Titian, Tintoretto and Veronese, the weight of works by Tintoretto in collections being perhaps more particularly marked. There was considerable interest in the Bassani and in Andrea Schiavone whose style had obvious affinities with Tintoretto's. Works of Giovanni Bellini were not often found, but those of Giorgione were evidently prized. The reverence for the fifteenth century, which had been so marked in the period of the *Anonimo Morelliano* seems to have now disappeared. There was little interest in other Italian schools. The main exception was the seventeenth century Bolognese school, notably Guercino, who was evidently regarded as being 'in the Vene-

K

tian manner'. Certain connoisseurs showed a marked interest in recent Venetian painters who could have appeared as revivers of the great sixteenth-century Venetian tradition.[14]

That Venice had a distinctive artistic tradition appears to have been essentially a discovery of the mid-seventeenth century. Ludovico Dolce, for instance, appears to have had no particular consciousness of this. Even if he did so, he was scarcely in a position to declare it, since his defence of Titian hinged upon that of Raphael. It was, perhaps, only after the experience of Tintoretto that the development of Venetian painting from Giorgione onwards could be seen as having a distinctive character. A new vision of Raphael may also have been crucial and here Roman and Bolognese artistic theory and propaganda may have disposed Venetians to envisage their native artistic tradition in terms more akin to our own. Among the moderns, Raphael became the great hero of those who proclaimed the duty of the artist to seek out the 'Idea of the Beautiful' while laying a primary stress upon plastic values. Once it was implied that Guido Reni and Domenichino were Raphael's heirs, the conceptual linkage between his name and that of Titian was liable to dissolve. In the Venetian Mario Boschini's *Carta del navegar pittoresco* of 1660, Raphael's name was coupled not with Titian's but, more extraordinarily still, with that of Giovanni Bellini: 'Zambelin is at least a Raphael,' Boschini wrote.[15] Boschini perhaps saw Bellini and Raphael as pioneers in the revival of painting, representing, with their cautious diligence, a relatively primitive stage in the evolution of art which had subsequently been superseded by Giorgione and Titian. At any rate, he pointedly related that Velasquez regarded Titian as the greatest of all painters while not being at all impressed by Raphael.[16] The contrast of Titian with Raphael was potentially far more illuminative of the distinctive features of the Venetian tradition than Dolce's contraposition of Titian and Michelangelo.

The Veronese critic Carlo Ridolfi in his *Meraviglie dell' arte* of 1648 used the term *maniera veneziana*, but his critical comments are not particularly illuminating and it is difficult to make out what the term meant for him. It was used repeatedly by the Venetian Mario Boschini in the *Carta del navagar pittoresco* of 1660 and in his *Breve istruzione*, the preface to the second edition of his *Ricche miniere* of 1674. What Boschini meant by the *maniera veneziana* is best understood by examining in the first instance his discussion of *disegno* and *colore* at the end of the *Breve istruzione*.

For Boschini, *chiaroscuro* and colour are crucial elements in the crea-

tion of pictorial form and line is only a relatively minor constituent of
disegno:

> *Disegno* is the principal base and foundation of the fabric; and just as
> a building cannot exist without foundations, likewise painting is an
> edifice that cannot be constructed without *disegno*. Some believe that
> *disegno* consists solely of line. . . . I say, however, that while line is
> certainly necessary to *disegno*, it must be used like the ruled sheet that
> one places under the paper one is writing on, which one uses as long
> as one is writing, but then puts aside, for painting must be delicate, of
> a mellow softness and without hard outlines (*tenera, pastosa e senza
> terminazione*), as nature teaches us. . . . Line can also be compared to
> the skeleton of the human body, which must be covered with flesh
> to be perfect, and this is one of the important parts of *disegno*, for the
> painter must, upon the basis of line, create the flesh with *chiaroscuro*.

Boschini proceeds to discuss the role of colour and *chiaroscuro* in creating
an impression of three-dimensional form. Further on he writes:

> *Disegno* is reinforced by the art of projection and recession (*l'artificio
> del dentro e fuori*), which is the supreme element of *disegno*, colour and
> invention, a true trinity of perfection, for this consort is both union
> and distinction of figures in separation and together in harmony,
> making them stand out from one another by virtue of lights,
> shadows, reflections and highlights, above all in the Venetian manner.

In discussing colour, Boschini described the working method of Venetian painters. Their ideas, he indicates, were essentially worked-out on
the canvas. In the first instance, they sketched out a design upon it,
without a model, working from the idea in their minds, paying particular attention to recession. (*La cura loro maggiore era concertare il dentro
e il fuori.*) Here *chiaroscuro* was the essential instrument. Only when they
had achieved the 'concert' of background and foreground did they turn
to their models, whether natural or artistic, and to these they did not
oblige themselves totally. They proceeded upon the basis of the sketch
with bold brush strokes (*a colpeggiare*), showing a preference for earth
colours and abhorring the shriller ones, going on to accentuate the
relief by reinforcement of lights and shadows. 'There is no doubt,'
Boschini writes, 'that by the maxims understood by these excellent
painters there has been established a *maniera* in itself.'

For Boschini, it appears, the *maniera veneziana* consisted in the first
instance of the *artificio del dentro e fuori*, the exploration of three-dimen-

sional space and the creation of a striking illusion of relief and recession, both in harmony with one another. Here *chiaroscuro* was all-important. The *maniera veneziana* also involved a method by which a painting was essentially worked out from start to finish on the canvas, keeping *chiaroscuro* and colour in constant symbiosis, rather than by transferring to the canvas ideas already developed in drawings. Aretino had been aware that Titian put down colours prior to his *disegno*, but only with Boschini was this supremely 'painterly' working method seen as the distinctive feature of a style. With Boschini, the sensitivity to freedom and boldness of handling had evidently become acute. Terms he constantly used in his writings were *colpeggiare* and *macchia*. The latter word, whose root-meaning is 'stain', is almost untranslateable in an artistic context. In some measure it equates to the word 'daub', but in a totally non-pejorative sense, being suggestive of bold, impressionistic handling. The term *colpeggiare* and *macchia* reinforced that of *sprezzatura*, which had been used by Dolce. For Dolce, however, the great hero had been Titian and he ignored Tintoretto, while with Boschini the term *sprezzo di penello* is specifically applied to the work of the latter, being linked to an assertion that his paintings were designed to be seen at a distance. Far from being signs of indolence, Tintoretto's free brush stroked were '*colpi* of a learned artificer'. In general, the stress on colourism was marked in Boschini's writings and like Dolce he did not regard good colour as meaning mere lusciousness of hue: with both critics, the preference was for a sober palette. No more than any sixteenth-century apologist for the Venetian school did he regard colourism in itself as its distinctive feature; the latter for Boschini lay rather in the combination of colour and *chiaroscuro* in the creation of three-dimensionality. This linkage of colour with *chiaroscuro* and the *artificio del dentro e fuori* does perhaps, however, distinguish Boschini from sixteenth-century critics who primarily linked it to the concepts of *naturalezza* and *convenevolezza*. Boschini does not appear to have had any particularly clear idea of the qualities which colours acquire in juxtaposition with one another, of the interplay of warm and cool hues and of the colouristic illusions which thereby arise, for instance the way in which grey pigment acquires the character of an 'optic blue' in certain contexts. Basically it was to be left for modern criticism to realise that the exploitation of chromatic illusions was one of the distinguishing characteristics of the great Venetian colourists.

The *Carta del navegar pittoresco* and the *Ricche miniere* were paeans to the glories of the Venetian school. Ridolfi in the *Meraviglie* of 1648 had provided the first true history of the school from the fifteenth century to the mid-seventeenth, but he did not assign to it any particular role in the history of painting; rather, like Andrea Vendramin, he commenced with an account of the great painters of antiquity and then went on to discuss the Venetians without a pause. Boschini, in the *Breve istruzione*, reversed Vasari's picture of the Tuscans as the pioneers of the 'modern manner' with a jingoistic arrogance of which not even Vasari had been capable. After the decline of painting in the post-antique era, the muse of painting had wandered about the world seeking shelter, until her good star had lead her to Venice. There she settled and received nourishment. It was Giovanni Bellini who discovered 'the sound foundations of perspective' and raised painting from the darkness. It was Giorgione who 'placed a diadem upon her brow'. As far as the fifteenth and sixteenth centuries went, Boschini's artistic culture was to all appearances an extremely narrow one, rigidly confined to the Venetian school. With regard to the seventeenth century, however, he was well aware of artistic developments in Italy and Europe as a whole. In the *Carta del navegar pittoresco*, he called Velasquez and Rubens as witnesses to the distinctions of the Venetian school, referring to the Spanish painter's admiration for Titian and Tintoretto and that of the Fleming for Titian. Rubens had learnt in Venice what he could not learn in Rome[17] and Boschini perhaps regarded him as a continuator of Venetian tradtion, thereby anticipating the vision of late seventeenth-century French defenders of the rights of colour.

For Boschini, the great heroes appear to have been Giorgione, Titian, Tintoretto and Jacopo Bassano. In describing the 'method' of Venetian painters, it was above all the working practices of Titian and Tintoretto that he set forth. It was evidently the achievement of the mid-seventeenth century to have apprehended the true greatness of Tintoretto and Bassano. Ridolfi had devoted one of the longest sections of the *Meraviglie* to Tintoretto and put forward the picture of him as a heroic figure who had triumphed in the face of hostility. In general, however, he praised him for his more academic qualities. He prefaced his life of *Tintoretto* by a section asserting that figure painting was the highest form of art. He lovingly elaborated the myth that he had combined the colour of Titian with the *disegno* of Michelangelo. Like Aretino, Ridolfi mildly censured him for not having known how to restrain his impetuosity. Boschini, on the other hand, clearly admired Tintoretto's *sprezzo di penello*. There is no reason for thinking that the references to his *bizarreria* and *capriccio* were in any way tinged by a penchant for

Michelangelo; indeed he appears to have had no particular enthusiasm for the latter. For Boschini, it seems, Tintoretto's panache was essentially one with his *artificio del dentro e fuori*: 'he endeavoured,' wrote Boschini, 'with subterranean mines, bombs, grenades and the like to make his figures jump from the canvases.'[18] It was, however, in Boschini's remarks on Jacopo Bassano that a new taste most clearly revealed itself. 'Bassano,' he wrote, 'was the arbiter of lights, for it was he who left an eternal light of artifice which has revealed to all how they should work, having made night shine even more than the day.' Here Boschini was evidently referring to Jacopo's *chiaroscuro* night scenes. For Boschini, 'this great classic master had so bold a brush (*è stato di così fiero colpo di penello*) that in this technique he has had no equals and no like . . . spurning diligence and finish, with, so to speak, a chaos of obscure colours in confused medley'.[19] By contrast, while Boschini praised Paolo Veronese highly, he was unable to express his admiration for him in a vocabulary that was either concrete or particularly suggestive.

·With Francesco Algarotti[20] in the middle years of the eighteenth century there was a conscious reaction against the Baroque and in his examination of the Venetian tradition the stress was primarily upon the sixteenth-century masters, to an even greater degree than with Ridolfi and Boschini. Algarotti had, in his own mind, a clear notion of what the Venetian school stood for, in this case colourism, which he conceived in terms essentially different from those of Boschini. Algarotti was perhaps the first Venetian critic to see colourism pure and simple as the distinguishing feature of the Venetian school and he fully assumed a dichotomy between Tuscan *disegno* and Venetian colour, seeing the Venetian masters as definitely weak in *disegno*. Here his vision was evidently conditioned by a debt to seventeenth-century Roman and French theorists of classical idealism who put forward the primacy of *disegno*. His links were with a tradition that had taken a rather patronising attitude towards the Venetian school, but Algarotti was in fact highly appreciative of the merits of the latter. For him, Raphael represented the supreme artistic achievement, but he did not set him up as a canon by which other artists should be judged. He regarded it as virtually impossible for any artist to combine all the elements of good painting and it was dangerous for aspirant artists to concentrate in their studies too heavily upon one artist or one school;[21] in his criticism he showed persistence in attempting to define the merits of each particular school.

In his *Saggio sopra la pittura* (1762), addressed to the British Royal Academy of Art,[22] while indicating classical sculptures as the models for young students in their apprenticeship in *disegno*, he suggested that they should also have models in the art of colouring. Here the great masters were Giorgione, Titian, Veronese and Jacopo Bassano, along with Correggio and Van Dyck; above all Titian. Algarotti's *colore*, however, was not the *colore* of Boschini. For one thing, Algarotti evidently assumed that *colore* and *disegno* were separate entities, an outlook alien to Boschini. An amateur, a man of letters, a rationaliser, his concept of colour was essentially unpainterly. He never perhaps comprehended the symbiosis of *disegno*, *chiaroscuro* and *colore* in creating an illusion of three-dimensional form that had been crucial to Boschini's concept of the Venetian *maniera*. He did not really explore the relationship between colour and brushwork. Rather he attempted to apply to discussion of pictorial colour the discoveries of Newtonian optics and gave the British Academy a disquisition on the effects of reflected light. He admitted, however, that Titian, Correggio and Van Dyck were excellent colourists without knowing about these subtleties and that the great colourists would be preeminently the books of study of the young painter: 'Giorgione and above all Titian succeeded in discovering in nature what others were not given to see.' In Titian, he wrote, there could be seen 'that smoothness of colour that comes of union, the charm that does not ignore truth, the insensible transitions, the lovely clothing and modulations of all the tints'. After Titian, the prizes went to Jacopo Bassano and Paolo Veronese, on account of 'their bravura, boldness of touch and lightness of brush'.[23] Here Algarotti was already moving away from his grand scientific theories, but his rather half-hearted attempts to apply the rules of Newtonian optics to the art of painting may account for his analysis of Titian's colouring primarily in terms of tints and transitions of tints. Furthermore, Algarotti's theories of light may have influenced his colouristic taste. It has been suggested that he may have encouraged Tiepolo to lighten his palette and move away from the marked *chiaroscuro* of his earlier work.[24]

Algarotti was fully conscious of the importance of brushwork, but he always applied to it less forceful and daring terms than *macchia* and *colpo di penello*. He was incapable of Boschini's vision of Tintoretto. The latter, he wrote, 'was inferior to none of the Venetians when he did not execute hack-work or slovenly pieces, to say the best, but showed what he knew'. He quoted with obvious agreement Aretino's advice to the painter to reduce his rapidity and show more patience in his work. His greatest admiration was for the *Miracle of the Slave*, a work which perhaps showed Tintoretto's academic qualities at their highest.

This combined '*disegno*, colour, composition, light-effects, movement, expression, all brought to their highest level'.[25] When he listed the most outstanding works of Tintoretto to be found in Venice,[26] it was hardly surprising that he should not have mentioned the shoddily executed cycles in the Ducal Palace, but what is significant is that he should also have omitted his cycles in the Scuola di S. Rocco. Evidently he was unsympathetic to Tintoretto's extreme *bravura* and admired the more academic qualities of his art. Like Ridolfi, he subscribed to the myth that Tintoretto combined the colour of Titian with the *disegno* of Michelangelo.

In Algarotti's view, Titian 'depicted truth in its most natural effects', 'Tintoretto in its most extraordinary', while Veronese 'enriched it with his magnificent fantasies'.[27] For Algarotti, Paolo was above all an artist of 'fantasy', a quality which also highly attracted him in the work of Tiepolo, although his own penchant for it in some measure ran counter to his more theoretical and a-priorist conceptions of the learned task of the artist. Paolo was also, for Algarotti, one of the great models for the draped figure and the supreme model for architectural backgrounds. The affinities between these and the buildings of his beloved Palladio were doubtless evident to him. Algarotti did not, however, suggest the more generally architectonic features of Paolo's work. In certain respects, Veronese encountered his strong censure: he was 'incorrect in *disegno* and even more so in *costume*'.[28] Algarotti's *costume* had certain affinities with the sixteenth-century concept of *convenevolezza*: it referred to the appropriateness of depiction to subject matter, but in Algarotti's case it was imbued with a specifically archaeologising tone and meant, among other things, that treatment of dress, architectural detail and so on should be appropriate to the period in which the scene of a picture was set. The Venetian painters in general were deficient in respect of *costume*.[29] Whatever his other failings, however, Veronese showed 'facility', 'charm' and 'a touch that which enamours'. Perhaps Algarotti was attracted by Paolo more than he cared to admit. It is in his descriptions of the latter that his language breaks out of his normally conventional mould and becomes most strikingly alive:

> What Paolo has achieved above all other painters is that everyone wishes to enter . . . his pictures and walk at ease there, see those parts that remain hidden to the eye; those graceful sites, those rich and graceful fields and the best conceived buildings imaginable invite and with sweet magic call the beholder to them.[30]

The Algarotti who wrote here was not the academic theorist who believed that history-painting and figure-composition were the highest form of art but the Algarotti who admired Canaletto and commissioned him to compose a *fantasia* on the work of Palladio.

If the greatness of Tintoretto had been the discovery of the seventeenth century, Veronese, with his refinement, architectonic rationality and clear palette—the 'harmony and clarity of his colour' that Goethe so much admired—might have been expected to appeal to the taste of the eighteenth. A Palladian enthusiast might well have been sympathetic to his work. Here it is significant that Goethe's primary artistic passions revealed in the course of his sightseeing tour in the Veneto were for Paolo and Palladio. Algarotti, however, did not have the same asceticism of taste as Goethe in his immediate post-Weimar period and just as he made concessions to Palladio's 'caprice', he relished the element of delicate 'fantasy' in Paolo's work. No less than his neo-Palladianism in its more purist aspects, this appreciation of fantasy, which was in some measure related to his hankerings after the picturesque, marked Algarotti as a child of his age. His vision of Veronese was perhaps coloured by his experience of the work of G. B. Tiepolo, whom he regarded as painting in Veronese's manner. In the sixteenth or seventeenth centuries, the term 'fantasia' would hardly have been applied to Paolo. At that time it primarily signified an almost superhuman force of imagination and *invenzione*. It had been applied to Michelangelo in the sixteenth century and might well have been applied to Tintoretto in the seventeenth, although the terms used by Ridolfi and Boschini of his work were *bizzarro, capriccioso, stravagante*. Only in the eighteenth century, perhaps, did it acquire more delicate overtones, although the term as used by Algarotti probably still carried strong suggestions of th grandiose and heroic and was some way removed from the concept of the 'fanciful'. Furthermore, it is doubtful whether earlier ages had seen an element of extravagance in Paolo's work. It was perhaps only an eighteenth-century critic that could see his 'fantasy'.

That Algarotti should have regarded G. B. Tiepolo as painting in the manner of Veronese, which he had combined with those of Salvator Rosa and Castiglione,[31] underlines the role of tradition in the development of Venetian painting in the post-Renaissance period. Throughout the seventeenth century, the influence of the sixteenth-century heritage had been strong. Quite apart, however, from the fact that the traditions that derived from it were merged with the Baroque–the heritage itself perhaps even being seen with a vision coloured by Baroque importations—it is unwise to speak simply of a regional conservatism. In the seventeenth century, the 'Venetian manner' was no longer a purely Venetian or Veneto affair: it had become a pictorial language common to much of Italy and found its echoes elsewhere in Europe. In Naples and Genoa, there were schools whose *colpo* and *macchia* had strong affinities with Veneto tradition. Even in Rome, the polished classicism associated with Bolognese painters such as Guido Reni and Domenichino was challenged from the 1620s by a high Baroque current which showed a certain allegiance to Venetian richness of colour, although not perhaps to Venetian *sprezzo* and *macchia*, its most notable exponent being Pietro da Cortona. Of the imitators of the great sixteenth-century Venetian masters working in the City of the Lagoons, a number were in fact products of other Italian schools, most notably the Genoese Bernardo Strozzi and the Roman Antonio Ruschi, who can be regarded in some measure as revivers of the manners of Tintoretto and Veronese respectively. In general, the traditions followed were more particularly those of Giorgione, Titian, Palma Vecchio, Tintoretto, the Bassani and Palma Giovane, but in the latter decades of the seventeenth century, there was a marked revival of the Veronese manner.[32]

In the eighteenth century, with Piazzetta and G. B. Tiepolo, the heritage of the past was evident, but held in symbiosis with revolutionary elements. In his early figure compositions, with their violent action and strong *chiaroscuro*, Piazzetta appeared in many respects as the continuator of seventeenth-century traditions, although with his rejection of colouristic charm and subtle chromatic modulation and in his play of whites, acid indigos and ochres against a red priming, his affinities were less with any Venetian master than with the Bolognese Guercino, significantly the non-Venetian painter most sought after by seventeenth-century Venetian collectors. Piazzetta's grandiose 'Baroque' phase was a relatively early one which he abandoned around 1720 for a calmer and more intimate manner in his genre pictures. Nevertheless, the pearly luminosity of the works of his later period, the loving and undeniably sensual treatment of flesh, were dependent upon the techniques evolved in his earlier *tenebroso* manner. The accentuated lusciousness and luminosity of effect was achieved by the contrast of the light tones with rich browns and slaty greys and by the play of colours and tones against the traditional red priming. In Tiepolo's early work of the period *c.* 1717–22, the affinities with the Baroque, more particularly with Guercino, were again marked, but the rather heavy *chiaroscuro* and splashes of violet colour soon gave way to a lighter palette in some ways reminiscent of Veronese's. Coming of a tradition primarily based upon oil painting, it was perhaps natural that Tiepolo, when he came to paint frescoes, should have looked back to the fresco tradition of six- teenth-century Venetia, not merely to Paolo Veronese, but more generally to the group of his contemporaries who had decorated the villas of the Terraferma. Reminiscences of Paolo constantly recur in Tiepolo's work, in the colouring, in the use of *di sotto in sù* illusionist perspective, in the picturesque landscapes and in the taste for theatrical antique costume and lavish sixteenth-century dress, although in the latter case Fasolo is a rather more obvious model. Even in what was perhaps the most revolutionary aspect of his art, the exploitation of void space, Tiepolo may have learnt lessons from Veronese. Tiepolo did not merely introduce an element of lightness into his compositions by making them open in form with large areas of canvas devoted to a delicate azure sky. He also gave a clearly defined compositional role to the void spaces between the solid forms and in certain cases his com- positions can be envisaged as harmonies of the shapes formed by these voids just as much as architectural structures created out of solid objects. In certain of Veronese's works, notably the Louvre *Cana* and the Accademia *Feast in the House of Levi*, the voids clearly form part of the overall pattern, notably in the latter work, where the segments of sky are partly defined by the curves and lines of the arches through which they are glimpsed and partly cut into fantastic shapes by the outlines of buildings. This particular device was employed by Tiepolo on a number of occasions. Tiepolo, of course, took the exploitation of void space very much further than Veronese had ever done. Of all European artists in the mid-eighteenth century, he was perhaps the most revolu- tionary and, at the same time, the most strongly linked to tradition: on the one hand he looked back to Veronese, on the other he pointed forward to Goya.

A clear line of tradition ran from the Baroque and the work of Magnasco, through Sebastiano Ricci of Belluno (1659–1734), the painter of picturesque, rugged Dalmatian vistas, to the Guardi. With Francesco Guardi's fantasy figure paintings, such as the *Argente and Tancred* (London) and the *Tobias* scenes in the church of the Angelo Raphael in Venice, a Rococo element can be seen which still has a strong tinge of the Baroque, and in which the qualities of *macchia* and *sprezzo di penello* are taken to their extreme point. While the roots of Canaletto's style can be clearly seen in late seventeenth-century vedutist tradition, his works, by contrast, ultimately have a rational quality peculiar to the eighteenth century.

The *vedutisti* had, to all appearances, a limited appeal for Venetian aristocratic connoisseurs. The main purchasers of their works appear to have been dealers, unpretentious plebeians and foreigners.[33] Tiepolo was the artist who preeminently catered for the tastes of aristocratic patrons prone to ostentation, while in the last three decades of the Republic's existence, a strong penchant for neo-classicism was evident among the outstanding patrician patrons of 'enlightened' outlook.[34] Significantly, however, Pietro Longhi, hailed by Goldoni as a fellow-searcher after 'truth', was highly regarded in advanced circles. It is even possible that his works were regarded as somewhat subversive. This is not to say, however, that he did not have an appeal among the aristocracy that extended far outside the limits of the 'enlightened' group.[35]

★ ★ ★

Pietro Longhi, in his genre paintings, depicted scenes of everyday life with sympathy and charm; the foibles of his age he revealed with a merciless eye. 'It is significant,' writes Professor Haskell, 'that the most enthusiastic praise of his work should have come from men who were anxious to look more steadily at the actual circumstances of Venetian life than was usual at the time.' There could scarcely have been a stronger contrast with Tiepolo who was always prepared to transport his patrons into the empyrean or invite his viewers into a fairyland where splendidly dressed Venetian ladies of the sixteenth century consorted with antique heroes. Here it was still the golden age of Venice. Tiepolo, however, could not celebrate this golden age with the seriousness of Veronese or Tintoretto.

In the sixteenth century, Venice had been a city of myth: the *stato di libertà*, the prime exemplar of the *stato misto*. Whatever their pride in her institutions, however, most Venetian statesmen realised that her power of action in the international field had very definite limits. Consciousness of the need to evaluate in a realistic spirit the situation in which she found herself, combined with hopes for an effective if circumscribed role in European affairs, gave a major impulse to what was perhaps the finest historiographical tradition in Counter-Reformation Italy. In the eighteenth century, realists were not lacking among the Venetian patriciate. Reformers like Andrea Memo addressed themselves to limited objectives in the slow task of economic and administrative repair. With Andrea Tron, attachment to Venetian tradition was combined with a weary scepticism regarding the active role to which Venice could aspire. A realistic assessment of the contemporary scene could help to ensure survival, but it hardly pointed towards a restoration of former glories. Where realism was not accompanied by genuine hope and the sense of a lost age of felicity was not so immediate as to provoke enquiries into the causes of misfortune, there was perhaps less impulsion towards an analytical historiography like that of Nicolò Contarini. In the event, eighteenth-century Venice produced a wealth of antiquarian studies, but scarcely any political historiography of note. The Venetian dominions in that century did not undergo an intellectual awakening or administrative overhaul comparable to those in the Italian states ruled by Habsburg and Bourbon powers. The contribution of the Venetian intelligentsia to the thought of the Enlightenment was limited. It was in the realms of comedy, of popular journalism and of painting that Venice made her great contributions to eighteenth-century culture, in the Guardis' romantic relish for squalour and decay, in the cool precision of Canaletto, in the fantasy of Tiepolo, in the robust naturalism of Goldoni and the sardonic realism of Longhi. It was a cultural tradition that drew upon the riches of the past and yet, even with Tiepolo, it had abandoned the old Venetian aspiration towards grandeur. Tiepolo's extravagance and fantasy were very different in character from the pictorial rhetoric of the great sixteenth-century masters. He was not, like Tintoretto and Veronese, in their apotheoses of Venice, the minister to a living mythology. Mythology was no longer possible, only nostalgia and escapism. A Venetian myth could only again arise when, in the post-Risorgimento period, hopes, faltering ones perhaps, of a national regeneration lead patriotic historians to look to the great Venetian past for reassurance.

Notes

[1] M. Petrocchi, *Il tramonto della Repubblica di Venezia e l'assolutismo illuminato* (Venice 1950); A. Fanfani, 'Il mancato rinnovamento economico' in *La Civiltà veneziana del Settecento* (Florence 1960), pp. 27–68

[2] On the Venetian and Veneto nobilities in this period, see: M. Berengo, *La Società veneta alla fine del Settecento* (Florence 1956), Ch. I; J. C. Davis, *The Decline of the Venetian Nobility as a Ruling Class* (Baltimore 1962), Ch. v. Information on the 1647–69 aggregations is to be found in Osterreichische Nationalbibliothek, Vienna, *Fond. Foscarini*, Cod. III, n. 6144

[3] Petrocchi, *op. cit.*, pp. 31–40

[4] See especially G. Tabacco, *Andrea Tron (1712–85) e la crisi dell' aristocrazia senatoria a Venezia* (Trieste 1957)

[5] See especially Berengo, *La Società veneta*

[6] G. Ortolani, *La Riforma del teatro nel Settecento* (Venice–Rome 1962), pp. 1–37

[7] *Elementi dell' architettura lodoliana* (Rome 1786)

[8] F. Haskell, *Patrons and Painters. A Study in the Relations between Art and Society in the Age of the Baroque* (London 1963), p. 322

[9] F. Algarotti, *Saggi*, ed. G. da Pozzo (Bari 1963), pp. 33–4

[10] A. M. Gabrieli, 'L' Algarotti e la critica d' arte in Italia nel Settecento', II, *La critica d' Arte*, III (2) (1939), pp. 24–31 at p. 26

[11] *Saggi*, pp. 91–2

[12] Haskell, *op. cit.*, p. 357

[13] Gabrieli, *loc. cit.*, p. 31

[14] Savini-Branca, *Il collezionismo veneziano*, esp. pp. 82–5

[15] 1660 ed., p. 30. *The Carta* together with the *Breve istruzione* is reproduced in M. Boschini, *La Carta del navegar pittoresco Edizione critica*, etc., ed. A. Pallucchini (Venice–Rome 1966). Here page-references will be taken from the 1660 edition, these being indicated in the 1966 critical edition

[16] *Carta*, p. 58

[17] *Ibid.*, pp. 56–60

[18] *Breve istruzione*

[19] *Ibid.*

[20] For Algarotti as a connoisseur and critic of painting see Gabriele, 'L' Algarotti e la critica d'arte', etc., I, *La Critica d' Arte*, III (1938), pp. 155–69; Haskell, *Patrons and Painters*, pp. 347–60

[21] *Saggio sopra l'Accademia di Francia ch' è in Roma*, in *Saggi*, *cit.* p. 22

[22] Reproduced in *Saggi*, pp. 53–114

[23] *Ibid.*, pp. 80–5

[24] Haskell, *Patrons and Painters*, p. 354

[25] *Saggi*, pp. 134–5 (*Sagg. pitt.*)

[26] *Ibid.*, p. 12 (*Sagg. Accad. Franc.*)

[27] *Ibid.*, p. 22 (*Sagg. Accad. Franc.*)

[28] *Ibid.*, p. 134 (*Sagg. pitt.*)

[29] *Ibid.*, pp. 93–5 (*Sagg. pitt.*)

[30] *Opere*, VIII (Venice 1792), p. 187; letter to Mariette 10 June 1761, *c.f. Saggi*, p. 134

[31] *Saggi*, p. 22 (*Sagg. Accad. Franc.*)

[32] See especially N. Ivanoff, 'Arte e critica d' arte nella Venezia del Seicento', in *La Civiltà veneziana nell' Età Barocca* (Florence 1959)

[33] Haskell, *Patrons and Painters*, p. 372 and seq.

[34] *Ibid.*, pp. 361–72

[35] *Ibid.*, p. 323

Appendix

Some Major Art-Patrons of the Sixteenth and Early Seventeenth Centuries in Venice and the Veneto (c. 1520–1630)

Abbreviations: f.—son of (e.g. Daniele Barbaro f. Francesco); Kr.—Cavaliere di S. Marco; Proc.—Procuratore di S. Marco.

Sources

(a) Primary

A. S. Ven, *Barbaro Albori*, 7 vols. (Genealogies of patrician families) Bibl. Marciana Ven. Mss. Italiani. Capellari-Vivaro, *Il Campidoglio veneto.*

Anonimo Morelliano. Published versions include *Der Anonimo Morelliano. Marcantonio Michiels Notizie d'opere del disgeno*, ea. T. Frimmel (Vienna 1888) and an English translation as *The Anonimo*, ed. G. C. Williamson (London 1903)

Vasari, G., *Le vite de' più eccelenti pittori scultori e architetti*. The references in this appendix are to the London 1950 (Everyman) four-volume edition of the *Lives* which gives in translation the Venice 1568 edition. The latter gives considerably more information on the Venetian school than the Florence 1550 edition.

Guisconi—Bardi—Goldioni, *Tutte le cose notabili e belle che sono in Venice* ecc. and variants of this title.

First ed. *Tutte le cose notabili e belle che sono in Venetia cioè usanze antiche pitture e pittori . . . di M. Anselmo Guisconi* (pseud. F. Sansovino) (Venice 1556)

Ibid., 1560 (anon.)

Delle cose notabili ecc. (1560) pref. F. Sansovino

Ibid. with adjoined *Dichiaratione di tutte le istorie . . . nel Gran Consiglio di Gerolamo Bardi* (1565, 1566, 1567, 1569, 1583, 1587)

Le cose meravigliose . . . riformate, raccomodate . . . da Leonico Goldioni (pseud. N. Doglioni) (1592, 1603)

Delle cose notabili ecc. (1606) (Goldioni)

Le cose meravigliose (1624) (Goldioni)

There were numerous later editions.

Palladio, A., *I quattro libri dell' architettura* (Venice 1570)

Sansovino—Stringa—Martinoni.

> *Venetia città nobilissima e singolare . . . da M. Francesco Sansovino* Venice (1581)
>
> *Ibid. (corretta, emendata . . . e ampliata del M. R. don Giovanni Stringa* (Venice 1604)
>
> *Ibid. (con aggiunte di tutte le cose notabili della stessa città fatte e occorse dall' anno 1588 fino al presente 1663 da D. Giustiniano Martinoni* (Venice 1663)

Marzari, G., *La historia di Vicenza* (Venice 1591)

Scamozzi, *L'idea dell' architettura universale* (Venice 1615).

Ridolfi, C., *Le maraviglie dell' arte ovvero le vite degli illustri pittori veneti e dello stato*, first published Venice 1648.

> Modern critical edition with notes by D. von Hadeln, 2 vols (Berlin 1914–24, reprint Rome 1965). The references here are to the latter edition

Boschini, M., *Carta del navegar pittoresco* (Venice 1660) is invaluable for mid-seventeenth-century locations but not in fact cited below

Foscarini, M., *Della letteratura veneziana* (1st ed. Padua 1752, citations here are from the Venice 1854 ed.)

Temanza, T., *Vite dei più celebri architetti e scultori veneziani che fiorirono nel secolo decimosesto* (Venice 1778)

Cicogna, E. A., *Delle inscrizioni veneziane*, 7 vols in 6 (Venice 1824–53)

Fapanni, *Elenco dei musei, delle pinacotheche e della varie collezioni pubbliche e private che un tempo esistettero e che esistono oggidi in Venexia* (1877–89, Ms. in Bibl. Marciana Ven. Cod. It Ser VI (10479)

(b) Collections of documents

Lorenzi, G. B., *Monumenti per servire alla Storia del Palazzo Ducale* Pt. I *1253–1600*, (Venice 1868)

Cheyney, E., *Original Documents Relating the Venetian Painters and their Pictures in the Sixteenth Century*, Miscellanea of the Philobiblion Society, XIV (1872–6)

Italienische Forschungen herausgegeben vom Kunsthistorischen Institut Florenz. Band IV. Archivialische Beitrage zur Geschichte der venezianischen Kunst, ed. W. Bode, G. Gronau, D. v. Hadeln, (Berlin 1911)

(c) Secondary sources

Morsolin, B., *Le collezioni di cose d'arte nel secolo decimosesto in Vicenza* (Vicenza 1881)

Levi, C. A., *Le collezioni veneziane d' arte e d' antichità dal secolo XIV ai nostri giorni* (Venice 1900)

Ferriguto, A., 'I committenti di Giorgione', *Atti del R. Istituto Veneto di Scienze, Lettere ed Arti*, LXXXV (1925–6)

Ferriguto, A., *Attraverso i 'misteri' di Giorgione* (Castelfranco Veneto 1933)

Barbieri, F., Cevese, R., Magagnato, L., *Guida di Vicenza* (Vicenza 1953)

Savini-Branca, S., *Il collezionismo veneziano del Seicento* (Padua 1954)

Gallo, R., 'Contributi su Jacopo Sansovino', *Saggi e Memorie della Storia dell' Arte*, I (1957), pp. 83–105

Gallo, R., 'Michele Sanmicheli a Venezia', in *Michele Sanmicheli. Studi raccolti dall' Accademia di Agricoltura, Scienze e Lettere di Verona per la celebrazione del IV centenario della sua morte* (Verona 1960)

Zorzi, G. G., 'La problematica palladiana in relazione alle più recenti scoperte', *Bollettino del Centro Internazionale di Studi di Architettura Andrea Palladio*, V (1963), pp. 87–97

Mazzotti, G., *Palladian and Other Venetian Villas* (London–Rome 1966)

Almerigo, Paolo f. Conte Domenico Kr. (*b.* 1514), Vicentine noble and Canon of Vicenza Cathedral.

He commissioned the Villa Rotonda (later Capra) Vicenza, designed by Palladio *c.* 1550–1. It was richly adorned with sculptures and contained valuable paintings. A canon lawyer by training and a man of letters, Paolo was Papal Referendary under Gregory XIII.

Palladio, p. 16; Marzari, pp. 202–3; G. Mantese, 'Tristi vicende del Canonico Paolo Almerigo' etc. in *Studi in onore di A. Bardella* (Vicenza 1964), pp. 161–86.

Aretino, Pietro (1492–1556) of Arezzo, resident in Venice 1527–56 (see above, pp. 132–6, 223).

He had close links with Titian, Jacopo Sansovino and Danese Cattaneo. The contents of his collection are uncertain, although drawings would appear to have bulked large. There are portraits of him by Titian, Sebastiano del Piombo and Danese Cattaneo. In 1545, Jacopo Tintoretto executed paintings on the ceilings of his Venetian house. These are now partly dispersed and partly lost. The *Apollo and Marsyas* is in Wadsworth Coll., Hertford, Connecticut.

Lettere sull' arte di P. Aretino, ed. F. Pertile and E. Camasasca, 3 vols in 4 (Milan 1957–60), including vol. III (1) *Biografia dell' Aretino*; Vasari, III, p. 116, IV, pp. 203–6; Ridolfi, I, pp. 169–70, 172, 174–6, 183, 193; Schulz, p. 46.

Barbarano, Conte Montano, Vicentine noble.

He commissioned the Palazzo Barbarano, Vicenza, designed by Palladio some time before 1570. The stucchi were perhaps by Vittoria or Rubini and it was decorated with paintings by Alessandro Maganza and Andrea Vicentino.

Palladio, II, pp. 20–1; Barbieri-Cevese-Magagnato, p. 108.

Barbarigo dalla Terrazza in S. Polo. Venetian noble family.

The ceilings of the palace were decorated in the 1550s with paintings from the studio of Bonifazio Veronese.

Barbaro Albori, I f. 107v.; Capellari-Vivaro, I f. 97v; Schulz, pp. 118–19.

Cristoforo f. Daniele f. Daniele (*b.* 1544).

He bought numerous works from the studio of the deceased Titian in 1581, referring to them in his testament.

Testament 1600, A. S. Ven, *Notarile. Testamenti*, B. 1194 prot. VI, pp. 57r.-59r; Ridolfi, I, p. 200 and note by Hadeln.

Daniele f. Domenico (1582–1625).

The nephew of Cristoforo, he inherited his collection. He possessed works by Gentile Bellini, Titian, L. Bassano, F. Bassano, Palma Vecchio, Palma Giovane and Tintoretto *inter al.*

Savini-Branca, pp. 183–6.

The family collection remained largely intact until 1845. See: Bibl. Correr, Ven., *Cod. Cicogna*, 3281 fasc. IV n. 45, *Letteri F. Caffi, Cod. Cicogna*, 3345 col 3006, *Barbarigo della Terrazza. Elenco di quadri di casa*; Savini-Branca, p. 183.

Barbaro di. S. Maria Mater Domini. Venetian noble family.

The family had a collection of modern and antique works of art in the late fifteenth century, which was admired by Politian. The family had Carpaccio and Giorgione work in the scuole under its protection, including S. Ursula.

Barbaro Albori, 1 f. 199; Levi, p. xliv; Savini-Branca, p. 13.

Daniele f. Francesco (1513–70), Patriarch Elect of Aquilea (see above, pp. 59–61, 77–8, 145–6, 173–4, 179, 185).

The great scholar and editor of Vitruvius. Together with his brother Marcantonio, he commissioned the Villa B. Maser (Trevigiano) designed by Palladio *c.* 1555–9, decorated with paintings by P. Veronese and sculptures and stuccoes by A. Vittoria and school. He commissioned a tomb in S. Francesco della Vigna with an altarpiece by Battista Franco. Note that the nearby tomb of the Patriarch Giovanni Grimani, whose coadjutor he was and to whom he appears to have been related, was also decorated by B. Franco.

P. Aretino, *Lettere sull' arte*, ed. F. Pertile and E. Camasasca, II (Milan 1957) *passim*; L. Dolce, *Dialogo della pittura* in P. Barocchi (ed.), *Trattati d'arte del Cinquecento*, I (Bari 1960) at p. 159; Ridolfi, I, pp. 302–3, 322; P. Laven, *Daniele Barbaro Patriarch Elect of Aquilea, with Special Reference to his Circle of Scholars* (University of London Ph.D. Thesis 1957, modern history); P. Paschini, 'Daniele Barbaro letterato e prelato veneziano veneziano del Cinquecento', *Rivista di Storia della Chiesa in Italia*, XVI (1962), pp. 73–107.

Marcantonio Proc. f. Francesco (1518–95), brother of Daniele (see above, pp. 173–4, 187, 191–2).

Aretino in a letter of April 1546 referred to his exercises in painting, engraving and stucco-work. Together with his brother, he commissioned the Villa Maser. In 1555 he was *Provveditore alla fabrica del Palazzo*. In 1577, in the course of the debates on the form of the votive church of the Redentore, he revealed himself as a partisan of the circular temple-type form. He was one of the Procuratori di sopra responsible for the erection of the Procurazie Nuove.

Marcantonio possessed a Paduan doctorate and had an outstanding governmental career, being ambassador in England, France and Constantinople.

A. S. Ven, *Procuratori di Supra*, B. 65 *passim;* Aretino, *Lettere sull' arte* (*ed. cit.*) doc. CCXLI; Lorenzi, p. 599; Ch. Yriarte, *Vie d'un patricien de Venise au XVIe siècle* (Paris 1884); Davide da Portogruaro 'Il Tempio e il Convento del Redentore', *Rivista di Venezia* (April–May 1930), p. 156.

Belli, Valerio, Vicentine engraver of gems.

He possessed a collection of antique and modern works of art.

Morsolin, *Le collezioni*, pp. 7-8.

Bembo, Pietro f. Bernardo (1489–1547), Venetian noble and cleric (see above, p. 51–2, 95–102, 132, 150–1, 156, 227, 229–30).

The great latinist and *volgare* writer, Secretary to Leo x, who became a cardinal in 1539. In 1521 he retired from Rome and settled in his villa in Padua. The collection that he formed there was described by the *Anonimo Morelliano*. It included paintings by Memlinc (two works including a *St John the Baptist*, probably the one in the Pina-kothek Munich), Raphael (a portrait-drawing of Bembo and a double portrait of his friends Navagero and Beazzano, of which the one in the Doria Gallery Rome may be a copy), Jacopo Bellini, Mantegna (a *Circumcision*, now in Querini-Stampaglia Gallery Venice, and a *St Sebastian*, now in Ca d'Oro, Venice) and Domenico Campagnola. There were also numerous antique marbles and bronzes. A great admirer of Raphael, he was a friend of Sanmichele and showed favour to G. M. Falconetto, whom he introduced to Alvise Corner.

Anonimo Morelliano; Vasari, III, pp. 51–2; IV, pp. 203, 210; Temanza, pp. 134, 137, 161.

Bernardo, Francesco f. Marcantonio, Venetian noble (see above. p. 187,) His collection of antique marbles and medals was mentioned in his testament of 1589 as having been commenced over twelve years previously. He was mentioned by Ridolfi as one of the *deputati* appointed in 1577 with responsibility for the decorative schemes in the *Sala del Scrutinio* and the *Sala del Maggior Consiglio* in the Ducal Palace. In his testament, he provided for a tomb in the Frari church with sculptures by A. Vittoria.

He was *Capitaneo* at Verona and Padua and *Savio del Consiglio*.
Testament of 1589 in A. S. Ven, *Notarile. Testamenti*, B. 194 n. 432; Sansovino, I, p. 371; Scamozzi, I, p. 305; Ridolfi, I, p. 326; Capell-ari-Vivaro, I, p. 158.

Capella, Alessandro, of Borgo Zuzzo, Padua.

His collection was described by the *Anonimo Morelliano*. It included antique bronzes and marbles and paintings ascribed to Cimabue and Montagna.

Chierigato, Gerolamo, Vicentine noble.

A friend of Palladio. He was among the first supporters of the Palladian plan for the *logge* of the Basilica in Vicenza and in 1550 was one of the superintendents of the project. Around 1550, he commissioned the Palazzo Chierigati from Palladio. This was decorated with stuccoes by Bartolomeo Ridolfi and with paintings by Domenico Rizzo and Battista Franco.

Palladio, II, p. 4; F. Barbieri, *Il Museo Civico di Vicenza* (Venice 1962), p. 9; Zorzi, 'La problematica palladiana', p. 94.

Contarini, Alessandro, Venetian noble.

A correspondent of Ludovico Dolce, he was mentioned by him in the *Dialogo della pittura* (1557) as a lover of painting. He was probably the same person as the noted numismatist. He was *Capitaneo General del Armar* and Procurator.

L. Dolce, *Dialogo della pittura*, reference in P. Barocchi (ed.), *Trattati d'arte del Cinquecento*, I (Bari 1960), p. 159; see also editor's note in *ibid.* at p. 448; Bardi (1952), p. 37; Foscarini, p. 409; Ravà in *Nuovo Archivio Veneto*, n.s., XXXIX (1920), p. 155.

Contarini, Federigo Proc. f. Francesco (1538–1613), Venetian noble (see above, pp. 161, 186, 192, 264–6).

He possessed an important collection of antiques and paintings. An inventory was made in 1613. He probably possessed works by Titian, Tintoretto and Veronese. Flemish works are mentioned in the inventory. See above.

Testament 1601 in A. S. Ven, *Notarile. Testamenti*, B. 1252 f. 51 and seq.; Stringa (1604) ff. 258r–259v; Capellari-Vivaro, I, p. 291; G. Cozzi, 'Federico Contarini: un antiquario veneziano tra Rinascimento e Controriforma', *Bollettino dell' Istituto di Storia della Società e dello Stato Veneziano*, III (1961), pp. 190–220; M. T. Cipollato, 'L' eredità di Federico Contarini: gli inventari della collezione e degli oggetti domestici' in *ibid.*, pp. 221–53; *c.f.* Savini-Branca, pp. 200–1.

Contarini, Giacomo f. Pietro f. Giacomo of S. Samuele (1536–95), Venetian noble (see above, pp. 154, 159–60, 179–80, 186, 187–9).

He possessed an important collection of paintings, antique marbles and vases, together with mathematical and cosmographical instruments and a major library. According to Ridolfi, he commissioned Veronese's *Rape of Europa* (now in the Ducal Palace) and Francesco

Bassano's *SS. Anthony and Sebastian*. Jacopo Bassano's *Return of Jacob from Canaan* (Ducal Palace) may have also been in the collection, together with work by Tintoretto and works of the schools of Giorgione, Titian, Tintoretto and Palma Giovane. These suggestions are made on the basis of the 1714 inventory (see above, p. 160). Contarini mentioned the collection in his testament of 1595 and subjected it to *fidecommesso*, specifying that it was to go to the state if the family line died out. It passed into the hands of the state in 1713. Contarini was the legatee of Palladio's drawings and was the special protector of Francesco Bassano.

In 1572 he was *Provveditore alle fortezze* and Senator in 1574, being in that year one of the three nobles responsible for the festivities on the occasion of Henry III's visit. Following the fire in the Ducal Palace of 1577, Contarini, together with Giacomo Marcello presented a memorandum on the decorative scheme for the *Maggior Consiglio*, *Sala del Scrutinio* and *Antepregadi*.

Testament 1595 in A. S. Ven, *Notarile. Testamenti*, B. 1194 prot v f. 2r and seq.; *Barbaro Albori*, II, f. 462; Capellari-Vivaro, I, f. 292; Sansovino, p. 138; Ridolfi, I, pp. 326, 337, 392, 395, 404, 408, II, pp. 66, 189, 225; Bibl. Marciana, *Cod. Lat.*, Cl xiv n. 21 (4553) *Catastico della Biblioteca Contarini 1714*, inventory of paintings and statues at ff. 62r–64v; A. S. Ven., *Index Secreta. Archivio proprio Giacomo Contarini*, introduction by M. F. Tiepolo; Temanza, pp. 356–7; Savini-Branca, pp. 31–2, 201–2; P. L. Rose, 'Two Venetian patrons of the Renaissance of Mathematics—Francesco Barozzi and Giacomo Contarini', *Studi Veneziani*, XIII (1971).

Contarini, Michele della Misericordia, Venetian noble.

His collection was mentioned in the *Anonimo Morelliano* in 1543. It contained antique marbles and recent paintings, including a *Madonna and Child* ascribed to Leonardo and a copy from Raphael. He is possibly identifiable with Michele f. Marcantonio f. Michele (1507–49) (*Barbaro Albori*, II, p. 464).

Contarini, Taddeo f. Sigismondo f. Domenico da SS. Apostoli (1478–1537) Venetian noble.

His collection of paintings was described by the *Anonimo Morelliano* in 1525. It included works ascribed to Giorgione (three pictures, including the Vienna *Three Philosophers*), Giovanni Bellini (three) and Jacopo Palma.

Anon. Morelliano 1525; *Barbaro Albori*, II, p. 498; Ferriguto, *Attraverso i 'misteri' di Giorgione*, pp. 185–6, 191.

Corner, Alvise (1475–1566). Of a Venetian noble family, he lost his noble status and settled in Padua (see above, pp. 23–4, 150–1, 167–70). The author of the *Della vita sobria* (1558), agricultural theorist and writer on architecture. He was the friend and patron of Angelo Beolco (Ruzzante) and G. M. Falconetto. Together with Ruzzante's theatrical company, he housed an atelier of artists including Falconetto's son-in-law Ottaviano Ridolfi and his pupils A. della Valle and Tizian Minio. Corner possessed villas at Campagna and Codevigo and a town house in Via del Santo Padua (no. 21 Via Melchiore Cesarotti). Falconetto did work on the Codevigo villa and built an arcade at Campagna (now both lost). In the town house he produced the loggia and odeon, still in existence, and the sides to the courtyard (now destroyed). The sculptures on the loggia were by Giovanni Mocca *et al.* and the stuccoes and fresco decorations in the odeon by Bartolomeo Ridolfi, Giovanni da Udine and probably also Domenico Campagnola. Temanza (1778) indicated that Corner commissioned Falconetto to design a great palace at Luvigliano (given as Luvigano), but causes confusion by saying that it no longer existed. The magnificent Villa dei Vescovi, Luvigliano, planned by Falconetto *c.* 1534 but probably executed in large part by A. della Valle, is still extant. Temanza appears to indicate that it passed to the Corner Piscopia (Alvise's only child Chiara married Giovanni Corner della Piscopia) but *c.f.* Mazzotti, p. 9. A portrait of Corner in advanced age, usually ascribed to Tintoretto, is in the National Gallery, London.

Anon. Morelliano; Temanza, pp. 137–44; G. Fiocco, 'La casa di Alvise Cornaro', *Miscellanea in onore di R. Cessi*, II (Rome 1958), pp. 69–78; G. Fiocco, *Alvise Cornaro, il suo tempo e le sue opere* (Venice 1965). The latter reproduces his treatises on architecture.

Corner Di Ca Grande and di S. Maurizio. Venetian noble family. *Barbaro Albori*, II, pp. 34, 47, 61.

The Corner and their palaces of S. Cassian, S. Maurizio, S. Polo and S. Angelo

A palace at S. Polo was acquired in 1453, and one at S. Cassian in 1458. The latter became the *Ca Grande di statio*, i.e. the principal family palace. Giorgio (b) (*d.* 1527) acquired a palace at S. Maurizio.

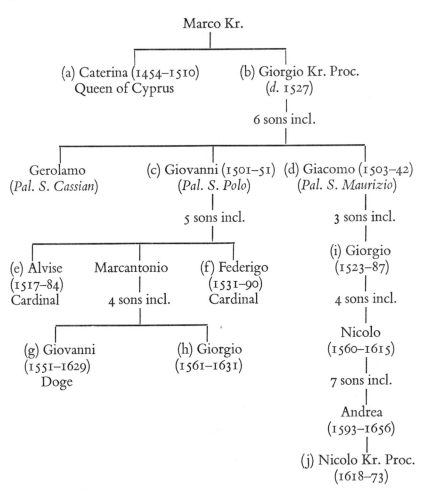

The first palace at S. Maurizio was burnt in 1532 and rebuilding on Sansovino's designs began in the same year. The first palace at S. Polo was destroyed by fire in 1535. Between 1540 and 1545 a division of goods was made between the sons of Giorgio. The Palazzo S. Cassian went to Gerolamo, the site at S. Polo to Giovanni and the Palazzo S. Maurizio to Giacomo. The new Palazzo S. Polo is believed to have been the work of Sanmicheli. Meanwhile, following the burning of the S. Polo home, Giovanni had been forced to seek a new abode and in 1542 he acquired a palace at S. Angelo (Palazzo Corner

Spinelli). This fine late fifteenth-century building is normally ascribed to Coducci.

R. Gallo, 'Michele Sanmicheli a Venezia', pp. 113–18.

(a) Caterina, f. Marco (1454–1510), wife of Jacques de Lusignan last
king of Cyprus.

> In 1488, she retired to Altivole near Asolo, where she kept her
> 'court'. She gave hospitality to artists and was allegedly painted by
> Giovanni Bellini and Giorgione.

> Ridolfi, I, pp. 65, 72; A. Centelli, *Caterina Corner e il suo regno*
> (Venice 1892); Mazzotti, *Palladian and other Venetian Villas*, p. 8.

(b) Giorgio, Kr. Proc. f. Marco (*d.* 1527).

> He commissioned a *Christ at Table* from Giovanni Bellini and was
> allegedly painted by Giorgione. He was *Podestà* at Padua and
> Verona and was Ambassador to France and to the Emperor. His
> wealth was stupendous.

> *Barbaro Albori*, II, p. 34; Vasari, II, pp. 45, 50; Ridolfi, I, p. 72.

(c) Giovanni, f. Giorgio (1501–51).

> He built the palace at S. Polo, normally attributed to Sanmicheli,
> of uncertain dating but finished in 1564. He purchased the palace
> at S. Angelo and commissioned Vasari to execute murals there.
> There were also certain re-modellings by Sanmicheli. Giovanni
> was a Senator.

> *Barbaro Albori*, II, p. 47; testament of 1557 in A. S. Ven, *Notarile*.
> *Testamenti*, B. 1217, prot. VII f. 88v.; Gallo, 'Michele Sanmicheli a
> Venezia', pp. 116–18; *Michele Sanmicheli. Catalogo Mostra d'arte
> della città di Verona*, ed. P. Gazzoli (Venice 1960), pp. 135–9, 148–
> 50, 169–70.

(d) Giacomo, Proc. f. Giorgio (1503–42).

> He commissioned the Palazzo Corner di S. Maurizio from designs
> of Jacopo Sansovino. He was Luogotenente Udine, Capitaneo
> Padua, Capo del Consiglio dei Dieci. In 1537, he bought the Pro-
> curacy for something between 12,000 and 16,000 ducats.

> *Barbaro Albori*, II, p. 61.

(e) Alvise, f. Giovanni (1517–84), Cardinal (1550), Archbishop of
Zara and Bishop of Bergamo.

> Presumably the Cardinal Cornaro who was protector to G. B.
> Ponchino on his return to Venice in 1558.

> Pertile-Camasasca, III (2), p. 416.

(f) Federigo, f. Giovanni (1531–90), Bishop of Trau, Bergamo and Padua, Cardinal 1585.

> According to Scamozzi, he was commissioned by Cardinal Federigo Corner to make designs for a palace at S. Maurizio.
> Scamozzi, pp. 244, 246.

(g) Giovanni, f. Marcantonio (1551–1629), Doge.

> With his brother Giorgio (h), he commissioned designs for a villa at Poisulo near Castelfranco from V. Scamozzi.
> Scamozzi, pp. 494–7.

(i) Giorgio, f. Giacomo (1523–87).

> Presumably he was responsible for commissioning the Villa Cornaro, Dese, from Palladio. Giorgio was a member of the Consiglio and the Council of Ten.
> *Barbaro Albori*, II, p. 61; Palladio, II, p. 51.

(j) Nicolò, Proc. f. Andrea (1618–73).

> His collection included works by Titian, Palma and Tintoretto. He bought the Procuracy in 1645 for 24,000 ducats.
> *Barbaro Albori*, II, p. 61.

> For the picture-gallery of the Corner di S. Maurizio in the seventeenth century, see Savini-Branca, pp. 26–7.

Crasso, Venetian citizen family.

(A. S. Ven, ms. G. Tassini, *Cittadinaza veneta*, II, f. 127).

Nicolò the Elder (*d.* 1595), 'il filosofo', celebrated jurist.

> A portrait of him, now lost, was painted by Titian. Titian also painted for him a *St Nicholas* for the Church of S. Sebastian, and a *Venus at the Mirror with Cupids* (? Budapest) and a *Girl with a Basket of Fruit*; the latter two works were mentioned by Ridolfi as being in the hands of his grandson Nicolò. He wrote a poem on Veronese.
> Vasari, IV, p. 209; Ridolfi, I, pp. 193–4 and notes by Hadeln; *ibid.*, p. 351; Cicogna, IV, p. 159.

Marco, f. Nicolo (*d.* 1626).

> A substantial number of pictures were mentioned in the inventories of his Venetian town house and his villa at Riese made in 1626. Indications of subject matter were given but not of authorship. Certain attributions are however possible on the basis of Ridolfi's descriptions of pictures possessed by his son. Marco became Grand Chancellor of Candia in 1612 and was painted as such by Domenico Tintoretto.

Ridolfi, II, p. 260; Levi, p. lxix (for inventories); Savini-Branca, pp. 116–17 (for inventories).

Nicolò, f. Marco f. Nicolò (1586–1655).

An orator poet and *erudito* with historical interests, he possessed an important collection of pictures, in part inherited. The pictures were mentioned in the inventories made of the contents of his Venetian house and villa at Riese in 1656–7. Details of authorship were not given. Ridolfi indicates that he possessed paintings by Giorgione, Palma Giovane (two), Titian, Peranda, Jacopo Tintoretto (four), Dom, Tintoretto (see under Marco I) and Veronese. He was *avvocato fiscale* in Candia.

Ridolfi, I, pp. 102, 194, 339; *ibid.*, II, pp. 55, 199, 260, 272; Foscarini, pp. 65n., 2, 151, 332, 350; Savini-Branca, pp. 130–4, 147 (for inventories) and p. 209.

Delfin, Giovanni, Venetian noble.

He commissioned a palace from Jacopo Sansovino (Pal. Delfin-Manin). According to Vasari, it cost 30,000 ducats.

Vasari, IV, p. 222.

Emo, Leonardo f. Alvise, Venetian noble.

He commissioned the Villa Emo at Fanzolo (Trevigiano) designed by Palladio and decorated by Veronese and Zelotti. He was a senator and one of those responsible for organising the festivities on the occasion of Henri III's visit in 1574.

S. Rumor, *Storia breve degli Emo* (Vicenza 1910), pp. 39–40.

Erizzo, Francesco, Venetian noble.

He commissioned a Venetian palace at S. Cancian, according to Ridolfi on the designs of Palladio. The portico was painted by Veronese with paintings of antique buildings and landscapes. Stucco statues were executed by Veronese and A. Vittoria.

Ridolfi, I, p. 324.

Fabri, Ottaviano, merchant, living in Venice early seventeenth century.

He possessed an important collection including paintings by Giovanni Bellini, Raphael, Giorgione, Titian, Dossi, Tintoretto and Palma Giovane; sculptures by Sansovino and Giambologna *et al.*; plaster copies from Michelangelo, together with antique vases, mathematical and cosmographical instruments and globes. The instruments were referred to by Stringa as 'all pertaining to his special profession in this honoured art'.

Stringa (1604), pp. 259–60; an inventory of 1606 which is not very informative on works of art is in Levi, pp. lxvi–lxvii; U. Tucci, 'The psychology of the Venetian merchant' etc. in *Venetian Studies*, ed. J. R. Hale (London 1972).

Godi, Gerolamo, Vicentine.

He commissioned the Villa Godi (later Valmarana), Lonedo (Vicentino) from Palladio. It was decorated by Gualterio Padovano, Battista del Moro and Battista Franco. This was Palladio's first domestic commission. In Vicenza, Godi lived in the same parish of S. Luca as Palladio.

Palladio, p. 63; G. G. Zorzi, 'La problematica palladiana', p. 94.

Grimani, di S. Maria Formosa, Venetian noble family (see above, pp. 31–2, 150–1, 155–6, 158, 160–1, 177–9, 183–5). *Barbaro Albori*, IV, pp. 145–6.

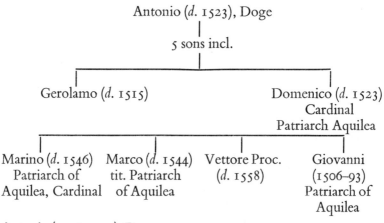

Antonio (1436–1523), Doge 1521.

He was painted by Titian.

Domenico, f. Antonio (*c.* 1461–1523), Cardinal 1493, Bishop of Paphos, Archbishop of Nicosia, Patriarch of Aquilea, Bishop of Urbino and Ceneda.

His collection was described by the *Anonimo Morelliano* in 1521. It comprised valuable antique marbles and bronzes and paintings. The antiques which passed to the state included some exceptionally fine Pergamene works or Roman copies thereof (note especially nos. 55, 57, 98 in Mus. Archaeol. Venice). The paintings included ones by Memlinc (several panels), Joachim Patenir (three), Hieronymus Bosch (two works only listed in the *Anonimo Morelliano*), Dürer, Gerard of Harlem, Raphael (an unknown cartoon) and the famous Grimani Breviary containing illuminations ascribed to Memlinc and Gerard of Ghent *et al.* Of Domenico's Boschs, some are still on display in the Palazzo Ducale (*Fall of the Damned, Inferno, Paradise, Ascent to the Empyrean, S. Giuliana, Hermits*). A portion of the antique collection passed to his nephew Marino.

Anonimo Morelliano 1521; details of pictures and antiques left to the Republic in inventory of 22 December 1523, reproduced in Levi, pp. 3–4; P. Paschini, 'Le collezioni archaeologiche dei prelati Grimani', *Rendiconti della Pontificia Accademia di Archaeologia*, v (1927), pp. 149–90; P. Paschini, *Domenico Grimani Cardinale di S. Marco* (+1523) (Rome 1943); R. Gallo, 'Le donazioni alla Serenissima di Domenico e Giovanni Grimani', *Archivio Veneto*, L–LI (1952), pp. 34–77.

Marino, f. Gerolamo (*d.* 1546), Bishop of Ceneda, Patriarch of Aquilea, Bishop of Concordia and Città di Castello, Patriarch of Constantinople.

He possessed an antique collection, mostly of medals, the marble pieces apparently being small. He was also interested in illuminated codices. According to Ridolfi, he called Pordenone to Ceneda to paint the Loggia della Giustizia there, although the paintings are usually ascribed to Pordenone's son-in-law, Pompeo Amalteo. He had connections with Sebastiano del Piombo and greatly appreciated Giovanni da Udine, whom he employed to make designs for certain projects which were not in fact executed. He appears to have been responsible for obtaining employment for Sansovino on the repair of the cupola of St Mark's. In 1539, he appears to have brought Giovanni da Udine and Cechin Salviati to Venice to decorate the *salotti* of the palace at S. Maria Formosa.

Vasari, IV, p. 221 (given erroneously as Domenico Grimani); Ridolfi, I, pp. 98–9 and notes by Hadeln; Paschini, 'Le collezioni archaeologiche', *cit.*; P. Paschini, 'Il mecenatismo del Cardinale Marino Grimani' in *Miscellanea in onore di R. Cessi*, II (Rome 1958), pp. 79–88; Pertile-Camasasca, III (2), pp. 321–2.

Grimani patronage in the mid-sixteenth century

The palace of S. Maria Formosa was substantially completed by 1539. Its authorship is uncertain. Temanza (1778) attributed it partly to Sanmicheli, but neither Vasari nor F. Sansovino did so. A contemporary reference appears to indicate the Patriarch Giovanni as its author. The palace was decorated with an ambitious series of mural cycles. The Cardinals Domenico and Marino had relatively little to do with the new palace and the brothers Vettore and Giovanni had a fairly free hand. In 1532, the house had been divided between the two brothers, each taking separate floors.

The role of the Grimani in the promotion of central Italian artistic currents has been discussed above. The artists with a central Italian training whom they employed in the family palace and in their chapel at S. Francesco della Vigna included Danese Cattaneo, Bartolomeo Ammanati, Giuseppe Salviati (della Porta), Battista Franco and Federico Zuccari.

Temanza, pp. 177–8; L. Coletti, 'La crisi manieristica nella pittura veneziana', *Convivium*, II (1941), p. 118; W. R. Rearick, 'Battista Franco and the Grimani Chapel', *Saggi e Memorie della Storia dell'Arte* (1960), p. 199 *et seq.*; R. Gallo, 'Michele Sanmicheli', pp. 125–9; Schulz, p. 142.

Vettore, f. Gerolamo, Proc. (*d.* 1558).

A great admirer of Sansovino, he was responsible for the building of the loggia on the Piazza S. Marco.

Vasari, IV, p. 225; Bardi (1592), p. 40; testament 1551, A. S. Ven, *Notarile. Testamenti*, B. 1218 prot. x, f. 71r *et seq.* (not of particular interest).

Giovanni, f. Gerolamo (1506–93), Bishop of Ceneda and Patriarch of Aquilea.

Giovanni reacquired part of his brother Marino's collection of antiques. Much of what Marino left at his death had to be alienated to pay his debts and also many of his works passed into the hands of the Papacy through *ius spolii* until Giovanni was able to redeem them for 3,000 gold ducats in 1557. Giovanni built up his antique collection further on his own account and imported statues into Venice from Rome. Vasari in 1563 recorded three paintings by Giorgione in his collection. In addition to work on the S. Maria Formosa Palace, Giovanni was substantially responsible for the embellishment of the

family chapel at S. Francesco della Vigna which had paintings by
Battista Franco and Federico Zuccari and sculptures by Tiziano
Aspetti. According to Temanza (1778), he commissioned Palladio's
façade of S. Francesco della Vigna.

In his testament of 29 August 1592, he referred to 'Titian pittore e
sculptore (i.e. Tiziano Aspetti) e Uberto Fiandrese mei domestici,
amici e servitori'. In this testament, he expressed the fear that he
might have offended God by his expenditure on cameos, medals, etc.
He ordered that they were to be sold and the proceeds given to the
poor, exception being made for the contents of an ebony cabinet.
This cabinet, containing cameos and antique bronzes, was bequeathed
to the Republic. In his testamentary codicil, Grimani revoked the
order regarding sale of cameos and medals and directed that they
should go to his nephew Antonio. The antique marble pieces were
given to the state, note of intention to this effect having been given
in 1587. They constitute the larger part of the contents of the present
Museo Antichita, Venice.

Testament of 1592 and codicils, A. S. Ven, *Notarile. Testamenti*, B.
658 no. 396; A. S. Ven, *Procuratori di Supra*, B. 68 *registro* 4. *Vestibilo
appresso la pubblica libreria*, f. 15r. *et seq.*, *Aventario fatto per il Mco
Massa Sectr. delli marmi ritrovati nel Palazzo della fe. me. di Mons.
Patriarca di Aquilegia Grimani oct. MCXCIII*; Vasari, IV, pp. 22–3, 90;
Temanza, p. 355; P. Paschini, 'Il mecenatismo artistico del Patriarca
G. Grimani', in *Studi in onore di A. Calde ini e R. Paribeni* (Milan
1956), pp. 851–62; Rearick, *loc. cit.*; Savini-Branca, p. 29.

Grimani, Gerolamo Kr. Proc. (*d.* 1570), of S. Luca, Venetian noble.
He commissioned the palace at S. Luca probably designed by Sanmicheli shortly before his death in 1559 and continued by Giacomo
de Grigis. A contract for its completion was made in 1561. The total
cost must have been between 40,000 and 50,000 ducats.

Gallo, 'Michele Sanmicheli a Venezia', pp. 120–5.

Gritti, Andrea (1455–1538), Doge 1523 (see above, pp. 182, 196, 263).
Described by Vasari as 'a great patron of genius', he was allegedly a
friend of Titian and a patron of Sansovino. He was supposed to have
given Titian the commission for the great battle-piece in the Maggior
Consiglio usually known as the *Battle of Cadore* (burnt in 1577) and it
was probably at his behest that Titian painted a fresco of *St Christopher*
in the *chiesetta* of the Ducal Palace. Titian painted a portrait of him

(Czernin Gal) and a votive portrait (later burnt). According to Vasari, he was responsible, on the advice of Cardinal Grimani, for appointing Sansovino to repair the cupola of St Mark's. He certainly intervened to ensure the appointment of Adriaan Willaert as Maestro di Capella of St Mark's in 1527. Gritti's career was mainly military and diplomatic.

Vasari, IV, pp. 203, 204, 221, 225; Ridolfi, I, p. 200; Cheyney, pp. 53–4, 65.

Gualdo, noble family of Vicenza (see above, p. 162).

The family collection of paintings and sculptures was probably the most important in Vicenza and perhaps even in the Terraferma as a whole. Its origins were in the late fifteenth century. A major role in its development was played by the Canon Gerolamo Gualdo (1492–1566). A description of the collection was drawn up by another Gerolamo in 1650. At that time it contained paintings dating from periods between the late thirteenth and the mid-seventeenth centuries and large numbers of modern sculptures.

Morsolin, *Le collezioni*, pp. 11–15; B. Morsolin, 'Il Museo Gualdo in Vicenza', *Nuovo Archivio Veneto*, VIII, pp. 173–220, 373–440. The latter reproduces the 1650 catalogue.

Da Hana, Flemish family with Venetian citizenship. Giovanni, Paolo and Martin.

Giovanni

He was, according to Vasari, a close friend of Titian. The latter painted for him a group portrait of the family in adoration of the Virgin, a *Crucifixion* and an *Ecce Homo* (the latter is normally identified with the one in the Kunsthistorishes Museum Vienna, dated 1543). This is thought to have been the same as the 'picture by Titian for which Henry III offered 800 ducats', (?c. 1575) mentioned in what is apparently an appendage of the *Anonimo Morelliano* as being in the possession of Paolo da Hana.

Anon. Morelliano (final entry); Vasari, IV, pp. 200, 210; Ridolfi, I, p. 102.

Martin

He brought Pordenone from Friuli to Venice to paint the façade of the Palazzo d'Anna.

Ridolfi, I, p. 102.

Lando, Simone, Venetian noble.

He bequeathed pictures by various painters to the church of S. Maria Maggiore. Cicogna lists the subjects of these but not the authors. From Ridolfi it emerges that four of them were by Veronese and that they included the *Entry of the Animals into the Ark* by Jacopo Bassano. Ridolfi, I, pp. 330, 391, 391 n.; Cicogna, III, p. 419.

Da Legge, Giovanni, Proc. (1575), Venetian noble (see above, pp. 184–5).

He is mentioned by Vasari as having been one of the special admirers of Sansovino and he was one of the Procurators chiefly responsible for the Sansovino buildings on the Piazza. Sansovino erected a Mausoleum for his family in the Crociferi Church (now Gesuiti), the bust of the Procurator Priamo da Legge being by Sansovino, although that of Giovanni is attributed to Giovanni de Moro.

Testament of 1575, A. S. Ven, *Notarile. Testamenti,* B. 1263 prot. VI, ff. 17r–19v, *Barbaro Albori,* IV, f. 236; Vasari, IV, p. 225; Mariacher, *Il Sansovino,* pp. 150–1.

Loredan of the Palazzo Non Nobis Domine (Pal. Vendramin-Calergi) S. Marcuola, later of S. Pantalon, Venetian noble family.

Andrea, f. Nicolo (*d.* 1513).

He ordered the construction of the palazzo in 1481, the architect being, it is generally believed, Mauro Coducci. Andrea was the protector of the monastery of S. Michele Murano and doubtless encountered Coducci there.

P. Paoletti, *L'architettura e scultura del Rinascimento in Venezia* (Venice 1893), pp. 187–8; M. Luxoro, *Il Palazzo Vendramin-Calergi* (Florence 1957), pp. 5–17.

Giovanni Bellini painted in the house two great pictures of cosmography, with the figures of Ptolemy, Strabo, Pliny and Pomponius Mela. In the portico, Titian painted arms and two figures of virtues. He also painted a *Flight into Egypt* for the house.

Vasari, IV, p. 200; Ridolfi, I, pp. 72, 155.

Andrea II.

A great lover and collector of antiques and a noted numismatist. He bought some of Gabriele Vendramin's medals in 1565 and tried to acquire his collection of antiques. Andreas *studio* was mentioned by

L

Scamozzi as one of the finest seen by him in his youth. A bust was made of him by Alessandro Vittoria.

The *Palazzo Non Nobis Domine* was sold by the Loredan in 1581 to the Dukes of Brunswick (subsequently passing to the Calergi and then to the Grimani) and the Loredan moved to S. Pantalon.

Vasari, IV, p. 230; Scamozzi, p. 305; Foscarini, pp. 409–10; Ravà in *Nuovo Archivio Veneto*, N.S., XXXIX (1920), p. 155; Fapanni, *Elenco dei musei*, etc., p. 76.

Bernadino, f. Andrea.

In his testament of 1608, he referred to acquisitions by himself and his father of 'antiques, bronze medals, fossils and pictures'.

A. S. Ven, *Notarile. Testamenti*, B. 840, referred to in Levi, lxvi; *c.f.* Foscarini, p. 409.

Marcello, Geronimo f. Antonio f. Giacomo (*b.* 1476) of S. Tomà, Venetian noble.

His collection in 1525 was described in the *Anonimo Morelliano*. It included works ascribed to Giorgione (two pictures including the Dresden *Venus*), Titian, Giovanni Bellini (two pictures) and Lorenzo Costa. He had almost certainly commissioned the *Venus* himself.

Anonimo Morelliano, 1525; *Barbaro Albori*, IV, p. 475; Ferriguto, *Attras verso i 'misteri' di Giorgione*, pp. 185–6, 193.

Mocenigo, Giovanni, alla Carità, Venetian noble.

According to Scamozzi (1615), he had 'a good quantity of statue- and busts of various sorts, medals and paintings'. A Giovanni Mocenigo was *Provveditare alla Fabbrica del Palazzo Ducale* in 1560, 1579 and 1580.

Scamozzi, p. 306; Foscarini, p. 411 Lorenzi, p. 594.

Mocenigo, Leonardo (identity unclear), Venetian noble.

Palladio (*iv libri*, II, p. 52) states that he designed the Villa Marocco between Venice and Treviso for the Cavalier Leonardo Mocenigo. He also refers (*ibid.*, p. 76) to a design for a site on the Brenta for one Leonardo Mocenigo, but does not refer to him as Cavalier. A large number of Leonardo Mocenigos are listed in *Barbaro Albori*, but the designation 'cavaliere' suggests Leonardo, Kr. f. Antonio Proc. f. Alvise Kr. (*Barbaro Albori V*, p. 20) as the commissioner of the Villa Marocco.

Capellari-Vivaro (III, f. 95v, referring to tree at f. 100r) mentions this Leonardo Mocenigo as having begun construction of a chapel in S. Luca which was unfinished and as the possessor of a fine collection of antiques. The latter was mentioned by Sansovino, *Venezia città* (1581), p. 139, and Scamozzi (p. 305). Leonardo f. Antonio f. Alvise (*b.* 1522) was Senator, *Consigliere* and *Savio Grande*.

Della Nave, Bartolomeo, resident in Venice, of Bergamese family which subsequently acquired Venetian nobility in 1653.

According to Scamozzi, 'Signor Bortolomeo della Nave, an honoured merchant in this city, has gathered together nearly thirty statues and busts, part of which belonged to the Rev. Cardinal Bembo, and also a hundred pictures of various sizes, of which there are twenty rare ones of Titian, besides many drawings. There are also clay models and a rare S. Sebastian by Vittoria.' Bartolomeo was a protector of Palma Giovane.

Capellari-Vivaro, p. 161; Scamozzi, p. 306; Ridolfi, 1, p. 201; II, p. 203; Savini-Branca, pp. 251–4.

Nis, Daniele. Flemish merchant resident in Venice.

Scamozzi referred to his collection as containing some 40 statues and nearly 80 heads, together with busts and bas-reliefs, and 60 paintings plus twenty portraits by celebrated painters, as well as a cabinet of small pieces, miniatures and enamels and 'all the drawings (presumably engravings) of Albert Dürer and Luke of Holland and a great number by the hands of the most excellent painters'. He estimated the value of the collection at 10,000 scudi.

Nis attempted to purchase Titian's *St Peter Martyr* from the Dominicans of SS. Giovanni e Paolo. A friend of Paolo Sarpi, he helped to transmit the mss. of the *History of the Council of Trent* to England and he was Charles I of England's agent in the purchase of the collection of the Duke of Mantua in 1627.

Scamozzi, p. 306; Cheyney, *Original Documents*, p. 45; G. Cozzi, 'Paolo Sarpi' in *Storia della Letteratura Italiana*, v, *Il Seicento* (Milan, 1967), p. 451; H. Trevor-Roper, *Plunder of the Arts in the Seventeenth Century* (London 1971), pp. 29–35.

Odoni, Andrea f. Rinaldo and son Alvise, Venetian.

Andrea

His collection, described by the *Anonimo Morelliano* in 1532, comprised various antique statues and fragments, antique vases, modern vases of precious stones, gold and porcelain, medals, many of the latter from the Zio collection, and paintings, including works ascribed to Giorgione, Vincenzo Catena (two portraits), Savoldo, Jacopo Palma (two), Lorenzo Lotto (Odoni portrait, Windsor) and Titian (*Virgin and Child with St John*, probably identifiable with the work in the National Gallery). The Lotto portrait shows Andrea with his antiques. His testament of 1555 is uninformative.

Alvise, f. Andrea.

An inventory of his collection of 1555 lists marbles, precious effects and pictures but without indications of authorship.

Anon. Morelliano, 1532; *Archivialische Beitrage zur Geschichte der venezianische Kunst*, p. 56 for Andrea's testament, pp. 55–71 for inventory of Alvise's collection. It is not possible to obtain an idea of the development of the Odoni collection between 1532 and 1555.

Pasqualino, Antonio, Venetian.

His collection described by the *Anonimo Morelliano* in 1529 and 1532 contained works ascribed to Gentile da Fabriano (two portraits), Antonello da Messina (the *St Jerome* now in the National Gallery and two portraits), Giovanni Bellini and Giorgione.

Pellegrini, Pietro, Venetian citizen, Secretary of the Council of Ten.

Scamozzi described his collection as containing 30 statues and busts and perhaps the same number of paintings by 'good masters', Scamozzi, p. 306.

Pisani, Francesco, Venetian noble.

He commissioned the Villa Pisani Montagnana from Palladio. Palladio, p. 50.

Pisani dal Banco, Venetian noble family.

Brothers Daniele (1525–84), Vettore (1525–(?)76) and Marco (1545–1602) sons of Giovanni f. Vettore.

They commissioned the Villa Pisani, Bagnolo, from Palladio. Daniele was a Senator, Marco a member of the *Zonta*. Palladio, II, p. 45; *Barbaro Albori*, VIII, p. 129.

Plovenio (Piovene), Guido, Cavalier, and Giuliano, brothers, Vicentine nobles.

They built a palace in Vicenza, designed by Palladio. At the time of its construction, one of them was *Provveditore* responsible for the loggia of the Basilica. Guido was a jurist and noted orator. Giuliano is described as 'letteratissimo' by Marzari.

Marzari, pp. 205–6; Zorzi, 'La problematica palladiana', p. 141.

Da Porto, Francesco 'Il Collaterale' (? f. Giovanni) and son Giambattista, Vicentine nobles.

Francesco is described by Marzari as *letteratissimo* with interests in antique statues and in buildings and gardens. He commissioned the Villa da Porto, Thiene. He and Giambattista developed the fine gardens begun by Giovanni and collected antique statues and objets d'art.

Marzari, p. 168; Morsolin, *Le collezioni*, p. 7.

Da Porto, Giuseppe (Iseppo), Vicentine noble.

He commissioned the Palazzo Porto (later Biego) Vicenza from Palladio. Here he was evidently inspired by the success of the Basilica project. He was the brother-in-law of Gerolamo Chierigato.

Palladio, II, pp. 6–7; Zorzi, 'La problematica palladiana', p. 94.

Ram, Giovanni, Catalan resident in Venice and son Alessandro.

Giovanni's collection, as described by the *Anonimo Morelliano* in 1531, included works ascribed to Rogier van der Weyden, Jan Scorel, Vincenzo Catena (two works and a portrait of Ram), Giorgione (two) and a St John Baptising ascribed by the *Anonimo* to Titian but usually attributed to Paris Bordone (Capitoline Gal.), together with numerous antique marble heads and busts, earthen and porcelain vases and modern bronzes. There is an inventory of Alessandro's collection dated 10 November 1592. Although authorship of paintings is not given, a number of the works in Giovanni's collection are clearly identifiable.

Anon. Morelliano, 1531; *Archivialische Beitrage zur Geschichte der venezianischen Kunst*, pp. 74–82 for the 1592 inventory. There is an almost illegible testament of a Catalan Giovanni Ram in A. S. Ven, *Notarile. Testamenti*, B. 22 no. 255. It does not appear to contain a reference to the collection.

Rangone, Tomaso di Ravenna called 'il Rangone', resident in Venice.

Medical scholar and practitioner and philologist. See above pp. 198, 205–7.

In 1552, Tomaso asked Sansovino to work on a project for the façade of S. Geminian on the Piazza S. Marco. The façade was to contain a monument with his statue. The project was, however, forbidden by the Senate.

In 1553, he obliged himself to provide 1,000 ducats for the façade of S. Giulian and for the general improvement of the church on condition that he could place a bronze statue of himself over the door at his own expense. The project was entrusted to Sansovino in the first instance. Alessandro Vittoria certainly had a hand in the statue and eventually took over the work on the church. Rangone also commissioned Sansovino to construct the door of the nunnery of S. Sepolcro in 1570. Vittoria was a friend of his and in his testament of 1566 left him a statue of St Thomas by his own hand. Tomaso was *Guardian Grande* of the Scuola di S. Marco. It was during his tenure of office, in 1562, that Alessandro Vittoria became a member of the Scuola. Following disagreements in the Scuola about acceptance of Tintoretto's cycle of the *Miracles of St Mark*, Tomaso received permission to have three pictures painted at his own expense.

Ridolfi, II, p. 22 and note by Hadeln; Cheyney, *Original Documents*, pp. 21–3; Gallo, 'Contributi su Jacopo Sansovino', pp. 96–105; F. Cessi, *Alessandro Vittoria, bronzista* (Trent 1961), p. 28; Mariacher, *Il Sansovino*, pp. 115–16, 181.

Ruzzini, Carlo, f. Domenico f. Carlo (1554–1644) and son Domenico (1584–1651), Venetian nobles.

Carlo was the son-in-law of the great antiquarian Federico Contarini (*d.* 1613). According to Martinoni (1663), he inherited the latter's collection, but in fact Contarini had bequeathed it to Domenico (see Cipollato's article). Already in 1604, Stringa had referred to Carlo as possessing a fine picture collection, including works by Giovanni Bellini, Giorgione, A. Schiavone, Titian and Veronese, also mentioning a large collection of antique medals and precious effects. Scamozzi (1615) referred to a large number of antique marble and bronze pieces, nearly 3,600 medals, cameos and engraved jewels and 120 paintings, 18 of them 'by the hands of the most excellent masters'. Domenico was *Luogotenente* Udine, *Podestà* Brescia, *Savio del Consiglio*.

Barbaro Albori, VI, f. 254; Capellari-Vivari, IV, f. 33v.; Stringa (1604), p. 259v.; Scamozzi, p. 305; Martinoni (1663), p. 374; Savini-Branca,

p. 277; Cipollato, *L'eredità di Federico Contarini* (cited under Contarini), pp. 221–4.

Thiene, Francesco and sons Odoardo and Teodoro, Vicentine nobles.
Commissioned Villa Cicogna from Palladio.
Palladio, II, p. 60; Zorzi, p. 93.

Thiene, Marcantonio (*d.* 1574) and son Ottavio, Vicentine nobles.
Marcantonio was one of Palladio's supporters in the Basilica project.
Palladio began the Palazzo Thiene in Via S. Gaetano Thiene for him
and Ottavio had the work completed after his death. The palace is
richly decorated with paintings by Bernardo India and Anselmo
Canera and stuccoes by A. Vittoria and Ottaviano Ridolfi.
Palladio, II pp. 10–13; Barbieri—Cevese—Magagnato, pp. 122–4
Zorzi, p. 94.

Thiene, Orazio, Vicentine noble.
Palladio's Palazzo Orazio Thiene at Castello was erected at the time
that Orazio was *Provveditore* of the loggia of the Basilica.
Zorzi, p. 94.

Tomeo, Leonico of Padua, philosopher.
His collection, described by the *Anonimo Morelliano* included two
paintings by Giovanni Bellini and one Flemish work ('John of
Bruges'), together with various antique sculptures and antique medals,
vases and cameos. Tomeo was first master of Greek at Padua.
Anon. Morelliano (under Padua); Ferriguto, *Ermolao Barbaro*, pp. 211–
16; *id. Attraverso i 'misteri' di Giorgione*, p. 227.

Trevisan, Camillo, Venetian noble.
His palace at Murano was said to be built on a design of Daniele
Barbaro. It had frescoes by Veronese and stuccoes by Alessandro
Vittoria. A bust of Trevisan by Vittoria is in SS. Giovanni e Paolo.
Vasari, IV, p. 230; Ridolfi, I pp. 322–3.

Trissino, Giangiorgio, Vicentine noble.
The distinguished humanist and *volgare* poet. His collection comprised medals, cameos and other unspecified objets d'art. Between
1530 and 1538, he built the villa at Cricoli; Trissino himself and
Palladio have both been suggested as its authors. He was the first
known patron of Palladio (see above, pp. 170–2).

B. Morsolin, *Giangiorgio Trissino* (Vicenza 1878); Morsolin, *Le collezioni*, pp. 5–6; G. Piovene, 'Trissino e Palladio nell'umanesimo vicentino', *Bollettino del Centro Nazionale di Storia dell' Architettura A. Palladio*, v (1963), pp. 13–23.

Trissino, Francesco and Ludovico, Vicentine nobles.

They commissioned the Villa Trissino, Meledo, from Palladio.

Zorzi, p. 94.

Valmarana, Alvise (*d.* 1534) and son Leonardo, Vicentine nobles.

Alvise had been one of Palladio's supporters over the Basilica project. Palladio did not execute a building for him before his death in 1558, although it is possible that a building was projected. In 1565, however, Alvise's widow Isabella took measures for the erection of a building designed by Palladio. The palace, in the present Corso Fogazzaro, was completed by Leonardo. Leonardo was a member of the Vicentine academic circles especially interested in architecture. It was he who commissioned the Loggia Palladiana in his gardens, which he opened to the public in 1572.

Barbieri—Cevese—Maganato, p. 14; Zorzi, p. 94.

Vendramin, Andrea, Venetian noble (see above, pp. 161–2).

He was the possessor of an outstanding collection of paintings of which he made a catalogue around 1627. The paintings were predominantly those of the sixteenth-century Venetian masters. He also had collections of antiques and coins and a natural history museum.

His collection was distinct from that of Gabriele Vendramin (see below), although it is possible that he was a relative. He is possibly identifiable with Andrea (*b.* 1561) f. Federigo f. Andrea f. Leonardo, who was a great nephew of Gabriele f. Leonardo.

Fapanni, II, p. 183; T. Borenius, *The Picture Gallery of Andrea Vendramin* (London 1923) (this reproduces Vendramin's catalogue); Fapanni, 'More about the Vendramin Collection', *The Burlington Magazine*, LX.

Vendramin, Gabriele (*b.* 1484) f. Leonardo f. Luca, of S. Fosca, Venetian noble (See above pp. 156–7).

His collection was described in 1530 by the *Anonimo Morelliano*. He referred to it in his testament of 1547, where he ordered that it should be kept under seal until one of his heirs should reveal himself a lover of antiquities and specified that an inventory should be made. It was finally compiled 1567–9. Scamozzi in 1615 referred to the collection as still being sealed. The pictures in his collection included works by Giovanni Bellini (several), Giorgione (four, including the *Tempestà* and *The Artist's Mother*), Titian (five, including the family picture now in the National Gallery), Palma Vecchio, Dürer (engravings, woodcuts and two portraits), Raphael (an engraving, drawing and a portrait) and the odd Flemish work. He also possessed numerous marbles (mostly fragments), vases and porcelains.

Capellari-Vivaro, IV, p. 158; *Anon. Morelliano*, 1530; Testament of 1547 in A. S. Ven, *Notarile. Testamenti*, B. 1208 n. 403, copy in B. 1217 Prot. VIII ff. 21r–30v, reproduced in *Archivialische Beitrage zur Geschichte der venezianisches Kunst*, pp. 72–4; Bardi (1592), p. 36; Scamozzi, p. 305; Foscarini, pp. 410–11; A. Ravà, 'Il camerino di anticaglie di Gabriele Vendramin', *Nuovo Archivio Veneto*, n.s. XXXIX (1920), pp. 155–81; (this reproduces the 1567–9 inventory); Ferriguto, *Attraverso i 'misteri' di Giorgione*, pp. 185–7, 193.

Venier, Giovanantonio, Venetian noble.

His collection, described by the *Anonimo Morelliano* in 1528 included works ascribed to Giovanni Bellini, Giorgione and Titian.

Verdizotti, Giovan Maria, Venetian.

A lover of painting and a friend of Titian. He possessed an *Apollo and Diana* of Titian. Bardi praised him as a poet.

Vasari, IV, p. 211; Bardi (1592), p. 137; Ridolfi, I, pp. 188–9.

Vittoria, Alessandro (1524–1608), Trentino living in Venice, sculptor.

He possessed a collection of paintings by major Venetian masters. Savini-Branca, pp. 287–8.

Zio, Francesco. His collection of paintings was described by the *Anonimo Morelliano* in 1512. It included works ascribed to (?) Savoldo, Mantegna, Palma Vecchio (three pieces) and a few antique marble pieces and fragments, antique vases and medals.

Bibliography

GENERAL HISTORIES AND SERIES

S. Romanin, *Storia documentata di Venezia*, 10 vols. (1st ed. Venice 1853–61, 2nd ed. Venice 1919–25)

P. Molmenti, *La storia di Venezia nella vita privata dalle origini alla caduta della Repubblica* (1st ed. Turin 1880, 7th ed., 3 vols., Bergamo 1927–9). This is translated by H. F. Brown as *Venice: Its Individual Growth from the Beginnings to the Fall of the Republic* (3 vols., London 1906)

R. Cessi, *Storia della Repubblica di Venezia* (2 vols., Milan 1944–6)

Storia della Civiltà veneziana, series edited by the Centro di Cultura e Civiltà della Fondazione Giorgio Cini, Venice (8 vols., Venice, 1955–62). For the period from the fifteenth to the eighteenth centuries see:

> *La Civiltà veneziana del Quattrocento* (1957)
> *La Civiltà veneziana del Rinascimento* (1958)
> *La Civiltà veneziana nell' età barocca* (1959)
> *La Civiltà veneziana del Settecento* (1960)

Civiltà europea e civiltà veneziana, series edited by the Centro di Cultura e Civiltà della Fondazione Giorgio Cini, Venice (Florence 1963–)

> 1. *Barocco europeo e barocco veneziano*, ed. V. Branca (1963)
> 2. *Umanesimo europeo e umanesimo veneziano*, ed. V. Branca (1963)
> 3. *Rinascimento europeo e rinascimento veneziano*, ed. V. Branca (1967)
> 4. *Venezia e l'Oriente fra tardo Medioevo e Rinascimento*, ed. A. Pertusi (1966)
> 5. *Sensibilità e razionalità nel Settecento*, ed. V. Branca (2 vols., 1967)

There are two main periodicals dealing with the history of Venice: *Archivio Veneto* which is concerned with the Veneto region and *Studi Veneziani*, formerly *Bollettino dell' Istituto di Storia della Società e dello Stato Veneziano* (henceforth referred to as *BISSSV*); this is more concerned with Venice as seen within a general European and Mediterranean framework.

LATE FIFTEENTH TO EARLY SEVENTEENTH CENTURIES

(a) General

English readers will perhaps find the following most useful: D. S. Chambers, *The Imperial Age of Venice 1380–1580* (London 1970) and J. R. Hale (ed.), *Venetian Studies* (London 1972)

(b) Political History

For general surveys see the works of Romanin and Cessi cited above. G. Cozzi, *Il Doge Nicolò Contarini. Ricerche sul patriziato veneziano agli inizi del Seicento* (Venice–Rome 1959) is a crucial work which examines political divisions within the ruling class from the 1580s to the 1620s. See also W. J. Bouwsma, *Venice and the Defence of Republican Liberty* (California 1968). For studies on the 'Venetian myth', see above Ch. I n. 10

(c) Religious History

While there is a large body of published work on detailed aspects of this, there is a lack of general studies.

For a discussion of major problems and of the learned contributions made to date, see P. Prodi, 'The Structure and Organisation of the Church in Venice: Suggestions for Research', in *Venetian Studies, cit.* For a discussion of the published material on piety and religious sentiment see I. Cervelli, 'Storiografia e problemi intorno alla vita religiosa e spirituale a Venezia nella prima metà del '500', *Studi Veneziani*, VIII (1966).

The juridical relationships between Church and State were dealt with in B. Cecchetti, *La Repubblica di Venezia e la Corte di Roma nei rapporti della religione* (2 vols., Venice 1874); this is now somewhat out of date. On Veneto-Papal relations, see A. Stella, *Chiesa e Stato nelle relazioni dei nunzi pontifici a Venezia: ricerche sul giurisdizionalismo veneziano dal XVI al XVIII secolo*, (Vatican 1964); this in fact primarily concentrates on the late sixteenth and early seventeenth centuries. Professors F. Gaeta, A. Stella and other, under the auspices of the Istituto Storico Italiano per L'Età Moderna e Contemporanea have been engaged in the editing for publication of reports from the Venetian Nunciature in the series *Nunziature di Venezia*; since 1958, vols. I, II, V, VI, and VIII have been published, covering the periods 1533–5, 1536–42, 1550–4, 1556–9. For an account of church-state relations based primarily upon secondary works see Bouwsma, *Venice and the Defence of Republican Liberty, cit.*

On Sarpi, see perhaps more particularly L. Salvetorelli, 'Le idée religiose di Fra Paolo Sarpi', *Memorie dell' Accademia Nazionale dei Lincei. Classe di scienze morali, storiche e filologiche*, Ser. VIII, vol. V (1953), pp. 311–60, and F. Chabod, *La politica di Paolo Sarpi* (Venice-Rome 1962).

For an introduction to the history of piety in Venice, see H. Jedin, 'Gasparo Contarini e il contributo veneziano alla Riforma Cattolica' in *La Civiltà veneziana del Rinascimento, cit.*

On Protestantism in Venice, the standard work is K. Benrath, *Geschichte der Reformation in Venedig* (Halle 1887), but see especially E. Pommier, 'La société vénitienne et la Réforme protestante au XVIe siècle', *BISSSV*, I (1959).

On the Greek religious minority in Venice see G. Fedalto, *Ricerche storiche sulla posizione giuridica ed ecclesiastica dei Greci a Venezia nei secoli XV e XVI* (Florence 1967).

The most active researcher in the field of Venetian religious history was the late Mgr. Pio Paschini. A bibliography of his publications is to be found in *Rivista di Storia della Chiesa in Italia*, XVII (1963), pp. 259–304.

Fairly general aspects of Venetian religious history are dealt with in my Ph.D. thesis, *Studies in the Religious Life of Venice in the Sixteenth and Early Seventeenth Centuries: the Venetian Clergy and Religious Orders, 1520–1630*, Cambridge University 1964; it may be consulted in the University Library, Cambridge.

(d) Economic History

A valuable collection of some of the most important articles on the Venetian economy in the sixteenth and early seventeenth centuries is contained in B. S. Pullan (ed.), *Crisis and Change in the Venetian Economy* (London 1968). On general aspects see also the following: F. Braudel, *La Méditerrannée et le monde méditerranéen a l'époque de Philippe II* (Paris 1949, 2nd ed. 1966); G. Luzzatto, 'La decadenza di Venezia dopo le scoperte geografiche nella tradizione e nella realtà', *Archivio Veneto*, Ser. V, n. LXXXIX–XC (1954), pp. 162–81; A. Stella, 'La crisi economica veneziana della seconda metà del secolo XVI', *Archivio Veneto*, Ser. V, n. XCIII–XCIV (1956), pp. 17–69; F. Braudel, 'La vita economica di Venezia nel secolo XVI', in *La Civiltà veneziana del Rinascimento, cit.* pp. 81–102; *Aspetti della decadenza economica veneziana nel secolo XVII*, proceedings of the *Convegno* of June–July 1957 at S. Giorgio Maggiore, Venice (Venice-Rome 1961); F. C.

Lane, *Venice and History: the Collected Papers of Frederic. C. Lane* (Baltimore 1966). On more specific aspects, see F. C. Lane, *Venetian Ships and Ship-Builders of the Renaissance* (Baltimore 1934); R. Cessi, 'Alvise Cornaro e la bonifica veneziana nel secolo XVI', *Rendiconti dell' Accademia dei Lincei, classe di scienze morali*, etc., Ser. VI, XII (1936), pp. 301–23; A. Tenenti, *Venezia e i corsari* (Bari 1961), translated by J. and B. Pullan as *Piracy and the Decline of Venice* (London 1967); D. Beltrami, *Storia della popolazione di Venezia dalla fine del secolo XVI alla caduta della Repubblica* (Padua 1954); idem, *Saggio di Storia dell' agricoltura nella Repubblica di Venezia durante l' età moderna*, (Venice–Rome 1956); idem, *Forze di lavoro e proprietà fondiarie nelle campagne venete dei secoli XVII e XVIII*, (Venice–Rome 1961); D. Sella, *Commerci ed industrie a Venezia nel secolo XVII* (Venice–Rome 1961).

(e) Venetian Society

Scientific studies of Venetian social history have been mainly orientated towards examination of the nobility. Here see J. C. Davis, *The Decline of the Venetian Nobility as a Ruling Class* (Baltimore 1962) and also: E. Rodenwalt, 'Untersuchungen uber die Biologie des venezianischen Adels', *Homo, Zeitschrift fur die vergleichende Forschung am Menschen*, VIII (1957), pp. 1–26; B. S. Pullan, 'Service to the Venetian State: Aspects of Myth and Reality in the Early Seventeenth Century', *Studi Secenteschi*, V (1964), pp. 95–148; idem, 'The Occupations and Investment of the Venetian Nobility in the Middle and Late Sixteenth-Century' in *Venetian Studies*, ed. Hale, *cit.*; U. Tucci, 'The Psychology of the Venetian Merchant in the Sixteenth Century', in the same volume, is most welcome for the attention it gives to *cittadini* alongside nobles. On social problems and philanthropy see B. S. Pullan 'Poverty, Charity and the Reason of State: Some Venetion Examples', *BISSSV*, II (1960), pp. 17–60 and idem, *Rich and Poor in Renaissance Venice, the Social Institutions of a Catholic State to 1620* (Oxford 1971); the latter work devotes extensive attention to the *Scuole Grandi* and the role of the *cittadini* therein. An indispensable handbook for the study of Venetian social history is M. Ferro, *Dizionario del diritto commune et veneto*, 10 vols. (Venice 1778–81).

(f) The Venetian Dominions

On the Terraferma in general, see C. G. Mor, 'Problemi organizzativi e politica veneziana nei riguardi dei nuovi acquisti di terraferma', in *Umanesimo europeo e umanesimo veneziano, cit.* and A.

Ventura, *Nobiltà a popolo nella società veneta del'400 e'500* (Bari 1964). On specific regions see: M. Borgherini-Scarabellin, *La vita privata a Padova nel secolo XVII* (Venice 1917); G. Marzari, *La Historia di Vicenza* (Venice 1591); G. Mantese, *Memorie storiche della chiesa vicentina*, III (2) (*1404–1563*), (Vicenza 1964), which gives valuable information on the city; P. Paschini, *Storia del Friuli*, III (Udine 1936). On Venice's non-Italian territories, note especially G. F. Hill, *A History of Cyprus*, III (London 1948) and G. Praga, *Storia di Dalmazia* (3rd ed. Padua 1954).

(g) Scholarship and Literature

M. Foscarini, *Della letteratura veneziana* (Padua 1752, Venice 1854) is still a valuable manual of references to Venetian scholars, antiquarians and historians.

On the printing-press, see H. F. Brown, *The Venetian Printing-Press* (London 1891) and *Scritti sopra Aldo Manuzio* (various authors), (Florence 1955). On academies, see M. Battagia, *Delle accademie veneziane. Dissertazione storica* (Venice 1826) and P. L. Rose, 'The Accademia Venetiana, science and culture in Renaissance Venice', *Studi Veneziani*, XI (1969), pp. 191–242. On erudite circles around the turn of the seventeenth century, see A. Favaro, 'Un ridotto scientifico a Venezia al tempo di Galileo Galilei', *Nuovo Archivio Veneto*, IX (1893), pp. 199–209 and idem, 'Fulgenzio Manfredi e Galileo Galilei', *Nuovo Archivio Veneto*, n.s. XIII (1907), pp. 34–67.

On the University of Padua, see E. Troilo, *Averroismo e Aristotelismo padovano* (Padua 1939); B. Nardi, *Saggi sull' Aristotelismo padovano dal secolo XIV al XVI*; J. H. Randall Jr., *The School of Padua and the Emergence of Modern Science* (Padua 1961). See also A. Favaro, *Galileo Galilei e lo Studio di Padova* (2 vols., Florence 1883, 2nd ed. Padua 1966).

On Venetian humanism, see especially the previously cited volumes *Umanesimo europeo e umanesimo veneziano*, *Rinascimento europeo e Rinascimento veneziano* and *Venezia e l'Oriente fra tardo medioevo e Rinascimento* and also A. Ferriguto, *Almorò Barbaro, l'alta cultura del settentrione d'Italia nel'400. I 'sacri canones' di Roma e le 'sanctissime leze' di Venezia* (Venice 1922) and D. J. Geanakoplos, *Greek Scholars in Venice* (Cambridge Mass. 1962). On scholarship and currents of thought in the middle and latter years of the sixteenth century see P. Laven, *Daniele Barbaro Patriarch Elect of Aquilea, with special reference to his circle of scholars and to his literary achievement*, Ph.D. thesis, 1957,

London, fac. Modern History, available for consultation in the Senate House Library; G. Cozzi, 'La società veneziana del Rinascimento in un opera di Paolo Paruta: "Della perfettione della vita politica" ', *Atti della Deputazione di Storia Patria per le Venezie* (1961); Bouwsma, *Venice and the Defense of Republican Liberty, cit.*

On historiography, see G. Cozzi, 'Cultura politica e religione nella "pubblica storiografia" veneziana del '500', *BISSSV*, v (1965); Bouwsma, *Venice and the Defense of Republican Liberty, cit.*; A. Pertusi (ed.), *La storiografia veneziana fino al secolo XVI* (Florence 1970).

On *volgare* prose, poetry and drama, see G. Toffanin, *Il Cinquecento. Storia letteraria d'Italia*, IV (Milan 1941); *Storia della Letteratura Italiana*, IV, 'Il Cinquecento' (Milan 1967); v, 'Il Seicento' (Milan 1967); D. Valeri, 'Caratteri e valori del teatro comico' and W. Th. Elwert, 'Pietro Bembo e la vita letteraria del suo tempo', both in *La Civiltà veneziana del Rinascimento, cit.*; W. Th. Elwert, *Studi di letteratura veneziana* (Venice-Rome 1960); C. Dionisotti, introduction to P. Bembo, *Prose della volgar lingua* (Turin 1960); E. Lovarini, *Studi sul Ruzzante e la letteratura pavana* (Padua 1965); L. Zorzi, introduction to Ruzzante, *Teatro. Prima edizione completa* (Turin 1967); G. Padoan, 'La Veneixiana: non fabula non comedia ma vera historia', *Lettere Italiane*, XIX (1967), pp. 1–54.

(h) Art criticism and Theory

For primary sources, see Ch. VII and footnotes; particularly important modern editions of sources are P. Aretino, *Lettere sull' arte*, comment, F. Pertile, ed. E. Camasasca (3 vols. in 4, Milan 1957), and P. Barocchi (ed.), *Trattati d'arte del Cinquecento, fra manierismo e controriforma*, I (Bari 1960); note also M. W. Roskill, *Dolce's 'Aretino' and Venetian Art-Theory of the Cinquecento* (New York 1968). For a general discussion, see R. Pallucchini, 'La critica d'arte a Venezia nel Cinquecento', *Quaderni del Rinascimento Veneto*, I, n.d.

(i) Art-patronage and Collecting

See Appendix.

(j) The visual arts

Periodicals

The main periodicals devoted more specifically to the study of Venetian art are *Arte Veneta* (1947–) and *Saggi e Memorie della Storia dell' Arte* (1957–).

328 BIBLIOGRAPHY

Painting: general discussions

F. Saxl, *A Heritage of Images. A Selection of Lectures by Fritz Saxl*, ed. H. Honour and J. Fleming (London 1970); these lectures were mostly given in the 1930s and are also to be found in F. Saxl, *Lectures* (London 1957); see 'Jacopo Bellini and Mantegna as Antiquarians', 'Titian and Pietro Aretino', 'A Humanist Dreamland'. L. Coletti, 'La crisi manieristica della pittura veneziana', *Convivium* (1941), pp. 109–26. *Venezia e l'Europa. Atti del XVIII Congresso Internazionale della Storia dell' Arte* (Venice 1956). E. H. Gombrich, *Norm and Form. Studies in the Art of the Renaissance* (London 1966); see especially the chapter entitled 'The Renaissance Theory of Art and the Rise of Landscape'. J. Schulz, *Venetian Painted Ceilings of the Renaissance* (California 1968).

Individual painters

Giovanni Bellini: G. Robertson, *Giovanni Bellini* (Oxford 1968). Note also E. Wind, *Bellini's Feast of the Gods. A Study in Venetian Humanism.* (Cambridge Mass 1948).

Giorgione: Readers are referred to T. Pignatti, *Giorgione*, (Venice 1969) which contains a comprehensive bibliography.

Titian: Th. Hetzer, *Tizian, Geschichte seiner Farbe*, (Frankfurt a.M. 1935, 1948, 1969); note also idem, 'Studien uber Tizians Stil', *Jahrbuch fur Kunstwissenschaft*, I (1923) pp. 202–48. E. Panofsky, *Problems in Titian, Mostly Iconographic*, (London–New York 1969). Tintoretto: For a general discussion of the bibliography, see R. Pallucchini, 'Tintoretto nella luce della critica', in *Rinascimento europeo e Rinascimento veneziano, cit.* pp. 233–60. Readers are also referred to H. Tietze, *Tintoretto, the Paintings and Drawings*, (London–New York 1948). Note also the extremely useful article by J. Wilde, 'Die Mostra del Tintoretto zu Venedig', *Zeitschrift für Kunstgeschichte*, VII (1937) pp. 140–43; it is helpful to refer for illustrations to the exhibition catalogue *La Mostra del Tintoretto, catalogo delle opere*, (Venice 1937).

Paolo Veronese: R. Pallucchini, *Veronese*, (Rome–Leipsig, n.d.). T. Pignatti, *Le pitture di Paolo Veronese nella chiesa di S. Sebastiano in Venezia*, (Milan 1966) is extremely valuable on Veronese's early development.

Architecture and sculpture

P. Paoletti, *L'architettura e scultura del Rinascimento in Venezia* (4 vols., Venice 1893) is a valuable standard work but only covers the period *c.* 1470–1520. An excellent brief summary on Venetian

architecture from late fifteenth to mid-sixteenth centuries is given in
P. J. Murray, *The Architecture of the Italian Renaissance*, (London 1963,
1969) and again for sixteenth-century Venetian sculpture see J. Pope-
Hennessy, *An Introduction to Italian Sculpture: Italian Renaissance
Sculpture*, (London 1958). Idem, *Italian High Renaissance and Baroque
Sculpture*, (London 1963). Note also G. Mazzotti, *Palladian and other
Venetian Villas*, (Venice-Rome 1966).
Early Renaissance architects and sculptors: L. Angelini, *Le opere in
Venezia di Mauro Coducci*, (Milan 1945). Idem. *Le opere di Bartolmeo
Bon e Guglielmo d'Alzano*, (Bergamo 1961). U. Donati, *Artisti ticinesi
a Venezia*, (Lugano 1961). F. Cessi, *Andrea Briosco detto Il Riccio,
scultore (1470–1532)*, (Trent 1965).
Sansovino: G. Mariacher, *Il Sansorino*, (Milan 1963).
G. M. Falconetto: See G. Fiocco, *Alvise Cornaro, il suo tempo e le sue
opere*, (Venice 1965).
Palladio: The reader is referred in the first instance to J. Ackerman,
Palladio, (London 1966) and to the valuable bibliography. See also
R. Wittkower, *Architectural Principles in the Age of Humanism*,
(London 1949, 1952, 1962) pts. iii and iv and R. Pane, *Andrea Palladio*,
(Turin 1948, 1961), a comprehensive study, which is well-illustrated.
The periodical *Bollettino del Centro Internazionale di Studi di Archi-
tettura Andrea Palladio* is specifically devoted to the architect and his
milieu.
Sanmicheli: *Michele Sanmicheli. Studi raccolti dall' Accademia di Agri-
coltura, Scienze e Lettere di Verona per la celebrazione del IV centenario
della sua morte*, (Verona 1960).
Vittoria: F. Cessi, *Alessandro Vittoria, bronzista* (Trent 1960). Idem,
Alessandro Vittoria, architetto e stuccatore (Trent 1961). Idem, *Alessandro
Vittoria, scultore*, (2 vols. Trent 1961).
Scamozzi: F. Barbieri, *Vincenzo Scamozzi* (Vicenza 1952).

Music and music-patronage

General

F. Caffi, *Storia della musica sacra nella già Capella Ducale di S. Marco in
Venezia dal 1318 al 1797* (2 vols., Venice 1855). S. T. Worsthorne,
Venetian Opera in the Seventeenth Century (Oxford 1954). G. Barblan,
'Aspetti e figure del Cinquecento musicale veneziano' in *La Civiltà
veneziana del Cinquecento, cit.* L. Ronga, 'La musica' in *La Civiltà
veneziana nell. età barocca, cit.* D. M. Arnold, 'Music at the Scuola di
S. Rocco', *Music and Letters*, XL (1959), pp. 229–41. G. F. Malipiero—

R. Cumar, 'Il barocco e la musica', in *Barocco europeo e barocco veneziano, cit.*

The Gabrieli: G. Benvenuti, *Andrea e Giovanni Gabrieli e la musica strumentale in S. Marco* (Milan 1931–2).

Monteverdi: G. F. Malipiero, *Claudio Monteverdi* (Milan 1929); this publishes Monteverdi's letters. L. Schrade, *Monteverdi, Creator of Modern Music* (London 1951) and D. M. Arnold, *Monteverdi* (London 1963).

MID-SEVENTEENTH TO LATE EIGHTEENTH CENTURIES

(a) General

M. Berengo, *La società veneta alla fine del Settecento* (Florence 1956). N. Jonard, *La vie quotidienne à Venise au XVIIIe siècle* (Paris 1965). Note also the previously cited volumes *La Civiltà veneziana nell' età barocca, La Civiltà veneziana del Settecento, Barocco europeo e barocco veneziano* and *Sensibilità e razionalità del Settecento*, the latter two being mainly concerned with the arts.

(b) Political history

M. Petrocchi, *Il tramonto della Repubblica di Venezia e l' assolutismo illuminato* (Venice 1950). G. Tabacco, *Andrea Tron (1712–85) e la crisi dell' aristocrazia senatoria a Venezia* (Trieste 1957). G. F. Torcellan, *Una figura della Venezia settecentesca, Andrea Memmo. Ricerche sulla crisi dell' aristocrazia veneziana* (Venice–Rome 1963). G. Cozzi, 'Politica e diritto nei tentativi di riforma del diritto penale veneto nel settecento' in *Sensibilità e razionalità del Settecento, cit.*

(c) Social history

See Berengo, *La società veneta, cit.*

(d) Religion

A. Vecchi, *Correnti religiose nel Sei-Settecento veneto* (Florence 1962).

(e) Literature

G. Ortolani, *La riforma del teatro nel Settecento* (Venice–Rome 1962).

(f) Art-patronage and collecting

S. Savini-Branca, *Il collezionismo veneziano del '600* (Padua 1954). F. Haskell, *Patrons and Painters. A Study in the Relations Between Art and Society in the Age of the Baroque* (London 1963), pt. iii.

(g) The visual arts

Painting

M. Levey, *Painting in Eighteenth-Century Venice* (London 1959).

R. Pallucchini, *La pittura veneziana del Settecento* (Venice 1960).

Architecture

C. Semenzato, *L'architettura di Baldessare Longhena* (Padua 1954).

E. Bassi, *Architettura del Sei e Settecento a Venezia* (Naples 1968).

Index

Italian proper names are listed alphabetically without regard to the prefixes: da, di, de' etc. (e.g. for Da Ponte, see Ponte). Netherlandish proper names are listed without regard to the prefix: van. The prepositions: da, di, de' are not treated alphabetically. Buildings are listed under location.

Abbondi, *see* Scarpagnino
Accademia della Fama, *see* Accademia Veneziana I.
Accademia Filosofica, 71
Accademia degli Infiammati, Padua, 73, 102, 104, 109
Accademia Olimpica, Vicenza, 46, 72–3, 258
Accademia Veneziana I (della Fama) (1557), 71–2, 84, 267
Accademia Veneziana II (1593), 72, 267
Acquapendente, Fabrizio, 70–1
Adria, 47
  bishopric, 30
Aemiliani, *see* Miani
Agnadello, battle of, 4, 6, 63, 109, 227
Alberti, Leon Battista, 129, 136, 143–4, 146, 170, 246
Aldus, *see* Manutius
Alexander VIII, Pope, 27
Alexandrism, 70, 80
Algarotti, Francesco, 280–1, 286–9
Almerigo, Paolo, 297
Altivole, 150
Amalteo, Pompeo, 179
Amiraglio dell' Armar, 27
Amiral al Arsenal, 260
Ammanati, Bartolomeo, 233, 310
Andrea Vicentino, 189, 207, 298
Annibale Padovano, 263
Anonimo Morelliano, 131–2, 154–8, 163–4
Antelmi family, 27
Antonello da Messina, 132, 224–5, 316
Apelles, 130–1, 139–40, 164, 229

Aquilea, 47
  bishopric, 30, 32, 60
  cathedral, 178
Arabia, 21–2
Aretino, Pietro, 129, 131–6, 141, 180–1, 184, 230, 233, 267, 284, 297–9
  in Dolce's *Dialogo*, 138–40, 144–5.
Arciero, Alvise, 262
Ariosto, Ludovico, 230
Aristotelianism, 46, 50–52, 54, 57, 59–60, 68–70, 80–3, 145–6, 157, 228
Armonio, Fra, 262–3, 267
Asolani, see Bembo, Pietro
Asolo, 95, 106, 150
Aspetti family, 45
Aspetti, Tiziano the Elder ('Minio'), 303
Aspetti, Tiziano the Younger, 151, 159, 178–9, 311
Assonica, Francesco, 242
Aurelio, Nicolò, 229
Austria, *see* Habsburgs
Averroism, 70, 80
Avogadori di commun, 25

Badoer, Federigo, 71–2, 267
Bagnolo, Villa Pisani, 316
Barbarano, Montano 298
Barbarigo dalla Terrazza family, 213–15, 298
Barbaro family of S. Maria Mater Domini, 31–2, 77–9, 180, 206, 211, 298–9
  Daniele, 56, 59–61, 65, 73–4, 77–9, 113, 118, 145–6, 159, 173–6, 179–80, 185,

Barbaro, Daniele—*cont.*
  243, 267, – in Paruta's dialogue, 56–8
  Ermolao the Elder, 77, 89
  Ermolao the Younger f. Zaccaria, 50,
    53, 59, 65, 71, 81–4, 87, 95, 157
  Ermolao f. Marcantonio, 78
  Francesco f. Marcantonio, 78
  Marcantonio, 61, 173–4, 179, 187,
    191–2
barchesse, 167, 175
Bardi, Gerolamo, 154–5, 188–9
Baronio, Cesare, 73
Bassano, 44
Bassano (Da Ponte) family, 44
  Francesco, 159–60, 179–80, 189–90,
    207, 211, 245, – items by, 298, 301–2
  Jacopo, 234, 239, 245, 256, – items by,
    302, 313 – references to 285–7
  Leandro, 298
Bazzacco, *see* Ponchino
Beccadelli, Ludovico, 97
Bellarmino, Roberto, 73
Belli, Valerio, 300
Bellini family, 45, – references to, 141,
    162
  Gentile, 182–3, 188, 205–6, 298
  Giovanni, 43, 97, 150, 156, 182–3,
    205–6, 224–5 – items by, 281, 302,
    305, 307, 313, 316, 318, 319, 321 –
    references to, 132, 137, 162, 282, 285
  Jacopo, 223–4
Bembism, 102
Bembo family, 51–2, 77
  Bernardo, 50–1, 53, 77, 82, 157
  Carlo, 97–8
  Pietro, 51–3, 71, 75, 77, 84, 87, 90,
    93–102, 116, 126, 132, 150–1, 155–8,
    214, 227, 229–31, 300, 315
Bembo type, 75
Benedictines, 196, 200, 202
Beolco, Angelo, called 'Il Ruzzante', 46,
    104–10, 111, 126, 151, 267, 277–8
Bertotti-Scamozzi, Ottaviano, 280
Bessarion, Cardinal, 73, 75
Bergamo, 20, 25, 43–5
  bishopric, 30
  school of painting, 43–4
  sculptors and master-builders, 45, 48

Bernardo, Francesco, 187, 213, 300
Black Sea, 21
Boccaccio, Giovanni, 94–5, 99–101
Boccalini, Traiano, 6–7
Bodin, Jean, 7
Bolognese school of painting, 281, 290
Bon, Bartolomeo of Venice (d. 1508)
  not cited
Bon, Bartolomeo of Bergamo (d. 1529),
    44, 183, 204–6, 245–7
Bonifazio Veronese, 298
Bordone, Paris, 206, 218, 256, 317 –
  references to, 135, 137
Borromeo, St Charles, 16–17, 61
Bosch, Hieronymus, 156, 309
Boschini, Mario, 135, 141, 155, 162, 212,
    220, 282–7, 289
Botero, Giovanni, 6, 203–4
Bramante, Donato, 166
Bregno, Antonio, 48
Brescia, 20, 25, 33–5, 43, 47, 193
  bishopric, 30
  school of painting, 43
Briosco, *see* Riccio
Bruni, Leonardo, 49
Bruno, Giordano, 64
Buora, Giovanni, 48, 205
Burchiello, il, *pseud.* (Antonio Molin), 267
Buus, Jaches, 261
Byzantine culture, 39, 47, 256

Calergi, Zacharia, 75
Caliari family, 236
  Benedetto, 43
  Paolo, *see* Veronese
Calmo, Andrea, 111, 267, 277
Camaldolese Order, 14, 52, 188, 194–5;
  see also Venice, S. Michele in Isola
Cambrai, Holy League of, 4
  War of the League of, 4–5, 63, 117
Campagnola, Domenico, 169, 300
Canaletto, il, *pseud.* (Antonio Canal), 281,
    291–2
Cancelliere Grande, 6, 27–8
Cancelliere Inferiore, 27
Candia, archbishopric, 30–1
Canera, Anselmo, 43, 237, 319
Canons Regular, 196, 200

Cape-route, 22
Capella, Alessandro, 300
Capello, Bernardo, 102
Capello, Michiel Antonio, 184, 198, 211
Capitanei, 34
Capitaneo General del Mar, 27
Capuchins, 191, 194, 196, 202
Caraffa, Gianpietro, 14–15
Caravia, Alessandro, 204–5
Carleton, Dudley, 24
Carpaccio, Vittore, 45, 83, 183, 205–6, 226, 299
case vecchie, 3, 32
Castiglione, Baldassare, 139, 144
Catena, Vincenzo, 45, 316–17
Catholic reform, 14–17, 52, 242–3, *see also* Counter-Reformation
Cattaneo, Danese, 45, 132–3, 233, 251–3
– items by 297, 310
Cavaleriato, 25
Cavalli, Francesco, 260, 262
Ceneda, 179
  bishopric, 32
Chancery, *see* Ducal Chancery
Charles V, Emperor, 132
Chierigato, Gerolamo, 172–3, 301
Church, 9–13
  benefices and preferments, 29–33
  see also Catholic Reform; Counter-Reformation; Papacy; Rome – Court
Church Fathers, 15, 42, 60, 86
Ciceronianism, 90–99
Cima, Giambattista, da Conegliano, 43, 225
Citizens of Terraferma cities, 33
Citizens of Venice, 4, 7–8, 25–8, 30, 53, 203
–*de intus* and *de extra*, 25
cittadini originarii, 4, 8, 26–7
Coducci, Mauro, 44, 48, 165–6, 194–5, 197, 205, 220, 245–9, 313
Codussi, *see* Coducci
Collegio, 2, 3, 7, 25, 191, 198
Colonna, Fra Francesco, 245–6
Commedia dell' Arte, 277, cf. 111–12
Concio, 2
Concordia, bishopric, 32

Consiglio (Minor Consiglio), 2, 10, 25
Consiglio dei Dieci, *see* Council of Ten
Constantinople, 21, 39
Contarini family, 29, 78
  branch of S. Samuele, 160, 301–2
Contarini, Alvise (Luigi), 61–3, 78, 87, 118
Contarini, Alessandro, 301
Contarini, Carlo, 276
Contarini, Federigo, 159, 161, 186, 192, 213, 215, 264–6, 301
Contarini, Gasparo, 1, 5–6, 15–17, 52–4, 64–5, 76, 78
Contarini, Giacomo, 74, 90, 154, 159–60, 179–80, 186–90, 211, 213, 215, 243, 301–2
Contarini, Michele, 158, 302
Contarini, Nicolò, 13, 17, 59, 63–5, 72, 113, 116, 118–22, 192–3
Contarini, Taddeo, 302
Contin, Antonio, 207
Cornaro, *see* Corner
Corner family di Ca Grande, S. Maurizio & S. Polo, 31–3, 177–8, 205, 303–6
  Caterina, 95, 100, 150, 177, 227, 305
  Francesco, 31
  Giorgio, 215, 306
  Marco, 105–7
Corner, Alvise (Luigi), 23–4, 104–5, 111, 145, 150–1, 157, 167–71, 175, 300, 303
Corner, Flaminio, 276
Cortese, Gregorio, 14–15, 51, 76
Coryat, Thomas, 1, 213
Cose notabili della città di Venezia (and variants), 141–2, 154–5, 295–6
Council of Ten, 3, 7, 25, 32–3, 274
  commissions of, 182
Council of Trent, 12, 15, 28, 54, 60, 115, 122, 242, *see also* Sarpi
Counter-Reformation, 16–17, 85–90, 111, 242, 257, *see also* Catholic Reform
Crasso family, 306–7
Crete, 20, 39
  art, 48
  Cretans in Venice, 39–40, 75
Crivelli, Carlo, 39

Crociferi (Crutched Friars), 199
cultura filosofica, 82, 84
Cyprus, 20
Cremonino, Cesare, 64
Croce, Giovanni della, 261–5

Dalmatia, 20–1, 30
  Dalmatian community, 205
Dandolo, Matteo, 56
Dante Alighieri, 16, 75, 86, 94–5, 99–100
Davila, Enrico, 112–13
Delfin family, 32–3
Delfin, Caterina, 376
Delfin, Giovanni, 307
Delfin, Giovanni, bishop of Vicenza, 33
Delfin, Pietro, 194
De Piles, Roger, 140
Dogado, 11, 20
Doge, 2–3, 6, 150, 260
Dolce, Ludovico, 131, 135, 137–41, 144–5, 159, 162, 238, 282
Dolfin, *see* Delfin
Dominicans, 200, 202, 245, 265
Donà, Gerolamo, 50–1, 77, 82, 84, 157
Donà, Leonardo, 13, 17, 72, 196
Donà, Pietro, 194–5
Donati, Baldassare, 259, 261–2, 264, 267
Donato, *see* Donà
Ducal Chancery, 7, 26–8, 53, 69
Ducal secretariat, 53, *see also* secretaries
Dufresnoy, Charles, 140
Dürer, Albrecht, 60, 136–7, 156, 225–6, 309, 321

Egnazio, Giovan Battista, 71
Egypt, 21–2, 39, 246
El Greco (Domenico Theotocopoulos), 40
Emo, Leonardo, 186, 307
England – English, 11, 22–3, 41, 59, 120, 280–1
Erasmus, Desiderius, 71, 78, 82, 85–7, 98
Erizzo, Francesco, 307
Erizzo, Sebastian, 90
Este, 47
Este house
  Alfonso, duke of Ferrara, 230
  Isabella, duchess of Mantua, 39, 42,

156, 164, 215
Eyck, Jan van, 48, 224

Fabri, Ottaviano, 159, 161, 307–8
Falconetto, Giovan Maria, 42, 45, 149, 151, 166, 169–70, 174–6, 180, 220, 247, 300, 303
Fanzolo, Villa Emo, 186, 307
Farinati, Paolo, 43
Farsetti, Filippo, 280
Fasolo, Giovan Antonio, 44, 180, 210, 236–7
Ferrara, 38–9, 77, 95, 127, 262, 266
Ferriguto, Arnaldo, 80, 228
fidecommesso, 29, 153
Filelfo, Francesco, 69
Flaminio, Marcantonio, 96
Flemings – Flemish art, *see* Netherlands
Florence, 39, 77, 84, *see also* Tuscany
Fondaco dei Tedeschi, 40, 182, 225–6
Foppa, Vincenzo, 43
Fortunio, Giovan Francesco, 94, 100
Foscari, Alvise and Nicolò, 215, 409
Foscarini, Sebastiano, 54
Fossis, Petrus de, 40, 256–62 passim.
Fracastoro, Gerolamo, 231
France, 4, 22, 41
  art theory in, 140–1, 286
  culture, 82–4, 277–8
  Venetian interest in, 41, 120
  views of Venice in, 1, 6–7, 11–12
Francesco di Giorgi, *see* Groppi
Franciscan Minors, 199–200
Franciscan Observants, 195–6, 280
Franco, Battista, 61, 163, 176, 178–80, 185–6, 211 – items by, 299, 301, 308, 310–11
Fra Paolo, *see* Sarpi
fraterna, 29, 65
Fratta Polesine, Villa Badoer, 175
Friuli, 20, 25, 30, 34, 40, 43, 233
Fugger family, 40

Gabriel, Trifon, 62
Gabrieli family, 257–8
  Andrea, 258, 262–4, 267
  Giovanni, 257, 262, 264–6
  Costanzo, 265

Galilei, Galileo, 71–3, 159
Gambara, Villa Foscari (la Malcontenta), 173, 215
Genoa, 21–2
George of Trebizond, 69
Germany, 21–2
    art, 225–6, 244
    German community in Venice, 21, 28, 40, 225; see also Fondaco dei Tedeschi
Giambologna, 161, 307
Giannotti, Tommaso, 5–6
Giolito, Gabriele, 71, 75
Giorgione da Castelfranco, 43, 77, 79–81, 100, 150, 165, 210, 225–9, 256, 299
    Sleeping Venus, 157, 165
    Tempestà, 157, 165, 227–8
    Three Philosophers, 79–81, 227–8 – items by, 156–8, 161, 281, 302, 305, 307, 314, 316–18, 321 – references to, 132, 136–9, 141, 285, 287
Giovani, 3, 10, 13, 16–17, 33, 41, 54, 63–4, 72
Giovanni da Udine, see Ricamatori
Giulio Romano, 39, 42, 175, 177, 180, 232–7, 244–5
Giunta family, 76, 141
Giustiniani family, 31
Giustiniani, Tomaso (Fra Paolo), 14–15, 52, 71, 76, 194
Giustiniani, Orsato, 102
Giusto, Paolo, 262
Godi, Gerolamo, 308
Goes, Hugo van der, 156
Goethe, 281, 289
Golden Book, 25
Goldioni, Leonico, pseud. (Nicolò Doglioni), 154, 295–6
Goldoni, Carlo, 277–9, 292
Gonzaga, Federico II, 39, 42
Gradisca, War of, 120
Grandi, Alessandro de, 266
Great Council, see Maggior Consiglio
Greek area, 47
Greek community in Venice, 10, 39, 205
Greek press, 74–5
Grigi, Giacomo de, 311
Grillo, Giambattista, 257, 262, 266

Grimani family of S. Maria Formosa, 31–2, 77–8, 149–52, 155–6, 158, 177–80, 185, 211–12, 233–4, 244, 308–11
    Antonio, 155, 308
    Domenico, 31–2, 73–4, 78, 155–6, 158–9, 179, 223, 308–9
    Giovanni, 32, 55, 60–1, 78, 113, 151, 156, 160–1, 175, 177–8, 196, 215, 223, 251, 310–11 – in Paruta's dialogue, 55–8
    Marco, 32, 78
    Marino, Cardinal, 32, 73–4, 78, 151, 160, 176–9, 193, 309
    Vettore, 178–9, 184–5, 198, 211, 310
Grimani, Gerolamo of S. Luca, 237, 310
Grimani, Marino, Doge, 265–6
Grimani ara, 223
Grimani Breviary, 156, 158, 309
Grimani Gauls, 223, 232
Gritti, Andrea, Doge, 179, 181, 183, 196, 263, 311–12
Groppi, Fra Francesco (F. di Giorgi), 196
Groppino, 215
Gualdo family, 162, 312
    Gerolamo, 162–3
    Giuseppe, 172
Guardi family, 291
Guarino Veronese, 38
Guercino, 281–2, 290
Guicciardini, Francesco, 58, 113–15, 118–19, 121, 125
Guisconi, Anselmo, pseud., see Sansovino, Francesco

Habsburgs, 4, 20, 34, 119–20
Hana family, 312
Harvey, William, 71
Hellenistic art, 222
Henry III of France, 18, 186, 257
Hermeticism, 228
Hieronymite friars, 195, 199, 202
Holy Roman Emperor, see Habsburgs
Horace, 95
humanistae, 68–9
Hypnoteromachia Polifili, 245–6

Index, Clementine, 74, 76

Index, Tridentine, 76
India, Bernardo, 43, 237, 319
Inquisition, 9–10, 201
Inquisitori di Stato, 274
Interdict of 1509, 9
Interdict of 1606, 9, 11, 120
Istria, 20, 30

Jenson, Nicholas, 74
Jesuits, 11, 73, 111, 194, 197, 200, 217
Jews, 276
John of Speyer, 74
Josquin des Près, 257
Julius II, Pope, 9

Labia family, 28, 274
La Boétie, Etienne, 7
Lando, Simone, 313
Laocöon, 232–3
Lateran Canons, 196
Legge, Giovanni da, 184–5, 313
Leonardo da Vinci, 132, 137, 156, 302
Leoni, Leone, 133, 233
Lepanto, battle of, 117, 186–7
Levant, 21–2, 39, 47–8, 246
Lodoli, Padre Carlo, 280
Liburnio, Nicolò, 94, 100
Libro d' oro, see Golden Book
Licinio, Giulio, 185
Livy, 85, 113–16
Lombardo (Solaro) family, 48, 165
    Antonio, 48, 226
    Pietro, 48, 183, 195, 197, 205, 245, 247
    Sante, 204–5
    Tullio, 48, 226
Lombardy, 4, 20
Longhena, Baldassare, 150, 192, 279
Longhi, Pietro, 292
Longueil, Christophe, 96
Lonigo, Villa Pisani, 174
Loredan family of S. Marcuola, 195, 214, 313–14
Lotto, Lorenzo, 43–4, 226, 316
Lucian, 221
Lupato, Pietro, 263
Luther, Martin, 8, 15, 52
Luvigliano, Villa dei Vescovi, 149, 169, 174–5

Manin family, 273–4
Maffei, Scipione, 277
Maganza, Alessandro, 44, 298
Maganza, Giovan Battista, 44, 172, 180, 236
Maggior Consiglio, 2–3, 6, 24–5
    commissions of, 183–4
    magistrati, 25
Magistrato alla Petizion, 154
Magistrato al Sal, 182
Magno, Celio, 28, 102
Malcontenta, see Gambara
Mannerism, 233–6, 241, 244
Mantegna, Andrea, 42, 137, 153, 156, 223–5, 300, 321
Mantua, 38–9, 42, 44, 46, 232–3, 235, 237, 262, 266
Manzino, Benedetto, 198
Manutius (Manuzio) family
    Aldus, 39, 71, 75–6
    Paolo, 71–2, 75
Marcello, Geronimo, 157, 165, 314
Marcello, Giacomo, 187–9
Marches, 39, 225
Marco da Mantova, 157
Marocco (Brenta), Villa Mocenigo, 314
Marot, Clément, 1
Martinengo, Giulio Cesare, 261, 266
Martinoni, Giustiniano, 155, 296
Maser, Villa Barbaro, 60–1, 173–5, 179, 243, 251, 298–9
Massari, Giorgio, 279–80
Mauro Bergamasco, see Coducci, Mauro
Medici family, 77, 153–4, cf. 98–9
Mediterranean trade, 21–4
Memlinc, Hans, 48, 156, 224, 300, 309
Memo, Andrea, 280, 292
Merula, Giorgio, 69
Merulo, Claudio, 262–7, passim
Miani, Gerolamo, 1, 14
Micanzi, Fra Fulgenzio, 64, 72–3
Michelangelo Buonarotti, 133–41 passim, 156, 162, 231–45 passim, 285
Michelozzi, Michelozzo, 246
Michiel, Marcantonio, 131, 154, *see also* Anonimo Morelliano
Milledonnis, Antonio, 28, 115
Milan, city, 16, 43

Milanese State, 4–5, 43, 45
ministeri, 25
Minor Consiglio, see Consiglio
Mio, Giovanni da, 185
Mocenigo family, 258
Mocenigo, Filippo, 55, 61
Mocenigo, Giovanni, 214, 314
Mocenigo, Leonardo, 314–15
Molin, Antonio, see Burchiello
Montagna, Bartolomeo, 300
Montagnana, Villa Pisani, 316
Montaigne, Michel de, 1
Monteverdi, Claudio, 193, 258–62 passim, 265–6
Moretto, il, pseud. (Alessandro Buonvicino), 43
Moro, Battista del, 43, 308
Morosini, Andrea, 59, 63–4, 76, 118
  his circle, 64, 72, 76
mortmain laws, 10
Musurus, Marcus, 71
Muttoni, Pietro, 279–80

Nanto, Pietro da, 215
Navagero, Andrea, 102, 230, 300 – in Fracastoro's Naugerius, 231
Nave, Bartolomeo della, 214, 315
Neacademia, 71
Neoplatonism, 196, 228–30
Netherlands, 11, 22–3, 40, 47 – United Provinces of, 22, 41, 120
  art, 30, 132, 156, 158, 160–4, 224–5, 244
  community in Venice, cf. 312, 315
  music, 256–7
nobles of Terraferma, 33–5, 272–3
  of Brescia, 33–5
  of Friuli, 34, 36
  of Verona, 44
  of Vicenza, 33–6, 44–6, 167
nobles of Venice, 2, 6, 24–8, 35, 272–4

Ochino, Bernardino, 8
Odoni, Alvise and Andrea, 315–16
Olmo, Fortunato, 196
Orsini, Leone, 73
Ottobon family, 27
Ovid, 221, 230

Padavin family, 27
Padovano, 23, 34, 167
Padua, 4, 13, 20, 25, 33–4, 39, 43, 45–7, 64, 68, 104, 126, 157, 193, 223, 226
  academies, 72–3, 231
  bishopric, 30, 32
  botanical garden, 59, 77
  Casa Cornaro, 151, 169, 303
  S. Giustina, 202
  University, 46–7, 50, 54, 59, 68–71, 231
Palladio, Andrea, 45–7, 59–60, 73, 77, 145, 151, 159–60, 166, 169–70, 172–4, 176–80, 186–7, 191–3, 196–7, 210, 212, 220, 249, 267
  separate works, 297–320 passim
  references to, 280–1
Palladianism, 279–81, 289
Paolo della Pergola, 69
Palma, Giacomo, il Vecchio, 43–4
  items by 206, 218, 298, 302, 306, 321
  reference to, 137
Palma, Giacomo, il Giovane, 45, 159, 163, 199, 201–2, 207, 209–10, 231
  items by, 189–90, 205, 207, 298, 302, 307, 315–16
Papacy, 4, 9–13, 31, 120, 193
  Papal Curia, 35; see also Rome, Court of
Papal States, 9
Parabosco, Gerolamo, 262, 267
Parma, school of painting, 241
Parmigianino, 234–5, 241, 243
Paruta, Paolo, 54–9, 61, 63, 65, 76, 113, 117–18
  his circle, 72
Pasqualino, Antonio, 316
Patenir, Joachim, 156, 309
Patrizi, Francesco, 71, 117
Paul V, Pope, 9–10
Pellegrini, Pietro, 214, 316
Pergamene art, 221–2
Peruzzi, Baldassare, 166, 172
Pesaro, Francesco, 275–6
Petrarch, 16, 49, 57, 75, 77, 85–7, 94–5, 99–101
  Petrarchism, 102–3, 126
Philip II, 230, 242
Philostratus, 230

Piazza, Paolo (Fra Cosimo), 192
Piazzetta, Giambattista, 290
Pinelli, Giovan Vincenzo, 73, 159, 267
Pino, Paolo, 129, 131, 136–7, 141, 143–4, 238
Piombino Dese, Villa Cornaro, 173, 215, 306
Pisa, 232
Pisani family dal Banco, 316
Pisani family of S. Maria Zobenigo & S. Stefano, 31–2, 269–70
Pisani, Francesco, 316
Pisani, Giorgio, 274–5
Pius V, Pope, 16
Platonism, 51, 82, 145, 267; *see also* Neoplatonism
Plautus, 109, 162
Pliny, 50, 83–4, 130, 164, 221, cf. 138–9
Plovenio, Giuliano & Guido, 316–17
Podestà, 34
Pole, Reginald, 15, 57, 96
Polesine, 34, 167
Poliziano (Politian), Angelo, 51, 82
Pomponazzi, Pietro, 52, 70
Ponchino, Giambattista, called 'il Bazzacco', 151, 178, 180, 185, 211, 305
Ponte family of Bassano, *see* Bassano
Ponte, Antonio da, 45, 187, 191
Ponte, Nicolò da, 13, 54–5
Pontecasale, Villa Garzoni, 174
popolani, in Terraferma, 33
Pordenone, Giovan Antonio Regillo da, 43, 141, 178, 233–4, 309, 312
references to, 137, 141
Porta, Giuseppe della, called 'il Salviati', 178, 185, 207, 309–10
Porto, Francesco & Giambattista da, 317
Porto, Giuseppe da, 317
Portugese, 22
Praglia, Abbey of S. Maria, 202
Pregadi, see Senate
Previtale, Andrea, 43, 227
Priuli, Gerolamo, 23, 213
Procuratori di S. Marco, 25, 181–2, 192
–*de Supra* (*di Sopra*), 181–2, 184–6, 192, 211, 259–66
Protestantism, 8–10, 12, 15

Protho (*protomaestro*) (of public works), 182–4, 187
Provveditori alla fabrica del Palazzo, 182, 187
Provveditori alle fortezze, 182

Quarantia, 2, 274–5
Querini family, 31
Querini, Angelo, 274
Querini, Andrea, 280
Querini, Vincenzo (Fra Pietro), 14, 52, 194
Quintilian, 143–4

Ragusa, 20
Ram, Giovanni & Alessandro, 215, 317
Ramusio, Giovan Battista, 28, 71
Rangone, il, *pseud.* (Tomaso di Ravenna), 198, 205–7, 210, 317–18
Raphael Sanzio, 48, 131–45 passim, 156–69 passim, 212, 231–45 passim, 282, 286, 300, 302, 307, 309, 321
relazioni of ambassadors, 59, 115
rettori, 36, 182
Rezzonico family, 269–70
Ricamatori, Giovanni, da Udine, 43, 169, 176, 178–80, 220, 309
Ricci, Sebastiano, 291
Riccio, il, *pseud.* (Andrea Briosco), 48, 226
Riccoboni, Lelio, 277
Ridolfi, Bartolomeo, 169, 301
Ridolfi, Carlo, 155, 162, 212, 220, 238, 282, 284–5, 289
Ridolfi, Ottaviano, 151, 180, 303, 319
Rimini, 39, 246
Rizzo, Antonio, 48, 183, 245, 247
Robusti, *see* Tintoretto
Rome, 48, 77–8, 95, 156, 172–3, 177, 179, 232, 237, 246, 263
architecture in, 166, 169
art theory in, 130, 282, 286
court of 9–10, 13, 32–3, 127
school of painting, 178, 180, 222, 231–4
Rore, Cyprian, 40, 257, 261–3
Rossi family of Brescia, 43
Cristoforo, 186

Rossi, Francesco, called 'il Salviati', 162, 178

Rosso Fiorentino, 233

Rovigo, see Adria

Rucellai circle, 5

Rubens, 285

Ruschi, Antonio, 290

Rusconi, Giovan Antonio, 45, 187, 191

Ruzzante, see Beolco

Ruzzini, Carlo & Domenico, 161, 214, 318

Sabellico, Marcantonio, 71, 74, 116

Salò, 74

Salutati, Coluccio, 49, 57, 85

Salviati, see Rossi and Porta

Sangallo, Antonio, the Younger, 166, 169

Sanmicheli, Michele, 45, 166, 174–5, 177–8, 215–16, 220, 248–9, 300
individual works, 305, 310–11

Sannazaro, Jacopo, 86, 227

sansaria of Fondaco dei Tedeschi, 182–3, 187

Sansovino, Francesco, 71, 141–2, 154–5, 161, 188–9, 230, 295–6

Sansovino, il, *pseud.* (Jacopo Tatti), 45, 132–3, 161, 166, 174, 177, 179–81, 183–6, 196, 198, 205–7, 211–12, 216, 233, 238, 247–51, 305, 307, 313, 318
references to, 133, 280
studio, 250

Santorio, Gerolamo, 70–71

Sanudo, Marino, the Younger, 58, 63, 71, 112, 116–17

Sarpi, Fra Paolo, 10–12, 41, 64, 72, 115–16, 121–7

Savii, 2
–di Terraferma, 25

Savoldo, Giovan Gerolamo, 43, 316, 321

Savorgnan family, 34–5

Scamozzi, Giovan Domenico, 215, 250

Scamozzi, Vincenzo, 45, 146, 155, 161, 174, 177, 191, 197, 215–16, 250, 305

Scarpagnino, lo, *pseud.* (Antonio Abbondi), 48, 195, 206

Schiavone, Andrea, 185, 207, 318
reference to, 137

Scuole Grandi, 6–7, 27, 200–1, 203–10,

211, 257, 266; *see also* Venice, Compagnia-, Scuola-

scuole di sacramento, 200

Sebastiano del Piombo (S. Luciani), 45, 227, 238, 309
items by, 297
references to, 137, 141

secretaries, 6–7, 26–8, 53

Senate, 3, 6–7, 10, 25, 197–8
commissions of, 184, 191–2, 198

Seneca, 85

Serlio, Sebastiano, 196, 248, 250

serrata, 2, 25, 29

Seyssel, Claude de, 7

Signoria, 2–3, 10, 13

Smeraldi, Francesco, 193

Solari family, see Lombardo

Soranzo, Giacomo, 187–8

Sorella, Simone, 45, 196

Sorte, Cristoforo, 142–3, 180

Spain, 4, 41, 119–20

Spalato, 119

Spavento, Giorgio, 45, 245, 249

Speroni, Sperone, 70, 73, 94, 100, 102, 104

Spira, Fortunato, 196

Squarcione, Francesco, 154

Stampa, Gaspara, 102

Stoics, 85

Stra, Villa Pisani, 269–70

Stringa, Giovanni, 155, 296

Strozzi, Bernardo, 290

Surian, Michele, in Paruta's dialgoue, 55–8

Syria, 21–2, 39

Tasso, Bernardo, 71, 132

Tebaldeo, Antonio, 227

Tedaldo, Francesco, 209

Tatti, Jacopo, see Sansovino

Temanza, Tomaso, 220, 280

Terraferma, 4, 10–11, 20–21, 23–4, 30–31, 33–6, 42–7, 150, 271–2
art in, 43–5, 166–8, 220, 236–7

Theatine order, 14, 194, 197, 199, 202

Theocritus, 227

Thiene family, 319

Thomism, 54, 61

Thucydides, 58, 113–14
Tiepolo, Giambattista, 269–70, 287–93
Tintoretto (Robusti) family, 45
    Domenico, 72, 190, 210; items by 205,
        207, 306–7
    Jacopo, 72, 159, 181–3, 185–7, 189–90,
        207–12, 234, 238–42, 244–5, 256,
        267; references to, 134–5, 137, 141–2,
        238, 284–6, 287–8; items by, 160–3,
        202, 205–7, 281, 297–8, 302, 306–7,
        318
Titian (Tiziano Vecellio), 43, 100, 151,
        180–6, 196, 212, 221–3, 225–7, 230–
        6, 238–9, 244, 256, 312
    Bacchus and Ariadne, 230–2
    Diana and Actaeon, 230–1, 235–6
    Diana and Callisto, 230–1, 235–6
    Sacred and Profane Love, 100, 229–30, 232
    items by, 97, 156, 161, 165, 183, 186,
        188, 200, 205–6, 214, 281, 297–8,
        306, 311–21 passim
    references to, 130–41, 144–6, 156,
        162, 282–5, 287–8
Tomaso di Ravenna, see Rangone
Tomeo, Leonico, 70, 157, 319
Torcello, 47
Torlone, Fra Bernardo, 199
Torre, Michele della, 55–6, 61
Trevigiano, 23, 34, 43, 167
Trevisan, Camillo, 173, 319
Treviso, 4, 25, 33, 43
    bishopric, 32
    studium, 46
Trissino, Francesco & Ludovico, 236,
        320
Trissino, Giangiorgio, 46, 73, 102, 146,
        150–1, 170–2, 175, 180, 277, 319–20
Tron, Andrea, 275–6, 292
Turks, 20, 22, 120
Tuscany, 12
    art, 222, 224, 231–4
    art theory in, 129 ff., 143, 238–9
Tutte le cose notabili, see Cose notabili
    etc.

Uberto of Flanders, 151, 311
Udine, 178–9
United Provinces, see Netherlands

Urbino, 39, 51, 96, 127
Uskoks, 119–20

Valle, Andrea della, 303
Valier, Agostino, 16–18, 54, 56, 59, 61–3,
        73, 78–9, 85–7, 113, 118, 126
Valla, Giorgio, 69
Valmarana, Alvise & Leonardo, 320
Vasari, Giorgio, 129, 131–2, 137–9, 141,
        145, 151, 154, 177, 181, 216, 233,
        240, 244, 305
Vecchi, 41
Velasquez, 282, 285
Vendramin, Andrea, 161–3, 165, 214, 320
Vendramin, Gabriele, 155–8, 163, 165,
        213–14, 228, 270, 313, 320–1
Veneto, see Terraferma
Venexiana, La, 110–11, 278
Venice
    Ca Pesaro, 279
    Ca Rezzonico, 269–70, 279
    Compagnia della Giustizia, 207, 209
    Convertite, 197
    Doges' Palace, see Ducal Palace
    Ducal Chapel, see S. Marco
    Ducal Palace, 150, 160, 180, 182–3,
        186–90, 211, 234, 243, 249
    Ducal Seminary, 257, 262
    Frari Church, see S. Maria Gloriosa
    Gesuati, see S. Maria del Rosario
    Libreria Sansoviniana, see Public Lib-
        rary
    Marciana Library, 73, 159, 184
    Museo d' Antichità, 156, 160, 223, 311
    Palazzo Corner, S. Cassian, 303–6
    Palazzo Corner, S. Maurizio, 247–8,
        279, 303–6
    Palazzo Corner, S. Polo, 248, 303–6
    Palazzo Corner-Spinelli, S. Angelo,
        166, 177, 246, 304–5
    Palazzo Delfin–Manin, 307
    Palazzo Ducale, see Ducal Palace
    Palazzo Grimani, S. Luca, 248, 311
    Palazzo Grimani, S. Maria Formosa,
        175, 178, 310
    Palazzo non nobis Domine, see Palazzo
        Vendramin-Calergi
    Palazzo Trevisan, Murano, 319

Palazzo Vendramin–Calergi, 166, 195, 214, 246–8, 313–14
Patriarchate, 10, 30, 258
Piazza S. Marco, 149–50, 182, 198; Loggietta in, 182, 184
Procurazie Nuove, 192
Procurazie Vecchie, 183, 185–6
Public Library, 182, 184–6, 192, 247, 251
Redentore church, 191–3, 249–50
Rialto bridge, 182
S. Francesco della Vigna, 178–9, 195–6, 250, 299
S. Geminian, 184, 198
SS. Giovanni e Paolo, 200–2, 207
S. Giorgio Maggiore, 14–15, 196, 200, 202, 249–50
S. Giovanni Crisostomo, 245
S. Giulian, 198
S. Marco (St. Mark's), basilica, 181–4, 245, 258, 263; capella musicale in 257–66
S. Maria della Carità, 196–7
S. Maria Formosa, 245
S. Maria Gloriosa dei Frari, 199
S. Maria dei Miracoli, 197, 245
S. Maria della Pietà, 280
S. Maria del Rosario (Gesuati), 280
S. Maria della Salute, 192–3, 279
S. Maria dell' Umiltà, 197, 200, 217
S. Michele in Isola, 194–5, 245–6
S. Nicolò ai Frari, 200
S. Nicolò dei Tolentini, 197, 199
S. Pietro di Castello, 193, 200, 258
S. Salvador, 245
S. Sebastian, 195, 198, 200, 202
S. Spirito in Isola, 200
S. Zaccaria, 197
School (academy) of Rialto, 54, 61, 68–9
School (academy) of S. Marco, 28, 53, 68–9
Scuola Grande della Carità, 203–4, 206
Scuola Grande di S. Giovanni Evangelista, 203–5
Scuola Grande di S. Marco, 203, 205–7, 209, 218

Scuola Grande della Misericordia, 203–4, 206–7
Scuola, Grande di S. Rocco, 203–9, 246–7, 257
Scuola Grande di S. Teodoro, 203
Scuola di S. Giorgio dei Schiavoni, 206, 209
Scuola di S. Maria del Rosario in SS. Giovanni e Paolo, 207
Scuola di S. Orsola, 206, 209
Teatro Nuovo S. Cassian, 258, 266
Zecca, 184, 247
Venier, Domenico, 72, 267
Venier, Giovan Antonio, 321
vera historia, 88–9, 113, 115, 119
Verdizotti, Giovan Maria, 321
Vergerio, Pietro Paolo, the Elder, 49, 85
Vernia, Nicoletto, 70
Verona, 20, 25, 33–4, 40, 43–4, 47, 167, 248
  bishopric, 30
  Palazzo Bevilacqua, 248
  school of painting, 44, 177, 210, 236–7
Veronese region, 174, 271
  Villa Sarego, 175
  Villa della Torre, Fumane, 175
Veronese, il, pseud. (Paolo Caliari), 43, 173–4, 177, 179–80, 187, 189–90, 210–11, 233–4, 236–7, 241–4, 256, 291
  items by, 160–1, 173–4, 183, 185, 187, 189–90, 198–202, 207, 281, 298–9, 301, 307, 313, 318–9
Vesalius, Andrea, 70–1
Vicentino region, 167, 172, 271
  Villa Godi-Valmarana, Lonedo, 308
  Villa da Porto, Thiene, 317
  Villa Trissino, Cricoli, 168, 171–2, 319–20
  Villa Trissino, Meledo, 320
Vicenza, 4, 20, 25, 33–6, 43–6, 162, 167, 211, 258, 279–80
  academies, 72–3, 170–1, 258
  Basilica (Palazzo della Ragione), 172, 211
  bishopric, 30–2
  cathedral, 249, 258
  master-builders, 45

painters, 44, 210, 236–7
Palazzo Barbarano, 298
Palazzo Chierigati, 301
Palazzo Porto, 317
Palazzo Thiene, via S. Gaetano, 319
Palazzo Thiene, Castello, 319
Palazzo Valmarana, 320
studium, 46
Teatro Olimpico, 73
Villa Capra (la Rotonda), 168, 174, 279
Vida, Giacomo, 86
Vidman family, 28
Virgil, 95, 227
Vitruvius, 59, 60, 77, 145–6, 167–8, 170–3
Vittoria, Alessandro, 45, 72, 163–4, 177,
    179, 190, 209, 212, 220–21, 251–3,
    267, 321
  items by, 173, 186, 190, 198, 206–7,
    298–300, 315, 318–19
  school of 180

Vittorino da Feltre, 38, 87
Vivarini, Bartolomeo & Ludovico, 205
volgare, 93–5, 98, 100, 102, 112

Weyden, Rogier van der, 132, 224, 317
Willaert, Adriaan, 40, 256–7, 260–3, 267

Zarlino, Giuseppe, 72, 259, 261–4, 267
Zelotti, Giambattista (called Battista
    Veronese), 43–4, 180, 185–6, 210,
    236–7, 307
Zeno, Apostolo, 277
Zeno, Renier, 4
Zeno, Simone, 214
Zerman, Fra Marco, 199
Zio, Francesco, 321
Zonta of Council of Ten, 3
Zonta of Senate, 3
Zuccari, Federico, 178–9, 207, 310–11